Bobby's Guide to SAT Writing: 22 Grammar & Writing Rules Explained 7 Practice Tests

Kukhon Uddin (Bobby)

&

Sakib Hussain

ISBN   9781074249793

BOBBY TARIQ TUTORIAL INC.

SAT® is a trademark registered by the College Board, which is not affiliated with, and does not endorse, this product

TABLE OF CONTENT

PRACTICE TESTS & ANSWERS EXPLANATIONS

22 TOPICS

&

PRACTICE QUESTIONS

FOR WRITING SECTION

TOPIC 1: PREPOSITIONS & IDIOMS

<table>
<tr><td>

What is a preposition?
A preposition is a short word that is usually placed before a noun or a pronoun to demonstrate the relationship between the phrase the preposition is in and the other word(s) in the sentence.

</td><td>

What is an idiom?
An idiom is a phrase that is particular to a language that does not always translate in meaning if those words were to be considered separately.

</td></tr>
</table>

What is a prepositional idiom?
An idiom that begins with a preposition is called a prepositional idiom and can be used at the beginning, middle, or end of a sentence to describe a noun or a verb.

Idioms that use the preposition *about*	Idioms that use the preposition *against*	Idioms that use the preposition *as*	Idioms that use the preposition *at*
anxious about ask about bring about curious about hear about think about talk about worry about	advise against argue against count against decide against defend against go against rebel against	celebrate as regard as see as view as	aim at arrive at laugh at look at succeed at
Idioms that use the preposition *by* accompanied by amazed by confused by followed by go by impressed by organized by struck by by and large	**Idioms that use the preposition *from*** abstain from different from excuse from far from obvious from protect from	**Idioms that use the preposition *into*** enter into look into inquire into read into	**Idioms that use the preposition *in*** engage in fall in love in A as in B interested in succeed in take in case in point
Idioms that use the preposition *on* base on draw on focus on impose on	**Idioms that use the preposition *over*** argue over rule over talk over think over	**Idioms that use the preposition *with*** agree with bargain with correlate with familiar with	**Idioms that use the preposition *of*** approve of capable of certain of characteristic of

insist on move on prey on rely on		identify with in keeping with interfere with sympathize with trust with	combination of A and B cure of deprive of die of a fan of
Idioms that use the preposition *of* [continued] in danger of in the hope of in recognition of made up of a model of an offer of on the border of remind of a selection of a source of suspicious of take advantage of an understanding of a wealth of	**Idioms that use the preposition *to*** able to accustomed to adapt to adhere to admit to adjacent to agree to as opposed to belong to central to come to contribute to devoted to in addition to	**Idioms that use the preposition *to* [continued]** in contrast to listen to object to prefer A to B partial to reluctant to reply to see to similar to a threat to try to (NOT try to) unique to	**Idioms that use the preposition *for*** advocate for ask for blame for famous for known for last for meant for named for necessary for pay for ready for responsible for tolerance for strive for wait for watch for for all intents and purposes

TOPIC 1: PRACTICE QUESTIONS

Questions 1-8 are based on the following passage:

Running Injuries: Causes and Prevention

Running is a popular form of exercise. With only a minimal amount of specialized equipment needed, it is regarded **1** for an activity with a low barrier to entry. Apart **2** to its popularity and simplicity, injuries remain very common among runners.

For **3** any intents and purposes, running is a safe sport because it does not involve contact or high speeds. However, each year about half of all runners experience an injury. Running injuries originate **4** from any of several common causes. Excessive mileage and anatomical factors are both major contributors to running injuries.

Running more than 40 miles per week is strongly associated with injury. To help prevent injury, runners who insist on routes with high mileage should slowly and gradually build up their running miles per week. This requires adhering **5** with a consistent training schedule. Though still unproven in scientific studies, pre-exercise stretching, warm-up and cool down are

Question 1
A) NO CHANGE
B) as
C) for
D) like

Question 2
A) NO CHANGE
B) with
C) from
D) of

Question 3
A) NO CHANGE
B) all
C) every
D) DELETE the underlined portion

Question 4
A) NO CHANGE
B) among
C) within
D) during

Question 5
A) NO CHANGE
B) on
C) in
D) to

recommended by running experts to prevent injuries.

Anatomical factors are also associated with increased injury. Particular physical characteristics such as muscle weakness, unequal leg length, and high-arched feet may all contribute to running related injuries. Hip strengthening exercises combined with custom shoes and orthotics may decrease injuries associated with anatomical factors. However, by **6** in large, the research proving the effectiveness of these treatments is lacking. Running experts offer several suggestions for reducing injury risk among runners, but few have been verified through research. The ongoing stresses running puts on the body can interact in complex ways that are not effectively addressed by sports clinics. Many medical establishments that take new patients on a **7** first come, first serve basis are not equipped to deal with many running-related injuries. Case **8** and point, when it comes to running injuries, prevention is the best treatment.

Unfortunately for the runners of the world, there are no simple solutions to prevent running injuries. However, runners who focus on prevention may be able to avoid future injury. By taking injury prevention seriously, runners can take control of their own health and find solutions that work for them.

Question 6

A) NO CHANGE

B) as

C) and

D) DELETE the underlined portion

Question 7

A) NO CHANGE

B) first-come, first-serve

C) first come, first served

D) first-come, first-served

Question 8

A) NO CHANGE

B) with

C) in

D) within

Topic 1: Practice Questions (Answers & Explanations)

Question 1

B is the best answer. "As" is used **when referring to the role/purpose of a person or a thing** (usually a noun). Here, the noun being referred to is the "activity" of running and the role/purpose described is running's "low barrier to entry."

A & C are incorrect. While "for" is used as a preposition in various conditions, its most common uses are: when **something is to be given to someone** (for example: "This is a gift for Mila."), when **describing the purpose of some object/idea** (for example: "What is this machine used for?"), to **explain consequence** (for example: "Sepiso was scolded for painting on the wall").

D is incorrect. When used as a preposition, "like" **indicates a comparison** (i.e., "The Harry Potter movies are like the books."), **it is used as an equivalent for "as if"** (i.e., "Ahmed looked like he could use a nap").

Question 2

C is the best answer. "From" is a versatile preposition, but its most common uses might be said to be: **to refer to the origin of something/someone** ("Cesar is from the region of Chiapas in southern Mexico."), **to show difference** ("It is hard to tell the original from the fake."), **to show distance** ("We are about fifteen minutes away from the park".) In this case, since the identified statement seeks to show difference (i.e., the injuries that occur despite the "low barrier to entry"), "from" is the best preposition choice.

A is incorrect because "any" is **not a preposition.** A preposition is used to show a **relationship** between two parts of a sentence – here the relationship is between "popularity and simplicity" and "injuries." Since "any" is not a preposition, it cannot be an accurate choice.

B is incorrect. "With" is commonly used **to imply togetherness/support/relationships** ("My mother has been with my father for over 45 years."), it is used **to refer to how something is done** ("This dress has been created with silk from Tamil Nadu."), it is used **to imply a cause** ("Ana Lucia is at home with a bad case of the chicken pox."). Since none of these conditions apply here, "with" is not an appropriate choice.

D is incorrect. As a preposition, "of" most often is used to show: **the belonging of something/someone to someone/something else** ("Have you read any of Arundhati Roy's political writing?"), to **show the cause of something** ("Francesca's grandfather died of a heart attack."), to **show comparison** ("Of all of Harjo's poetry, *How to Write a Poem in a Time of War* is my personal favorite.").

Question 3

B is the best answer. "For all intents and purposes" is a prepositional idiom that is used to mean "in all cases," "whatever the reason," or "from what could be observed." It is an idiomatic phrase that cannot be explained grammatically and is best memorized beforehand!

All other answers are incorrect because, for an idiomatic phrase, there is only one answer that should be immediately apparent.

Question 4

A is the best answer. "From" is a versatile preposition, but its most common uses might be: **to refer to the origin of something/someone** ("Cesar is from the region of Chiapas in southern Mexico"), **to show difference** ("It is hard to tell the original from the fake"), **to show distance** ("We are about fifteen minutes away from the park.") In this case, since the identified statement seeks to show origin (i.e., how running injuries originate), "from" is the best preposition choice.

B & C are incorrect because using the words "all" or "every" between "originate" and "any" would render the sentence **meaningless.**

Similarly, D is incorrect because **without** a preposition between "originate" and "any" no relationship is established between the phrase about the origin of running injuries and the subsequent phrase that expands on the previous one.

Question 5

D is the best answer. "Adhere to" is a prepositional idiom that is used to mean "follows" or "sticks to certain conditions." It is an idiomatic phrase that cannot be explained grammatically and is best memorized beforehand!

All other answers are incorrect because, for an idiomatic phrase, there is only one answer that should be immediately apparent.

Question 6

C is the best answer. "By and large" is a prepositional idiom that is used to mean "in most cases" or "most of the time." It is an idiomatic phrase that cannot be explained grammatically and is best memorized beforehand!

All other answers are incorrect because, for an idiomatic phrase, there is only one answer that should be immediately apparent.

Question 7

D is the best answer. In this use of an idiom, what is being tested is the use of **punctuation** and **tense.** From the sentence construction, because the words "first come" and "first serve" are unusual phrasings, linking them with a **HYPHEN** would enable the reader to better understand how to read the sentence. Furthermore, we can **imply** that the idiom means to say that someone/something that comes "first" (the earliest), will get "served" (before the others). Therefore, the **PRESENT TENSE** of "come" **needs to be contrasted** with the **PAST TENSE of** "served". In this case, therefore, even though the idiom is not one that has been mentioned in the list above, we can **understand based on context** the best of the grammatical choices that are made available to us.

All the other answers are incorrect because they either do not use a hyphen to clarify the connection between "come" and "served" and the "first" before each of them, or they use the **present tense** to conjugate both "come" and "serve" which makes the phrase meaningless.

Question 8
C is the best answer. "Case in point" is an **idiomatic phrase** that is used to provide an example of a previously stated idea or concept i.e., it is the same as saying "for example," or "for instance.

All other answers are incorrect because, for an idiomatic phrase, there is only one answer that should be immediately apparent.

TOPIC 2: SUBJECT-VERB AGREEMENT

What is a subject?	**What is a verb?**
A subject is the person/thing/idea that is being discussed/described in a sentence.	A verb is a word that describes or is an "action," i.e., what a subject does/did/will do. Verbs are conjugated based on the subject and the time described in a sentence.

What is subject-verb agreement?

The subject and verb must agree in number, i.e., they both need to be singular or plural. Pay attention to the following cases.

The non-essential clause that comes between a subject and its verb	**The prepositional phrase that comes between a subject and its verb**	**The subject follows the verb**
Ravi, while mediocre in academic classes, **is** a phenomenal athlete.	**Changes** to the weather **are** becoming more frequent due to global warming.	On the park benches **is** where you're most likely to find **Goran**.
Make sure that the verb following the non-essential clause agrees with the subject (i.e., "is" agrees with "Ravi," not "academic classes").	*Make sure that the verb following the prepositional phrase ("to the weather") agrees with the subject (i.e., "are" agrees with "changes," not "weather").*	*Make sure that the verb agrees with the subject (i.e., "is" agrees with "Goran," not "park benches").*
The collective nouns	**The gerund as a subject**	**The compound subjects**
The school's **theatre club is** incredibly talented.	**Changing** the world **requires** determination.	**Aliya** and **Samar have** been best friends since childhood.
Although there are many (plural) people in the "theatre club," it is being referred to as a collective (a single entity). Therefore, the verb needs to be singular.	*Since "changing" is used as a gerund, the verb should be singular. The subject in this sentence is "changing."*	*Make sure that the verb agrees with the subject (i.e., "have" agrees with "Aliya and Samar" – two subjects).*

STRATEGIES TO USE

First, identify the subject(s) and see if it is singular or plural.

Second, ignore any non-essential phrases/clauses/words that come between the subject and the verb.

Then, use the appropriate verb.

TOPIC 2: PRACTICE QUESTIONS

Questions 1-8 are based on the following passage.

Starry Night, Van Gogh's Unexpected Masterpiece

Starry Night is one of the most iconic and recognized pieces of art in the world. It has inspired songs, limericks, and memorabilia throughout various cultures. The famous image **1** had been painted by one of the most widely recognized artists in the world, Vincent van Gogh. Van Gogh created his masterpiece during his stay at the asylum of Saint-Paul-de-Mausole in 1889.

The **2** asylums, which was near the Saint-Rémy-de-Provence region, offered Van Gough a fair degree of freedom. He was permitted to leave the hospital grounds if he **3** were attended, and he was given a studio where he spent his days reading and painting.

Unfortunately, during his time at the asylum, Van Gogh **4** suffered from paranoia and epileptic fits. The treatment he received helped greatly, but Van Gogh relapsed just as he

Question 1

A) NO CHANGE

B) was

C) were

D) had

Question 2

A) NO CHANGE

B) asylum's

C) asylums'

D) asylum

Question 3

A) NO CHANGE

B) is

C) had been

D) was

Question 4

A) NO CHANGE

B) suffering

C) suffer

D) suffers

appeared to be on the cusp of recovery. Due to the shift in his mental health, Van Gogh <u>begins</u> to incorporate darker colors into his artwork, similarly to the artwork he created in the beginning of his career. As the painter became more depressed, he splattered his emotions and personal conflicts across his canvas. Ultimately, these challenges brought forth a timeless masterpiece, *Starry Night*. Artistic, historical, and psychological experts [6] <u>offers</u> a number of interpretations on what Van Gogh intended to portray in *Starry Night*. The masterpiece is said to be a dreamy interpretation of the night view outside of Van Gogh's asylum room. The village depicted in the painting also appears to be a representation of Saint-Rémy-de-Provence. Despite the clear depiction of the village, experts around the world disagree on the significance of the painting's contorted night sky. Some believe that the sky is a realistic portrayal of how the stars were positioned in June 1889. Others, however, explain the depiction as symbolic, citing the expressive and furious brush strokes in the piece as evidence.

Starry Night's color scheme is dominated by variations of blue that blend the hills, mountains, and olive trees in the painting seamlessly into the night sky. The brush strokes in the night sky create intricate swirls, where each 7 swirls rolls in tune with the other components of the sky and a lone cypress tree. Many observers believe that swirling brush strokes in night sky, in combination with the fiery appearance of the cypress tree, 8 portrays an apocalyptic motif.

Despite how popular it is today, Van Gogh actually considered *Starry Night* to be a failure. The painting was finished only after the artist attempted to depict the view from his window 21 times before. However, Van Gogh's "failed artwork" has stood the test of time. Since 1941, the masterpiece has held its place in the permanent collection in New York City's Museum of Modern Art.

Question 8

A)   NO CHANGE

B)   portray

C)   had portrayed

D)   DELETE the underlined portion

Topic 2: Practice Questions (Answers & Explanations)

Question 1

B is the best answer. The subject is **singular** ("the image") and is being referred to in the **PAST TENSE** (since the sentence describes who painted this work of art). Therefore, "was" – as the **SIMPLE PAST SINGULAR** conjugation – is the best choice.

A is incorrect. The term "had been" is in the **PAST PERFECT** tense and used for a **singular subject**. **Past perfect** is used when describing something that happened **before** something else. Since there is nothing to compare "had been" to, it is an incorrect choice.

C is incorrect. "Were" would be used to refer to **multiple subjects** (i.e., it is in the plural form).

D is incorrect. By using "had" to replace the underlined section, the sentence is rendered **meaningless**.

Question 2

D is the best answer. The clue to locating this answer lies in the verb "was" that is used later in the sentence. This conjugation is **in the singular** and, therefore, **the subject it refers to** ("the asylum") should also be singular.

A is incorrect. Currently, the subject is **plural** (indicated by the "s" that ends the word "asylum"). This is in **disagreement** with the verb "was," which is singular. Therefore, this cannot be the correct answer.

B & C are incorrect because they both use the **apostrophe** to indicate a **possessive quality in the subject.** They could only be used accurately if the content following the subject was described as belonging to it in some way (for example: "the asylum's origin" would be the singular form, and "the asylums' origin" would refer to multiple asylums' origins). Since that is not the case here, both these answers can be ignored.

Question 3

D is the best answer. As indicated by the multiple uses of "was" in this sentence, the **SIMPLE PAST** is best used in this **context** while referring to its **singular subject** ("Van Gogh").

A is incorrect because "were" refers to **multiple subjects** and in this sentence, there is only one.

B is incorrect because it uses the **PRESENT TENSE** and this would cause a **VERB TENSE INCONSISTENCY** with the rest of the statement, which clearly talks about a past event.

C is incorrect. The **past perfect** is necessary only when referencing an event that occurred **before** another event being described. In this sentence, all parts of it are referring to the "same" moment/event, Van Gogh's departure from the asylum. Therefore, the **PAST PERFECT** is not necessary.

Question 4

A is the best answer. There is a singular subject ("Van Gogh") and the events being referred to are in the past. Therefore, the current verb usage is completely accurate.

B is incorrect. In order to use the **gerund** "suffering," the verb needs to be preceded by "was," i.e., "was suffering." Without the "was," the sentence would be **meaningless.**

C is incorrect. "Suffer" is in the **present tense**, which would be **inaccurate** in the context here (of describing Van Gogh's life, which is an event of the past). Furthermore, "suffer" would be used to refer to multiple subjects. For a single (third-person) subject, the correct use of the verb in the present tense would be "suffers."

D is incorrect because, like the previous answer, it uses the **PRESENT TENSE** to refer to the past.

Question 5

C is the best answer. Once again, we are looking for the verb form that is used to refer to a single subject and that is conjugated in the **simple past tense.** "Began" is the only appropriate choice here.

A is incorrect. By using the present tense, there is an **immediate VERB TENSE INCOSISTENCY** that occurs with the use of "created" later in the sentence. Therefore, this answer is not a suitable choice.

B is incorrect. "Beginning" is the **noun** form of the word "begin." Since we need a verb in this position – since the underlined portion signifies an action – a **noun** would be **misplaced** and **grammatically inaccurate.**

D is incorrect. "Begun" is the **PAST PARTICIPLE** form of the verb "to begin" and in order to be accurate, it needs to be preceded by an **auxiliary verb like "had,"** i.e., "He had begun [to do something]." Without the auxiliary verb, the sentence would be **grammatically inaccurate.**

Question 6

B is the best answer. There are multiple subjects in this sentence, "artistic" experts, "artistic" experts, and "psychological" experts. Therefore, the **verb** needs to agree with the **plural** nature of the subjects. "Have offered" is the only answer choice that agrees with this condition.

A is incorrect. While the **present tense** could be a viable option in this sentence, this is **an exceptional case** where the **multiple subjects** would be addressed (in the present tense) as a **compound noun** (i.e., as a singular entity of the "experts") rather than as three different subjects.

C is incorrect. "Had offered" is the **past perfect conjugation** and would be necessary only **if** the sentence was referencing an event that occurred **before** another event being described. Since that condition is not met in this statement, this option can be eliminated.

D is incorrect. By using offer as a gerund or a noun, the sentence is rendered meaningless.

Question 7

D is the best answer. In addition to none of the options presented being grammatically correct and since the subject ("swirls") has been referenced immediately before the underlined portion, it is **sufficient** to refer to the "swirls" with "each" (without repeating the word).

A is incorrect. The word "each" implies **a singular subject** and, therefore, what follows should be "each swirl" – without the "s" at the end of the word.

B is incorrect. If "each of the" were to be used accurately, the word "swirl" would need to be in the plural ("each of the swirls"). Here, "each of the swirls" becomes the subject that needs to correspond with the verb "rolls."

C is incorrect. By using "swirling" either as the **present continuous** form of the verb "to swirl," or as a noun, it would **render the sentence ineffective and meaningless.**

Question 8

B is the best answer. Notice the use of the **non-essential clause** (indicated by the commas, i.e., "in combination with…"). While the use of "in combination with" **might lead you to think that this sentence has multiple subjects,** notice that it is presented as a non-essential clause. Therefore, the subject is **singular,** i.e., "the swirling brush strokes in night sky," and the verb "portray" is the only one that agrees with it.

A is incorrect because it references the content of the **non-essential clause** (about the "cypress tree") as an additional subject, which as stated in the rules earlier, **is a common error that should be looked out for.**

C & D are incorrect because they both use the **apostrophe** to indicate a **possessive quality to the subject.** They could only be used accurately if the content following the subject was described as belonging to it in some way. And even in that case, we would speak of "the portrayal's," not the "portray's." **Both these answers would be inaccurate and make the sentence meaningless.**

TOPIC 3: DANGLING MODIFIERS

| **What is a modifier?** A modifier is an optional element that modifies (adds to/describes) another part of the sentence. It is an element that can be removed without negatively affecting the grammar (or content) of that sentence. | **What is a dangling modifier?** A dangling modifier describes a case in which a modifier is used ambiguously and is unclear about which part of the sentence it is referring to. |

The introductory modifier

<u>Error</u>
Walking toward the café, a man was playing the guitar.
→
No subject is being referred to.
Who is walking toward the café while a man plays the guitar?

<u>A possible correction</u>
Walking toward the café, Ramona saw a man playing the guitar.

An introductory modifier needs to:
- **Be followed by a comma**
- **Explicitly refer to the subject of the sentence, i.e., whatever follows the comma should be the noun that the introductory modifier is describing**

The misplaced modifier

<u>Error</u>
My mother sent a package to me of my favorite chocolate.
→
What is "of my favorite chocolate" modifying? Clearly, it is meant to modify "a package."

<u>A possible correction</u>
My mother sent me a package of my favorite chocolate.

A modifier needs to be next to whatever it is modifying.

STRATEGIES TO USE

Locate the modifier
To do so, ask yourself if the sentence would make grammatical sense without this phrase/clause.
If the answer is yes, you are looking at a modifier.

Identify what the modifier is modifying
The subject being modified should be next to the modifier.
If this is not the case, or if the subject itself is unclear, there is a modifier error present in the statement.

TOPIC 3: PRACTICE QUESTIONS

Questions 1-8 are based on the following passage.

Curcumin: Powerful Medicine from a Tasty Herb

1 A tasty herb that is used to add a smoky, turmeric adds earthy flavour to many dishes. In recent years, turmeric is expanding from a delicious food additive to a key ingredient in many modern home remedies. A key compound in this flavourful spice called *curcumin* may have important medical benefits. However, this insight is nothing new. Ancient civilizations began using turmeric for its medicinal properties long before people in the 21st century started adding the ancient spice into their daily supplements.

2 Found throughout the tropics although its specific origin remains unknown, turmeric is native to Southeast Asia. Most of the world's turmeric supply comes from India.

Question 1

A) NO CHANGE

B) A tasty herb that is used to add a smoky, turmeric adds earthy flavour to many dishes.

C) Turmeric, a tasty herb, is used to add a smoky, earthy flavour to many dishes.

D) Adding earthy flavour to many dishes, turmeric is a tasty herb.

Question 2

A) NO CHANGE

B) Although its specific origin remains unknown, turmeric is native to Southeast Asia and can be found throughout the tropics.

C) Turmeric is native to Southeast Asia, although its specific origin remains unknown and can be found throughout the tropics.

D) Its specific origin remains unknown and can be found throughout the tropics, but turmeric is native to Southeast Asia.

3 Such as curry, turmeric is a key ingredient in many popular dishes in India. However, Indian turmeric is considered to be the best in the world due to its naturally high content of the bioactive compound *curcumin*. **4** *Curcumin* has powerful antioxidant and anti-inflammatory effects, and it has become popular for its anti-cancer properties. The compound has also been recognized for its ability to help lower cholesterol and prevent heart disease.

5 Nearly four thousand years ago, Southeast Asian cultures started using the turmeric plant in religious ceremonies and as a common spice in foods. Ancient Indians would burn turmeric and inhale the fumes to alleviate congestion, and they would apply the paste or juice from the plant to wounds, bruises, and for the treatment of various skin conditions such as eczema and shingles.

[6] Ayurvedic medicine around 500 BCE, an ancient Indian practice of natural healing, that is still practiced today, began integrating turmeric in its practices.

Due to its popularity, *curcumin* has found a place in many cultural practices common across Southeast Asia. For example, in traditional Indian wedding ceremonies, the groom ties a string that has been dyed yellow with *curcumin* from turmeric paste around his bride's neck. [7] The necklace, called a *mangala sutra,* is meant to symbolize that a woman is married.

Turmeric's use as a flavor, a healthcare treatment, a dye, and a culturally-valuable spice extends back thousands of years. [8] Now that turmeric and the medicinal compound *curcumin* have caught on in the West, they have become increasingly popular over the past few years. Much of this popularity is due to *curcumin,* which is still valued for its health benefits.

Question 6

A) NO CHANGE

B) around 500 BCE Ayurvedic medicine, which is an ancient Indian practice of natural healing, that is still practiced today

C) Ayurvedic medicine, which is an ancient Indian practice of natural healing still practiced today, around 500 BCE

D) around 500 BCE, Ayurvedic medicine, an ancient Indian practice of natural healing, that is still practiced today,

Question 7

A) NO CHANGE

B) The *mangala sutra,* meant to symbolize that a woman is married, is a necklace.

C) The necklace meant to symbolize that a woman, called a *mangala sutra,* is married.

D) Meant to symbolize that a woman is married, the *mangala sutra* is a necklace.

Question 8

A) NO CHANGE

B) Increasingly popular over the past few years, turmeric and the medicinal compound *curcumin* have caught on in the West.

C) Turmeric and the medicinal compound *curcumin* have caught on in the West, which has over the past few years made the ancient spice increasingly popular.

D) Turmeric and the medicinal compound *curcumin* have caught on in the West because they have been increasingly popular over the past few years.

Topic 3: Practice Questions (Answers & Explanations)

Question 1

C is the best answer. This option is the clearest. The position of "a tasty herb" as a modifier is clearly established through the use of commas. Furthermore, it is very clear that this modifier describes "turmeric," the noun that is placed right next to it. Because of its clarity, this is the most appropriate answer.

A is incorrect. This sentence is **missing** a subject. By beginning the line with "a tasty herb that," we are not told what this information is in reference to. The lack of punctuation also makes this sentence difficult to understand – what is **the essential information here? What is the non-essential information?** Clearly, we cannot tell either of those things without knowing the subject. Therefore, this structure needs to be changed.

B is incorrect. The use of the phrase "to add a smoky" without a sufficient noun/adjective following "smoky" (like "flavour," for example) renders the sentence **meaningless.**

D is incorrect. The modifier is a **non-essential part of a sentence.** In this case, if the suggested modifier is taken out, all we are left with is "Turmeric is a tasty herb." Clearly, essential information about the taste that is added through the use of turmeric cannot be entirely **non-essential.** The only viable non-essential phrase in this sentence is "a tasty herb." If this phrase were to be removed from the sentence, the reader would still understand the main point (the kind of flavor that turmeric adds, which **implies** its tastiness).

Question 2

B is the best answer. By accurately demarcating the modifier ("Although its specific origin remains unknown"), this sentence is the only option that retains the focus on the origins of turmeric (in Southeast Asia and throughout the tropics).

A is incorrect because the modifier is **misplaced.** By placing the phrase in the middle of the sentence, the logic in the sentence is disrupted. The modifier is preceded and followed by information about regions in which turmeric is found. This geographical information **should be placed next to each other** without being interrupted by the modifier.

C is incorrect. By placing **essential information** as part of the modifier (that turmeric is found in the tropics), this choice does not follow the rule that generally requires modifiers to only include **non-essential** components to the sentence (i.e., components that would not alter the grammar or the meaning in negative ways).

D is incorrect since the sentence does not have a logical flow and is unclear what the **subject** of this statement is (i.e., where turmeric can be found).

Question 3

B is the best answer. "Such as curry" is clearly the modifier in this sentence since even without the inclusion of this statement, the reader would understand the **essential point,** the importance of turmeric to food in India.

A is incorrect because using a modifier that begins with "such as" at the beginning of the statement is **unclear to the reader.** Since turmeric is the noun immediately following the comma, is the statement saying that turmeric is a form of curry? Because of this lack of clarity, this is not a good answer choice.

C is incorrect because in this case, turmeric (by itself) is used as a dependent clause. From the information that has come before, we know that turmeric is the **subject** of this passage. By giving it a passive position, the sentence is almost **meaningless.**

D is incorrect because, in this case, the reader is led to think that "such as curry" modifies "turmeric" (by its placement right next to the word) rather than modifying "most popular dishes."

Question 4

D is the best answer. By clearly demarcating the introductory modifier with a comma, and by following this comma immediately with the subject that is being referred to (i.e., *"Curcumin"),* this is the most grammatically accurate choice.

A is incorrect because the use of the modifier at the end of the sentence does not effectively communicate the subject that is being referred to. The word "it", in this case, is ambiguous and does not **effectively transition the reader** between the different ideas being presented.

B is incorrect. In addition to the lack of punctuation, this choice **alludes to** a cause-effect relationship between "antioxidant and anti-inflammatory effects" to "anti-cancer properties." Since we have not been given any other information to substantiate this claim, choosing this answer would involve the reader making an ASSUMPTION.

C is incorrect. This sentence construction **changes the meaning of the sentence** and suggests that the spice "has become popular" rather than "contains," i.e., changing the relationship between ingredient properties, their potential effects, and the perception of those properties and effects.

Question 5

A is the best answer. By placing the modifier as an introductory clause that is followed by a comma and followed by the subject ("Southeast Asian cultures"), this choice **effectively demarcates** the **essential and non-essential elements of this sentence.** The essential elements are that these cultures have been using turmeric for religious and culinary purposes; the non-essential element that would not affect the grammar/logic of the sentence even if removed is "nearly four thousand years ago."

B is incorrect. The modifier in this sentence is constructed to refer to "cultures" (the noun immediately following it) but, clearly, this **contradicts with how this modifier begins** ("A common spice").

C is incorrect. Without the use of appropriate punctuations, this sentence is **meaningless**. All the information is "mashed" together making it difficult for the reader to understand its **different components.**

D is incorrect since **non-essential and essential parts of the sentence are placed interchangeably,** and the **modifier cannot be taken out** without affecting the grammatical correctness and the meaning of the sentence.

Question 6

C is the best answer. Let's start by identifying the different parts of the content in this sentence. There is information about when Ayurveda originated, a description of Ayurveda, its continuing use today, and its integration of turmeric. Given this diversity of content, identify **KEYWORDS that might imply a better order.** For example, the term "began" tells us that the following information should be associated with "around 500 B.C.E." – leaving a description of Ayurveda and its ongoing use. Given the answer choices, this is the only option that connects a dependent clause dealing with time with a following clause which reflects emphasis on a time period. Therefore, this is the most appropriate answer. Although this sentence construction is not ideal, it is much more suitable than the other choices.

All the other answer choices are **far more difficult to understand since phrases/clauses that are not connected by specific subjects and/or modifiers are all mixed together.**

Question 7

A is the best answer. By using the Sanskrit name for the necklace as a modifier while using this to directly refer to the preceding noun (the necklace), this answer is both clear and grammatically accurate.

The remaining answers are incorrect because they **do not place the subject being modified** ("the necklace") near the phrase that functions as the modifier ("the *mangala sutra*"). In choice B, the modifier seems to refer to "meant to symbolize," choice C seems to refer to "the woman" or "married," and choice D changes the nature of the modifier such that the sentence would lose meaning/accuracy if it were to be taken out. Remember that a modifier is a part of the sentence that will NOT **affect the rest of the statement** grammatically (or in terms of **essential content**) if it is removed.

Question 8

B is the best answer. The modifier ("Increasingly popular over the past few years") is used as an introduction. Furthermore, the modifier is followed by a comma and is immediately followed by the subjects that it refers to (turmeric and *curcumin*). Therefore, this is the best answer.

A is incorrect because the modifier here ("they have become increasingly popular over the past few years) is **not** placed next to the subject it is modifying. Furthermore, removing this modifier would make the sentence grammatically incorrect and, as we know, the removal of a modifier should **not affect** the grammatical accuracy of the statement.

C is incorrect. The sentence structure does not allow clarity. The particular lack of clarity lies in the section "which has over the past few years made […]," and the lack of punctuations here makes the ideas hard to follow.

D is incorrect. This structure **alters the meaning of the sentence** and suggests a causal relationship between the popularity of the spice and its popularity in the West (through the use of the word "because"). What is stated here, however, is an **additional** relationship, i.e., the spice is popular **and** has caught on in the West.

TOPIC 4: COMMA PHRASES

What is a comma phrase?	

As the term suggests, a comma phrase is one that is preceded and/or followed by this punctuation mark.

There are a few rules to remember about the comma.

A non-restrictive relative clause should always be surrounded by commas.

A relative clause describes a noun and starts with a relative pronoun or adverb: *which, that, who, where.* A **non-restrictive clause is not integral to the meaning of a sentence.**

For example: Nilofer, **who is a junior in high school**, is something of a savant at computer programming.

If "who is a junior in high school" is removed, the sentence would still retain its meaning (just a little less information).

An appositive clause should always be surrounded by commas.

An appositive is a descriptive phrase that does not contain a verb. And like a non-restrictive clause, an **appositive is not integral to the meaning of a sentence.**

For example: Nilofer, **a junior in high school**, is something of a savant at computer programming.

If "a junior in high school" is removed, the sentence would still retain its meaning (just a little less information).

Introductory phrases and clauses should always be followed by a comma.

Introductory phrases are **dependent or descriptive sections** that begin a sentence.

For example: **When Nilofer was a junior in high school,** he became something of a savant at computer programming.

Here, "when Nilofer was a junior in high school" is a dependent, introductory clause and must be followed by a comma.

Items in a list of three or more items should be separated by commas.

For example: Nilofer is extremely skilled at **computer programming, dance, and philosophy.**

When a sentence includes a COMPLETE thought, do NOT use a comma.

For example: Nilofer is skilled at computer programming, she is extremely adept in this discipline.

The comma separates two complete thoughts and, therefore, creates an **error** *called the "comma splice."*

Do NOT include a comma between an adjective and a noun.

For example: Nilofer is a skilled, programmer.

ASK YOURSELF THE FOLLOWING QUESTIONS

Does the text include a non-restrictive clause?
If yes, it needs to be surrounded by commas.

Does the text include an appositive?
If yes, it needs to be surrounded by commas.

Does the text include an introductory phrase?
If yes, it needs to be followed by a comma.

Does the text include a list of three or more items?
If yes, the items need to be separated by commas.

Does the comma connect two complete thoughts?
If yes, the comma needs to be deleted.

Is the comma placed between a noun and an adjective?
If yes, the comma needs to be deleted.

TOPIC 4: PRACTICE QUESTIONS

Questions 1-8 are based on the following passage.

The Library of Alexandria

The greatest library of the ancient world was located in Alexandria, Egypt. The city was founded in 330 BCE by Alexander the Great. After his passing in 323 BCE, Alexander's Empire was passed on to his generals. This Empire was great, and it boasted one of the most famous libraries the world has ever known.

1 For millennia the Library of Alexandria has been a fascinating and heated subject among scholars and historians alike. Even though the Library of Alexandria is considered to be one of the most significant ancient libraries in history, its origin is shrouded in mystery.

At its peak, the Library contained works by some of the greatest minds and writers of antiquity. The Library's collection would have been **2** vast and contained works from Homer Plato Socrates, and many other inspiring writers and philosophers. The Library was a part of a much larger research institution called

Question 1

A) NO CHANGE

B) For millennia, the Library of Alexandria, has been a fascinating and heated subject among scholars and historians alike.

C) For millennia, the Library of Alexandria has been a fascinating and heated subject among scholars and historians alike.

D) For millennia, the Library of Alexandria, has been a fascinating and heated subject among scholars, and historians, alike.

Question 2

A) NO CHANGE

B) vast and contained works from Homer, Plato, Socrates, and many other inspiring writers and

C) vast, and contained works from Homer, Plato, Socrates and many other inspiring writers, and

D) vast, and contained works from Homer, Plato, Socrates, and many other inspiring writers and the **3** Mouseion which was created in dedication the nine goddesses of the arts, "the Muses."

Question 3

A) NO CHANGE

B) Mouseion, which was created in dedication the nine goddesses of the arts,

C) Mouseion which was created in dedication the nine goddesses of the arts

D) Mouseion, which was created in dedication the nine goddesses of the arts

4 Around 295 BCE, a scholar and exiled governor of Athens named Demetrius Phalerum, proposed the idea of a universal library to the ruler of Alexandria. The leader was convinced and allowed Demetrius to begin construction on the library.

Question 4

A) NO CHANGE

B) Around 295 BCE, a scholar and exiled governor of Athens, named Demetrius Phalerum, proposed the idea of a universal library to the ruler of Alexandria

C) Around 295 BCE a scholar and exiled governor of Athens named Demetrius Phalerum, proposed the idea of a universal library to the ruler of Alexandria

D) Around 295 BCE, a scholar and exiled governor of Athens named Demetrius Phalerum proposed the idea of a universal library to the ruler of Alexandria

Eventually, the library housed more the 100 scholars. These scholars had many **5** jobs, including carrying out research, translating and copying documents, and performing lectures. The scholars were charged with collecting Hebrew **6** scriptures, Buddhist texts, and manuscripts from Greek authors, as well as translations of works from Assyria, Persia, and Egypt.

Nearly half of a million documents were estimated to have been held in the great Library. Eventually, the library's collection became so great that a daughter library had to be established to contain the flood of documents and books that continued to flow. **7** As impressive as it must have been to the observer's eye the Library of Alexandria no longer stands today. The story behind the Library's devastating demise is one that continues to elude scholars all over the world. The most popular belief is that the original Library of Alexandria was destroyed in a fire during Caesar's occupation of the Egyptian city. Speculators have come to different

Question 5

A) NO CHANGE

B) jobs, including carrying out research translating and copying documents and performing lectures

C) jobs including carrying out research, translating, and copying documents, and performing lectures

D) jobs including carrying out research, translating and copying documents, and performing lectures

Question 6

A) NO CHANGE

B) scriptures, Buddhist texts, and manuscripts from Greek authors, as well as translations of works from Assyria Persia and Egypt

C) scriptures Buddhist texts and manuscripts from Greek authors, as well as translations of works from Assyria, Persia, and Egypt

D) scriptures Buddhist texts and manuscripts from Greek authors, as well as translations of works from Assyria Persia and Egypt

Question 7

A) NO CHANGE

B) As impressive as it must have been, to the observer's eye the Library of Alexandria no longer stands today.

C) As impressive as it must have been to the observer's eye, the Library of Alexandria no longer stands today.

D) As impressive as it must have been to the observer's eye the Library of Alexandria no longer stands, today.

conclusions over the years. **8** <u>Regardless the loss of the vast collection of priceless knowledge and history that once sat on the shelves of the Library of Alexandria haunts scholars and bibliophiles to this day.</u>

A) NO CHANGE

B) Regardless, the loss of the vast collection of priceless knowledge and history that once sat on the shelves of the Library of Alexandria haunts scholars and bibliophiles to this day.

C) Regardless the loss of the vast collection of priceless knowledge and history, that once sat on the shelves of the Library of Alexandria, haunts scholars and bibliophiles to this day.

D) Regardless, the loss of the vast collection of priceless knowledge and history that once sat on the shelves of the Library of Alexandria haunts scholars and bibliophiles, to this day.

Topic 4: Practice Questions (Answers & Explanations)

Question 1
C is the best answer. "For millennia" is an introductory phrase that is accurately followed by a comma (without the inclusion of extra commas in other parts of the sentence). Therefore, this is the most accurate choice.

A is incorrect. Since there is no comma following the introductory phrase, this sentence is grammatically inaccurate.

B is incorrect because of the comma that comes after "the Library of Alexandria." Because of this additional punctuation, this phrase is demarcated as an **appositive** (which, as we know, is information that is **not** integral to the meaning of this sentence). Since this information **is integral** in this sentence, it should **not be followed by a comma.**

D is incorrect. In addition to the extra comma after "Alexandria," this sentence also includes a list of **two items** that currently has commas to separate those elements. Since commas are only used **in lists of three or more items,** this choice is not accurate.

Question 2
B is the best answer. This sentence accurately places commas to separate "Homer," "Plato," and "Socrates" without adding commas in unnecessary parts of the sentence.

A is incorrect. The current sentence does not include commas to separate the three or more items (the names of the philosophers) that are listed here.

C is incorrect because of the comma following "vast." Here, we see that there are **two complete thoughts** that are included. The first talks about how the collection in the library could have been vast; the second discusses the work that it contains. As we have learned earlier, **commas should not be used to separate two complete ideas.** Furthermore, this sentence also includes a comma after the word "writers," which is not necessary since what follows is a list of **two** items ("writers and philosophers").

D is incorrect. Although this choice does not include the comma after "writers," it does (like the choice above) place an extra comma after the word "vast" and thus separates two complete thoughts that do not need punctuation between them.

Question 3
B is the best answer. As mentioned in the rule earlier on, a **RELATIVE NON-RESTRICTIVE CLAUSE** should always be surrounded by commas. In this case, the word "which" indicates that what follows is a relative clause that describes the noun, "Mouseion". Furthermore, even if the information about the nine goddesses was to be taken out, the sentence would still remain relevant to the paragraph (hence it being a non-restrictive clause). Since this is the only option in which **commas are found before and after the relative non-restrictive clause, it is the only accurate answer.**

A is incorrect. The comma is only placed before the relative non-restrictive clause and not after it.

C is incorrect. There are no commas around the relative non-restrictive clause. There should be one at the beginning and one at the end of the relative non-restrictive clause.

D is incorrect. The comma is only place after the relative non-restrictive clause and not before it.

Question 4

D is the best answer. In this sentence, a comma needs to follow the introductory clause "Around 295 BCE." All the other information in the sentence, however, is **restrictive,** i.e., there is nothing else in the sentence that, if removed, would contain all the necessary bits of information: the name of the governor, the fact that he was exiled, and that it was he who propose the idea of the library. Therefore, since this is the only answer choice that limits the use of the comma to after the introductory clause, it is the only viable option.

A is incorrect. In this option, by placing a comma on either side of "a scholar and exiled governor of Athens named Demetrius Phalerum," this information becomes **non-integral** to the sentence. However, without this information, the content of this statement would be negatively affected. Therefore, the text should not be surrounded by commas.

B is incorrect because the comma is overused in multiple parts of the sentence that are **restrictive clauses.**

C is incorrect because the use of the comma here demarcates this entire phrase as being the introductory clause: "Around 295 BCE a scholar and exiled governor of Athens named Demetrius Phalerum." Clearly, this clause does not simply introduce the sentence but alters its logic. Therefore, this is not a suitable option.

Question 5

A is the best answer. There are two elements to pay attention to here. The first is the phrase that introduces the list of items ("These scholars had many jobs") – and as **an introductory phrase**, this selection needs to be followed by a comma. In addition, "including" is followed by a list of three items: (1) carrying out research (2) translating and copying documents (3) performing lectures. Therefore, there needs to be commas following items (1) and (2). Since the current sentence structure includes all the necessary commas, it is the most accurate choice.

B is incorrect because there are no commas separating the items on the list.

C & D are incorrect because neither of these choices includes the mano comma after the introductory phrase.

Question 6

A is the best answer. By using commas to separate the (three) items on each list, this choice is the most accurate. Note that the first list includes the items "scriptures, Buddhist texts, and manuscripts from Greek authors," and the second list includes the items "Assyria, Persia, and Egypt."

Furthermore, this is the only choice that uses a comma before "as well as" to introduce the second part of the sentence (which is **not** a complete sentence by itself, thus rendering the comma use correct).

B is incorrect because there are no commas separating the items in the second list that are included in the sentence.

C is incorrect because there are no commas separating the items in the first list that are included in the sentence.

D is incorrect since there are no commas used in either of the lists that are included in the sentence.

Question 7

C is the best answer. The introductory phrase here is "As impressive as it must have been to the observer's eye" – a phrase that helps describe the clause that follows it ("the Library of Alexandria no longer stands today). Therefore, as the comma rules suggest, this introductory dependent clause needs to be followed by a comma.

A is incorrect because there is no comma that demarcates the introductory dependent clause, whose only purpose is to **contextualize** the clause that follows it.

B is incorrect because the placement of the comma here alters the meaning of the sentence. By framing "as impressive as it must have been" as the introductory clause, the reader is given to understand that the Library no longer stands to "the observer's eye" **implying** that the Library stands for others. This would, clearly, change the meaning of the sentence.

D is incorrect because it places an unnecessary emphasis on "today" without clearly demarcating the introductory clause.

Question 8

B is the best answer. In the sentence, the introductory phrase is "Regardless," a word that serves the primary purpose of transitioning the reader from the idea in the preceding sentence. All the other information in this sentence is **restrictive** and thus, no more commas are needed in the text.

A is incorrect since it does not place a comma after the introductory phrase.

C is incorrect for two reasons. First, it does not place a comma after the introductory phrase. Furthermore, by placing commas on either side of "that once sat on the shelves of the Library of Alexandria," this information is shown as being **non-restrictive**. However, we know that this information is integral to the sentence since the statement would not make sense without it.

D is incorrect. The use of commas in this choice signifies that everything between "Regardless" and "to this day" is **not integral to the text**. Clearly, this cannot be the case since this part of the sentence is where most of its information is located. Therefore, this cannot be a viable answer choice.

TOPIC 5: RUN-ON SENTENCES

What is a run-on sentence?
A run-on sentence is one in which two or more complete sentences are **not** connected by an appropriate conjunction or punctuation mark. To fix a run-on sentence, consider the following:

If a comma connects the two sentences, is the comma followed by: For; And, Not, But, Or, Yet, So?

Remember the acronym, FANBOYS.

Guillermo couldn't say no to the job offer, he had always wanted to live in Seoul. → *Incorrect use of the comma*

Guillermo couldn't say no to the job offer, for he had always wanted to live in Seoul. → *Correct use of the comma since it is followed by "for."*

Will a semicolon or a period solve the problem?

Guillermo couldn't say no to the job offer he had always wanted to live in Seoul. → *Incorrect. No punctuation or conjunction between the two sentences.*

Guillermo couldn't say no to the job offer; he had always wanted to live in Seoul. → *Correct. The sentences remain independent but are connected by a semicolon.*

Guillermo couldn't say no to the job offer. He had always wanted to live in Seoul. → *Correct. The sentence is split into two statements that are separated by a period.*

Can the semicolon be followed by a conjunctive adverb?

A semicolon can be followed by a conjunctive adverb like: "However" (to imply a contrast), or "Therefore" (to imply a cause-effect relationship). In such cases, the conjunctive adverb **must be followed by a comma.**

Guillermo couldn't say no to the job offer; **moreover,** he had always wanted to live in Seoul. → *Correct. The word "moreover" is used to strengthen the causal relationship between the clauses. Note the use of the semicolon between the ideas <u>and</u> the comma that follows "moreover"*

Can the sentence be rewritten with a subordinate clause?

Having always wanted to live in Seoul, Guillermo couldn't say no to the job offer. → *Correct. Here, Guillermo's interest in Seoul has been made a subordinate (dependent) clause that introduces the main (independent) clause that follows.*

Can the repeated subject be removed?

Guillermo had always wanted to live in Seoul and so, couldn't say no to the job offer. → *Correct. Notice that the subject ("he") is not mentioned again.*

REMEMBER
Complete sentences have a **subject, verb,** and **object.** If two sentences -- each with their own subject, verb, and object -- are placed next to each other **without** a conjunction or a punctuation mark, you are looking at a **run-on sentence.**

TOPIC 5: PRACTICE QUESTIONS

Questions 1-8 are based on the following passage.

The Library of Alexandria
Julius Robert Oppenheimer – a Committed Man of Science

Julius Robert Oppenheimer was a theoretical physicist who made a number of significant contributions to mathematics and science, primarily in the fields of physics and chemistry. **1** He conducted his undergraduate studies at Harvard University, where he worked side-by-side with some of the world's most prestigious physicists, including Albert Einstein, Niels Bohr, Werner Heisenberg, and Pascual Jordan. Oppenheimer's greatest contributions include the Tolman-Oppenheimer-Volkoff limit and the Oppenheimer-Philips process, but the scientist is most famously known as "the father of the atomic **2** bomb," a nick-name he acquired for his position in the Manhattan Project during World War II as wartime head of the Los Alamos Laboratory.

Robert Oppenheimer was born to Julius Oppenheimer and Ella Friedman in New York on April 22, 1904. Oppenheimer's family was of Jewish descent, and his father immigrated from Germany to America in 1888.

Question 1

A) NO CHANGE

B) He worked side-by-side with some of the world's most prestigious physicists having conducted his undergraduate studies at Harvard University, including Albert Einstein, Niels Bohr, Werner Heisenberg, and Pascual Jordan.

C) Conducting his undergraduate studies at Harvard University he worked side-by-side with some of the world's most prestigious physicists, including Albert Einstein, Niels Bohr, Werner Heisenberg, and Pascual Jordan.

D) The world's most prestigious physicists, including Albert Einstein, Niels Bohr, Werner Heisenberg, and Pascual Jordan were at Harvard while Oppenheimer was conducting his undergraduate studies.

Question 2

A) NO CHANGE

B) bomb;" a nick-name he acquired

C) bomb." He acquired this nickname

D) bomb," which is a nick-name he acquired

Oppenheimer displayed an interest in academia very early in life. By age 10, he had already begun to sink his teeth into more advanced subjects in school, physics and chemistry in particular.

Oppenheimer was at the top of his high school class, and he graduated as valedictorian in 1921. Oppenheimer enrolled at Harvard University as a chemistry major in 1922 but shortly thereafter realized that physics was his true calling. Oppenheimer graduated with a degree from Harvard after only three **3** years, then in 1925 he began pursuing his graduate studies in physics under the supervision of J.J. Thompson at the Cavendish Laboratory in Cambridge, England.

During his studies with Thompson, Oppenheimer discovered his talent for theoretical physics. He accepted an invitation from Max Born, the Director of the Institute of Theoretical Physics, to study at the University of Göttingen in **4** Germany and in 1927, Oppenheimer received his doctorate and returned to the U.S. to teach physics at the California Institute of Technology, and the University of California, Berkeley.

Question 3

A) NO CHANGE

B) years, then, in 1925, he

C) years. In 1925 he

D) years; in 1925, he

Question 4

A) NO CHANGE

B) Germany; in 1927

C) Germany, and, in 1927,

D) Germany. In 1927,

5 Oppenheimer may have been a man of science, but he shared his time with a famously ambitious dictator named Adolf Hitler, who invaded Poland in 1939 after rising to power in Germany years earlier. In this time of conflict, many world leaders were looking at nuclear science as a possible solution.

Famed European physicists – including Albert Einstein, Eugene Wigner, and Leo Szilard – warned the United States and its allies of what would ensue if Germany made the first nuclear bomb. **6** American leaders heeded their warning and, in 1942, the Manhattan Project was launched for the purposes of developing nuclear weapons, and Oppenheimer was appointed director of weapons development.

Question 5

A) NO CHANGE

B) Oppenheimer he shared his time with a famously ambitious dictator named Adolf Hitler, who invaded Poland in 1939 after rising to power in Germany years earlier, although he may have been a man of science.

C) Oppenheimer, who invaded Poland in 1939 after rising to power in Germany years earlier, may have been a man of science, but he shared his time with a famously ambitious dictator named Adolf Hitler.

D) Oppenheimer shared his time with a famously ambitious dictator named Adolf Hitler who may have been a man of science, but invaded Poland in 1939 after rising to power in Germany years earlier.

Question 6

A) NO CHANGE

B) American leaders heeded their warning; in 1942, they launched the Manhattan Project for the purposes of developing nuclear weapons and appointed Oppenheimer the director of weapons development.

C) Heeded their warning, in 1942, the Manhattan Project was launched by American leaders for the purposes of developing nuclear weapons, and Oppenheimer was appointed director of weapons development.

D) American leaders heeded their warning and, in 1942, the Manhattan Project was launched for the purposes of developing nuclear weapons; Oppenheimer was appointed director of weapons development.

7 Under Oppenheimer's leadership, the Manhattan Project was a success; the physicists developed the world's first nuclear bomb, which had a major impact on world history. The weapons developed in the Manhattan project were used in the bombings of Hiroshima and Nagasaki in 1945, which led to Japan's surrender and the end of World War II. After the war, Oppenheimer and his colleagues Albert Einstein, Joseph Rotblat, and Bertrand Russell established the World Academy of Art and Science – an institution committed to peaceful progress in academia. Oppenheimer continued lecturing on physics until his **8** passing in 1967, and his name will live on in history as one of the scientific minds behind the development of nuclear weapons, as well as the many peaceful uses of nuclear energy that have followed.

A) NO CHANGE

B) The Manhattan Project was a success, because under Oppenheimer's leadership the physicists developed the world's first nuclear bomb; this had a major impact on world history.

C) The Manhattan Project was a success under Oppenheimer's leadership, the physicists developed the world's first nuclear bomb, which had a major impact on world history.

D) The Manhattan Project was a success, because under Oppenheimer's leadership the physicists developed the world's first nuclear bomb; which had a major impact on world history.

A) NO CHANGE

B) Passing. In 1967, his

C) passing in 1967; and his

D) passing in 1967. His

Topic 5: Practice Questions (Answers & Explanations)

Question 1

A is the best answer. The clauses in this sentence are all well connected with commas and, as such, is not a run-on sentence that needs to be corrected.

B is incorrect. This particular answer choice is **not coherent.** The different clauses are mixed in together, and it is hard to understand the point that is being put forward. For a sentence like this one, just reading it should be enough to let the reader know that it **does not make sense.**

C is incorrect. In this case, notice the lack of connection (either through a punctuation or a conjunction) between the following clauses: "Conducting his undergraduate studies at Harvard University" and "he worked side-by-side with some of the world's most prestigious physicists."

D is incorrect. Once again, notice the lack of connection (either through a punctuation or a conjunction) between the following clauses: "The world's most prestigious physicists, including Albert Einstein, Niels Bohr, Werner Heisenberg, and Pascual Jordan were at Harvard" and "while Oppenheimer was conducting his undergraduate studies."

Question 2

C is the best answer. By separating the different ideas in this sentence into two clear statements, this is the **clearest** choice among all those that have been presented.

A is incorrect. This run-on sentence is not incorrect for the lack of punctuation or conjugation but because the length of its various dependent and independent clauses makes the **content** extremely difficult for the reader to engage with. Furthermore, the comma is placed before the quotation mark, rather than being placed after it.

B is incorrect because of the placement of the semicolon before the quotation mark (;") instead of placing it after the quotation mark (";)

D is incorrect. Once again, the punctuation is placed before the quotation mark, rather than being placed after it. Furthermore, the inclusion of "which" makes the description of his nick name **NON-ESSENTIAL** (i.e., not integral to the meaning of the sentence). However, from the **context** we know that this is important information.

Question 3

D is the best answer. By using the semicolon to separate the two independent clauses and by using the comma effectively after the introductory phrase to the second clause (i.e. "in 1925,"), this is the most accurate choice.

A is incorrect. The current sentence structure shows a comma splice error. By using the **FANBOYS** acronym, we can immediately tell that ", then" is not an effective way of connecting two complete sentences. Therefore, this is not a viable answer.

B is incorrect. The placement of multiple commas right after each other makes the logic of the sentence extremely difficult to follow. It is hard to tell from a sentence like this one, which information is **integral,** and which is **not integral** to the text.

C is incorrect. While splitting up the two clauses here, it would have been the clearest choice. The error in this answer lies in the **comma that is missing** after the introductory clause "in 1925."

Question 4

D is the best answer. By using the period to separate the two independent clauses into different sentences, and by using the comma effectively after the introductory phrase to the second clause (i.e., "in 1927,") this is the most accurate choice.

A is incorrect. The current sentence structure shows a comma splice error. By using the **FANBOYS** acronym, we can immediately tell that ", then" is not an effective way of connecting two complete sentences. Therefore, this is not a viable answer.

B is incorrect. While splitting up the two clauses, using a semicolon would be grammatically accurate (though still hard to follow because of the sentence length). The error in this answer lies in the **comma that is missing** after the introductory clause "in 1927."

C is incorrect. The placement of multiple commas right after each other makes the logic of the sentence extremely difficult to follow. It is hard to tell from a sentence like this one, which information is **integral,** and which is **not integral** to the text.

Question 5

A is the best answer. By using commas to effectively demarcate between the different ideas presented in this statement, this answer choice is more accurate than any of the others that are provided here.

B is incorrect. The "he" that is included right after the name "Oppenheimer" immediately makes this answer choice unviable.

C is incorrect. This sentence **misattributes** information and says that Oppenheimer "invaded Poland" while it is Hitler who did so.

D is incorrect. This sentence **misattributes** information and says that Hitler is a "man of science" while it is Oppenheimer who is being referred to as such (**context** that has been established throughout the passage).

Question 6

B is the best answer. By using the semicolon to separate the two independent clauses and by using the comma effectively after the introductory phrase to the second clause (i.e. "in 1942,"), this is the most accurate choice.

A is incorrect. The placement of multiple commas right after each other makes the logic of the sentence extremely difficult to follow. It is hard to tell from a sentence like this one, which information is **integral,** and which is **not integral** to the text.

C is incorrect. The very first word of the sentence "Heeded" is grammatically inaccurate. The only way for this term to be used accurately would be as "In heeding." Because of this immediate inaccuracy, this answer choice can be quickly eliminated.

D is incorrect because of the placement of the comma **after** and ("and,") rather than being used accurately **before** the conjunction (", and").

Question 7

A is the best answer. This sentence uses a semicolon to separate two independent clauses and accurately uses commas after the introductory phrases in each of them ("Under Oppenheimer's leadership" and "the physicists developed the world's first nuclear bomb").

B is incorrect. By placing an unpunctuated dependent clause within the independent clause ("because under Oppenheimer's leadership"), this choice makes the sentence unclear and hard to follow.

C is incorrect. This answer is clearly an example of a run-on sentence. It does not contain accurate punctuation marks and lacks clarity.

D is incorrect. A semicolon is needed to separate two independent clauses. In this choice, "which had a major impact on world history" is **not an independent clause** (i.e., it does not work on its own, as a complete sentence). Therefore, this is not a suitable answer.

Question 8

D is the best answer. By using the period to separate the two independent clauses into different sentences, this choice improves the **clarity** of the sentence and is grammatically correct.

A is incorrect. Although ", and" fits the **FANBOY** rule, this conjunction is clearly not **relevant** given the **tone** of the two sentences. One talks about the date of Oppenheimer's death; the second talks about how his legacy lives on. "And", therefore, is not the appropriate conjunction to **connote** the meaning of the sentence.

B is incorrect for two reasons. First, there is an **irrelevant capitalization** of the term "passing." Furthermore, adding "In 1967" to the second sentence is an **error** since the date is clearly mentioned to **reference** the year of Oppenheimer's passing.

C is incorrect because of the conjunction "and" that follows the semicolon. Only conjunctive adverbs can be used as connectors after this punctuation mark.

TOPIC 6: REDUNDANCY

What is redundancy?
Redundancy is cause when a word/phrase **repeats** content that has already been mentioned/described/implied earlier in the text.

Identify the main idea being conveyed by the sentence	Is there a word or phrase that seems to be repeating what the rest of the sentence is saying?	Can you remove the repeated section without affecting the meaning of the sentence?
Example 1		
Harry found Foucault's *Discipline & Punishment* to be inaccessible and he found it difficult to understand the ideas that were being communicated by the author. *The main idea of this sentence to describe Harry's difficulty in understanding the author's writing. When a text is referred to as being "inaccessible," the implication is that the ideas in it are hard to understand.*	In this example, the word "inaccessible" seems to be communicating the same idea as "found it difficult to understand the ideas that were being communicated by the author" → *the second phrase essentially restates the idea being put forward by the first part of the sentence.*	By removing the repeated section, the revised sentence would read: "Harry found Foucault's *Discipline & Punishment* to be inaccessible" or, better yet, "Harry found Foucault's *Discipline & Punishment* to be an inaccessible text." *By making this change, the redundancy is removed, and the sentence is made clearer and more concise.*
Example 2		
Due to her unrelenting dedication, Yijing woke up at dawn every morning and dedicated herself to running 10 kilometers every day. *The main idea of this sentence is to evidence Yijing's daily dedication in training for the marathon. It demonstrates this by telling us the runner's daily schedule of waking up early is to run 10 kilometers.*	There are two ideas that are repeated here: Yijing's dedication, and that she went running every morning.	By removing the repeated ideas, the revised sentence would read: "Due to her unrelenting dedication, Yijing woke up at dawn every morning to run 10 kilometers". (or)

| | | "Yijing woke up at dawn every morning and dedicated herself to running 10 kilometers."

In both the revisions above, we see how simple edits can help remove the redundancy in a given sentence. |
| --- | --- | --- |

TOPIC 6: PRACTICE QUESTIONS

Questions 1-8 are based on the following passage.

Man's Search for Meaning

What if the meaning of life is to give life meaning? Victor Frankl, author of the book, *Man's Search for Meaning*, might say exactly that. Frankl came to this remarkably simple conclusion while **1** living his life in one of the most horrific places history has ever seen: the Nazi concentration camps. Not only did Frankl endure the horror **2** and survive, he also found deep meaning in his and his fellow inmates' experiences. His perspective may be hard to understand, but it offers profound lessons that apply to the modern world.

Frankl was born in Austria and trained as a psychiatrist. He lost his entire family **3** during World War II, including his wife. Despite his suffering, Frankl was a man of deep insight. He believed there were two types of men: **4** decent men and indecent men. He recounted Nazi guards who were compassionate and kind, and he encountered prisoners who were cruel and manipulative.

Question 1

A) NO CHANGE

B) living life

C) living

D) live

Question 2

A) NO CHANGE

B) while surviving

C) as a survivor

D) DELETE the underlined portion

Question 3

A) NO CHANGE

B) during World War II.

C) including his wife.

D) DELETE the underlined portion

Question 4

A) NO CHANGE

B) decent men and indecent.

C) decent and indecent men.

D) decent and indecent.

Concentration camp life was a hard existence, and prisoners were literally starving. On top of this, they wore thread-bare clothes in freezing conditions and were forced to do intense manual labor each day at dawn. Many of the prisoners found small joys even under these appalling circumstances. For some it was the simple beauty of a sunrise on a cloudless morning. For others, it was a **5** <u>vivid memory</u> of a loved one or joking with a fellow prisoner about the absurdity of their lives. These everyday experiences are what Frankl believed compelled people to continue living. Frankl did not lose faith in life's beauty; rather, he found it even under the most desperate places.

Frankl's possessions, freedom, and even his family were taken away from him. But the one thing he believed could not be taken away was the freedom of choice. A person can determine how they respond to their circumstances – even in the **6** <u>worst imaginable conditions or most dire circumstances</u>. Frankl believed that those who could find a sliver of meaning in camp life were ultimately the ones who survived.

Thankfully, the conditions of concentration camps are **7** <u>exceedingly rare</u> in modern life. But the lessons learned from Frankl's

Question 5

A) NO CHANGE

B) memory

C) vividly-recalled memory

D) visualization

Question 6

A) NO CHANGE

B) worst conditions imaginable.

C) worst, most dire circumstances.

D) most dire imaginable circumstances.

Question 7

A) NO CHANGE

B) very, very rare

C) rare

experiences still apply today. He believed that to find fulfilment, one needs to make his or her **8** <u>life meaningful and live with purpose.</u> According to the insights of the brilliant philosopher Victor Frankl, it is through deep personal connection, enduring suffering for a cause, and intensely personal projects that brings true meaning to life.

D)   DELETE the underlined portion

A)   NO CHANGE

B)   life meaningful.

C)   life lived with meaning and purpose.

D)   meaning and purpose.

Topic 6: Practice Questions (Answers & Explanations)

Question 1

C is the best answer. The use of the term "living" while speaking about a single subject ("Frankl") is sufficient to **imply** that the life that is being described is "his." Furthermore, the notion of "living" directly **connotes** the concept of life (i.e., "life" is the noun which corresponds to the verb "to live"). Therefore, all that is needed in this sentence – to prevent redundancy – is the term "living."

WRONG CHOICES ARE NOT NOTED BUT DESCRIBED COLLECTIVELY.

Question 2

D is the best answer. To "endure" something means to live through that condition, to survive it despite hardship and struggle. In this case, therefore, just saying that Frankl "endured" the Holocaust **implies** his survival of it. Including an additional term/phrase like "survived" and/or "as a survivor" would therefore create redundancy.

WRONG CHOICES ARE NOT NOTED BUT DESCRIBED COLLECTIVELY.

Question 3

B is the best answer. Since the previous sentence speaks about where Frankl was born, it is important to restate **when** and **how** he lost his family. Therefore, the phrase "during World War II" needs to continue to be mentioned. However, by stating that Frankl "lost his entire family," the **implication** is that everyone in his family died. Therefore, "including his wife" is an unnecessary redundancy.

WRONG CHOICES ARE NOT NOTED BUT DESCRIBED COLLECTIVELY.

Question 4

D is the best answer. The redundancy here is the repetition of the term "men." Since it's already been mentioned that there are two types of "men," simply stating "decent and indecent" is more than sufficient to qualify what types of people are being referred to.

WRONG CHOICES ARE NOT NOTED BUT DESCRIBED COLLECTIVELY.

Question 5

A is the best answer. There is no redundancy here since "vivid" is an adjective (meaning intense) that qualifies the "memory." Therefore, by describing something as a "vivid memory," the idea is given an intense quality.

An example to the contrary can be seen in option C, which references a "vividly-recalled memory," which contains a **redundancy in the use of the term "recalled" alongside the term "memory."** Memories, by their very nature, are "recalled" and, therefore, this option contains a redundancy.

Choice B **deletes an added quality to the "memory," thus affecting the information provided.**

Choice D speaks of a "visualization," which **alters the meaning of the statement.** To visualize something means to create a mental image. This does not always mean the image is clear ("vivid") or that the image is being recalled (a "memory" rather than a visualization of something in the present or the future).

Question 6
B is the best answer. There are two **redundancies** to consider here. The first is the use of the words "worst" and "most dire." Both mean essentially the same thing in this **context** – that the circumstances being described are dreadful/horrible. In addition to this redundancy, we find repetition in the use of terms like "conditions" and "circumstances," which once again are synonyms to refer to a particular event/context. By eliminating these redundancies, therefore, choice B is the better answer and is preferable to those in choices A and C (which use both "worst" and "most dire" in different ways).

D is incorrect because of the sentence construction. In order for the phrase to be grammatically correct, it should read "the most dire circumstances imaginable," rather than placing "imaginable" between "dire" and "circumstances." This is an **idiomatic sentence construction** that should be learned.

Question 7
A is the best answer. The term "exceedingly" is an adjective that adds to the word "rare" and qualifies the latter by describing the extreme degree of its rareness. Therefore, there is no repetition here and the statement does not need to be corrected. "Exceedingly" is far more efficient as a word choice than the repeated use of "very." It also adds a quality to "rare" that would be absent if the word is completely deleted.
WRONG CHOICES ARE NOT NOTED BUT DESCRIBED COLLECTIVELY.

Question 8
A is the best answer. To make life "meaningful" and to "live with purpose" cannot be said to be the same concept, i.e., each of those ideas can be defined in different ways, based on the person that has used them. Therefore, there is **no redundancy** in the use of these phrases.

B is incorrect. This answer assumes that "meaningful" implies "living with purpose." However, this would be an **ASSUMPTION** since "meaningful" might mean different things to different people.

C is incorrect because replacing the underlined section with this answer would make the sentence **meaningless.**

D is less suitable. Leaving out the words "life" and "live" from the underlined sections would make the sentence a little harder to understand. "[H]is or her meaning and purpose" would also only work if the preceding verb was "find" rather than "make." "To make" one's meaning and purpose does not read clearly.

TOPIC 7: PARALLELISM

What is parallelism?

A sentence is said to have parallel structure when the items it contains – two or more ideas/ words/ phrases – follow the same pattern.

Parallel Lists

When two or more items are presented as a list, the words used should have the same grammatical form.

Adarsh was known in the neighborhood for his being brilliant, independence, and creativity. → *Incorrect. Here, there are three items in the list: "being brilliant," "independence," and "creativity." We can see that the first item is a gerund followed by an adjective, while the other two are nouns.*

Adarsh was known in the neighborhood for his brilliance, independence, and creativity. → *Correct. Here, all items in the list are in the noun form and thus, exhibit parallel structure.*

Parallel Phrases

Phrases on either side of a conjunction must match in their structure.

Remember the conjunction acronym **FANBOYS** (**F**or, **A**nd, **N**or, **B**ut, **O**r, **Y**et, **S**o) and whenever you see these words, make sure that the phrases on either side of them have the same structure.

Adarsh was well-known in his neighborhood and his brilliance, independence, and creativity were being famous by the community at large. → *Incorrect. In the first part of the sentence, the verb ("was") is followed by the adjective ("well-known"). In the second part of the sentence, the verb is as past continuous ("were being"), followed by an adjective ("famous").*

Adarsh was well-known in his neighborhood and his brilliance, independence, and creativity were famous in the community at large. → *Correct. In this case, both parts of the sentence are conjugated in the simple past, and the verb – in both cases -- is followed by an adjective.*

STRATEGIES

When looking at a list of items, make sure that each item follows the same grammatical structure.

Are they all nouns?
Are they all gerunds?
Are they all adjectives?
If the answer is no, you have a parallelism error.

When looking at phrases that come on either side of a conjunction (FANBOYS), break each phrase down into its different components and their order. Pay particular attention to:
The conjugation of the verb

The item following the verb
The use of nouns versus adjectives
The placement of the preposition
If the use of any element on one side of the conjunction varies in structure from the use on the other side, you have a parallelism error.

TOPIC 7: PRACTICE QUESTIONS

Questions 1-8 are based on the following passage

Quitting Tobacco the Evidenced-Based Way

Tobacco use is the leading cause of preventable death in the United States. Tobacco harms nearly every organ in the body and is known **1** for causing cancer, heart disease, and other health problems. Quitting tobacco is the most important thing a person can do to be healthy. Research suggests that nicotine, the addictive drug found in tobacco, is among the most difficult drugs to quit. Despite the challenge, tobacco users can succeed **2** in quitting by beating their habit forever if they use the right approach.

Tobacco is both physically and psychologically addictive. In other words, when people are addicted to tobacco, their bodies and brains are actually changing **3** to become dependent on the substance. To maximize the chances of success, any attempt to quit tobacco should address both the physical and psychological aspects of the health issue.

Behavioral counselling from a trained professional might occur **4** talking online or over the phone to help with the psychological addiction to tobacco. The effectiveness of

---

Question 1

A) NO CHANGE

B) cause

C) to cause

D) for having caused

Question 2

A) NO CHANGE

B) quit

C) to quit

D) for having quit

Question 3

A) NO CHANGE

B) and becoming

C) and become

D) become

Question 4

A) NO CHANGE

B) in-person

C) through human interactions

treatment increases along with the number and length of counseling sessions. Other popular strategies for quitting like "going cold turkey," hypnosis, and substitution may work for some people. However, the robust scientific evidence shows tobacco users will have the most success quitting [5] with a combination of medications and behavioral counseling.

To the surprise of many, some prescription medication can help people who are trying [6] to give up the habit and quit smoking. Medications, including nicotine replacement products, bupropion SR, and varenicline tartrate, will target the physical addiction by reducing cravings and easing symptoms of withdrawal.

Tobacco users in the United States who are seeking help can call their state quitline at 1-800-QUIT-NOW or ask their doctor for help quitting tobacco. With the right approach – which could include both medication and [7] counseling, anyone can succeed.

D) conversationally

Question 5

A) NO CHANGE

B) taking medicine and behavioural counselling

C) medication and attending counselling

D) DELETE THE UNDERLINED SECTION

Question 6

A) NO CHANGE

B) quitting smoking

C) to quit to smoke

D) quitting to smoke

Question 7

A) NO CHANGE

B) to counsel

C) to seek counseling

D) council

The health benefits of quitting include 8 a reduction in your risk for cancer and lowering the likelihood of lung disease, heart attack, and stroke. Quitting tobacco is hard, but it is an important health goal – and remember, it is never too late to quit.

A) NO CHANGE

B) lowering your risk for cancer, lung disease, and heart attack, and stroke.

C) a reduction in cancer, lung disease, and heart attack, and stroke

D) DELETE THE UNDERLINED SECTION

Topic 7: Practice Questions (Answers & Explanations)

Question 1

C is the best answer. The first verb in this sentence is used in the **SIMPLE PRESENT TENSE** ("harms") and, therefore, to maintain parallel structure, the following verb should also follow that conjugation. In this case, since the next verb is preceded by "known" – and something is always known "for" or "to" something else – "to cause" is the choice that both is grammatically accurate, keeps the sentence's meaning, and retains the verb tense from the first part of the sentence. Therefore, this is the most accurate choice and all the others would violate one of these conditions.

A is incorrect for using the gerund form ("causing).

B is incorrect because when "cause" immediately follows "known" without a "for" or "to" between the words, the sentence loses all meaning.

D is incorrect. "For having caused" is in the **IMPERFECT tense** that causes both a **VERB TENSE INCONSISTENCY and an issue with PARALLELISM in the sentence.**

Question 2

A is the best answer. Here, both verbs are used in their **gerund forms,** i.e., followed by "ing." Therefore, since "in quitting" and "beating" show a parallel structure on either of side of the conjugation "and," it is already the most accurate answer. All other choices would cause an error in parallelism.

B is incorrect for its used of the **SIMPLE PRESENT tense.**

C is incorrect because it uses the **INFINITIVE form of the verb.**

D is incorrect because it uses the **IMPERFECT form of the verb.**

Question 3

B is the best answer. The sentence as it is does not convey information in a way that is easy to understand. By trying out all the other answers to replace the underlined section, we immediately see that the sentence gains more clarity with the use of the conjunction "and" – which then makes the verbs "to change" and "to become" as part of a two-item list that necessitates both verbs having the same form (in this case, the **PRESENT CONTINUOUS TENSE**).

A is incorrect. "Changing to become" is not an accurate way of constructing the sentence (since the **tone** and **meaning** are altered in this choice) leading to the sentence being much harder to understand.

C is incorrect. By adding "add," the verbs "to change" and "to become" are part of a two-item list that necessitates both verbs having the same form.

D is incorrect. Adding the word "become" to replace the underlined section makes the sentence **meaningless** since there is not a sufficient connection being made between the ideas.

Question 4
B is the best answer.

Notice that "online" and "by phone" refer to particular **modes** in which behavioral counselling might occur, i.e., the **mediums through which these sessions occur, through technology like the internet or the telephone.** Therefore, to maintain parallel structure, the first item in this three-item list needs to also refer to a "mode" of counselling rather than a verb like "talking," an adverb like "conversationally," or a phrase like "through human interactions." Thus, "in-person" is the best option here.
WRONG CHOICES ARE NOT NOTED BUT DESCRIBED COLLECTIVELY.

Question 5
A is the best answer. Notice that the list here consists of two items – "medications" and "behavioral counselling"— both of which are used as nouns. Therefore, no change is needed.

B & C are incorrect because the items on the list are not used in the same way. In both cases, one item is qualified with a preceding gerund ("taking" medications and "attending" counselling), while the other term is used as a noun. This would affect the parallel structure and render the sentence **grammatically inaccurate.**

D is incorrect. By deleting the underlined section, the sentence **would be incomplete and lose meaning.**

Question 6
A is the best answer. "To give up" and "quit" are both conjugated in the infinitive, allowing parallel structure.

In this case, the most efficient way to arrive at the correct answer is to go through a process of elimination and by replacing the underlined section with the different answers provided. Immediately, we see that none of these options make grammatical sense:
- To the surprise of many, some prescription medication can help people who are <u>quitting smoking.</u> → **Using a gerund (like "quitting") is more passive that using the active infinitive ("to quit").**
- To the surprise of many, some prescription medication can help people who are <u>to quit to smoke.</u> → **Grammatically incorrect**
- To the surprise of many, some prescription medication can help people who are <u>quitting to smoke.</u> → **Grammatically incorrect**

Question 7

A is the best answer. Here, "medication" and "counselling" are both nouns that are used in a two-item list. Since both of these words adhere to the same grammatical form, no change is needed.

Note that "counselling" might sound like a verb (because of the "ing"); however, in **context** we understand that what is being addressed is the assistance of a mental health/behavioral counsellor. In this case, "counselling" is not used as an action word; it is used to name a particular activity (i.e., a noun).

Two of the incorrect choices (options B & C) that use "counsel" as a verb can be ignored. The final choice, "council," **alters the meaning of the word entirely** and therefore, cannot be considered a viable option.

Question 8

B is the best answer. By combining **redundant** phrases like "reduction" and "lowering," this sentence effectively improves the **clarity and tone** of the underlined section.

A is incorrect. Apart from unnecessarily splitting the clause into two parts that speak to the reduction in risks that come from quitting smoking, this sentence also does **not contain parallel structure.** Notice the difference between "reduction in" and "lowering," i.e., the different grammatical forms that these verbs take on either side of the conjunction **"and."**

C is incorrect because it changes the meaning of the sentence by deleting the word "risk," i.e., quitting smoking does not reduce the disease itself; it reduces the risk of the disease occurring.

D is incorrect because deleting the underlined section would render the sentence **incomplete and meaningless.**

TOPIC 8: PRONOUNS

What is a pronoun?
A pronoun is a word that can take the place of a noun.

A pronoun must agree with its antecedent (i.e., the noun that the pronoun is replacing).

PERSONAL PRONOUNS
Note the agreement that needs to occur between the pronoun and the gender and number of the noun(s) it replaces.

I/me/my: first person singular
*I spent all evening watching the election results unfold because **I** knew that the the outcome would affect **me** and **my** family.*

We/us/ours: first person plural
*We spent all evening watching the election results unfold because **we** knew that the outcome would affect **us** and **our** families.*

You/your: second person (singular and plural)
*You should spend the evening watching the election results unfold because the outcome will affect **you** and **your** family.*

He/him/his: third person masculine (singular)
*Akram spent all evening watching the election results unfold because **he** knew that the outcome would affect **him** and **his** family.*

She/her: third person feminine (singular)
*Anastasia spent all evening watching the election results unfold because the outcome would affect **her** and **her** family.*

It/its: third person neutral (inanimate objects)
*The television was in use all evening because we were using **it** to watch the election results unfold.*

They/them/their — third person (plural) + multiple inanimate objects
*Akram's and Elizabeth's families spent all evening watching the election results unfold because the outcome would affect all of **them**.*

*The televisions were in use all evening because **they** were being used to watch the election results.*

RELATIVE PRONOUNS
Notice the agreement between the "type" of noun(s) being replaced, i.e., if the noun refers to a place, a time, or an idea.

Who and whom — a person
*As the newscaster got ready to announce **the winner of the election**, we wondered **who** it would be.*

When — a point in time

The newscaster will announce the winner of the election, **when** *all the votes* **have been counted.**

Where — a place
The winning candidate will deliver their speech from **the place where** *they first announced their candidacy.*

Which and that
The newscasters announced **the election results, which** *we had all been waiting nervously for.*
The newscasters announced **the election results that** *we had all been waiting nervously for.*

STRATEGY

Identify the number of nouns that the pronoun replaces
Singular/plural

Identify the gender of the nouns that the pronoun replaces
For personal pronouns: is the noun male/female/both/neither?
For relative pronouns: is the noun a place/a time/an idea?

Use the appropriate personal or relative pronoun based on the number and type of noun that you have identified.

TOPIC 8: PRACTICE QUESTIONS

Questions 1-8 are based on the following passage.

Salvador Dalí and The Persistence of Memory

Salvador Dalí was born May 11, 1904 in Figueras, Spain. He is famously known as a Surrealist painter and one of the most versatile artists of the twentieth century. Throughout the duration of **1** this long life, Dalí dabbled in a vast range of artistic outlets including printmaking, painting, fashion, advertising, writing, sculpting, and filmmaking. In fact, Dalí is most famously known for his filmmaking collaborations with other well-known creative professionals including the likes of Luis Buñucl and Alfred Hitchcock.

From an early age, Dalí received encouragement from his parents to pursue sophisticated art forms. His passion for art, **2** which eventually led him to drawing school, characterized Dalí's existence.

In 1922, Dalí was admitted into the Academy of Art in Madrid **3** when he drew attention to himself through his eccentric ways and art works. He allowed himself to be influenced by several different artistic styles. Despite his talents, Dalí was eventually expelled from the

Question 1
A) NO CHANGE
B) its
C) his
D) himself

Question 2
A) NO CHANGE
B) that
C) it
D) when

Question 3
A) NO CHANGE
B) who
C) what
D) where

Academy after being accused of instigating conflict.

Shortly after he was expelled, Dali visited Paris where he was introduced to Pablo Picasso. In his early years as an artist, Dalí's work reflected the motifs of **4** the fellow Spanish painters – particularly Picasso and Joan Miró – as well as his fascination with Renaissance and Classical art. Regardless, Dalí experimented with several styles of avant-garde painting. He began to display his work in galleries around Barcelona and Madrid. However, it wasn't until the late 1920s that Dalí began to dabble in the surrealist artistic style that **5** it is known for today.

Question 4

A) NO CHANGE

B) its

C) her

D) his

Question 5

A) NO CHANGE

B) the art

C) he

D) himself

Dalí was most famous for his surreal painting **6** he called *Persistence of Memory*, which he completed in 1913. Perhaps one of his most famous works, the Persistence of Memory was first shown at the Julien Levy Gallery in 1932. It featured a spectacle of hard objects becoming limp – thought to create the illusion of time bending. This painting became an icon for symbolism and one of the most famous and recognizable pieces of art in the 20th century.

Question 6

A) NO CHANGE

B) it

C) they

D) DELETE the underlined word

In 1929 Dalí met his wife Gala, **7** <u>whom</u> he claimed to be his muse and inspiration for a vast number of his artworks. She was not only his muse but also **8** <u>his</u> business manager. Dalí's health began to decline at age 76, and his career as an artist began to fade. Gala passed away in 1982, and Dalí followed a few short years later at the age of age 84.

A) NO CHANGE

B) that

C) who

D) which

A) NO CHANGE

B) its

C) her

D) the artist's

Topic 8: Practice Questions (Answers & Explanations)

Question 1

C is the best answer. The noun that is being referred to is Dalí – singular, masculine, third person (all of this information is provided through the **context** in the previous sentences; notice the use of "He" to begin the second sentence of the paragraph). Given this, "his" is the only possible answer. "This" and "it" would be used to replace inanimate objects; the **reflexive pronoun** ("himself") would only be used if the subject of the sentence was "He" (not Dalí, as indicated in the clause that follows the introductory clause).
WRONG CHOICES ARE NOT NOTED BUT DESCRIBED COLLECTIVELY.

Question 2

A is the best answer. The term "which" is used to refer to Dalí's "passion for art" (a phrase that communicates an idea/concept). "Who" would be appropriate only if the pronoun was being used to replace a person, "where" could be appropriate only if the pronoun was being used to replace a place, and "what" is generally used in a **noun clause** (a dependent clause that acts as a noun), not as a pronoun.
WRONG CHOICES ARE NOT NOTED BUT DESCRIBED COLLECTIVELY.

Question 3

D is the best answer. The noun being replaced here is a place, i.e., the "Academy of Art in Madrid." Therefore, "where" is the most appropriate pronoun choice. "When" would be appropriate only if the pronoun was being used to replace a time, "who" would be appropriate only if the pronoun was being used to replace a person, and "what" is generally used in a **noun clause** (a dependent clause that acts as a noun), not as a pronoun.
WRONG CHOICES ARE NOT NOTED BUT DESCRIBED COLLECTIVELY.

Question 4

D is the best answer. The "fellow painters" being referred to are those who were Dalí's peers. Therefore, the noun that this pronoun replaces is Dalí (as we know, Dalí is singular, male, and third person). "His" is the only accurate option.

"The" is an article, not a pronoun and, therefore, its use here would be inaccurate. "Its" would be used if referencing an inanimate object (not a person); "her" would be used only if the pronoun was replacing a noun that refers to a female (and as established throughout the passage, Dalí is male).
WRONG CHOICES ARE NOT NOTED BUT DESCRIBED COLLECTIVELY.

Question 5

C is the best answer. The noun that is being referred to is Dalí – singular, masculine, third person (all of this information is provided through the **context** in the previous sentences). Therefore, "he" is the best option.

A is incorrect because "it" would only be used if the noun being replaced was inanimate (i.e., the art itself).

B is incorrect because "the art" **is a noun** and using this phrase here would render the sentence meaningless.

D is incorrect. The **reflexive pronoun** ("himself") would only be used if the subject of the sentence was "He" (not Dalí, as indicated in the clause that precedes the use of the underlined pronoun).

Question 6

D is the best answer. The pronoun is unnecessary here since the sentence does not require its usage in order to communicate the necessary meaning. Although "he" agrees with the antecedent noun ("Dalí"), we can see that the sentence refers to the name of a painting (that is stated directly before the name of the work of art).
WRONG CHOICES ARE NOT NOTED BUT DESCRIBED COLLECTIVELY.

Question 7

C is the best answer. Since the pronoun here refers to a person ("Gala," Dalí's wife), the most appropriate relative pronoun would be who or whom – since all other options would not be used to refer to a person.

When trying to decide between **who** and **whom,** consider this. **If the person being referred to is the subject of the sentence, use "who." If the person being referred to is the object of a verb or preposition, use "whom."**

In this case, Dalí's wife is clearly the subject of the sentence. Therefore, "who" is the better choice.
WRONG CHOICES ARE NOT NOTED BUT DESCRIBED COLLECTIVELY.

Question 8

A is the best answer. Since the two subjects are of different genders, using "his" twice does not take away from the grammatical accuracy. In fact, clarity is maintained because of the use of consecutive pronouns – reminding the reader of who it is being referred to.

B is incorrect. "Its" is used to refer to a **NON-HUMAN** subject. In this case, since the person being referred to is a male person (Dalí), it would not be accurate to refer to this artist as "it."

C is incorrect. "Her" is used to refer to a **FEMALE** subject. In this case, since the person being referred to is **MALE** (Dalí), it would not be accurate to refer to this artist as "her."

D is incorrect. Restating "the artist's" would be necessary only if there would otherwise be a lack of clarity in who is being referred to (i.e., when both subjects in the sentence are of the same gender). Since that is not the case in this sentence – Dalí and his wife are of different genders – it is not necessary to restate "the artist" since we understand (**from the surrounding context**) who is being referred to.

TOPIC 9: VERB TENSES

> **What is a verb tense?**
> Tenses are categories that tell us **when** something happens/has happened/will happen. Tenses are usually made evident in how **verbs are conjugated.** While the list below is not exhaustive, below are the tenses that are most important to remember.

SIMPLE PRESENT	PRESENT PROGRESSIVE or PRESENT CONTINUOUS	PRESENT PERFECT
Used for sentences in which the action happens in the moment. Kashmir **is** a conflict zone between India, Pakistan, and China.	*Used for sentences in which the action is happening in the moment (i.e., it implies a continuity of the action that simple present does not).* An international conflict between India, China, and Pakistan **is occurring** in the region of Kashmir.	*Used to describe actions that began in the past but continue in the present. This is often indicated by the use of "has" or "have" (singular/plural subjects) + the past participle of the verb.* Since 1947, Kashmir **has become** a conflict zone between India, Pakistan, and China.
SIMPLE PAST	**PAST PERFECT**	**CONDITIONAL**
Used for sentences in which the action has already happened (i.e., it has been completed). Kashmir **became** a conflict zone between India, Pakistan, and China in 1947 after the Partition.	*Used in a sentence that describes **two** completed actions. The past perfect is used to describe the event that took place first. This is often indicated by the use of "had" + the past participle of the verb.* Kashmir **became** a conflict zone after the Partition between India & Pakistan **had occurred**.	*Used to describe things that could occur, or things that have not occurred from the perspective of the past. This is often indicated by the use of "would" + the verb.* No one knew that Kashmir **would become** a conflict zone between three of the world's nuclear powers.

FUTURE	GERUNDS & INFINITIVES
Used to speak about events that haven't happened yet and might/will take place in the future. This is often indicated by the use of "will" + the verb.	*Both these tenses function as nouns.* *Gerunds have an "ing" at the end of the verb ("becoming"); infinitives are preceded by "to" ("to become").*

It is likely that Kashmir **will continue** to be a flashpoint on the Indian subcontinent.	*The only way to choose between a gerund and an infinitive is to see which option sounds/reads better.* The governments of India, Pakistan and China have agreed on **disagreeing** about the issue of Kashmir. (or) The governments of India, Pakistan and China have agreed **to disagree** about the issue of Kashmir. *In the examples above, while both options are grammatically accurate, "agreed to disagree" sounds better that "agreed to disagreeing." Therefore, it is a better choice.* *When you have a gerund, try replacing it with the infinitive (and vice versa). Consider which option sounds better in the context of the given sentence.*

STRATEGY

Study the text for clues about the timing of an event that the sentence describes.

*Does the event **happen** now?* SIMPLE PRESENT

*Is the event **still happening** now?* PRESENT CONTINUOUS

*Has the event **happened** recently?* PRESENT PERFECT

*Has this event **occurred** in the past?* SIMPLE PAST

*Had it **happened** before some other event occurred?* PAST PERFECT

*Would this event **have been predictable** in the past?* CONDITIONAL

Will this event happen in the future? FUTURE

*Is the event **happening**, or is it about **to happen**?* GERUND versus INFINITIVE

Usually, all verbs in a given sentence have to be conjugated in the same tense so as to prevent a VERB TENSE INCONSISTENCY.

TOPIC 9: PRACTICE QUESTIONS

Questions 1-8 are based on the following passage.

Natural Antifreeze in Wood Frogs

The wood frog is an intriguing species. It inhabits forests spanning from the Appalachian Mountains all the way up into the Arctic Circle. Some areas of its range can fall as low as -4°C, and over the years experts **1** ponder how a species of frog could survive in such freezing temperatures. The answer can be found in the wood frog's surprising adaptive physiology: natural antifreeze.

When temperatures drop low enough, the fluid surrounding the blood and organ cells of an organism will begin to freeze. As a result, solute concentrations begin to increase, and the law of osmosis – the process by which water is drawn out of the cell – comes into effect. This process can be harmful to cells in extremely cold conditions. However, wood frogs **2** adapted physiologic features that prevent ice from forming. This allows wood frogs to survive extreme freezing temperatures, but how is this all possible?

Question 1

A) NO CHANGE
B) have pondered
C) will have pondered
D) pondered

Question 2

A) NO CHANGE
B) will adapt
C) adapt
D) have adapted

Much like the many other animals that hibernate, the frog **3** enters an inactive state. The frog's heart rate and breathing rate slow down, and its body temperature and metabolic rate begin to drop when temperatures lower.

Question 3

A) NO CHANGE
B) had entered
C) entered
D) will enter

Antifreeze proteins found in wood frogs prevent ice formation outside the frog's cells. These proteins bind to the surface of ice crystals found outside the cell. This limits the ice crystals' growth. The antifreeze proteins work in tandem with compounds call cryoprotectants. As the narrative explains below, crypto protectants **4** will play an important role in the wood frog's biology.

Question 4

A) NO CHANGE
B) play
C) had played
D) will have played

Cryoprotectants – which include glucose, glycerol, and urea – move through the aquaporins in the cell. Over time, this **5** will increase the solute concentration and hinders the harmful outflow of water during freezing. Ultimately, this **6** prevents the degree to which the cells will shrink in freezing temperatures.

Question 5

A) NO CHANGE
B) increases
C) had increased
D) will have increased

Question 6

A) NO CHANGE
B) prevented
C) will prevent
D) will have prevented

When the freezing temperatures let up, the frog essentially begins to thaw out. Wood frogs recover from their hibernation extraordinarily fast. The frog's basic behavioral and physiological functions generally return within hours of "thawing." In fact, the wood frog's heart begins to beat even before the ice inside the frog **7** has melted completely.

The wood frog can survive the harsh freezing temperatures of its extreme habitats using its own type of evolutionary hibernation. At the point of hibernation, the frog may appear to be either dead or frozen. However, by the end of winter, this frozen-looking wood frog **8** thaws out!

Question 7

A) NO CHANGE

B) melts

C) will melt

D) will have melted

Question 8

A) NO CHANGE

B) will have thawed

C) will thaw

D) had thawed

Topic 9: Practice Questions (Answers & Explanations)

Question 1

B is the best answer. Since the sentence describes events that have occurred "over the years" (implying a past event that is relevant in the present), the **PRESENT PERFECT tense** is the most appropriate answer.

A is incorrect. If "ponder" is used only in the **PRESENT TENSE**, it **implies that this event has not occurred before.** In this case, the **KEYWORDS** "over the years" tell us that this has happened in the past. Therefore, this answer cannot be suitable.

C is incorrect. Once again, using "will have" in relation to "over the years" leads to **INCONSISTENCY** in the statement. This sentence construction implies a **CONDITIONAL,** i.e., as if something could have happened but didn't.

D is incorrect. If "pondered" is used only in the **PAST TENSE**, it **implies that this event has terminated and has no current implications.** In this case, the **KEYWORDS** "over the years" tell us that this event continues to happen (the pondering). Therefore, this answer cannot be suitable.

Question 2

D is the best answer. In this sentence, the word "adapted" is used to refer to something that has happened in the past and that still occurs today (i.e., the way in which the cells adapted then, have resulted in the way that the cells function now). Therefore, the most appropriate tense choice would be the **PRESENT PERFECT TENSE,** i.e., "has" or "have," followed by the past participle of the verb. Since the subjects being referred to here are in the plural (i.e., "wood frogs"), the correct choice is "**have adapted.**"
WRONG CHOICES ARE NOT NOTED BUT DESCRIBED COLLECTIVELY.

Question 3

A is the best answer. Based on the **context** provided in the rest of the paragraph, we know that the hibernation behaviors being described in the text **happen in the present.** Therefore, the most appropriate choice here is the **SIMPLE PRESENT TENSE.** Since the current sentence already includes the most appropriate form of the verb conjugation, no change is needed.
WRONG CHOICES ARE NOT NOTED BUT DESCRIBED COLLECTIVELY.

Question 4

B is the best answer. The previous verb that is used in this sentence has been conjugated in the **SIMPLE PRESENT TENSE** (i.e., "explains"). Therefore, in order to prevent **VERB TENSE INCOSISNTENCY** is for the verb that follows to also be conjugated in the same way. This, in addition to the need for subject-verb agreement (with "the narrative below") tells us that "play" is the only accurate choice for an answer to this question.
WRONG CHOICES ARE NOT NOTED BUT DESCRIBED COLLECTIVELY.

Question 5

B is the best answer. The clue to this answer can be seen in the verbs that follow the underlined text ("hinders" and "prevents"). This immediately tells us that "increases" is the only possible option since any other choice would cause a **VERB TENSE INCOSISTENCY** within the paragraph.
WRONG CHOICES ARE NOT NOTED BUT DESCRIBED COLLECTIVELY.

Question 6

C is the best answer. Notice the use of all the other verbs that precede and follow the underlined section ("will increase" and "will shrink") – both of which use the **FUTURE TENSE**. Therefore, in order for the sentence to adhere to **VERB TENSE CONSISTENCY,** the underlined term should also be conjugated in the future tense (i.e., "will prevent"). Any other choice would cause the sentence to become grammatically inaccurate.
WRONG CHOICES ARE NOT NOTED BUT DESCRIBED COLLECTIVELY.

Question 7

A is the best answer. In this sentence, the best choice is not **consistency** because of the use of the **KEYWORDS** "even before." Since events that occur in different times are mentioned here, we see the need for the **PERFECT TENSE** (i.e., has/have/had + the verb).

However, since the first verb is conjugated in the **SIMPLE PRESENT**, we can tell that the verb that follows needs to be in the **PRESENT PERFECT (past perfect is used only when the previous event in the sentence is conjugated in the simple past tense)**. Therefore, "has melted" -- by being conjugated in the present perfect -- is the most accurate answer.
WRONG CHOICES ARE NOT NOTED BUT DESCRIBED COLLECTIVELY.

Question 8

B is the best answer. Notice that the event being referenced here happens in the future, i.e. "by the end of winter." Therefore, the verb "thaw" needs to be conjugated in the future tense. This leaves us with two options: "will thaw" and "will have thawed."

From what we know of the **PAST** and **PRESENT PERFECT TENSE** – indicated by the use of "has" or "have" or "had" – the PERFECT TENSE is used only when **two actions are being referred to in the same sentence.** So, in this case, **"will HAVE"** would only be used if there was another action being referred to in the same sentence (that takes place more recently that the action highlighted). **Since there is only one verb in this sentence, any form of the PERFECT TENSE can be ruled out.** Thus, we are left with one correct answer: "will thaw".
WRONG CHOICES ARE NOT NOTED BUT DESCRIBED COLLECTIVELY.

TOPIC 10: DASHES & COLONS

What is a dash?
Dashes (--) when used on both sides of a **non-essential phrase**, function like commas. When used on one side of a phrase, the dash functions like a colon (i.e., to introduce an explanation or a list).

What is a colon?
Colons (:) are generally used to introduce lists and explanations and **follow a complete sentence,** i.e., using a period in place of the colon should result in a sentence that makes sense.

USING THE COLON

Doug went to the store and bought groceries for the week, including: chicken, apples, and peanut butter.

→

Incorrect. Adding ", including" before the colon results in the first part of the sentence not being complete.

Doug went to the store and bought groceries for the week: chicken, apples, and peanut butter.

→

Correct. The colon is preceded by a complete sentence and is followed by a list of items.

Doug went to the store and bought groceries for the week: a weekly chore that was his responsibility.

→

Correct. The colon here is used to introduce an explanation that follows a complete thought.

USING DASHES

Doug, as a weekly chore – went to the store and bought groceries for his household.

→

*Incorrect. "As a weekly chore" is demarcated here as a non-essential clause. Therefore, it either needs to be surrounded by dashes on **both** sides or with commas on both sides of the phrase.*

Doug -- as a weekly chore – went to the store and bought groceries for his household.

→

Correct. The dashes are used on either side to demarcate the non-essential phrase.

Doug went to the store and bought groceries for the week -- a weekly chore that was his responsibility.

→

Correct. The dash here is used to introduce an explanation that follows a complete thought (just like the colon).

Choosing between a COLON and a DASH, as above, is often a matter of style. It is rare that both options will be provided as the potential correct answers for the same question.

TOPIC 10: PRACTICE QUESTIONS

Questions 1-8 are based on the following passage.

Highly Active Antiretroviral Therapy (HAART)

In the past, the human immunodeficiency **1** <u>virus the pathogen that causes the HIV infection</u> was believed to be nearly untreatable. Now, there are a number of effective treatments that greatly improve HIV patient outlook and quality of life.

Highly active antiretroviral **2** <u>therapy , or: HAART – is</u> a term that was coined in the late 1990's to describe the efficacy **3** <u>of – a particular combination – of</u> drugs used in the treatment of HIV. Before HAART was used to treat patients with HIV, doctors had not had much luck treating either the disease or the related autoimmune deficiency that often develops as a result.

Before HAART, an AIDs or HIV diagnosis was **4** <u>considered – a death sentence.</u> Instead of using a cocktail of antivirals to treat HIV, only one or two drugs were used to treat the devastating disease. When it was discovered, HAART was commonly known as a "triple drug **5** <u>cocktail:" the</u> discovery of this drug cocktail remains to be one of the most significant breakthroughs in the modern treatment of AIDs and HIV.

Question 1

A) NO CHANGE

B) virus, the pathogen that causes the HIV infection – was.

C) virus – the pathogen that causes the HIV infection, was.

D) virus – the pathogen that causes the HIV infection – was.

Question 2

A) NO CHANGE

B) therapy – or HAART – is

C) therapy : or HAART – is

D) therapy, or HAART is

Question 3

A) NO CHANGE

B) of, a particular combination, of

C) of: a particular combination of

D) of a particular combination

Question 4

A) NO CHANGE

B) considered: a death sentence

C) considered a death sentence

D) considered, a death sentence

Question 5

A) NO CHANGE

B) cocktail." The

C) cocktail" – the

D) cocktail," the

Before HAART, the HIV viral populations would spontaneously mutate. When this happened, the drugs available at the time were no longer effective in stopping the virus from 6 mutating – a phenomenon exhibited by a number of viruses with drug resistance. The antiretrovirals used in HAART suppress a wide range of HIV pathogens that exists within a single viral population. If one drug is rendered ineffective in treating a certain viral 7 type – then the other drugs pick up the slack. This suppresses the HIV virus population and reduces the chance that the virus will mutate within the blood stream. This is the key factor to treating HIV as it is near impossible to keep up with the variations of mutations that the virus is able to undergo when it exists in high populations within the blood stream.

Using HAART, scientists combine three or more drugs with protease inhibitors to effectively treat HIV patients. While researching, scientist observed that the antiviral cocktail effectively inhibited the HIV virus from replicating at certain different points in the virus' life cycle. Currently, there are five classes of antiretroviral 8 drugs: each one affects a specific stage of the virus's life cycle. Within only three years of the introduction of

Question 6

A) NO CHANGE
B) mutating a
C) mutating; a
D) mutating: a

Question 7

A) NO CHANGE
B) type, then
C) type: then
D) type then

Question 8

A) NO CHANGE
B) drugs; each
C) drugs, each
D) drugs each

HAART, doctors and scientists saw a 50% drop in the number of deaths related to AIDs and HIV in both the U.S. and Europe. All in all, HAART represents a major leap forward in the treatment of HIV and AIDs around the world.

Topic 10: Practice Questions (Answers & Explanations)

Question 1

D is the best answer. Unless being used to introduce a list or an explanation, DASHES are used on **BOTH sides of a NON-ESSENTIAL CLAUSE, i.e., information that adds to a sentence but that is not integral to the accuracy of that statement.** When used on one side of a clause, the information that comes before the DASH needs to be **able to stand alone as a complete thought.** Since none of the options with a single dash contain a preceding complete thought, the use of dashes on both sides of the non-essential clause is the best choice.
WRONG CHOICES ARE NOT NOTED BUT DESCRIBED COLLECTIVELY.

Question 2

B is the best answer. DASHES are used on **BOTH sides of a NON-ESSENTIAL CLAUSE, i.e., information that adds to a sentence but that is not integral to the accuracy of that statement.** When used on one side of a clause, the information that comes before the DASH needs to be **able to stand alone as a complete thought** (and in this case, the DASH functions like a COLON: to introduce a list or provide an explanation).

The answer choices that use a colon and a dash (A & C) can be immediately eliminated since this combination of punctuations would render the sentence meaningless.

D would be a viable option if the COMMA was used on either side of the non-essential phrase ("or HAART"). Since there is only one comma used in this option, it is clearly incorrect.

Question 3

D is the best answer. Here, the phrase "of a particular combination" is **an integral** part of the sentence and is not used to describe or qualify any information that comes before it. In fact, this phrase is simply part of the rest of the sentence. Therefore, no punctuations should be used here.
WRONG CHOICES ARE NOT NOTED BUT DESCRIBED COLLECTIVELY.

Question 4

C is the best answer. Here, the phrase "was considered a death sentence" is **an integral** part of the sentence and is not used to describe or qualify any information that comes before it. In fact, this phrase is simply part of the sentence itself. Therefore, no punctuations should be used here.
WRONG CHOICES ARE NOT NOTED BUT DESCRIBED COLLECTIVELY.

Question 5

B is the best answer. There are two complete sentences in this part of the text. The first sentence is "When it was discovered, HAART was commonly known as a "triple drug cocktail," and the second sentence is "The discovery of this drug cocktail remains to be one of the most significant breakthroughs in the modern treatment of AIDs and HIV." These two sentences, while linked by the

theme of the "drug cocktail," are clearly separate thoughts, i.e., neither of them is used to describe/explain/qualify the other, and neither of them is non-essential. Therefore, the only accurate option would be to split the sentences into two and separate them with a period.
WRONG CHOICES ARE NOT NOTED BUT DESCRIBED COLLECTIVELY.

Question 6

A is the best answer. Consider this. Does the clause "a phenomenon exhibited by a number of viruses with drug resistance" **explain** something that came before it? Not really. While the information provided here adds **context** to the earlier part of the sentence, it does not directly explain content that precedes it. Therefore, a DASH is a more accurate option than a COLON (since the latter would be a more identifiable explanation of a previously mentioned idea/concept).

Using no punctuation between "mutating" and "a" (choice B) renders the sentence meaningless.

Using a semicolon (choice C) is inaccurate since this punctuation is only used when the clauses on **both sides** of the mark are complete thoughts (each with its own subject, verb, and object). Since this condition is not met, this is not a viable answer choice.

Question 7

B is the best answer. Consider the clause preceding the underlined punctuation mark. "If one drug is rendered ineffective in treating a certain viral type." You'll immediately notice that this is **NOT a complete thought.** Therefore, we immediately know that neither a COLON nor a single DASH is an accurate choice (since they must be preceded by a complete thought). However, from reading the sentence, we know that some form of punctuation is required so as to make the **content** clearer to the reader. Therefore, the comma (choice B), becomes the best choice.

Question 8

B is the best answer. There are two complete sentences in this part of the text. The first sentence is "Currently, there are five classes of antiretroviral drugs" and the second sentence is "each one affects a specific stage of the virus's life cycle." These two sentences are clearly separate thoughts, i.e., neither of them is used to describe/explain/qualify the other, and neither of them is non-essential. Therefore, the only accurate option would be to split the sentences into two and separate them with a period or a semicolon.
WRONG CHOICES ARE NOT NOTED BUT DESCRIBED COLLECTIVELY.

TOPIC 11: APOSTROPHES

What is an apostrophe?
Apostrophes (') are mostly used with nouns to indicate **possession** of something.
They are also used to form contractions.

If a word is in the singular, then you add an apostrophe and an "s" AFTER the apostrophe.
For example: **Ana's** father cooks Peruvian food once a week to remind his children of their heritage.

If a word is in the plural but it doesn't end in "s", then you add an apostrophe and an "s" AFTER the apostrophe.
For example:
Ana and Jorge's father cooks Peruvian food once a week to remind his children of their heritage.
(or)
The children's father cooks Peruvian food once a week to remind them of their heritage.

If a word in the singular or plural ends in s, then you add an apostrophe to the end of the word.
For example: **The siblings'** father cooks Peruvian food once a week to remind his children of their heritage.

REMEMBER THAT THE APOSTROPHE IS MOSTLY USED TO INDICATE POSSESSION (i.e., something belongs to someone/something else)

In all other cases, the use of the apostrophe is incorrect.

To check if a noun should be in the possessive form, add the words "of the" between them.
For example: The father **of the children** cooks Peruvian food every week.

If the sentence makes sense by adding "of the" preceding the possessed word, the noun following "of the" should be in the possessive form.

THE APOSTROPHE IS ALSO USED TO INDICATE A CONTRACTION
It's = it is
They're = they are
Don't = do not
Can't = cannot
Shouldn't = should not
There'll = there will

Make sure to check whether the apostrophe is being used to indicate possession or a contraction.

TOPIC 11: PRACTICE QUESTIONS

Questions 1-8 are based on the following passage.

The Mysterious Platypus

The platypus is an unusual creature. It was discovered over two centuries ago, but the first evidence of the animal was suspected to be a hoax. A governor in Sydney sent illustrations of the **1** <u>platypus and the animals fur</u> to European biologists for further research. They thought that the animal was a fabrication due to its odd physiology. The governor described the platypus to the European biologists as a small, amphibious mole-like creature that burrowed in the banks of fresh water lakes. **2** <u>Regardless, the platypus – with its fur</u>, warm blood, webbed feet, egg laying properties, and slick duck bill – is most certainly an odd and mysterious creature.

Even today, people remain perplexed over the idea of a mammal that lays eggs and has a duck bill. Its unique traits, however, have proven critical to the **3** <u>platypus hunting abilities. Platypuses</u> stalk their prey in deep, dark waters, where the senses of sound, smell, and sight are of little use.

In 1802, scientists discovered that the **4** <u>platypus nervous system</u> includes a series of the trigeminal nerves that supply sensory

---

Question 1

A) NO CHANGE

B) platypus and the animals' fur

C) platypus's and the animal's fur

D) platypus and the animal's fur

Question 2

A) NO CHANGE

B) Regardles's, the platypus – with it's fur

C) Regardless, the platypus' – with its fur

D) Regardless, the platypus – with it's fur

Question 3

A) NO CHANGE

B) platypus' hunting abilities. Platypuses

C) platypus' hunting abilities. Platypus's

D) platypus hunting abilities. Platypus's

Question 4

A) NO CHANGE

B) platypus' nervous system

C) platypus' nervous's system

D) platypus's nervous system

stimulation to the brain from certain regions of the head.

Scientists in the nineteenth century learned a great deal about this mysterious anima, but researchers 5 didn't begin to fully understand the platypus's unusual bill until the 20th century. 6 Platypus's share a prominent facial feature that is actually a finely-tuned organ linked to the innervations of the trigeminal nerves. Pores on the bill have morphological similarities to the ampullary electroreceptors found in electric fish, which pick up on low frequency electric signals are generated by an 7 animals nerves and the beats of its heart.

The 8 platypus' bill may look odd, but its actually a finely-tuned sensory organ that can pinpoint the exact location of underwater prey. The electroreception of the platypus's bill was coined the "bill sense," which explains how platypuses are able to deftly navigate through dark waters to find prey. Platypus electroreception was first confirmed by scientists in Australia many years ago, but this mysterious animal continues to perplex researchers to this day.

Question 5

A) NO CHANGE
B) didnt fully understand the platypus's
C) didn't fully understand the platypus
D) didnt fully understand the platypus

Question 6

A) NO CHANGE
B) Platypus
C) Platypus'
D) Platypuses

Question 7

A) NO CHANGE
B) animals' nerves and the beats
C) animal's nerves and the beats
D) animal's nerves and the beats'

Question 8

A) NO CHANGE
B) platypus' bill may look odd, but it's
C) platypus bill may look odd, but it's
D) platypus' bill may look odd, but its'

Topic 11: Practice Questions (Answers & Explanations)

Question 1

D is the best answer. There are two things to consider here. First, we know that the fur belongs to the animal (by using the "of the" strategy, we see that "the fur of the animal" makes sense). Therefore, we know that there should be an apostrophe. Second, we need to consider if "animal" is in the singular or the plural form. From the previous and following sentences, we see that "the animal" is used in the singular form. Therefore, for **consistency**, this use of "the animal" would also be singular. The only correct answer is choice D that both indicates possession and uses the singular form.
WRONG CHOICES ARE NOT NOTED BUT DESCRIBED COLLECTIVELY.

Question 2

A is the best answer. The word "regardless" is a **connector** and apostrophes are only used with **nouns** to indicate possession of something/someone. Therefore, any answer choice that uses an apostrophe within the word "regardless" can be disregarded. Furthermore, remember that when the apostrophe is used with "it's," it is a contraction for "it is" and saying "it is fur" would clearly be inaccurate. Therefore, the only right answer would have **no apostrophe** either in the term "regardless" or in the word "its."

In the case of "it's," also try the "of the" strategy. With this replacement, the sentence would read "fur of the it," which clearly does not make sense. This is a way of double checking your use of the apostrophe when you are not sure if the word in question is a contraction.
WRONG CHOICES ARE NOT NOTED BUT DESCRIBED COLLECTIVELY.

Question 3

B is the best answer. This is the only answer that uses the apostrophe accurately for the first use of platypus in the underlined section, while also leaving the second use ("Platypuses") in the plural form. The second use should not be possessive since when saying that "Platypuses stalk their prey," there is no possession that is being described. This would be different, of course, if the second sentence were stated as "Platypuses' prey" – in this case, the apostrophe would be necessary.
WRONG CHOICES ARE NOT NOTED BUT DESCRIBED COLLECTIVELY.

Question 4

B is the best answer. The subject here is the "nervous system" **of the** "platypus." Therefore, there needs to be an apostrophe in "platypus." Since this word ends with an "s," the apostrophe should be placed at the end of the word (i.e., after the "s"). Note that it is not incorrect to say "platypus's," but it is less suitable than "platypus'."

The second aspect to consider is the use of the apostrophe within the word "nervous." As you can tell, saying "system" **of the** "nervous" does not make sense. Therefore, there should be **no apostrophe** in the word "nervous." Any answer choice that includes this can be immediately eliminated.
WRONG CHOICES ARE NOT NOTED BUT DESCRIBED COLLECTIVELY.

Question 5
A is the best answer. The use of the apostrophe in the word "didn't" functions as a contraction for "did not." Therefore, a correct answer **would retain the apostrophe between "n" and "t" in didn't.** Furthermore, since we are referring to the "bill" **of the** "platypus," the latter should contain an apostrophe at the very end of the word (since the word ends with an "s"). However, since there is no answer choice that places the apostrophe at the end of the word "platypus," "platypus's" is the most viable alternative.
WRONG CHOICES ARE NOT NOTED BUT DESCRIBED COLLECTIVELY.

Question 6
D is the best answer. The word should NOT be in the possessive since when saying that "Platypuses share" a facial feature, **there is no possession that is being alluded to.** This would be different, of course, if the sentence were stated as "Platypuses' facial features" – in this case, the apostrophe would be necessary.

Options A and C are incorrect because they refer to the animal in the **singular** when the **context tells us that there are plural subjects** (the **implication** is that all platypuses share a feature, i.e., many of them). Furthermore, they use the apostrophe to indicate possession when that is not necessary.

Option B is incorrect because it is in the **singular** when the **context tells us that there are plural subjects** (the **implication** is that all platypuses share a feature, i.e., many of them).

Question 7
C is the best answer.

The **KEYWORD** before the underlined section is "an," which tells us that we are talking about a **singular entity.** Therefore, the correct answer would have a singular subject – immediately ruling out option B (which refers to animals in the **plural**).

Furthermore, we know that the term "animal" needs to be followed by an apostrophe and "s" since the "nerves" and the "beats of the heart" belong to that animal. Therefore, because they don't have an apostrophe, option A can be eliminated.

When looking at option D, we see an extra apostrophe following "beats" which is unnecessary since the use of the term "of its" already **implies** possession. Therefore, this answer can also be eliminated.

Question 8

B is the best answer. The "bill" **of the** "platypus" necessitates the use of an apostrophe in the word "platypus," ideally at the end of the word (after the "s"). Furthermore, the word "its" in this context is clearly used as a contraction for "it is" since the sentence would only make sense if it read: "[…] but **it is** actually a finely-tuned sensory […]." Therefore, the correct answer would include "it's" and an apostrophe at the end of "platypus."

WRONG CHOICES ARE NOT NOTED BUT DESCRIBED COLLECTIVELY.

TOPIC 12: WORD CHOICE

What is word choice?

Word choice errors, or errors in **diction**, occur when words that sound similar (but that are different in meaning) are used incorrectly. These errors are hard to prepare for since they rely solely on the knowledge of the reader. Below is a list of words that are commonly confused.

accept & except *The former means an agreement/acceptance.* *The latter means an exclusion/exception to a rule/condition.*	**access & excess** *The former means permission or opportunity.* *The latter means that there is more than necessary.*	**addition & edition** *The former means something that is added on.* *The latter refers to a particular volume of something (usually the edition of a book).*	**adopt & adapt** *The former means to take on someone/something.* *The latter means to change according to a given circumstance.*
adverse & averse *The former means an unfavourable condition/circumstance.* *The latter refers to an opposition toward someone/something.*	**affect & effect** *The former means to influence someone/something.* *The latter is the result of an action/event.*	**afflict & inflict** *The former refers to suffering that is felt/experienced [by someone/something].* *The latter refers to suffering that is caused [toward someone/something else].*	**aisle & isle** *The former refers to a passageway (usually between rows of chairs/benches).* *The latter refers to an island.*
allude & elude *The former means an indirect reference.* *The latter implies an escape/avoidance.*	**allusion & illusion** *The former means an indirect reference to something/someone.* *The latter means a vision/something that is not necessarily real.*	**already & all ready** *The former means something that has already happened.* *The latter means to be completely prepared.*	**altar & alter** *The former means the table for a religious ceremony.* *The latter means to change.*
altogether & all together *The former means completely.* *The latter means things/people coming/working with each other.*	**ambivalent & ambiguous** *The former means to have no particular feelings toward/about someone/something (to be neutral).* *The latter means a lack of clarity in meaning.*	**anecdote & antidote** *The former means a short account of something.* *The latter is something that stops the negative effect of something else (antidote to snake venom, for example).*	**angel & angle** *The former means a spiritual creature.* *The latter is a mathematical term referring to how lines intersect.*
apart & a part *The former means separated.* *The latter means a section/piece of something.*	**appraise & apprise** *The former means to examine something.* *The latter means to tell someone about something (an update).*	**are & our** *The former is the third person plural form of "to be."* *The latter indicates possession of something/someone by the subject "us."*	**accent & ascent** *The former refers to the way someone speaks.* *The latter means a movement upwards.*
assistance & assistants *The former means help.* *The latter refers to helpers.*	**aural & oral** *The former refers to things that are related to hearing/the ears.* *The latter refers to matters related to the mouth.*	**bare & bear** *The former means something is uncovered.* *The latter refers to the animal and the act of carrying something.*	**berth & birth** *The former means a bed on a boat/train.* *The latter refers to someone/something being born.*
beside & besides *The former means "next to."* *The latter means "in addition to."*	**boar & bore** *The former means a wild pig.* *The latter means something/someone that is dull.*	**board & bored** *The former means a long, flat piece of wood.* *The latter refers to feeling disinterested.*	**born & borne** *The former means to have been birthed.* *The latter refers to being carried.*

bough & bow *The former means a large branch of a tree.* *The latter is an action that involves bending the upper body, or the shape in which something is tied (i.e., the ribbon was tied in a bow).*	**brake & break** *The former is the part of a vehicle that stops it.* *The latter means that something is destroyed/separated into pieces.*	**buy & by** *The former means to purchase.* *The latter is a preposition to show that something was done by someone.*	**canvas & canvass** *The former refers to a type of cloth/material.* *The latter refers to asking people for their opinions.*
censure & censor *The former means to criticize.* *The latter means to stop/prohibit someone/something.*	**capital & capitol** *The former refers to money or the city in which a government is located.* *The latter refers to a state legislature building.*	**climactic & climatic** *The former means an important or exciting time (related to climax).* *The latter relates to the weather (the climate).*	**coarse & course** *The former means rough and thick.* *The latter means a series of lessons or a path.*
collaborate & corroborate *The former means to work together.* *The latter means to provide evidence.*	**command & commend** *The former means to order.* *The latter means to praise.*	**complacent & complaisant** *The former means lazy.* *The latter means a willingness to please others.*	**complement & compliment** *The former means something that goes well with something else.* *The latter means praise.*
comprehensive & comprehensible *The former means thorough.* *The latter means something that is easy to understand.*	**conscience & conscious** *The former means refers to something within human beings that tells us the difference between right and wrong.* *The latter means to be awake or aware.*	**corps & corpse** *The former means a group of people.* *The latter means a dead body.*	**council & counsel** *The former means an elected group of people.* *The latter means to give advice.*
dairy & diary *The former means milk products.* *The latter means a book of personal notes/thoughts.*	**descent & dissent** *The former means a movement downward.* *The latter means to disagree.*	**dessert & desert** *The former means sweet food.* *The latter refers to a hot, dry, sandy area.*	**device & devise** *The former means equipment that is used for a particular purpose.* *The latter refers to designing or inventing something.*
discreet & discrete *The former means secretive.* *The latter means separate.*	**do, dew, & due** *The first indicates an action.* *The second refers to drops of water.* *The third refers to something that is expected or planned.*	**die & dye** *The former means to stop living.* *The latter means to change the colour of something.*	**elicit & illicit** *The former means to get information/a reaction from someone.* *The latter means something that is not legal.*
eminent & imminent *The former means respected.* *The latter refers to something that is about to happen.*	**emit & omit** *The former means to send out gas/heat/light.* *The latter means to exclude something/someone.*	**envelop & envelope** *The former means to cover something.* *The latter means the packet in which letters are sent.*	**exhaustive & exhausting** *The former means repetitive use.* *The latter means tiring.*
expandable & expendable *The former means to get bigger.* *The latter means to leave out.*	**explicit & implicit** *The former means something that is made obvious.* *The latter means something that is not obvious.*	**farther & further** *The former means far.* *The latter means more.*	**flaunt & flout** *The former means to show off/exaggerate.* *The latter means to ignore/disobey something intentionally.*
formally & formerly *The former refers to something that is done according to particular norms.* *The latter means something that has happened before.*	**foreboding & forbidding** *The former refers to something that is ominous/threatening.* *The latter means that something is not allowed.*	**forth & fourth** *The former refers to a movement forward.* *The latter relates to the number four.*	**gorilla & guerrilla** *The former refers to a large monkey.* *The latter refers to an unofficial group of rebels.*

hear & here *The former refers to sounds.* *The latter refers to a location.*	**heard & herd** *The former relates to sound and hearing.* *The latter refers to a large number of animals.*	**hoard & horde** *The former means to collect/store.* *The latter means a large group.*	**hole & whole** *The former means a hollow space in something.* *The latter means something that is complete.*
human & humane *The former means people/person.* *The latter means to show humanity (to be kind/noble).*	**implicit & complicit** *The former means something that is not obvious.* *The latter means involvement with/within something.*	**incur & occur** *The former means to take on something (to incur a cost).* *The latter means that something happens.*	**influence & affluence** *The former means to make an impression/have an effect.* *The latter refers to wealth.*
ingenious & ingenuous *The former means to be incredibly intelligent.* *The latter means to be honest.*	**its & it's** *The former refers to belonging.* *The latter means "it is."*	**knew & new** *The former means knowledge that is had.* *The latter means something that is not old.*	**later & latter** *The former refers to time and something that happens after something else.* *The latter means the last thing that was mentioned in a list of two.*
lessen & lesson *The former means to weaken.* *The latter refers to something that is taught.*	**lightning & lightening** *The former refers to the weather.* *The latter means that something is less dark.*	**loose & lose** *The former refers to something that does not fit tightly.* *The latter refers to not winning.*	**meat, meet, & mete** *The first refers to flesh.* *The second refers to an introduction/meeting/assembly.* *The third refers to an act that is carried out on someone/something (i.e., the punishment was meted out to him).*
miner & minor *The former means someone who works in a mine.* *The latter means something that is unimportant or someone who is not considered a legal adult.*	**moral & morale** *The former refers to right and wrong vis-à-vis someone's character.* *The latter refers to someone's enthusiasm/spirit.*	**passed & past** *The former means to qualify.* *The latter means an event that has happened already.*	**patience & patients** *The former means to stay calm.* *The latter refers to sick people.*
peace & piece *The former means tranquillity.* *The latter means a part of.*	**perpetrate & perpetuate** *The former means to do something bad.* *The latter means to carry something forward.*	**personal & personnel** *The former relates to an individual.* *The latter means staff on a team.*	**persecute & prosecute** *The former means to treat someone unfairly.* *The latter means to convict someone (usually in a court of law).*
perspective & prospective *The former means viewpoint.* *The latter means a possibility.*	**plain & plane** *The former means ordinary.* *The latter refers to the vehicle.*	**pore & pour** *The former means a small hole for sweat to pass through.* *The latter refers to the flow of liquid.*	**precede & proceed** *The former means to happen before something else.* *The latter means to go forward.*
precedent & president *The former means to set an example for others.* *The latter means the head/leader of something.*	**prescribe & proscribe** *The former means to give medical treatment.* *The latter means to not allow something.*	**presence & presents** *The former means being somewhere.* *The latter means gifts.*	**principal & principle** *The former refers to the most important part of something, or to the head of a school.* *The latter means a basic rule.*
quiet & quite *The former means no noise.* *The latter means completely.*	**rain, reign, & rein** *The first refers to the weather.* *The second refers to the period of rule of a particular leader/idea.* *The third refers to the straps that control a horse.*	**raise & raze** *The former means to lift.* *The latter means to completely destroy.*	**rational & rationale** *The former means the condition of being reasonable.* *The latter refers to the reasoning why something happens.*
reluctant & reticent *The former means unwilling.* *The latter means shy.*	**respectfully & respectively**	**right & rite** *The former means correct.*	**scene & seen** *The former refers to a view, or to a part of a theatre play.*

	The former means showing respect. *The latter refers to things that are referred to in the same order.*	*The latter means a practice in religion or custom.*	*The latter relates to the eyes and sight.*
sense & since *The former means logic.* *The latter refers to a time in the past.*	**sight, site, & cite** *The first relates to vision.* *The second refers to a place.* *The third means referencing something.*	**simulate & stimulate** *The former means to imitate.* *The latter means to cause a response.*	**stationary & stationery** *The former means to stay still.* *The latter refers to office supplies.*
taught & taut *The former relates to education.* *The latter means something is stretched tight.*	**than & then** *The former is used to compare two things.* *The latter refers to a specific time.*	**their, they're, & there** *The first refers to possession by "them."* *The second means "they are."* *The third refers to a specific location.*	**through & threw** *The former means from one end to the other (a passage of some sort).* *The latter is the past tense of "to throw."*
waist & waste *The former refers to the middle section of the human body.* *The latter means something that is left over/not used properly.*	**waive & wave** *The former means to remove a rule/condition.* *The latter means a movement of the hands.*	**weak & week** *The former means not strong.* *The latter refers to 7 days.*	**weather & whether** *The former relates to the climate.* *The latter refers to a condition that affects something else.*
whose & who's *The former refers to ownership of something, by someone.* *The latter means "who is."*		**your, you're, & yore** *The first means belonging to the person being spoken to ("you").* *The second means "you are."* *The third means a long time ago.*	

TOPIC 12: PRACTICE QUESTIONS

Questions 1-8 are based on the following passage.

Celebrated Novelist Ernest Hemingway

Nobel Prize winner Ernest Hemingway is regarded as one of America's greatest novelists. Born in Cicero, Illinois on July 21, 1899, Hemingway demonstrated a **1** knack for writing early in life. In high school, the aspiring writer worked on his school newspaper. After graduation, Hemingway went to work for the *Kansas City Star*, where he gained **2** experiences that would later help shape his distinctive writing style. However, much of Hemingway's writing was inspired by **3** real-life events.

Hemingway **4** worked as an ambulance driver in the Italian Army during World War I and was awarded the Italian Silver Medal of Bravery for his valiance. After taking some time to recover from injuries he suffered in the war, Hemingway returned to the U.S. and took a position at the Toronto Star.

Question 1

A) NO CHANGE

B) aptitude

C) skills

D) guidance

Question 2

A) NO CHANGE

B) aptitude

C) skills

D) guidance

Question 3

A) NO CHANGE

B) the author's real life.

C) experiences.

D) things the author actually experienced.

Question 4

A) NO CHANGE

B) was employed

C) gained experience

D) served

Hemingway met his first wife in Chicago, and the couple moved to Paris shortly after their wedding. In Paris, Hemingway worked as an international correspondent. He also mentored under Gertrude Stein, who introduced Hemingway to some of the greatest **5** influencers of the time including Scott Fitzgerald, Pablo Picasso, and Ezra Pound. In Paris, Hemingway became an integral **6** cog of what Stein famously called "The Lost Generation."

In 1925, Hemingway travelled to the festival of San Fermin in Pamplona, which later served as the basis for his first novel, *The Sun Also Rises*. The novel skilfully examined the post-war disillusions of the writer's generation using a perspective shaped by personal experience.

After the publication of his first novel, Hemingway and Hadley parted ways. Shortly after, Hemingway remarried and settled down in Key West, Florida. This is where Hemingway **7** did his acclaimed novel about World War I, *A Farewell to Arms*.

Later in life, Hemingway spent much of his time **8** chasing an adventurous lifestyle. His preferred activities included hunting big game in Africa and bullfighting in Spain. Never to stray too far from his roots, Hemingway travelled to Europe in 1937 to report on the Spanish Civil War. During this time,

Question 5

A) NO CHANGE
B) writers
C) artists
D) people

Question 6

A) NO CHANGE
B) participant
C) condition
D) component

Question 7

A) NO CHANGE
B) published
C) made
D) engaged

Question 8

A) NO CHANGE
B) going for
C) pursuing
D) perusing

Hemingway gathered material for his next novel, *For Whom the Bell Tolls.*

Hemingway served as a war correspondent again during World War II and, in 1951, Hemingway wrote his most famous novel, *The Old Man and the Sea.* In 1954, Hemingway won the Nobel Prize in Literature, and he published a memoir of his years in Paris, *A Moveable Feast,* shortly before his death in 1961.

Topic 12: Practice Questions (Answers & Explanations)

Question 1

A is the best answer. The **KEYWORD** to notice here is the "a" that comes before the underlined word. This tells us that what follows should be **singular** (i.e., not "skills"). It should not begin with a vowel (i.e., not "aptitude"). It should need a preceding article (unlike "guidance"). Therefore, the only choice that fits all these criteria is what has already been used.
WRONG CHOICES ARE NOT NOTED BUT DESCRIBED COLLECTIVELY.

Question 2

C is the best answer. There are two clues to the correct answer in his case. The first is the use of the word "gained" before experiences. "Gained" is a word that I used when something **countable** is being referred to. Experiences, by their very nature, contain many different parts that cannot be quantified. Unlike "skills" which could be listed, and thus, counted. Therefore, to say that someone "gained skills" is more accurate ("had experiences," for instance, would have been more accurate too).

The second clue to the correct answer lies in the use of the phrase "would later help shape." This turn of phrase **implies** that **more than one skill** was picked up by Hemingway during this time (otherwise, the specific skill would have been named, rather than being generalized as "experiences" or "skills"). Because we can **infer** the plural nature of the underlined text, "aptitude" and "guidance" can be eliminated as options.
WRONG CHOICES ARE NOT NOTED BUT DESCRIBED COLLECTIVELY.

Question 3

B is the best answer. "The author's real life" is the **most active and clear of all the provided choices.** "Real-life events" is **ambiguous** since the term does not clarify whose real-life is being referred to. "Experiences" is similarly unclear since it does not communicate specificity. "Things the author actually experienced" is a possible answer; however, the sentence construction is far more **passive** than "the author's real life." Remember, whenever two answers seem to communicate the same meaning, choose the one that is more **concise** (i.e., uses fewer words to make the same point).
WRONG CHOICES ARE NOT NOTED BUT DESCRIBED COLLECTIVELY.

Question 4

D is the best answer. While "worked" would be appropriate in most contexts, here, the **KEYWORD** is the "army." We do not say that someone "worked" in the army or that they "gained employment in"/were "employed by" the army. The only accurate term to refer to someone's participation in the armed forces is "serve" (which is why former soldiers are often thanked for their service when they return from war).
WRONG CHOICES ARE NOT NOTED BUT DESCRIBED COLLECTIVELY.

Question 5

A is the best answer. Scott Fitzgerald was a writer, Pablo Picasso was a painter, and Ezra Pound was a poet. Therefore, it would be too general to refer to these individuals as "writers," "people" or "artists," since their realms of influence encompassed different strands of society. "Influencers," therefore, is most appropriate in capturing these individuals' impact on the world surrounding them at the time.
WRONG CHOICES ARE NOT NOTED BUT DESCRIBED COLLECTIVELY.

Question 6

D is the best answer. The best way to arrive at this answer is to consider each answer and its **implications.** A "cog" is a part of a machine. It calls someone a "cog" in a particularly identified group. "The Lost Generation" would be inaccurate. Similarly, "participant" would imply a competition/event of which Hemingway was a more passive actor. "Condition" would render the sentence meaningless since it would not make sense to that "[…] Hemingway became an integral **condition** of what Stein famously called 'The Lost Generation'." Therefore, the only choice we are left with is "component" since this word more accurately captures **the tone** of what is being said here which is that Hemingway was **a part** of a movement of sorts and not only a participant.
WRONG CHOICES ARE NOT NOTED BUT DESCRIBED COLLECTIVELY.

Question 7

B is the best answer. Books are "written" or "published." They are not "done," "made," or "engaged." The right answer to this question is immediately obvious.
WRONG CHOICES ARE NOT NOTED BUT DESCRIBED COLLECTIVELY.

Question 8

C is the best answer. "To chase" implies to go after something that is getting away from you and, therefore, would be not entirely accurate when referring to a lifestyle (that cannot be caught through a chase). While "to pursue" also could be used in the context of a chase, this word also means to try and attain something (an idea/a goal/ that cannot necessarily be "caught." In this sense, "pursuing" **captures** the idea that is being put forward here more effectively than the correct answer.

The other two answer choices (B & D) are immediately unviable because of the words' meanings. "Going for" is ambiguous and is more a term that is used in slang ("Go for it", for example). "To peruse" means to browse through a range of materials (for example: "I perused the books in the library").

TOPIC 13: TRANSITION WORDS

What is a transition word?
Transition words are terms that are used to effectively take the reader from one idea to the next.

TRANSITIONAL WORDS
There are three kinds of transitions that are used most often; these transitions can occur between words, between parts of a sentence, or between sentences.

ADDITION
Words that elaborate on an idea or concept that was mentioned before

Most commonly used terms to indicate addition: Also, Moreover, In fact, Furthermore, In addition, Similarly, Indeed, In conclusion, In other words, Finally, Next, Likewise, Then, For example.

For example: **In addition** *to playing music, Selena is extremely skilled at martial arts.*

CONTRAST
Words that help introduce conflicting ideas

Most commonly used terms to indicate contrast: However, On the other hand, Nonetheless, Nevertheless, Still, Instead, Despite, Meanwhile

For example: Selena is extremely skilled at martial arts. **However,** *she is not only a fighter; she is also an artist!*

CAUSATION
Words that indicate a cause-effect relationship between two ideas, i.e., B happens because of A.

Most commonly used terms to indicate causation: Thus, As such, Therefore, Consequently, As a result

For example: Selena is extremely skilled at a variety of skills from martial arts to music. **Therefore,** *she is considered by all around her to be a well-rounded individual!*

STRATEGY
Understand the relationship between the words/phrases/sentences for which a transition word is being used.

Is it a relationship of addition?
Is it a relationship of contrast?
Is it a relationship of causation?

TOPIC 13: PRACTICE QUESTIONS

Questions 1-8 are based on the following passage.

China's Ancient Silk Road

The Silk Road was an ancient trade route that once ran along the northern borders of China to connect the nation with Persia, India, and Europe. **1** Eventually the trade route was most commonly referred to as a road, but this label is a bit misleading. **2** As a matter of fact, the Silk Road was a network of routes that spanned nearly 4,000 miles throughout Asia, Europe, Africa, and the Middle East. Ultimately, this vast network facilitated ancient trade practices that helped shape modern society.

The ancient trade routes that comprised the Silk Road originated in Xi'an, China and were formally established during the Han Dynasty. **3** For instance, silk trading was a major driving force behind the establishment of the Silk Road. For thousands of years before the route was officially established, China would use it to trade their world-famous silk thread and cloth throughout Asia and Europe. **4** So, the ancient Romans even referred to China as the "land of silk."

Question 1	
A)	NO CHANGE
B)	Before
C)	Although
D)	However

Question 2	
A)	NO CHANGE
B)	Nevertheless
C)	Regardless
D)	Eventually

Question 3	
A)	NO CHANGE
B)	Indeed
C)	In short
D)	Likewise

Question 4	
A)	NO CHANGE
B)	In fact
C)	Accordingly
D)	By the same token

Silk was the primary commodity traded on the silk road, but it was just one of many goods that made the trans-continental journey on the Silk Road. Eventually, China also exported tea, sugar, spices, salt, porcelain, and other goods to its foreign trading partners. Many of these goods were considered luxuries in ancient times, **5** thus making trade on the road very lucrative.

By connecting civilizations across Eurasia and North Africa, traders on the Silk Road could exchange both goods and ideas. **6** For example, the ancient trade routes helped generate trade and commerce between countries while simultaneously creating an outlet for the exchange of ideas, inventions, and religions, for ancient civilizations between the years of 130 BCE – 1453 CE. **7** So, much like other forms of trade and travel, the Silk Road brought challenges as well as opportunities.

The silk road gave cultures the ability to connect with one another. **8** By the same token, it also inadvertently facilitated the spread of disease throughout Europe and Asia. Historians theorize that travellers from the Silk Road may have introduced the Bubonic plague – also known as "the Black Death" - into Europe during the fourteenth century.

Question 5

A) NO CHANGE
B) despite
C) so
D) because

Question 6

A) NO CHANGE
B) For instance
C) Accordingly
D) DELETE the underlined word

Question 7

A) NO CHANGE
B) Likewise
C) Similarly
D) Even so

Question 8

A) NO CHANGE
B) Conversely
C) Likewise
D) In short

Parts of the silk road eventually became very dangerous after the Romans lost their territory in Asia, and its use began to dwindle. Centuries later, the Mongols revived the Silk Road and put security measures in place for merchants and travellers. It was at this time that famed explorer Marco Polo used the Silk Road to travel to China. Unfortunately, the only part of the Silk Road that still exists today is a paved highway used to connect Pakistan and China.

Topic 13: Practice Questions (Answers & Explanations)

Question 1

C is the best answer. The **KEYWORD** to pay attention to in this sentence is the term "misleading" that is used at the end of the sentence. This tells us that a relationship of **CONTRAST** is being introduced by eliminating "Eventually" and "Before" as potential options (since they are more often used to **connote CAUSATION** with reference to a timeline of events). Therefore, "However" and "Although" are the two possible answers. By using both of these words in the identified sentence, we immediately see that the sentence becomes **meaningless.** "However" renders the sentence meaningless and grammatically inaccurate. Thus, the only viable answer is "Although."
WRONG CHOICES ARE NOT NOTED BUT DESCRIBED COLLECTIVELY.

Question 2

A is the best answer. In this case, the transition word is used to imply an **ADDITION,** i.e., it tells us why "this label is a bit misleading." Thus, we need to use a transition of **ADDITION** in the underlined location. "Nevertheless" indicates CONTRAST. "Eventually" implies CAUSATION. "Regardless" (being close in meaning to "despite") also indicates CONTRAST. Therefore, the only viable option here is "As a matter of fact."
WRONG CHOICES ARE NOT NOTED BUT DESCRIBED COLLECTIVELY.

Question 3

C is the best answer. Let's look at the relationship between the two sentences. The first sentence tells us where the "ancient trade routes" originated and when they were "formally established." The second sentence adds to our understanding of the Silk Road, i.e., how silk trading "was a major driving force" behind the establishment of the Silk Road. Therefore, what we have here is a relationship of **ADDITION.** All the answers provided for this particular question could imply addition. Therefore, we need to analyze each one more carefully.

Choice A, "For instance" **connotes** an example that helps add to a previous idea; there is no example in this statement (only a statement).

Choice B, "Indeed" **indicates** that what follows is new information that adds to the previously mentioned idea.

Choice D, "Likewise" asks the reader to look for a similarity between two different ideas whereas what we have here is a summarized statement that seeks to strengthen the relationship between two concepts: the "ancient trade routes" and the establishment of the "Silk Road." Therefore, "In short" is the most viable answer choice.

Question 4

B is the best answer. The sentence "the ancient Romans even referred to China as the 'land of silk.'" functions as an ADDITION, i.e., the information in this sentence seeks to strengthen the preceding

statement about China's reputation in trading silk to Asia and Europe. Therefore, the transition word that is used here needs to **add** information in a way that **reinforces** (strengthens) the previous ideas that have been put forward. The strongest of the options, therefore, is "In fact" – since it gives the reader a factual statement (what Romans used to refer to China as) to reinforce what came before it.
WRONG CHOICES ARE NOT NOTED BUT DESCRIBED COLLECTIVELY.

Question 5

A is the best answer. The transition here reflects **CAUSATION,** i.e., trade on the route was "lucrative" because the items that were being transported were considered "luxuries." "Despite" indicates CONTRAST, while "so" and "because" are used to indicate ADDITION. The only choice for CAUSATION, therefore, is "thus."
WRONG CHOICES ARE NOT NOTED BUT DESCRIBED COLLECTIVELY.

Question 6

C is the best answer. The sentence in question ADDS to the previous sentence by **expanding on the ideas that it contains.** Since no examples are provided here, "for example" and "for instance" are inaccurate choices. Deleting the underlined word would now allow the reader to see the link between the sentences in question. Therefore, the most viable transition word here is "accordingly."
WRONG CHOICES ARE NOT NOTED BUT DESCRIBED COLLECTIVELY.

Question 7

D is the best answer. The previous sentences in the paragraph speak primarily to the benefits/advantages of the Silk Road. By introducing the idea of "challenges" in the last sentence, we know that the transition word to be used should indicate **CONTRAST**. "So," "likewise," and "similarly" are all transitions of ADDITION. Therefore, the only possible choice is "even so" since the use of the word "even" **implies** an emerging qualification/contrast.
WRONG CHOICES ARE NOT NOTED BUT DESCRIBED COLLECTIVELY.

Question 8

B is the best answer. The first sentence in this paragraph speaks to the connection that the Silk Road facilitated in a **positive tone.** However, by introducing the idea of "disease" in the next sentence, we know that the transition word to be used should indicate **CONTRAST**.

"By the same token," "likewise," and "in short" are all transitions of ADDITION. Therefore, the only possible choice is "conversely" since it is the only choice that **connotes CONTRAST.**
WRONG CHOICES ARE NOT NOTED BUT DESCRIBED COLLECTIVELY.

TOPIC 14: TRANSITION SENTENCES

What is a transition sentence?
Transition sentences, like transition words, are used to take the reader from the idea in one sentence/paragraph to the idea in a following sentence/paragraph.

TRANSITIONAL SENTENCES
There are three kinds of transitional relationships that are used most often (just as in the case of transition words).

ADDITION
Sentences that elaborate on an idea or concept that was mentioned before (and take the reader to a connected idea in the following sentence)

Most commonly used terms to indicate addition: Also, Moreover, In fact, Furthermore, In addition, Similarly, Indeed, In conclusion, In other words, Finally, Next, Likewise, Then, For example.

CONTRAST
Sentences that help introduce conflicting ideas (and take the reader to a contrasting idea in the following sentence)

Most commonly used terms to indicate contrast: However, On the other hand, Nonetheless, Nevertheless, Still, Instead, Despite, Meanwhile

CAUSATION
Sentences that help the reader transition between other clauses that speak to a cause and its effects

Most commonly used terms to indicate causation: Thus, As such, Therefore, Consequently, As a result

STRATEGY
Make sure you understand the question (is it asking about transitions **between** or **within** paragraphs).
Understand the relationship between the sentences in the paragraph (or between the paragraphs).
Try to identify the transitional relationships between the necessary texts (addition, contrast, causation).

TOPIC 14: PRACTICE QUESTIONS

Questions 1-8 are based on the following passage.

Kombucha: A Healthy Fermented Tea

Kombucha is delightful concoction made with a bacterial culture, tea, and sugar. [1] <u>The fermented tea most likely originated in ancient China, but</u> Kombucha continues to be popular all over the world. [2] <u>Plenty of people enjoy kombucha for its taste, but many kombucha drinkers seek out the beverage for its perceived health benefits.</u>

The exact origins of Kombucha remain unknown, but evidence dating back to 221 BCE traces the tea beverage to China's Qin Dynasty. [3] <u>Theories abound regarding the origins of Kombucha, but regardless many ancient</u> Chinese healers believed drinking

The author is considering deleting the underlined portion. Should the author make this change?

A) Kept, because it brings together prior information in the paragraph to a logical conclusion.

B) Kept, because it provides a transition to a point about kombucha.

C) Deleted, because it ignores the fact that kombucha's exact origin is unclear.

D) Deleted, because it interrupts the paragraph's description of kombucha.

The author is considering deleting the underlined portion. Should the author make this change?

A) Kept, because it provides an effective transition between paragraphs.

B) Kept, because it brings together prior information in the paragraph to a logical conclusion.

C) Deleted, because it ignores the fact that some people don't like kombucha.

D) Deleted, because it interrupts the flow of the passage.

A) NO CHANGE

B) Theories abound regarding the origins of Kombucha, but regardless of its exact origins, many

C) Ancient

D) OMIT the underlined portion

kombucha could rid the body of toxins. They referred to kombucha as the "elixir of life" as a reflection of the energizing effects many people observed after drinking the fermented tea. Many of these benefits result from the fermentation of kombucha's three main ingredients, which creates probiotics with immune-boosting effects.

4 By 414 AD, the fermented tea drink had made its way to Japan. **5** Specifically, kombucha made its way into the hands of Emperor Inkyo, a Japanese ruler who had severe digestive problems. Emperor Inkyo loved the stuff, and the fermented tea became a popular beverage health aid throughout Japan **6** from that time onward.

Question 4

The writer wants a transition from the previous sentence that highlights the transition from the introductory sentence to the remainder of the content in the paragraph. Which choice best accomplishes this goal?

A)   NO CHANGE

B)   Chinese trade routes brought the drink into neighboring parts of Asia; knowledge of kombucha's delightful flavor and medicinal applications began to spread.

C)   Chinese trade routes brought the drink into neighboring parts of Asia, and knowledge of kombucha's delightful flavor and medicinal applications began to spread.

D)   Once Chinese trade routes brought the drink into neighboring parts of Asia, knowledge of kombucha's delightful flavor and medicinal applications began to spread.

Question 5

A)   NO CHANGE

B)   Kombucha

C)   The tasty beverage

D)   Perhaps kombucha

A) NO CHANGE

B) since.

C) after.

D) OMIT the underlined portion.

7 Healers in Russia and Germany used kombucha as a homeopathic remedy for various ailments. They found kombucha to be particularly helpful in the treatment of inflammatory diseases and other metabolic disorders. Regardless, kombucha's health benefits were not common knowledge across Europe until the turn of the twentieth century.

The writer wants a transition from the previous sentence that highlights the transition from the introductory sentence to the remainder of the content in the paragraph. Which choice best accomplishes this goal?

A) NO CHANGE

B) During its travels around the world, kombucha eventually reached Europe.

C) Kombucha travelled around the world, and it eventually reached Europe.

D) Kombucha eventually found a new home in Europe.

8 Kombucha became a popular health aid throughout Europe until after World War II. Over time, commercial kombucha production fizzled out due to its high cost. However, kombucha resurfaced after research performed in the 1960s showed that the drink's natural immune-boosting properties could aid in certain disease preventions and treatments. Due to its health benefits and delightful flavour, kombucha remains a popular beverage in cultures across the globe.

A) NO CHANGE

B) Kombucha remained popular around the world, including throughout Europe.

C) Kombucha remained popular throughout Europe until after World War II.

D) OMIT the underlined portion.

Topic 14: Practice Questions (Answers & Explanations)

Question 1

B is the best answer. This sentence uses information about the origin of kombucha in China to then **ADD** information about its popularity all over the world today. Therefore, the sentence should be kept because it provides a transition (of ADDITION) to a point about kombucha.

A is incorrect because the information provided in this sentence does not provide a conclusion to any other idea. In fact, as part of the introductory paragraph, we have not been given much information that might lead to a conclusion of any sort!

C is incorrect because **this answer contradicts the information that has been given,** i.e., that there is an identified place of origin for kombucha.

D is incorrect because there is no interruption to the paragraph's focus. The underlined sentence is also **extremely relevant** to the content of the text.

Question 2

A is the best answer. In order to choose the most appropriate answer to this question, you need to read the following paragraph. Doing so, we find that the text that follows speaks about the health benefits of kombucha to eliminate "toxins" from the body. Therefore, the underlined sentence – in speaking about health benefits – effectively transitions the reader to the next paragraph.

B is incorrect because the information in this line introduces a new idea (about health benefits) rather than concluding previously shared information.

C is incorrect because it would be **irrelevant** to state, at this point in the passage, that some people do not like kombucha. As the introductory paragraph, the main function of it is to prepare the reader for what is to follow.

D is incorrect because there is no interruption to the paragraph's flow. The sentence effectively takes the reader from the idea about kombucha being "popular all over the world" to why people enjoy the drink. Therefore, the flow is effectively maintained.

Question 3

B is the best answer. This is the only choice that actually transitions the reader between the different ideas that are mentioned by the sentences in question (from information about the date of its origin, to its use by Chinese healers).
WRONG CHOICES ARE NOT NOTED BUT DESCRIBED COLLECTIVELY.

Question 4

D is the best answer. Since choices B, C, and D all contain the same information, look for the answer choice that is the most **active**. One of the ways to do this immediately is to look for the sentence that is the most concise and clear (i.e., the choice that uses the fewest number of words and clauses to make the same point). In this case, D is the immediate option since it uses the word "Once" to establish a **CAUSAL** connection between the two parts of the sentence rather than separating them with a semicolon or a conjunction like "and."

A is immediately unviable because the question asks for a sentence that would capture the content of the following paragraph and the current first line is clearly not a summary of ideas; it is simply a statement about when the drink arrived in Japan.

Question 5
A is the best answer. The sentence here **adds** information to the previous sentence by giving the reader a **specific** instance of the drink's reach in Japan. In so doing, the word "specifically" helps **frame** this new additional information for the reader – as compared to all the other answer choices. Now, please note that the other choices are not incorrect. They are simply less suitable because they do not as effectively transition the reader to a new idea.
WRONG CHOICES ARE NOT NOTED BUT DESCRIBED COLLECTIVELY.

Question 6
A is the best answer. Using a phrase like "from that time onward" helps the reader understand the influence that the Emperor had over the people, i.e., it was because he adopted tea that it became so popular.

Omitting this phrase (as choice D suggest) would take out this important **contextual information.**

Choices B & C are incorrect because using words like "since" and "after" without properly **associating** the time with the point being referenced (i.e., using a term like "that" to refer to the Emperor's preference for tea) creates a lack of clarity for the reader.

Question 7
D is the best answer.

The previous paragraph speaks about the presence of tea in Japan; the first sentence in the next paragraph speaks about "Russia" and "Germany." Therefore, it is important to add a line that tells the reader about this regional shift that is being addressed in the content. This immediately eliminates option A.

Of the remaining options, consider which one is the most **ACTIVE** and **CONCISE.** The former speaks about subjects as having agency (rather than being the recipients of actions), and the latter means using the least amount of words needed to make your point. From the options that are given here, the only option that does not use an additional clause that is not essential is option D.

Question 8
D is the best answer.

Given that the following information is more general, we can tell that this is the concluding paragraph. Using a Europe-centered topic sentence with specific information about Kombucha's popularity in relation to World War II, therefore, is **too specific** to be included in this concluding paragraph. Since all other answer choices refer to either Europe, or World War II, or both, the only option that remains viable is to omit the underlined text.
WRONG CHOICES ARE NOT NOTED BUT DESCRIBED COLLECTIVELY.

TOPIC 15: EVIDENCE & EXAMPLES

What is command of evidence?
Command of evidence requires test takers to be able to understand and interpret a particular passage based on examples that support stated ideas.

STRATEGIES

When being asked to identify examples that can act as evidence for particular ideas, consider implementing the following steps:

- See if you can predict an answer to the question <u>before</u> you look at the answer choices, i.e., locate an example from the text that you consider to be the strongest evidence in support of the question. Then, see if the example you have identified is one of the answers listed as a choice.

- Look for synonyms, i.e., see if there are **KEYWORDS** in the question that mean the same as words in the given passage (of course, sometimes, you'll see a **REPETITION OF KEYWORDS** in both the question and the answer and in that case, you can immediately identify the most viable answer choice).

- Read **ALL** the answer choices. Sometimes, there could be multiple correct answers to a particular question, and you should be looking for the **MOST accurate** answer – not the first one that you identify!

- Make sure to read the information **around** the text in question to make sure you understand the **context** in which that evidence is being presented.

TOPIC 15: EVIDENCE & EXAMPLES

Questions 1-8 are based on the following passage.

The Many Historical Uses of Garlic

Before building the formal institutions of modern medicine, people mostly tended to their healthcare at home. Often, this required getting a little creative to treat wounds and other common ailments. <u>This was particularly true for ancient civilizations</u>. As a result, ancient peoples often experimented with the medicinal properties of native plants. Garlic is a prime example of an effective home remedy ancient peoples discovered while finding ways to treat common health issues.

Garlic is grown around the world. It is used both as a savory seasoning and for health-related purposes. In fact, many people use garlic as a natural supplement to help lower blood pressure and cholesterol and to reduce the risk of cancer.

Question 1

A) NO CHANGE

B) Particularly true for ancient civilizations, this creativity gave rise to experimentation.

C) This was particularly true for ancient civilizations, who often lacked formal healthcare systems.

D) OMIT the underlined portion

Question 2

At this point, the writer is considering adding the following sentence:
"The species is native to northeastern Iran and Central Asia, and how it spread throughout Asia and the Middle East is a matter of speculation."

Should the writer make this addition here?

A) Yes, because it links two related ideas in the paragraph.

B) Yes, because it provides information that helps clarify other information presented in the paragraph.

C) No, because it provides redundant information.

D) No, because it provides irrelevant information.

Garlic has been used as both a food and health supplement for thousands of years. Ancient Egyptians used garlic for its medicinal properties but also as a staple food for the poor.

In ancient times, those living in poverty often had only porridge to eat, which did not contain much nutrition. By providing poor Egyptians with crucial vitamins, garlic helped prevent death from starvation.

Question 3

At this point, the writer is considering adding the following sentence:
"Ancient Egyptians officially recorded their first use of garlic as early as 3200 BCE."

Should the writer make this addition here?

A)   Yes, because it links two related ideas in the paragraph.

B)   Yes, because it provides information that helps clarify other information presented in the paragraph.

C)   No, because it provides redundant information.

D)   No, because it provides irrelevant information.

Question 4

At this point, the writer is considering adding the following sentence:
"In the ancient Egyptian culture, garlic was irreplaceable as a nutritional supplement."

Should the writer make this addition here?

A)   Yes, because it links two related ideas in the paragraph.

B)   Yes, because it provides information that helps clarify other information presented in the paragraph.

C)   No, because it provides redundant information.

D)   No, because it provides irrelevant information.

At this point, the writer is considering adding the following sentence:
"As a result, the poorest people in ancient Egypt primarily received their vitamins from garlic."

Should the writer make this addition here?

A)   Yes, because it links two related ideas in the paragraph.

B)   Yes, because it provides information that helps clarify other information presented in the paragraph.

C)   No, because it provides redundant information.

D)   No, because it provides irrelevant information.

The Egyptians were not the only ancient civilizations to recognize the value of garlic. Archaeologists found evidence that the Sumerians of Mesopotamia began using garlic for its medicinal and flavoring properties dating all the way back to around 2600 BCE. Ancient Israelis also used garlic as a parasite killer, body heater, and blood pressure enhancer in addition to a flavoring.

At this point, the writer is considering adding the following sentence:
"Garlic even found applications in ancient China, which recorded its first use of garlic for its medicinal applications around 2700 BCE."

Should the writer make this addition here?

A)   Yes, because it links two related ideas in the paragraph.

B)   Yes, because it provides information that helps clarify other information presented in the paragraph.

C)   No, because it provides redundant information.

D)   No, because it provides irrelevant information.

Garlic was used by ancient peoples for its many health effects, and it grew to become an important part of many traditional home remedies.   Some cultures still use garlic to treat digestive issues and stomach upset. Garlic remains an important part of many Eastern medical traditions including Chinese traditional medicine.

The history of people's relationship with garlic history spans throughout ancient civilizations and across the world. The properties of this delicious and savory plant continue to be a topic of interest to this day.

Question 7

At this point, the writer is considering adding the following sentence:
"Some cultures still use garlic to treat digestive issues and stomach upset."

Should the writer make this addition here?

A)   Yes, because it links two related ideas in the paragraph.

B)   Yes, because it provides information that helps clarify other information presented in the paragraph

C)   No, because it provides redundant information.

D)   No, because it provides irrelevant information.

Question 8

At this point, the writer is considering adding the following sentence:
"In fact, 80 percent of the world's garlic comes from China."

Should the writer make this addition here?

A)   Yes, because it links two related ideas in the paragraph.

B)   Yes, because it provides information that helps clarify other information presented in the paragraph.

C)   No, because it provides redundant information.

D)   No, because it provides irrelevant information.

Topic 15: Practice Questions (Answers & Explanations)

Question 1

D is the best answer. The underlined sentence makes a general statement about "ancient civilizations." This general statement is preceded by a statement about the requirement for these individuals to get "a little creative" and followed by "ancient peoples'" experimentation with the medicinal "properties of native plants." Thus, we can see that the statements before and after the underlined sentence link to each other – the underlined statement repeats generalized ideas that are also mentioned in the sentences that come before and after it. Therefore, the best choice would be to delete the identified section.

WRONG CHOICES ARE NOT NOTED BUT DESCRIBED COLLECTIVELY.

Question 2

D is the best answer. Although the first line speaks about how garlic is "grown around the world," the subsequent lines speak about the health-related benefits that come from its use. Therefore, adding information that speaks about the specific origin of garlic in this particular paragraph is **irrelevant** since it does not fit within the **context of the information** that is provided here. Although it is not redundant – in that no information is repeated – it does not help link or clarify any other idea on the surrounding text.

WRONG CHOICES ARE NOT NOTED BUT DESCRIBED COLLECTIVELY.

Question 3

B is the best answer. Given the second line's subject of "Ancient Egyptians," we can immediately tell that the correct answer must be either A or B (i.e., that the content that is proposed does connect to the text in the paragraph). When choosing between A and B, note that the former suggests a link between **two** ideas – what are those ideas? The text **does not contain** two ideas that could be connected by the proposed sentence since this new text only speaks of when garlic came to Egypt. Therefore, B is the only possible answer since the proposed text helps **frame** the use of garlic in this region.

WRONG CHOICES ARE NOT NOTED BUT DESCRIBED COLLECTIVELY.

Question 4

C is the best answer. An answer is considered **REDUNDANT** when the information in question is repetitive or useless in the paragraph. The proposed sentence, as we can see, repeats the same information that is provided in the second sentence, i.e., by saying that "garlic was irreplaceable as a health supplement" the statement is essentially restating how garlic provided Egyptians with "crucial vitamins" and "prevent death from starvation." Therefore, the proposed sentence is not necessary, for it is redundant.

WRONG CHOICES ARE NOT NOTED BUT DESCRIBED COLLECTIVELY.

Question 5

C is the best answer. Note the **KEYWORD** "adding" in the question. Then, look at the following sentence. Doesn't the sentence that the author wants to add say something that is repeated almost exactly in the following sentence? Since this is the case, the proposed line should be deleted because it provides **REDUNDANT** information.

Although this information is **RELEVANT** because it so clearly states an existing idea, it should immediately be discarded for creating redundancy.
WRONG CHOICES ARE NOT NOTED BUT DESCRIBED COLLECTIVELY.

Question 6

B is the best answer. The first sentence of this paragraph tells us that the focus is on ancient civilizations – **in addition to** the Egyptians – to use garlic. The first example speaks to Mesopotamia, the second example speaks to ancient Israelis, and the proposed line speaks to an example from ancient China. By bringing in **RELEVANT information** that has not been mentioned before, this proposed sentence would only help clarify other information presented in the paragraph. By functioning as an **extension** of a given idea rather than a **link between** two given ideas, this is the most viable answer.
WRONG CHOICES ARE NOT NOTED BUT DESCRIBED COLLECTIVELY.

Question 7

C is the best answer. Note the **KEYWORD** "adding" in the question. Then, look at the following sentence. Doesn't the sentence that the author wants to add say something that is repeated almost exactly in the following sentence? Since this is the case, the proposed line should be deleted because it provides **REDUNDANT** information.

Although this information is **RELEVANT** because it so clearly states an existing idea, it should immediately be discarded for creating redundancy.
WRONG CHOICES ARE NOT NOTED BUT DESCRIBED COLLECTIVELY.

Question 8

D is the best answer. The current sentences in the paragraph refer to the following: its general importance for ancient peoples and "traditional home remedies," the use of garlic in treating stomach issues, and the importance of garlic in "Eastern medical traditions." Given this **surrounding context,** including a line about where 80% of the world's garlic comes from, would be **IRRELEVANT in the current paragraph.**
WRONG CHOICES ARE NOT NOTED BUT DESCRIBED COLLECTIVELY.

TOPIC 16: RELEVANCE & PURPOSE

Questions about RELEVANCE and PURPOSE have four answer choices.

- Two that advocate for the sentence being KEPT (for two different reasons) and two that advocate for the sentence being DELETED (for two different reasons).

- First, decide if the sentence must be KEPT or DELETED (without looking at the reason).

- Once you've made that decision, you will only have two choices remaining as viable options.

How do you identify RELEVANCY?

- Irrelevant information is usually "random" and has nothing to do with the surrounding content in the paragraph/passage, i.e., there will be a sudden **SHIFT IN TOPIC.**

- Irrelevance can also be caused by a sudden **SHIFT IN SCOPE.** There is a shift from information that is extremely specific to information that is extremely general (and vice versa).

- Look at the **KEYWORDS** in the given sentence. Can you spot those **KEYWORDS** (or synonyms for them) in the sentences before/after the text that you are being asked to consider for retention/deletion? If there are no related words, it is likely that the provided text is irrelevant.

How do you identify PURPOSE?

- Read the sentences around the identified sentence and determine the **FUNCTION (purpose)** of the given text.

- The function/purpose of a sentence will usually fall into one of these larger categories:
  - The text serves as an explanation/emphasis/evidence of a certain term or phenomenon in the surrounding text (either before or after the section you are being asked to focus on).
  - The text serves as the introduction of a topic.
  - The text serves as an effective transition.
  - The text serves as the conclusion of a paragraph or passage.

TOPIC 16: PRACTICE QUESTIONS

Questions 1-8 are based on the following passage.

Nikola Tesla, the Unlucky Inventor

When mentioned in modern times, the word "Tesla" tends to elicit thoughts of speedy electric cars. However, these cutting-edge vehicles are actually named after a world-renowned scientist in the field of electrical engineering: Nikola Tesla.

[1] In his early years, Tesla pursued an education in philosophy at the University of Prague. He also studied math and physics at the Technical University of Graz. In 1884, Tesla came to the United States and briefly worked as an engineer at famed inventor Thomas Edison's Manhattan headquarters. Tesla worked under Edison for roughly a year before leaving Manhattan under less-than-friendly circumstances. [2]

Question 1

At this point, the writer is considering adding the following sentence:

"Nikola Tesla was born July 10, 1856 in modern-day Croatia."

Should the writer make this addition here?

A)   Yes, because it provides relevant details about Tesla's career.

B)   No, because it interrupts the paragraph's description of Tesla's career.

C)   Yes, because it provides an effective introduction to Tesla's personal history.

D)   No, because it ignores the fact that Croatia was not a country at the time.

Question 2

At this point, the writer is considering adding the following sentence:

"Specifically, Edison failed to uphold certain promises to implement Tesla's designs, and the two brilliant inventors had a falling out."

Should the writer make this addition?

A)   Yes, because it provides important details that clarifies information discussed earlier in the passage.

B)   No, because it groups together examples that are too different to be of use.

C)   Yes, because it offers another relevant example supporting the topic of the paragraph.

D) No, because it conflicts with information presented later in the sentence.

After leaving Edison's Manhattan headquarters, Tesla attempted to start his own company: the Tesla Electric Light Company. Unfortunately, his attempts failed. Despite his brilliant mind and years of training, the inventor was left destitute. **3** For a time, the only employment he found was digging ditches for only $2 per day.

Question 3

The writer is considering deleting the underlined sentence. Should the sentence be kept or deleted?

A) Kept, because it shows the impact of job conflicts on career.

B) Kept, because it provides a detail clarifying a key fact presented earlier in the passage.

C) Deleted, because it ignores the impact of inflation on wages.

D) Deleted, because it interrupts the paragraph's description of Tesla's professional challenges.

After a number of setbacks, Tesla finally found backers to support his research. **4** Between 1887 and 1888, Tesla received over 30 patents for his inventions. During this time, he was also invited to lecture at the American Institute of Electrical Engineers. Tesla's lecture sparked the interest of inventor George Westinghouse, who hired Tesla **5** immediately after hearing his lecture.

Question 4

At this point, the writer is considering adding the following sentence:

"Tesla was fascinated by alternating currents, which describes one way that electricity moves through power lines."
Should the writer make this addition?

A) Yes, because it provides important details that clarifies information discussed earlier in the passage.

B) Yes, because it provides information that describes a key term.

C) No, because it provides an irrelevant example.

D) No, because it conflicts with information presented later in the sentence.

A) NO CHANGE

B) immediately.

C) after hearing his lecture.

D) OMIT the underlined portion.

Westinghouse gave Tesla his own lab. After partnering with Westinghouse, Tesla released a number of new **6** inventions. In 1895, the two inventors partnered with General Electric to install power generators at Niagara Falls. This project resulted in the creation of the first modern hydroelectric power plant in the U.S., which powered all of Buffalo, New York **7** with clean, renewable electricity.

The writer is considering revising the underlined portion to the following:

"inventions: meters, improved lights, a high-voltage transformer that came to be known as "the Tesla coil," electric oscillators, and more."

Should the writer make this addition here?

A) Yes, because it offers examples that clarify information presented earlier in the passage.

B) No, because it creates a punctuation error.

C) Yes, because it sets up a topic that is discussed later in the passage.

D) No, because provides extraneous information that distracts from the main purpose of the passage.

A) NO CHANGE

B) with clean energy generated from renewable resources.

C) with renewable energy.

D) OMIT the underlined portion

Tesla had an unlucky streak that followed him much of his life. His lab in New York burned down in 1895. Taking the opportunity as a fresh start, Tesla briefly migrated to Colorado Springs **8**. Upon returning to New York, Tesla began work on building a global wireless system designed to provide free energy to the entire world. However, Tesla was forced to abandon the project, and he suffered a nervous breakdown shortly thereafter. Nikola Tesla passed away in New York City in 1943, and he remains a well-respected inventor and engineer to this day.

At this point, the writer is considering adding the following phrase:

"before returning to New York in 1900"

Should the writer make this addition?

A) Yes, because it links two related ideas in the paragraph.

B) Yes, because it provides information that helps clarify other information presented in the paragraph.

C) No, because it provides redundant information.

D) No, because it provides irrelevant information.

Topic 16: Practice Questions (Answers & Explanations)

Question 1

C is the best answer. The second line of this paragraph begins with "in his early years" telling us about the early life of Tesla; the rest of the paragraph goes on to give us biographical information about the scientist. Therefore, adding a sentence about the place of Tesla's birth at the beginning of this paragraph provides an **effective introduction** to the man's personal history. It connects effectively and relevantly with the following content and helps us learn about Tesla's **biographical information.**
WRONG CHOICES ARE NOT NOTED BUT DESCRIBED COLLECTIVELY.

Question 2

A is the best answer. The sentence that precedes the location of the proposed statement's inclusion tells us that Tesla left his work with Edison under less-than-ideal circumstances. By explaining the reason behind the falling out between the two scientists, the new statement would certainly help clarify information discussed earlier in the passage. Although this is not an example that supports the main topic of the paragraph – which is a general overview of Tesla's career – it is still **RELEVANT** information and has the purpose of clarifying an earlier statement.
WRONG CHOICES ARE NOT NOTED BUT DESCRIBED COLLECTIVELY.

Question 3

B is the best answer. The previous line ends by stating that "he was left destitute." Therefore, by telling us the job that Tesla had to take on ("digging ditches") and how much he was paid for that ("$2 per day"), this information helps provide evidence for a key fact, i.e., that Tesla was "left destitute."

Choice A is incorrect because the sentence does not tell us about the general impact of "job conflicts on careers." It gives us specific information about Tesla's destitution.

Choice C is incorrect because the topic of "inflation" is **irrelevant** in the current context and therefore, there's no need for the underlined sentence to refer to the theme.

Choice D is incorrect because this sentence rather than interrupting a description of Tesla's challenges **helps reinforce the ideas** that are presented before it.
WRONG CHOICES ARE NOT NOTED BUT DESCRIBED COLLECTIVELY.

Question 4

C is the best answer. By placing information about one of Tesla's research interests alongside information about how the scientist eventually began to overcome setbacks, the information in this proposed addition would be **irrelevant** in this particular context. Although the content in this statement is generally relevant to the topic of the passage, it is not relevant with the surrounding context in this portion of the text.

Choices A and B are incorrect because this proposed sentence does not clarify (or help define) any preceding information or terms. Nowhere in the surrounding text do we see reference to "alternating currents."

Choice D is incorrect because there are no conflicts with information provided later in the paragraph, simply because the topic that is included in the proposed sentence is not reflected anywhere else in this text.

WRONG CHOICES ARE NOT NOTED BUT DESCRIBED COLLECTIVELY.

Question 5

B is the best answer. The sentence tells us that Tesla's lecture sparked the interest of George Westinghouse. We can immediately understand that Westinghouse was at the lecture and was interested in Tesla's work because of the lecture. Referencing "after the lecture," therefore, is **unnecessary** since that information has already been established for the reader. However, the term "immediately" expresses the extent of Westinghouse's interest in Tesla's work – thus making it necessary to retain this term, to help the reader understand the intensity of Westinghouse's desire to work with Tesla.

WRONG CHOICES ARE NOT NOTED BUT DESCRIBED COLLECTIVELY.

Question 6

A is the best answer. Although the focus of the latter part of the paragraph is on the first "hydroelectric power plant" that Tesla and Westinghouse partnered on, the proposed information would be greatly beneficial in helping contextualize the "number of new inventions" that Tesla produced upon partnering with Westinghouse. If not for this information, the reader would not have information that helps **situate** the sheer scope of Tesla's inventions (in addition to the hydroelectric power plant).

WRONG CHOICES ARE NOT NOTED BUT DESCRIBED COLLECTIVELY.

Question 7

C is the best answer. The information in the underlined section is important in **contextualizing** why this project was particularly important, i.e., for the way in which it used energy. "Clean" energy is – by definition – drawn from renewable sources. It is precisely because of this use of renewable resources that this energy is "clean." Furthermore, in this context, the more appropriate vocabulary to use is "energy" rather than "electricity." While deleting the information here would result in a **loss of context,** what is important to focus on is the right – and efficient – use of vocabulary.

WRONG CHOICES ARE NOT NOTED BUT DESCRIBED COLLECTIVELY.

Question 8

A is the best answer. By telling us when Tesla returned to NYC, there is a link established between the previous line's mention of his move to Colorado Springs and his subsequent return to the city.

Although this sentence does not help clarify other information, neither is it relevant or redundant. Instead, the sentence helps the reader understand Tesla's movements with more clarity in relation to the timeline of his life and career.

WRONG CHOICES ARE NOT NOTED BUT DESCRIBED COLLECTIVELY.

TOPIC 17: CONCLUSION SENTENCES

What is a topic sentence?

A topic sentence introduces a paragraph by transitioning the reader from the previous one (if necessary).

What is a conclusion sentence?

A conclusion sentence ends a paragraph by transitioning the reader to the next one (if necessary).

Both topic and conclusion sentences are typically more general as compared to the specific information that might be included in the paragraph itself.

Let's assume, for example, that we have a three-paragraph essay
(excluding the introduction and conclusion)
where:
Paragraph 1 deals with Theme A
Paragraph 2 deals with Theme B
Paragraph 3 deals with Theme C

A paragraph structure that uses **strong topic and conclusion sentences** would look something like this:

Sentence 1 of Paragraph 1 introduces the reader very generally to Theme A and makes links to the thesis statement that ends the introduction.
This is followed by specific information about Theme A.
The last sentence of Paragraph 1 says something general about how Theme A connects to Theme B.

Sentence 1 of Paragraph 2 introduces the reader very generally to Theme B.
This is followed by specific information about Theme B.
The last sentence of Paragraph 2 says something general about how Theme B connects to Theme C.

Sentence 1 of Paragraph 3 introduces the reader very generally to Theme C.
This is followed by specific information about Theme C.
The last sentence of Paragraph 3 leads the reader from a consideration of Theme C into the concluding paragraph of the essay.

TOPIC 17: CONCLUSION SENTENCES

Questions 1-8 are based on the following passage.

The Origins of Tea

[1] <u>Save for water,</u> tea is the most commonly-consumed beverage in the world. Although nobody is certain exactly who brewed the first cup of tea, the beverage originated in China thousands of years ago. [2]

[3] Supposedly, in 2737 BCE, a Chinese emperor and his herbalist were served boiled water that had been contaminated by the leaves of a *Camellia sinensis* tree. This early legend has never been substantiated, but archaeologists have found tea containers in ancient Chinese tombs

---

Question 1

A)   NO CHANGE

B)   With the exception of water,

C)   Except water,

D)   Apart from water,

Question 2

At this point, the writer is considering adding the following sentence:
"Since that time, the beloved beverage has found a cherished place in cultures around the world."

Should the writer make this addition here?

A)   Yes, because it provides an effective introduction to the paragraph.

B)   Yes, because it provides new information that clarifies facts discussed later in the passage.

C)   No, because it provides redundant information.

D)   No, because it provides irrelevant information.

Question 3

At this point, the writer is considering adding the following sentence:
"According to legend, tea was discovered by accident."

Should the writer make this addition here?

A)   Yes, because it provides an effective transition from one paragraph to the next.

126

that date all the way back to the Han Dynasty around 200 BCE. **4**

5 As beloved as it was among the Chinese people, tea was not introduced into other Asian countries until hundreds of years later.

B) Yes, because it provides information that summarizes details presented earlier in the passage.

C) No, because it provides redundant information.

D) No, because it provides irrelevant information.

Which choice provides the most appropriate conclusion to the paragraph?

A) NO CHANGE

B) Thus, the Chinese definitively invented tea.

C) Thus, archaeological evidence shows that the Chinese were the first tea drinkers.

D) As a result of archaeological evidence, we now know that China made the first tea.

At this point, the writer is considering adding the following sentence:
"During China's Tang Dynasty – which spanned from 618 to 906 AD – tea became so popular it was formalized as the national drink of China."

Should the writer make this addition here?

A) Yes, because it provides information that summarizes details presented earlier in the passage.

B) Yes, because it provides an effective transition from one paragraph to the next.

C) No, because it provides redundant information.

D) No, because it provides irrelevant information.

6 People's knowledge of tea spread, and tea lovers began to emerge in other regions of Asia. Japanese Buddhist monks who had travelled to China on an educational mission brought tea back to Japan. The monks loved the stuff, and tea caught on quickly.

Tea spread from Asia to Europe when traders and missionaries from Portugal started to bring tea home from their journeys. While Portuguese traders may have been the first to bring tea into Europe, it was not introduced on a commercial scale until the Dutch set up a formal trade route. The Dutch were the first people who were able to economically ship tea to Europe.

7 In 1606, the Dutch's first commercial shipment of tea arrived. After its introduction to Holland, the trend of tea drinking began to spread to other countries throughout western Europe. Although, due to the high price, tea was often only consumed by the wealthy, and it became a highly fashionable drink.

At this point, the writer is considering adding the following sentence:
"Since its introduction into Japan, tea has become a crucial component of Japanese culture."

Should the writer make this addition here?

A)   Yes, because it provides information that summarizes details presented earlier in the passage.

B)   Yes, because it provides an effective transition from one paragraph to the next.

C)   No, because the revision is phrased as a conclusion, so it is not suitable here.

D)   No, because the revision presents irrelevant information.

The writer is considering revising the underlined sentence to:
"The Dutch shipped the first commercial container of tea from China to Holland in 1606."

Should the writer make this addition here?

A)   Yes, because the revision is more concise.

B)   Yes, because the revision improves clarity.

C)   No, because the revision is phrased as a conclusion, so it is not suitable here.

D)   No, because the revision presents irrelevant information.

Today, tea is a cultural staple in nations around the world. Across England and Ireland, people retire for tea between 3 p.m. and 5 p.m. each day and enjoy what has become an iconic British tradition. However, it was not until a fashionable Portuguese princess, Catherine of Braganza, married England's King Charles II did tea reach the United Kingdom. The princess' love of tea soon influenced other members of the court, and the tea drinking trend soon spread like wildfire. The British East India Company began to import tea from China in 1664, and the U.K. continues to be home to some of the most enthusiastic tea drinkers in the world. 8

Which of the following is the main purpose of this passage?

A) Tea is an ancient beverage that offers several health benefits.

B) People all around the world love tea, and it has been an important part of international commerce for centuries.

C) Tea was discovered in China thousands of years ago, and it has spread around the world over time.

D) Since its discovery, many cultures across the world have embraced tea, and it is still the drink of choice in many countries to this day.

Topic 17: Practice Questions (Answers & Explanations)

Question 1

D is the best answer. "Save for water" does not function well as an **idiomatic expression.** "With the exception of water" is less ideal since it begins the very first sentence of the passage with a preposition ("with") and takes more words than necessary to make the same point. Therefore, the two options we are left with are "Except water" and "Apart from water." The term "except" puts the emphasis on "water," i.e., that water is the exception to something. Using the term "apart from," however, shifts the focus from "water" to what it is being set apart from, i.e., "tea."
WRONG CHOICES ARE NOT NOTED BUT DESCRIBED COLLECTIVELY.

Question 2

B is the best answer. This is would be a concluding sentence to the paragraph (not its introduction) and in being so, it would help **frame the following content** for the reader, i.e., that the passage speaks to the global popularity of tea rather than a specific focus on China (as the current end of the paragraph currently suggests). By providing this **relevant** information that does not repeat anything that has been said before (hence making it **not** redundant), this sentence best serves to provide information that contextualizes facts that come later.
WRONG CHOICES ARE NOT NOTED BUT DESCRIBED COLLECTIVELY.

Question 3

A is the best answer. Rather than jumping directly into the Chinese emperor's accidental discovery of tea (an unsubstantiated legend), this proposed sentence should inform the reader that the paragraph deals with the discovery of tea. In so doing, this sentence would **effectively introduce** the reader to the content which follows. The information is **not a summary** of what comes before, and yet, it is not **irrelevant** or **redundant** – the information is absolutely in line with the following content and in fact, helps achieve **clarity** for the reader.
WRONG CHOICES ARE NOT NOTED BUT DESCRIBED COLLECTIVELY.

Question 4

A is the best answer. The phrase that is **KEY** here is "This early legend has never been substantiated," i.e., that these ideas have not been proven. Therefore, using words like "definitively" (as in choice B), or "shows that" (as in choice C), or "know that" (as in choice D) would require the reader to make **ASSUMPTIONS** that are not evidenced in the text.
WRONG CHOICES ARE NOT NOTED BUT DESCRIBED COLLECTIVELY.

Question 5

B is the best answer. Although the information in the proposed sentence does not summarize anything that came before it (since there is nothing earlier that has been said about the Tang Dynasty),

it is neither **irrelevant** (since it connects with previously mentioned information about the origin of tea in China), nor is it **redundant** (since the proposed inclusion does not repeat previously mentioned information). Therefore, B is the best answer – it takes the reader from information about the presence of tea in the Han dynasty to that in the Tang dynasty (in a later time period) to the subsequent dispersion of tea to different parts of the world.
WRONG CHOICES ARE NOT NOTED BUT DESCRIBED COLLECTIVELY.

Question 6

C is the best answer. The first line of this paragraph speaks about the spread of tea to other parts of Asia before speaking specifically about the use of tea in Japan. Therefore, the proposed sentence here would act as a more effective concluding statement to the paragraph (since, as established earlier, concluding sentences are also more general in scope while linking to material previously mentioned in the paragraph).

Although the information in this sentence is **not irrelevant,** neither does it help summarize previously mentioned information (since all focus on Japan comes after the position at which this statement would be included). It neither functions as an **effective transition** since it would take the paragraph from a focus on Japan to a sentence about Asian countries back to a focus on Japan.
WRONG CHOICES ARE NOT NOTED BUT DESCRIBED COLLECTIVELY.

Question 7

B is the best answer. By effectively connecting **previously mentioned information** and **explicitly making the links between the Dutch and the Chinese,** this choice would help improve clarity.

A is incorrect because the new sentence would **add** information and thus, cannot be called **more concise.**

However, this information is **EXTREMELY RELEVANT** (thus eliminating option D) to the topic that is being discussed in this passage – especially as an introductory sentence that **frames** the following information about the spread of tea from Holland to the rest of Europe (thus making option C unsuitable).
WRONG CHOICES ARE NOT NOTED BUT DESCRIBED COLLECTIVELY.

Question 8
D is the best answer.

A is insufficient in capturing the theme of the passage since it refers to "health benefits" as the main theme when in fact, the focus of the text tells us about the various regions/countries in which tea became popular (and how).

B requires an **ASSUMPTION** since, although the passage focuses on the global popularity of tea, it does not focus on the concept of "commerce." Commerce is mentioned in the context of Holland's introduction to tea, but otherwise, there are a variety of reasons that are explored as being the reason for tea's global popularity and availability.

While C does capture the **essence** of the passage, it is a less suitable answer than D because it does have the same **scope** as the latter. To say that something has "spread over the word" is different from speaking to how the drink has been "embraced" and become the "drink of choice" – phrases that are far more **relevant** in speaking to the theme of the passage as a whole.

THE CORRECT CHOICE IS NOTED BUT NOT DESCRIBE INDIVIDUALLY.

TOPIC 18: DEPENDENT CLAUSES

What is a dependent clause?
There are two types of clauses: independent and dependent.
An independent clause works as a complete sentence.
A dependent clause **has to be attached to an independent clause** to be complete.

REMEMBER THE FOLLOWING

When the dependent clause acts as the SUBJECT of a sentence, treat it as a singular noun.

For example: **Whoever has power needs** to wield it responsibly.

Notice the verb ("needs") agrees with "Whoever has power."
To check if this works, replace the subject with a more obvious singular noun and see if it makes sense.
*For example, "The President **needs** to wield it (his power) responsibly."*

Dependent clauses can be used to COMBINE two sentences

If there is a person, place, thing, or concept that both sentences are talking about
For example:
The President has great power. Whoever has power needs to wield it responsibly.
Those who have power, like the President, need to wield it responsibly.

If there is a chronological sequence that two sentences are describing
For example:
The President won the election. She then took office.
Upon winning the election, the President took office.

If one sentence defines the other
"With great power comes great responsibility." This is a quote made famous by the movie
Spiderman.
As mentioned famously in the *Spiderman* movie, "With great power comes great responsibility."

A dependent clause is incomplete by itself
Dependent clauses, when not attached to an independent clause, are **incomplete fragments.**

For example, consider the sentence above:
Upon winning the election, the President took office.

"Upon winning the election" cannot function as an independent sentence. Often, a clue to locate a dependent clause
*is the use of a **relative pronoun** (words like that, which, whoever) or a **subordinate conjunction** (words*
like after, although, because).

Generally speaking, sentences WITHOUT dependent clauses are CLEARER (and more ACTIVE).
So, if it is possible to eliminate a dependent clause
– and to a sentence entirely independent –
that would be the preferred option.

When a dependent clause is absolutely necessary,
use the most concise one!

TOPIC 18: PRACTICE QUESTIONS

Questions 1-8 are based on the following passage.

The Vampire Squid: A Unique Creature of the Sea

The vampire squid has piqued the interests of scholars and scientists all over the world. The creature has a highly unusual name: *Vampyroteuthis infernalis*, which roughly translates as the "vampire squid from Hell." [1] If its name is not interesting enough, what many people find even more fascinating about the vampire squid is that it is not actually a squid.

The vampire squid has features that are similar to squid, cuttlefish, and octopi. It has eights arms and two tentacles, and it is characterized by a unique brownish-red coloring. [2] Because of the vampire squid's name and appearance, it is easy to mistake this creature as part of the squid or octopus family, but it belongs to neither. In fact, scientists have classified the vampire squid into its own unique [3] order, *Vampyromorphida*, which the vampire squid is the only member of.

Question 1

A) NO CHANGE

B) The vampire squid's name and appearance make it

C) Thanks to the vampire squid's name and appearance, it is

D) Due to the unique name and appearance of vampire squid, it is

Question 2

A) NO CHANGE

B) The vampire squid's name and appearance make it

C) Thanks to the vampire squid's name and appearance, it is

D) Due to the unique name and appearance of vampire squid, it is

Question 3

A) NO CHANGE

B) order, *Vampyromorphida* which the vampire squid is the only member of.

C) order, *Vampyromorphida*, that the vampire squid is the only member of.

D) order, *Vampyromorphida*.

Unlike squids and octopi, the vampire squid does not release a black ink to escape predators. Instead, the vampire squid uses its unusual characteristics to deter potential threats. [4] When startled, the vampire squid inverts a cape-like webbing between its eight arms and displays the large spines that line the underside. It also secretes a bioluminescent [5] substance which confuses predators and allows the vampire squid to escape. [6] Vampire squids also produce a light at the tip of each arm to communicate with others of their kind. Although, the species is so rare that encounters are infrequent.

Question 4

A) NO CHANGE

B) Startled, the

C) The

D) If it is startled,

Question 5

Λ) NO CHANGE

B) substance to confuse predators and allows

C) substance to confuse predators and allow

D) substance that allows

Question 6

Which of the following most effectively combines the underlined sentences?

A) Also, vampire squids produce a light at the tip of each arm to communicate with others of their kind; although is so rare that encounters are infrequent.

B) Vampire squids also produce a light at the tip of each arm to communicate with others, and the species is so rare that encounters are infrequent.

C) The species is so rare that encounters are infrequent; even so, vampire squids also produce a light at the tip of each arm to communicate with others of their kind.

D) Although the species is so rare that encounters are infrequent, vampire squids also produce a light at the tip of each arm to communicate with others of their kind.

Although the appearance and name of the vampire squid make the creature sound intimidating, it is actually quite harmless. The vampire squid is a filter feeder meaning that it captures plant and animal matter floating around in the ocean rather than hunt. **7** If a vampire squid is hungry it uses the sticky cells on its filamentous tentacles to collect nutrients.

Vampire squids are fascinating. Unfortunately, however, these creatures are difficult to study because their natural habitats are in the deepest parts of the ocean. The unusual deep-sea creature is found in tropical to temperate climates in the open ocean, where it the occupies **8** meso to bathypelagic oceanic depths where light is very limited. As a result, little is known about the behavior of the elusive and unusual vampire squid. But as scientists continue to explore the depths of the ocean, they are uncovering more information about these unique deep-sea creatures.

Question 7

A) NO CHANGE

B) Hungry vampire squids use

C) Vampire squids that are hungry use

D) Whenever a vampire squid is hungry, it uses

Question 8

A) NO CHANGE

B) the dimly lit meso to bathypelagic oceanic depths.

C) meso to bathypelagic oceanic depths, in which light is very limited.

D) meso to bathypelagic oceanic depths.

Topic 18: Practice Questions (Answers & Explanations)

Question 1
A is the best answer. This choice **effectively** links the name of the squid with another interesting fact about it – enabling the reader to see a **flow in logic** from one sentence to another.

None of the other choices create this **flow**. By using **connectors like** "even though," "although," and "so" – without specifying what the following content is being said in relation to – there is a **less effective flow of logic** in the paragraph.
WRONG CHOICES ARE NOT NOTED BUT DESCRIBED COLLECTIVELY.

Question 2
B is the best answer. When possible, avoid beginning sentences with words like "because," "thanks to," and "due to" – all of these options result in the sentence becoming more **PASSIVE**. A choice like B, therefore, make the sentence more **DIRECT** and **ACTIVE** and thus, is the preferable choice.
WRONG CHOICES ARE NOT NOTED BUT DESCRIBED COLLECTIVELY.

Question 3
D is the best answer. The **KEYWORDS** to notice here are "its own" and "unique" – words that **immediately imply** that the vampire squid is the **only** member of this particular category. Therefore, using "only" would cause an **unnecessary redundancy**. As the only choice that omits the word "only," D is the only possible option.
WRONG CHOICES ARE NOT NOTED BUT DESCRIBED COLLECTIVELY.

Question 4
A is the best answer. The underlined section refers directly to what has been mentioned at the end of the previous sentence ("to deter potential threats"). Given this, using the significantly shorter (and more concise) dependent clause of "When startled" is sufficient – since "when" can immediately be connected to occasions in which potential threats need to be deterred.

Choices B and C, by taking away any reference to time, **alter the tone** of the sentence and **affect its clarity by not establishing a clear connection to the previous sentence** (given that it exists).

Choice D, while not incorrect, is less suitable because it takes more words to make the same point. As mentioned earlier, when dependent clauses are necessary for the meaning of a sentence, use the shortest one!

Question 5
C is the best answer.

The current sentence construction, while not incorrect, uses a more passive sentence construction (indicated by the use of "which") that – if possible – should be made more active. Not to mention, of course, that when the word "which" is used to introduce a dependent clause, it needs to be preceded by a comma. Since the comma has not been included here, there is a grammatical error. Therefore, **A is incorrect.**

While both B & C are more active in their use of the infinitive ("to confuse"), choice B has a subject-verb disagreement. The subject of this sentence is the "bioluminescent substance," in the singular form. Therefore, both "confuse" and "allow" need to be in the singular form in the sentence that follows. Therefore, C is the best option.

D is not a viable answer since it eliminates part of the information that is helpful for the reader to better understand the nature of the squid and the bioluminescent substance.
WRONG CHOICES ARE NOT NOTED BUT DESCRIBED COLLECTIVELY.

Question 6

D is the best answer. This answer is most effective in transforming the second sentence into a dependent clause ("Although the species is so rare that encounters are infrequent") that introduces the independent clause ("vampire squids also produce a light at the tip of each arm to communicate with others of their kind").

A is incorrect because semicolons are used only **when there are complete sentences on BOTH sides of the punctuation mark.** Since that condition is not met in this case – "although is so rare that encounters are infrequent" is both incomplete and grammatically inaccurate – the semicolon is not a viable choice.

B is incorrect because the use of the word "and" is misleading. "And" is used when ideas build on each other. Here what is provided is a **qualification** (a contrast, of sorts) to a previous idea.

C is incorrect. While the use of the semicolon in this case is not incorrect, compare this answer choice to answer D. It will immediately be noted that choice D is more active, clearer, and more concise. Therefore, it is the preferable choice.

Question 7

B is the best answer. Whenever possible, avoid using sentences that begin with "if" or "whenever." In this case, that would immediately rule out options A and C. Between options B & D then, we see a visible difference between **ACTIVE and PASSIVE voice.** In the former, the squids are more directly described as "hungry" rather than being recipients of the condition of hunger.

Question 8

B is the best answer. Whenever possible, look for the sentence structure that **transmits ALL the necessary information** in a way that uses as few **dependent clauses** and as **few words as possible.**

In this case, for instance, using the term "dimly lit" rather than using "where light is very limited" is preferred.

Choices A and C use additional terms that are not necessary to describe the same idea.

Choice D is less suitable because it takes away **necessary information** (about the nature of the light) in order to make the sentence shorter (i.e., it is shorter **BUT does NOT** communicate **ALL** the same information).

TOPIC 19: COMPARATIVES & SUPERLATIVES

What are comparatives and superlatives?

Comparatives are words that are used to compare two items.
These words often end with "-er."

Superlatives are used to compare three or more items.
These words often end with "-est."

STRATEGY

If you see a comparative
Make sure that only two items are being compared.
Make sure that a comparative word that ends with "-er," does **not** have the term "more" before it.

For example:
Correct: Between the two brothers, Diego is the **faster** runner.
Incorrect: Between the two brothers, Diego is the **more** faster runner.
Incorrect: Between the two brothers, Diego is the **fastest** runner.

If you see a superlative
Make sure that three or more items are being compared.
Make sure that a comparative word that ends with "-est," does **not** have the term "most" before it.

For example:
Correct: Among all the students in the class, Diego is the **fastest** runner.
Incorrect: Among all the students in the class, Diego is the **most** fastest runner.
Incorrect: Among all the students in the class, Diego is the **faster** runner.

TOPIC 19: PRACTICE QUESTIONS

Questions 1-8 are based on the following passage.

Famous Rivals Thomas Edison and Nikola Tesla

Thomas Edison and Nikola Tesla were both famous inventors who contributed great innovations to the fields of technology and electrical engineering. Each mans' work continues to impact the world even in today's advanced technological age. However, the two inventors were famous adversaries. The rivalry between Edison and Tesla still rages, and experts around the world debate to this day: **1** which was the more impressive inventor?

Despite their rivalry, the two inventors had some **2** rather similar characteristics. Neither Edison nor Tesla completed high school. Regardless, they would both go on to make incredible strides in the complex fields of science and engineering. Likewise, they were both key innovators during the early days of electricity.

Thomas Edison was an American inventor and businessman known for commercializing and capitalizing on his inventions. Until recently, Thomas Edison was the **3** more prolific inventor in history having held over 1,000 patents at the time of his death. **4** Much of

Question 1

A) NO CHANGE

B) who was the more impressive inventor?

C) who was the impressive inventor?

D) who was the more impressive inventor.

Question 2

A) NO CHANGE

B) relatively similar

C) more or less similar

D) similar

Question 3

A) NO CHANGE

B) prolificest

C) most prolific

D) best

Edison's inventions are still used today including the light bulb, phonograph, motion picture camera **5** and – perhaps most important of all – the system that transports electricity across America.

Question 4

A) NO CHANGE

B) Many

C) More

D) One

Question 5

A) NO CHANGE

B) and – perhaps more important than any other – the

C) and, perhaps, most important of all, the

D) and perhaps, most important of all, the

Like Edison, Nikola Tesla was an inventor, mechanical and electrical engineer, and physicist. Tesla was well known for his contributions to the design of the modern alternating current electrical supply system, which in many ways is **6** superior than Edison's direct current design. Tesla also invented many items commonly used today including the radio transmitter and the Tesla Coil.

Question 6

A) NO CHANGE

B) superior

C) superior to

D) better than

Tesla and Edison crossed paths when Tesla went to work as an engineer at Thomas Edison's Manhattan headquarters in 1884. Tesla had admired the American inventor greatly, and he even found ways to improve Edison's inefficient generators and motors. However, the two men who were once the **7** close colleagues had a falling out. The conflict arose when Edison allegedly offered the young Tesla a large amount of money – an amount that would equal one million dollars today – if he achieved a particular design improvement. As the story goes, Tesla succeeded, but Edison claimed his offer was a joke. Instead, he offered Tesla a meagre raise in pay. Feeling slighted, Tesla quit on the spot.

After Tesla resigned from Edison's company, the two inventors entered into an epic rivalry. In the late 1880s, the two geniuses waged what was known as a "War of Currents." The two inventors battled over whose electrical system would sustain the world's energy needs – Tesla's alternating current or Edison's direct current. Edison's direct current ultimately **8** proving superior, and most of today's electrical transmission infrastructure is based on direct current technology.

A)   NO CHANGE

B)   closer colleagues than ever

C)   closest

D)   closest of colleagues

A)   NO CHANGE

B)   proved superior

C)   proved itself

D)   itself superior

Topic 19: Practice Questions (Answers & Explanations)

Question 1

B is the best answer.

There are two people being compared here: Tesla and Edison. Therefore, we need to use the COMPARATIVE "more." This immediately eliminates choice C.

Since the underlined section refers to people rather than ideas or things, "who" is a better choice than "which." This helps us eliminate choice A.

Of choices B and D, we are asked to make a decision between the sentence as a question versus the sentence as a statement (that ends with a period). Since the phrase begins with an interrogatory word like "who," the question mark is the more viable choice.
THE CORRECT CHOICE IS NOTED, BUT IT IS NOT DESCRIBED INDIVIDUALLY.

Question 2

D is the best answer.

The word "similar" preceded by the word "some" already **implies** that the relationship is qualified as being "more or less," or "relatively." Therefore, to use such terms when "some" has already been used is unnecessary in describing the similarities between the two scientists.
WRONG CHOICES ARE NOT NOTED BUT DESCRIBED COLLECTIVELY.

Question 3

C is the best answer. Since Edison is being compared to all other scientists in history, there are certainly more than three items being compared. Therefore, we are looking for a **superlative:** a choice that is preceded by "most" or that ends with "est." In the choices presented, 'prolificest' is presented as an option. However, this word does not exist ("most prolific" is the superlative that would apply).

"More" prolific would not work since there are more than two points of comparison. "Best" is less viable since it is more general than "prolific." To be "prolific" means to be extremely productive; to the "best" means, more generally, to be good at something.
WRONG CHOICES ARE NOT NOTED BUT DESCRIBED COLLECTIVELY.

Question 4

B is the best answer. When the noun in question is countable – like "light bulb, phonograph, motion picture camera" – "many" is the correct choice.

Choices A and D are unviable because "much" is used when there is **more than "one" of something** and these **quantities are not countable.**

"More" is used as a comparative (which is not the case here) since all that is provided is a list of Edison's inventions that are still in use today.

Question 5
A is the best answer.

There are more than three items being compared in this sentence (all of Edison's inventions that are still in use; four that have been listed here). Therefore, a superlative like "most" is necessary. Therefore, B can be eliminated as an answer choice.

Of the three remaining choices that all use "most." we are asked to choose between the DASHES and COMMAS. Remember that when DASHES are used on either side of a phrase, they **add emphasis** to the text in question (unlike COMMAS, which are more often used on both sides to **show non-essential information**). In this case, given the extra emphasis on the **most** important invention, the DAHSES are the better option. Leaving us, with choice A.

Question 6
C is the best answer.

When using "superior" as a comparison, only "to" is idiomatically accurate. Using "than" following that word, or not using any preposition at all, are both grammatically incorrect.

"Better than," while grammatically accurate, does not carry the same **implication** as the word "superior." To be "better" is more benign and more ambiguous. To be "superior" though, alludes to a mark of higher status.
WRONG CHOICES ARE NOT NOTED BUT DESCRIBED COLLECTIVELY.

Question 7
D is the best answer.

This is a tricky question. There are only two people being referred to here – Edison and Tesla – and technically, if a comparison were being created between these individuals, the comparative would be the right choice. However, note what is being compared here is their closeness to the closeness of colleagues as a general category (a category that includes more than three items). Therefore, what is needed in this case is a **superlative.** Choices C & D are the only options that then remain.

Using both remaining options to replace the underlined text, we immediately see that choice C ("closest") renders the sentence meaningless since it does not clarify the term **in relation** to what it is being compared to. Choice D, therefore, is the most viable answer.

Question 8
B is the best answer.

A is incorrect because we are speaking of an event in the past. "Proved," therefore, is more suitable than "proving."

Any option that does not use the word "superior" is unviable because, without this word, no comparison is established between Tesla and Edison's work. Therefore, option **C can be eliminated.**

When deciding between "proved superior" and "itself superior," replace both terms in the underlined section. You'll immediately notice that the latter (answer D) makes the sentence meaningless — we need a verb like "proved" in order to complete the idea that is presented. Therefore, B is the most viable answer.

TOPIC 20: RELATIVE CLAUSES

What is a relative clause?

Relative clauses **begin with a relative pronoun**: with, whom, whose, which, that.

Relative clauses **add meaning** to a sentence,
but they are **not needed for the sentence to be complete.**

For example:
The ideas of "peace" and "non-violence", **which are now well-known concepts**, are attributed to
Mahatma Gandhi.
In this sentence, the relative clause "which are not well-known concepts" gives us extra information, i.e., that the ideas are
famous. However, even if this clause was to be deleted, the sentence would be grammatically correct.
"The ideas of 'peace' and 'non-violence' are attributed to Mahatma Gandhi.'

Relative clauses are sometimes bounded by COMMAS (as in the example above).
However, this is not always necessary.

For example:
The ideas of "peace" and "non-violence" **that are well-known concepts** are attributed to Mahatma
Gandhi.

Relative clauses, like dependent clauses, **can never stand alone as complete sentences.**

TOPIC 20: PRACTICE QUESTIONS

Questions 1-8 are based on the following passage.

Eat Your Vegetables

Depending on **1** who you ask, it seems like everyone has a different opinion about nutrition. Low-carb, high-fat, weight loss, raw, ketogenic, vegan, and a seemingly endless variety of other diets maintain their place in popular culture. It seems impossible to know **2** which is best. The effectiveness of any specific diet can be hard to pin down for an individual person, but there is one thing that every expert on food and nutrition can agree upon: vegetables are an integral part of any healthy diet.

Some of us may only eat our vegetables so that we can have dessert, but there are important reasons to make sure to include vegetables in every meal. Vegetables are nutrient dense; they contain high concentrations of vitamins, minerals, antioxidants, and dietary fiber. A diet rich in these nutrients may reduce the risk of heart disease and **3** cancer, which is a great reason to make sure to eat vegetables with every meal.

Question 1
A) NO CHANGE
B) whom
C) what
D) where

Question 2
A) NO CHANGE
B) what is best.
C) that is best.
D) best.

Question 3
A) NO CHANGE
B) cancer that is a great reason to make
C) cancer, which are great reasons to make
D) cancer;

If you think you do not like the taste of vegetables, consider trying a different variety. Vegetables are often divided into groups, including dark green, red and orange, beans and peas, and starchy. Vegetables from each subgroup offer their own unique benefits, and the various vegetable subgroups are filled with different types of important nutrients. Dark green vegetables are full of vitamins C and E, **4** which are antioxidants that help repair damaged cells and promote immune system health. Beta-carotene, **5** it helps keep eyes, skin and bones healthy, is plentiful in red and orange vegetables like carrots and sweet potatoes. Beans and peas are packed with fiber and protein, as well as minerals like magnesium and iron. Last but not least, starchy vegetables are good sources of the **6** B-vitamins which your brain needs to produce important chemicals.

Diets rich in vegetables offer many health benefits. For example, eating plenty of vegetables helps maintain healthy blood pressure levels. This helps people minimize their risk for stroke and heart **7** disease, which is the leading cause of death in the United States. Vegetables also have a positive impact

Question 4

A) NO CHANGE
B) that are antioxidants
C) antioxidants
D) and are antioxidants

Question 5

A) NO CHANGE
B) which helps keep eyes, skin and bones healthy,
C) that helps keep eyes, skin and bones healthy,
D) DELETE the underlined portion.

Question 6

A) NO CHANGE
B) B-vitamins, which your brain needs
C) B-vitamins, your brain needs
D) B-vitamins that your brain needs

Question 7

A) NO CHANGE
B) disease that is the
C) disease, a
D) disease, the

on physical traits that affect daily quality of life, such as vision and the functioning of the digestive system. Eating a lot of vegetables can even prevent some forms of [8] cancer, which is a potentially life-threatening disease.

For those seeking better health, increased vegetable intake should be among the first steps. Eating vegetables across the color spectrum as well as plenty of servings of beans and peas is the best way to ensure an effective dose of vitamins, minerals, antioxidants, and nutrients. With vegetables, more is better; any increase in daily vegetable servings tends to correlate with a decrease in disease risk. So, while some diets come and go with trends and fads, the solution to better health is simple: eat your vegetables!

Question 8

A)   NO CHANGE
B)   cancer is a
C)   cancer, a
D)   cancer, the

Topic 20: Practice Questions (Answers & Explanations)

Question 1

B is the best answer. From what follows the underlined word, we know that "everyone" refers to people. Therefore, the only two options that would be appropriate are "who" and "whom." "Whom" should be used when referring to the object of a verb or a preposition; "who" should be used to refer to the subject of the sentence. In this case we see that the underlined word refers to "everyone," which is the object of the sentence. Therefore, "whom" is the most appropriate choice.

WRONG CHOICES ARE NOT NOTED BUT DESCRIBED COLLECTIVELY.

Question 2

A is the best answer. In this case, the relative pronoun is being used to refer to the different "diets" that are mentioned in the previous sentence. So, consider this. If you were asking someone about their diet, how would you frame the question? "What diet do you follow?" "Which diet do you follow?" Immediately, you'll notice that "which" sounds a lot more accurate than the other option. That said, "what" is not grammatically incorrect. "Which" is simply more formal and better fits the **context** of this sentence.

Options C and D are not viable options to even consider since, when used in the sentence to replace the underlined word, the sentence loses meaning.

Question 3

A is the best answer.

Note the tricky subject number here. Initially, you might be likely to think that "heart disease" and "cancer" are **two** subjects. However, in reading the sentence more closely, you find that the subject is the "reduction of risk," i.e., a singular subject that needs to be followed by a singular verb ("is" rather than "are"). This immediately eliminates option C.

D is incorrect because it uses a semicolon incorrectly. Semicolons should only be used when there are complete sentences – each with its own subject, verb, and object – on either side of the punctuation. Since this condition wouldn't be met here, this choice is unviable.

So, we are left between A and B. The first uses ",which" to introduce the subsequent clause; the second uses "that" to introduce what follows. While both are accurate grammatically, reading the sentence aloud will tell you that the comma before "which" allows the reader to take a pause before reading information that is **NON-ESSENTIAL** but relevant. The lack of the comma with the option of "that" makes the sentence a little harder to follow. This is why A is the better choice.

Question 4

C is the best answer.

The "reason" being referred to here is the "reduction in risk" in "heart disease" **and** "cancer," i.e., the reductions in risk in **TWO** diseases (i.e., in the plural). Therefore, "are great reasons" is a **better choice** than "is a great reason." This immediately excludes A and C.

D is unsuitable because a **SEMICOLON** can only be used when there are complete sentences on **both** sides of the punctuation mark. Since that condition does not apply here, this choice is unviable.

Question 5

B is the best answer. Seeing the comma that follows "Beta-carotene," you can immediately tell that the word that follows the punctuation has to be "which." The use of "it" makes the clause independent; "that" would **not need to be preceded by the comma.** Furthermore, since the information that is provided here is **relevant** (although non-essential to the sentence's grammatical accuracy) there is no need for it to be deleted.
WRONG CHOICES ARE NOT NOTED BUT DESCRIBED COLLECTIVELY.

Question 6
D is the best answer.

A is grammatically incorrect because "which" always needs to be preceded by a comma.

B is incorrect because ",which" is often used to integrate a **NON-ESSENTIAL CLAUSE** while "that" is used to include **an ESSENTIAL CLAUSE.** Since the information provided in the underlined portion is essential to its form and content, "that" is a better choice. Hence, **D is a more viable answer.**

C is incorrect since the lack of a **relative pronoun** makes the sentence difficult to follow.

Question 7
A is the best answer. Notice that the sentence refers to two diseases as the "leading causes for death" **in the plural.** Therefore, any answer that is in the singular (like choice B) can be excluded. Similarly, the article "a" and "the" **connotes** a singular entity ("a" disease or "the" disease versus multiple diseases) and therefore, this answer would be unsuitable.
WRONG CHOICES ARE NOT NOTED BUT DESCRIBED COLLECTIVELY.

Question 8
A is the best answer.

Using B as the answer would **render the sentence meaningless;** "Eating a lot of vegetables can even prevent some forms of **cancer is a** potentially life-threatening disease."

D is unsuitable because of the use of "the" – which implies "only" rather than saying that it is "one of many" potentially life-threatening diseases.

Between A and C, we see the difference in the use of the relative pronoun "which." While, in this case, the absent relative pronoun is **not incorrect**, adding the "which" certainly helps ensure that there is no misunderstanding for the reader. Therefore, A is the better option.

TOPIC 21: COMBINING SENTENCES

There are multiple ways to combine sentences. Let us work with this example:
In order to manage her PTSD, Garima visits a counsellor every day. She does this alongside taking medications and following a strict exercise program.

USE A TRAILING PHRASE
In order to manage her PTSD, Garima visits a counsellor every day, alongside taking medications and following a strict exercise program.

USE A PREPOSITION
In order to manage her PTSD, Garima visits a counsellor every day **alongside** medications and a strict exercise program.

USE A DEPENDANT CLAUSE OR A MODIFIER
In order to manage her PTSD, in addition to medications and a strict exercise program, Garima visits a counsellor every day.

USE A CONJUNCTION
In order to manage her PTSD, Garima attends counselling, exercises regularly, **and** takes medication.

USE A RELATIVE CLAUSE
Garima attends counselling, takes medication, and exercises regularly – **all of which** help her manage her PTSD.

USE AN INFINITIVE
Garima attends counselling, takes medication, and exercises regularly to manage her PTSD.

Do NOT use more pronouns than absolutely necessary

Do NOT change the meaning of the sentence

Do NOT repeat words or use more words than necessary

TOPIC 21: PRACTICE QUESTIONS

Questions 1-8 are based on the following passage.

The Hard Lessons of Ernest Shackleton

In 1914, Ernest Shackleton and his crew started on a quest to achieve a **1** truly monumental goal. They sought to cross the Antarctic continent by foot. In the Antarctic, Shackleton proved an effective leader even under disastrous conditions. Despite his abilities, however, Shackleton's journey became both a symbol of the dangers of overestimating your abilities and the profound human capacity to survive seemingly unendurable conditions.

2 Shackleton was a seasoned explorer with a big ego. He had a thirst for fame, recognition, and adventure. He set off by sea with a crew of twenty-eight men, but it became apparent that their goal of crossing the southernmost continent would be impossible to achieve.

Before the expedition reached land, Shackleton's ship, the *Endurance*, got frozen in pack ice. Stuck in the sea ice, the party stayed on the ship for as long as they **3** could. After ten months, however, pressure from the surrounding ice crushed the massive ship.

A)   NO CHANGE

B)   truly monumental goal:

C)   truly monumental goal; they sought to

D)   truly monumental goal, to

A)   NO CHANGE

B)   Shackleton was a seasoned explorer with a big ego, as well as a thirst for fame, recognition, and adventure.

C)   Shackleton was a seasoned explorer with a thirst for fame.

D)   Shackleton was a seasoned explorer with a thirst for fame, recognition, and adventure – as well as a big ego.

A)   NO CHANGE

B)   could, but after ten months

C)   could; but after ten months

D)   could, and after ten months

Shackleton ordered his men to abandon the *Endurance*. [4] Without a ship, Shackleton and his crew were stuck. His goal changed entirely. Shackleton's new mission was to get himself and his crew back to civilization alive.

The crew set up camp on the sea ice. [5] Shackleton remained steadfast. He shifted his entire focus to their new goal of surviving the life-threatening conditions of the Antarctic seas. They lived on sea ice while soaking wet much of the time. It was desperately cold, and the men survived by hunting seal and penguin. [6] When temperatures eventually warmed, and sea ice began to break. When enough water was exposed, Shackleton ordered the men to launch the lifeboats from their abandoned ship.

Question 4

A) NO CHANGE

B) Shackleton and his crew were stuck without a ship, and the expedition's goals changed entirely.

C) Without a ship, Shackleton and his crew were stuck; goals changed entirely.

D) Without a ship, Shackleton and his crew were stuck, meaning that the expedition's goals changed entirely.

Question 5

The author is considering replacing the underlined with the following sentence:

"Shackleton remained steadfast, shifting his entire focus to their new goal of surviving life-threatening conditions."

Should the author make this replacement?

A) No, because it omits relevant information.

B) Yes, because it improves clarity.

C) No, because it includes a modifier error.

D) Yes, because it eliminates passive voice.

Question 6

The author is considering replacing the underlined with the following sentence:

"As time went on, temperatures warmed. This made the sea ice break."

Should the author make this replacement?

A) No, because it omits relevant information.

B) Yes, because it improves clarity.

C) No, because it is unclear.

In their lifeboats, the crew rowed nonstop for five **7** days. It was a harrowing journey in horrible conditions. They finally landed at the remote Elephant Island - merely a big, inhospitable rock.

After only a few days of rest, Shackleton and five crew members set sail once again. They embarked on an eight-hundred-mile journey through the most dangerous waters in the world to reach a remote whaling station. **8** Miraculously, they arrived at their island destination. However, the sea forced them to land on the wrong side. The men had to cross miles of glacial ice by foot to get to the Western side of the island where they finally found assistance. Two years after setting out on their mission to cross Antarctica by foot, the men were finally rescued from their makeshift camp on Elephant Island. They had never even reached the continent they had sought to conquer.

The tale of Shackleton and his men offer valuable lessons to modern adventurers. First, never underestimate a challenge laid before you. Second, human survival is possible under even the most challenging conditions so long as people work together to endure.

D)   Yes, because it eliminates passive voice.

Question 7

A)   NO CHANGE

B)   days; indeed, it was a harrowing journey in horrible conditions.

C)   days in horrible conditions.

D)   days – a harrowing journey in horrible conditions.

Question 8

A)   NO CHANGE

B)   Miraculously they arrived; but the sea forced them to land on the wrong side of the island.

C)   They arrived, but the sea ice miraculously forced them the wrong side of the island.

D)   The sea at their destination forced them to land on the wrong side of the island.

Topic 21: Practice Questions (Answers & Explanations)

Question 1

B is the best answer. The COLON is used in order to introduce a list of items or to clarify a preceding term/concept. In this case, the second sentence clarifies what the "monumental goal" was, i.e., to cross the Antarctic continent by foot. Since the clarification provided is so obvious and related to the first part of the clause, the COLON is the most appropriate way of combining the sentences.

While none of the other options provided are grammatically incorrect – the comma what we are looking for here is the **most** appropriate punctuation mark.
WRONG CHOICES ARE NOT NOTED BUT DESCRIBED COLLECTIVELY.

Question 2
D is the best answer.

We can immediately see that **A is not the most suitable answer** since both sentences share the same subject ("Shackleton") and both clauses also speak to his personality traits. Therefore, it would be more efficient to combine the two sentences.

C is not an appropriate answer since each item on the given list describes a different quality of Shackleton's and by including only his "thirst for fame," the reader does not get sufficient information.

Both B & D are suitable responses, so let us consider which option is **more** viable. Option B, by using commas to combine all four different characteristics into one sentence places less **emphasis** on his "big ego." Clearly, the author wants to highlight this particular characteristic more than the others (an assumption that can be made by this being listed first, and in the topic sentence). Therefore, an option that preserves this **tone** and **emphasis** would be preferable – a goal that is better achieved by the use of the dashes in option D.

Question 3
A is the best answer.

Option B, with its multiple subordinate clauses and uses of commas is harder for the reader to access.

Options C and D are not entirely viable because it is **unnecessary** to use a conjunction like "and" or "but" to follow the **semicolon** punctuation mark.

Therefore, it would be most appropriate to leave the sentences as they are – as two separate clauses.

Question 4

B is the best answer. By effectively using ",and" this answer is the clearest and most accurate of all the provide answers.

The current sentence structure (**A**) is less suitable because the second clause ("His goal changed entirely") is extremely brief and since the content is directly related to the preceding statement, the structure would be improved by attempting to combine the sentences.

C is incorrect because the use of the **SEMICOLON is incorrect.** Remember that the clauses on both sides of this punctuation mark need to have their own subject, verb, and object.

D is incorrect because the placement of "Shackleton and his crew were stuck" between commas creates the implication that this information is **NON-ESSENTIAL.** However, given the central role that this information plays in understanding the rest of the sentence, it cannot be considered non-essential.

Question 5

B is the best answer. By combining two sentences with related ideas, the new sentence is effective in improving the clarity of the text.

A and C are incorrect because no information is omitted in the combined sentence, and there is no modifier error.

D is incorrect because there was no passive voice used in the original sentence that needed to be eliminated. Both the underlined sentences describe the subject, "Shackleton," as the enactor of the actions ("remained" and "shifted") and thus are **ACTIVE** in their structure.

Question 6

C is the best answer. The choice that the author has made to split the sentence into two with the second one beginning with "This," makes the text unclear and hard to understand. The reader cannot tell if "this" refers to "time" or the temperatures.

The sentence does not omit relevant information (as option B suggests), but neither does it improve clarity or correct the passive voice. Therefore, C is the only answer that is suitable.
WRONG CHOICES ARE NOT NOTED BUT DESCRIBED COLLECTIVELY.

Question 7

C is the best answer. By telling us that the journey was "horrible," and with the surrounding **contextual information** (about the journey being nonstop for five days) about the nature of the journey, we understand that the conditions are "harrowing." Using the two words in the same sentence therefore, and to describe the same event, causes an **unnecessary redundancy.** As the only choice that avoids the use of both "harrowing" and "horrible," C is the most viable answer.

Question 8
A is the best answer.

When using semicolons, it is recommended that **conjunctions** (like "but") are omitted. Therefore, choice B is less suitable.

Choice C changes the meaning of the sentence and **implies** that it was the sea ice that was "miraculous" rather than the crew's feat of having arrived despite the conditions.

Choice D is **incomplete** since it takes away the information about the crew's "miraculous" arrival despite the ice. The **content** and **tone** are altered in unnecessary ways.

TOPIC 22: DATA ANALYSIS

STRATEGIES

Understand the data

If you are provided with a graph, look at the **title** of the figure.

Then, look at what the different data points **represent.**

Read the labels and the scales.

Before looking at the questions that are provided, try to ascertain the following:

What are the patterns in the data?

What are the anomalies (changes in the pattern)?

What is the story that the data tells you (in relation to the passage it is part of)?

Understand the question

Make sure you really know what the question is asking for. Then go to the data.

Look for the evidence **in the figure** and **not in the text** of the passage

(unless you are explicitly asked to do so).

Eliminate choices that are **IRRELEVANT** and/or require you to make **ASSUMPTIONS.**

Irrelevant choices will have nothing to do with the data that has been presented to you.

They will include ideas that have nothing to do with what the data represents.

*Other choices will **overstate** or **understate** information in the graph*

*and ask you to make assumptions about what the data **implies.***

*Remember that graphs and other pictorial representations of data very rarely are used for **implications.***

They are used to communicate "fact."

Understand the connection

Refer to the passage **only if** the question **explicitly asks you to do so.**

Look for **KEYWORDS** from the data in the text.

Make sure you understand the **context** of the text so that you are making accurate

(rather than contrasting or assumptive) associations between data and text.

TOPIC 22: PRACTICE QUESTIONS

Questions 1-8 are based on the following passage.

Global Warming and The Greenhouse Effect

1 Greenhouse gases are the primary cause of the greenhouse effect, which leads to globally increased temperatures.

2 Shortwave heat energy from the sun heats the surface of the Earth during the day. At the same time, some of the radiant heat - longer energy waves that have bounced off the earth – bounce back into the atmosphere. The earth's natural homeostatic systems allow these rays to radiate back into space. However, when greenhouse gasses are present on the Earth's surface, those gases trap the long wave energy in the lower atmosphere.

Greenhouse gasses trap heat so less of it radiates back into space. Instead, it stays trapped within the lower atmosphere, radiating higher levels of heat onto the Earth's surface and contributing to rising global temperature.

Question 1

At this point, the writer is considering adding the following sentence:
"Greenhouse gases are any gas found in the atmosphere that absorbs and releases radiation in the thermal infrared range."

Should the writer make this addition here?

A) Yes, because it defines a key term used in the passage.

B) Yes, because it summarizes key data.

C) No, because it provides redundant information.

D) No, because it provides irrelevant information.

Question 2

Which of the following creates the most effective transition?

A) Greenhouse gasses are accumulating in our atmosphere.

B) The greenhouse effect occurs because of human activity.

C) Greenhouse gases are emitted from many natural sources.

D) The greenhouse effect occurs because greenhouse gasses are accumulating in our atmosphere.

Figure 1: Greenhouse

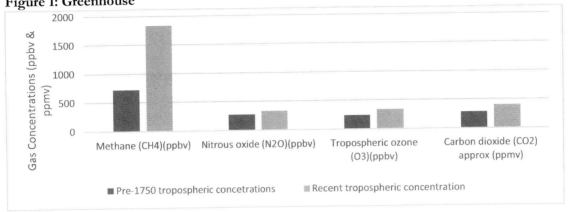

3 Figure 1 shows a comparison of greenhouse gas concentrations in the troposphere before the year 1750 and in recent times. The chart shows **4** increases in dangerous greenhouse gases. While a number of greenhouse gases do occur naturally, other harmful gases are emitted from human activities. A few examples of these manmade greenhouse gases are: chorofluorocarbons (CFCs), perfluorocarbons (PFCs), and hydrofluorocarbons (HFCs).

An American scientist, Dr. Charles Keeling, began sampling atmospheric concentrations of carbon dioxide – the most commonly-studied greenhouse gas – in 1958. Since that time, his findings have indicated human-caused contributions to global warming.

Question 3

At this point, the writer is considering adding the following sentence:
"Some of the most common greenhouse gasses are methane, nitrous oxide, ozone, and carbon dioxide."

Should the writer make this addition here?

A) Yes, because it links two related ideas in the paragraph.

B) Yes, because it provides information that clarifies data in the figure.

C) No, because it provides redundant information.

D) No, because it provides irrelevant information.

Question 4

A) NO CHANGE

B) little change in greenhouse gas levels.

C) no demonstrable relationship between economic activity and greenhouse gases.

D) an increase that will surely spell disaster.

Figure 2 shows the most abundant greenhouse gases in the atmosphere. **5** Across the board, levels are rising **6**

Figure 2: Greenhouse Gas Measurements

Which choice provides relevant information from the figure to support the writer's argument

A) Greenhouse gasses are accumulating at increasing rates.

B) Data collected on every major greenhouse gas shows universal increases.

C) Scientists measured increases in each of the key greenhouse gases.

D) Scientists measured increases in each of the key greenhouse gases except for carbon dioxide, which remained constant.

The writer wants to use data from the graph to create an effective transition sentence. Which of the following best accomplishes this goal?

A) Temperatures rise and fall, but greenhouse gas concentrations have certainly increased over time.

B) There is no evidence that greenhouse gases are primarily emitted from human sources.

C) Across the board, greenhouse gases are accumulating at increasing rates.

D) Temperatures rise and fall, but greenhouse gas accumulation is irreversible.

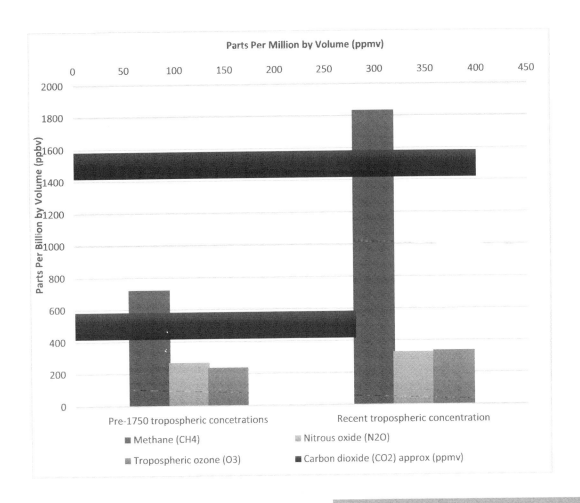

Parts Per Million by Volume (ppmv)

Pre-1750 tropospheric concetrations   Recent tropospheric concentration

■ Methane (CH4)   ■ Nitrous oxide (N2O)

■ Tropospheric ozone (O3)   ■ Carbon dioxide (CO2) approx (ppmv)

Carbon dioxide concentrations in the atmosphere are so high that they must be measured in per million(ppm). This is one thousand times greater than the units of measurement for other greenhouse gases, which are represented in parts per billion (ppb). Because it is so abundant, carbon dioxide is the most commonly-studied greenhouse gas. **7**

At this point, the writer is considering adding the following sentence:

"However, other greenhouse gases – methane in particular – are equally as dangerous."

Should the writer make this addition here?

A) Yes, because it links two related ideas in the paragraph.

B) Yes, because it provides information that helps transition to the next paragraph.

C) No, because it provides redundant information.

D) No, because it provides irrelevant information.

Typically methane is released into the atmosphere from low oxygen environments like swamps and bogs. However, recent increases in methane emissions are related to human activity, specifically mining, use of natural gases, and agricultural activities. 8

Which of the following summarized the main point of the passage?

A)   Atmospheric concentrations of greenhouse gases, which trigger the greenhouse effect, have been steadily increasing over time.

B)   Greenhouse gases have increased substantially, correlating to a rise in global temperature.

C)   Greenhouse gases are rising, and they show little to no signs of slowing down.

D)   If global temperatures continue to climb, we may continue to observe the loss of natural habitats in colder regions of the world.

Topic 22: Practice Questions (Answers & Explanations)

Question 1

A is the best answer. Since the term "greenhouse gases" introduces this passage, it would be necessary to first tell what these gases are. If not, the text immediately becomes inaccessible to the reader who is not already informed about the topic in question.

The other answers are incorrect because there is no data that has been presented yet that could be summarized (as choice B suggests); the sentence is not redundant since nothing has been said so far that could be repeated by this proposed sentence's inclusion (enabling the elimination of choice C). The sentence is clearly relevant to the text that follows (making choice D incorrect).

Question 2

D is the best answer.

Answers B & C can be immediately eliminated since the paragraph that follows says nothing about "human activity" or "natural sources."

Answers A and D both contain the **KEYWORDS** "greenhouse gases" and "atmosphere." Therefore, we must try to choose the better answer between these two choices. We see that that they both contain the same content except that choice D introduces the following information by saying "The greenhouse effect occurs because" – a phrase that immediately links to the last sentence of the previous paragraph (which mentions the greenhouse effect) and thus, creates a more **effective transition** for the reader.

Question 3

B is the best answer. Since the terms "methane, nitrous oxide, ozone, and carbon dioxide" have not been mentioned before their use in the figure, it would be useful for the author to include the proposed line in the indicated location. This would certainly help the reader better **contextualize** the data in the graph.

This information is not redundant since it has never been mentioned before; it is clearly relevant to the content of the figure. So, while we cannot say that it helps **link** ideas in the paragraph, it certainly helps **clarify** the data in the figure.
WRONG CHOICES ARE NOT NOTED BUT DESCRIBED COLLECTIVELY.

Question 4

A is the best answer. From the lighter shaded bars in the graph that are all above the darker shaded bars, we can say that there has been an increase in all the dangerous greenhouse gases (across the board).

B is incorrect because it contradicts the information that is provided in the graph by saying that "little change has occurred."

C is incorrect because the chart has nothing to do with "economic activity" and as such, saying that the chart "shows" this (as the sentence before the underlined section mentions) **would be inaccurate.**

D is incorrect because it invites the reader to make an **assumption** about how the increase might manifest (in disaster), which is **not** information that is out forward in the chart.

Question 5

C is the best answer. The best process to arrive at this answer is through a process of elimination.

D can be immediately eliminated because it contradicts data in the graph. Carbon dioxide, like all the other gases, has increased (i.e., not remained constant).

B is incorrect because it is an overstatement. By saying that the graph refers to "every major greenhouse gas," the reader is asked to make an **assumption** that the gases depicted here showcase every single gas.

A is incorrect because we are not told anything about the **rate** of increase (we are just shown the increase itself). Therefore, this too would invite the reader to **make an assumption.**

Question 6

A is the best answer. Once again, a process of exclusion is the best way to reach this answer.

B is incorrect because the graph does not give us any information about "human sources" and their relationship to the increase in gases.

C is incorrect since we are not told anything about the "rates" of increase and would involve making an **assumption.**

D is incorrect because no information has been presented about the effects being reversible or not.

Therefore, the only answer we are left with is A!

Question 7

B is the best answer. As we can see, the current paragraph focuses on carbon dioxide, while the next paragraph focuses on methane. Therefore, adding this sentence here would help the reader more **effectively transition** between the different ideas presented in the two paragraphs.

This immediately discounts all the other answer choices: **A** is unsuitable because the ideas that are linked are not in the same paragraph, **C** is incorrect because, in not repeating any previously stated information, **the sentence is NOT redundant, and D is incorrect** because, given the topic of the passage, the information in this sentence is **relevant to the themes of the text.**

Question 8

A is the best answer. Once again, a process of exclusion is the best way to reach this answer.

B is incorrect because the link between greenhouse gases/effect and temperature is not the main theme of the passage and is never explicitly stated.

C is incorrect because while we are told about how the gases are increasing/have increased over time, we are not told about future trends of that increase. To say this, therefore, would involve making an **assumption** from the data rather than reading what it provides to us.

D is incorrect because, like choice C, this choice would involve making an **ASSUMPTION** from the data rather than reading what it provides to us.

PRACTICE TEST 1

25 MINUTES, 44 QUESTIONS

DIRECTIONS

Each passage below is followed by a number of questions. For some questions, you will be asked to consider how the passage may be improved. For others, you will consider how the passage may be edited to correct errors in sentence structure, word usage, grammar, or punctuation.

Some questions will direct your attention to an underlined portion of the passage. Others will direct you to a location in a passage or ask you to consider the passage as a whole.

Read each passage carefully. After reading the passage, choose the answer to each question that most effectively improves the quality of writing of the passage or improves its conformance to standard written English. Most questions include a "NO CHANGE" option, which you should select if you think the best choice is to leave the applicable portion of the passage as-is.

Questions 1-11 are based on the following passage:

Writing Engaging Nonfiction

(1)

[1] The goal of nonfiction writing is to tell a true story. As important as effective nonfiction storytelling may be, many people simply find it boring. Great nonfiction writers such as acclaimed author, John McPhee, breathe life into the facts behind his stories.

Which choice best introduces the topic of this paragraph?

A) NO CHANGE

B) Nonfiction writing is dull and uninteresting for writers and readers alike.

C) Nonfiction works can be dull if authors do not write them in an engaging way.

D) Many great authors started their careers by writing nonfiction works.

(2)

2 McPhee's career as a nonfiction writer has spanned six decades. He has told stories about orange growing, birch-bark canoes, rafting the Grand Canyon, family physicians, farmers' markets, a school headmaster, and even the nation of Iceland. The topics of his stories may vary greatly, but they share one key **3** commonality: each is a subject about which McPhee himself became fascinated. **4** This fascination gives rise to a stylistic elegance, beauty, and humility unmatched in nonfiction writing.

Question 2

The writer is considering deleting the underlined sentence. Should the sentence be kept or deleted?

A) Kept, because it shows the impact of the investment of time on a career.

B) Kept, because it provides an effective transition between one concept in the passage and the next.

C) Deleted, because it ignores the fact that many fiction writers have had long careers.

D) Deleted, because it interrupts the paragraph's description of nonfiction writing.

Question 3

A) NO CHANGE

B) commonality each is

C) commonality, each is

D) commonality; each is

Question 4

A) NO CHANGE

B) The author's interest in the subject is reflected a

C) The fascination behind the writing was key to McPhee's

D) The writer's captivation allowed him to cultivate a

---

(3)

In recognition of his brilliance, **5** he has been nominated for the Pulitzer **6** Prize – the highest honor in literature, four times. He won the award once for his series *Annals of the Former World*, a set of books **7** written over the course of twenty years about the geology of North America. In McPhee's characteristic style, he presents the human side of the stories along with the facts in these encyclopedic tomes.

Question 5

A) NO CHANGE

B) he himself

C) McPhee

D) McPhee himself

Question 6

A) NO CHANGE

B) Prize, the highest honor in literature – four

C) Prize, the highest honor in literature, four

D) Prize, the highest honor in literature four

Question 7

A) NO CHANGE

B) about the geology of North America, which he wrote over the course of twenty years.

C) about the geology of North America written by him over the course of twenty years.

D) about the geology of North America that he wrote over the course of twenty years.

CONTINUE

(4)

8 McPhee is especially skilled at bringing a human element into his nonfiction storytelling. He focuses on the characters in his story rather than **9** himself. If the subject of his work is the factual history of a particular area, in conveying the tale he makes sure to include the people involved in the work. **10** By telling his stories through the experiences of common people, McPhee instills his work with an incredible authenticity.

As an author, McPhee excels at communicating the perspective of ordinary people. He has profiled numerous mid-level government scientists, a canoe maker, environmental activists, fishermen, and sailors – just to name a few. He famously documented a river trip down the Grand Canyon in which he joined two local experts who had vastly different ideas of what was best for the famous monument. Not only did McPhee effectively communicate the deep differences the two seemingly opposed figures had, but he was also able to highlight a surprising amount of similarities between them.

Question 8

To make this passage most logical, paragraph (4) should be placed:

A) where it is now

B) before paragraph (3)

C) before paragraph (2)

D) before paragraph (1)

Question 9

A) NO CHANGE

B) the facts alone.

C) the author.

D) anything else.

Question 10

At this point, the writer is considering adding the following sentence:

"For example, McPhee may introduce a new geological concept by highlighting his time spent road tripping with wacky geologists who explained the scientific information to him in the first place."

Should the writer make this addition here?

A) Yes, because it provides an effective transition.

B) Yes, because it provides information that helps clarify other information presented in the paragraph.

C) No, because it would be more effective as a conclusion at the end of the paragraph.

D) No, because it provides irrelevant information.

CONTINUE

Very few writers have McPhee's eclectic interests and wide-ranging abilities. However, his ability to emphasize others' views has proven to be the most important part of his legacy. He has been a prominent writer for over six decades and a respected professor for over forty years. **11** For decades, McPhee has passed his love for writing onto the next generation. Among his former students are best-selling authors, notable journalists, and even a Pulitzer Prize winner.

By expressing an authentic fascination with specific topics and an interest in the people whose lives center around those topics, McPhee has contributed a unique and important perspective to nonfiction writing.

Question 11

The writer is considering deleting the underlined sentence. Should the sentence be kept or deleted?

A) Kept, because it shows the impact of mentorship on a successful career.

B) Kept, because it provides an effective transition between one concept and the next.

C) Deleted, because it provides redundant information.

D) Deleted, because it ignores the fact that many people become successful writers without mentors.

Questions 12-22 are based on the following passage:

The Fierce and Mysterious Mountain Lion

Puma, cougar, catamount, **12** panther – each of these terms refers to a single type of cat: the mountain lion. Mountain lions are among the most solitary and reclusive animals in North America. But do not let their shyness fool you. They are also fearsome and capable predators. **13** In fact, these creatures were once so widely feared that they were nearly hunted to extinction. **14**

Question 12

A) NO CHANGE

B) panther: each of these terms refers to a single type of cat: the

C) panther – each of these terms refers to a single type of cat – the

D) panther – each of these terms refers to a single type of cat the

Question 13

A) NO CHANGE

B) For example,

C) Although,

D) Moreover,

Question 14

Which choice provides the best conclusion for this paragraph?

A) NO CHANGE

B) Fortunately, however, this species has proven resilient to the threats against it.

C) Mountain lions are resilient, fortunately, and their survival is almost certain.

D) Mountain lions have always been a critical part of the North American natural landscape.

CONTINUE

During the late nineteenth and early twentieth centuries, hunters pursued predators like wolves, bears, and mountain lions without regulation. Most U.S. states even placed a bounty on the big cats, offering cash rewards for their pelts. **15**

Over the years, hunting and habitat encroachment **16** had driven most of America's mountain lions outside of their native ranges. While they once roamed the entire country from coast to coast, by the mid-twentieth century mountain lions lived only in the mountainous American West or deep in the Florida swamps. **17** By the 1950s, mountain lion populations were measured and discovered to be historically low.

At this point, the writer is considering adding the following sentence:

"Unsurprisingly, this policy forced mountain lions into the most remote and rugged areas of North America."

Should the writer make this addition here?

A) No, because it provides a more effective introduction.

B) Yes, because it provides information that helps explain why hunters pursued predator species.

C) Yes, because it provides an effective conclusion.

D) No, because it provides irrelevant information.

A) NO CHANGE

B) drove

C) has driven

D) are driving

A) NO CHANGE

B) Mountain lion populations were considered historically low by the 1950s.

C) By the 1950s, mountain lion populations had sunk to historic lows.

D) DELETE the underlined portion

Mountain lions survived near-extinction thanks to their keen instincts and **18** <u>ability to adapt.</u> **19** <u>Mountain lions are graceful and powerful hunters.</u> <u>They</u> can see in the dark, walk almost silently, and leap long distances. These features allow them to pursue their favorite **20** <u>prey: deer, porcupines, raccoons, rabbits, rodents, elk, and even moose.</u> Their wide-ranging hunting skills combined with a keen hiding ability have helped mountain lions regrow their populations to healthy levels.

Fortunately, by the 1960s, most states had eliminated the bounty program and **21** <u>was starting to protect</u> mountain lions. Once these hardy animals received protection from hunters, they quickly began repopulating the lands where they once lived. Mountain lion populations have grown enough now so that encounters with humans have grown more frequent, which raises new problems for the tense relationship between these species.

Question 18

A) NO CHANGE

B) adept ability

C) adoption

D) adaptability

Question 19

A) NO CHANGE

B) Mountain lions can be graceful, powerful,

C) Mountain lions

D) Graceful and powerful hunters, mountain lions

Question 20

A) NO CHANGE

B) prey; deer, porcupines, raccoons, rabbits, rodents, elk, and even moose

C) prey – deer, porcupines, raccoons, rabbits, rodents, elk, and even moose

D) prey: deer, porcupines, raccoons, rabbits, rodents, elk – and even moose

Question 21

A) NO CHANGE

B) started protecting

C) protects

D) will protect

Mountain lion populations are spreading eastward from the mountainous West into Nebraska, South Dakota, and even New York. In suburban areas of Colorado, people will occasionally spot mountain lions in a backyard. Rarely, they are even found inside a car or a house. **22** As both mountain lion and human populations continue to expand, communities must strike a balance between human safety and mountain lion protection.

Question 22

A) NO CHANGE

B) Communities

C) Mountain lions continue to expand, and human communities

D) Both mountain lion and human populations continue to expand; communities

Questions 23-33 are based on the following passage:

The Northwest Passage

The Northwest Passage is an oceanic route that follows the northern coast of the North American continent. In the past, explorers thought that the passage would offer a valuable shortcut. If [23] possible, it would allow ships to travel from Europe to Asia without sailing around Africa or across the Pacific Ocean from South America. [24] Now, the Northwest Passage is [25] thawing. This is largely due to the impacts of global climate change.

Question 23

A) NO CHANGE

B) passable

C) plausible

D) probable

Question 24

At this point, the writer is considering adding the following sentence:

"Throughout most of known history, the Northwest Passage has been far too icy and treacherous to offer a reliable means of commercial transportation."

Should the writer make this addition here?

A) Yes, because it provides effective support for a prior assertion.

B) Yes, because it provides information that helps clarify other information presented in the paragraph.

C) No, because it provides a more effective conclusion.

D) No, because it provides irrelevant information.

Question 25

A) NO CHANGE

B) thawing; this is largely due

C) thawing due in large part to

D) thawing, largely due

By the 1800s, European explorers had been seeking a quick route to Asia by sea for centuries. Despite this great effort, the discovery evaded them. In 1850, a rescue mission **26** looking for an expedition that had gone missing stumbled across a sea route to Asia by way of the Northwest Passage. European shipping interests were ecstatic to hear the news, but unfortunately their discovery was nearly worthless.

27 The first successful completion of a sea voyage through the Northwest Passage was accomplished by a small crew in 1906. **(1)** Most early attempts at exploring the Northwest Passage ended in disaster. **(2)** Often, expeditions would go missing because the explorers' ships would freeze in the sea ice. **(3)** The frozen terrain would either crush the ship or leave **28** their crew members stranded. **(4)** As it turned out, the Northwest Passage was nearly impossible to cross because it was clogged with ice most of the year.

The writer is considering deleting the underlined sentence. Should the sentence be kept or deleted?

A) Kept, because it shows the impact of fate on discoveries.

B) Kept, because it provides an effective transition between one concept and the next.

C) Deleted, because it ignores the fact that the rescue mission was a success.

D) Deleted, because it provides redundant information.

To make this passage most logical, the underlined sentence should be placed:

A) where it is now

B) after sentence (1)

C) after sentence (2)

D) after sentence (4)

A) NO CHANGE

B) its

C) it's

D) his

Eventually, technology made commercial shipping through the Northwest Passage feasible. **29** However, rising temperatures have begun to melt the sea ice, and scientists speculate that the passage will become more maneuverable over time **30** and an icebreaker will be needed less and less. As a result, **31** we could see the Northwest Passage becoming a viable shipping lane during more months out of the year.

At this point, the writer is considering adding the following sentence:

"Today, an icebreaker is used to move through the passage during the colder months."

Should the writer make this addition here?

A) Yes, because it provides information that helps clarify other information presented in the paragraph.

B) No, because it provides a more effective introduction.

C) Yes, because it helps establish an appropriate summation of the passage.

D) No, because it provides irrelevant information.

A) NO CHANGE

B) meaning less and less icebreakers will be necessary

C) and thus, we'll need less icebreakers

D) DELETE the underlined portion.

A) NO CHANGE

B) the Northwest Passage is becoming

C) the Northwest Passage could become

D) we could see the Northwest Passage as

Experts believe that the combined effects of continued ocean warming and thawing of sea ice will open the Northwest Passage and the northern passage through the Canadian archipelago. In 2007 – for the first time in history – the Northwest Passage opened up to vessels without an icebreaker escort. With global temperatures on the rise, more areas of the Northwest Passage will open up. This may allow ships to circumnavigate the polar ice cap and cut hundreds of miles off of current transport lines.

Question 32

A) NO CHANGE

B) in

C) with

D) when

Question 33

A) NO CHANGE

B) 2007, for the first time in history – the

C) 2007: for the first time in history, the

D) 2007, the

CONTINUE

Questions 34-44 are based on the following passage:

Renewable Energy on the Rise

Whether it comes from a plug, a battery, or some other source, **34** it's hard to even imagine what life would be like without electricity. People everywhere rely on electrical power to cook, heat their homes, and light their streets. Without it, the world would be a much darker and more dangerous place. Unfortunately, however, a great deal of the infrastructure that provides the electricity people rely on every day **35** are unsustainable.

At this point, the writer is considering revising the underlined part to the following:

"electricity powers our world."

Should the writer make this revision here?

- A) Yes, because it provides an effective introduction.
- B) Yes, because it improves clarity, voice, and tone.
- C) No, because it provides irrelevant support.
- D) No, because it is a less effective transition.

- A) NO CHANGE
- B) will be
- C) is
- D) may become

A great deal of the electricity produced in the United States originates from raw resources that are not easily replenished. **36** The most common unsustainable resources tapped for electricity production include fossil fuels - such as coal, natural gas, and crude oil – as well as nuclear fuels like uranium and plutonium. Generating electricity from these resources generally requires **37** combustion, that releases potentially dangerous chemicals into the air and water. These chemicals can have a devastating impact on human health and the environment. Fortunately, however, America is experiencing a boom in renewable energy production that may improve the environmental outlook for electrical production nationwide.

Question 36

At this point, the writer is considering adding the following sentence:

"According to federal agencies, over ninety-two percent of the electricity generated in the United States in 2018 originated from non-renewable resources."

Should the writer make this addition here?

A) Yes, because it provides an effective transition.

B) Yes, because it provides information that helps clarify other information presented in the paragraph.

C) No, because it provides a more effective conclusion.

D) No, because it provides irrelevant information.

Question 37

A) NO CHANGE

B) combustion, which

C) combustion, and

D) combustion, this

The figure below shows the total amount of solar energy produced from sources distributed across the country. This includes solar panels installed on residential rooftops, community-scale solar farms, and other sources of photovoltaic electricity that **38** does not originate from a power plant owned by a utility.

Figure 1: Total Distributed Solar Energy Production

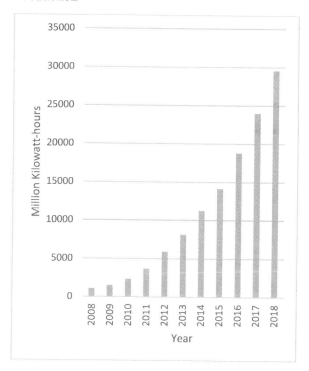

The U.S. has seen a clear increase in the deployment of distributed solar energy over time. **39** This gives many people reason to hope that our energy mix is improving over time.

Question 38

A) NO CHANGE

B) doesn't

C) do not

D) don't

Question 39

Which of the following provides the most effective support from Figure 1?

A) In 2008, the amount of distributed solar energy production did not even reach the 5,000 million kilowatt-hour mark.

B) Much of this is due to a boom in residential rooftop solar as more and more people are installing solar panels on the roofs of their homes and businesses.

C) Energy from all sources has increased by multiples just over the past decade.

D) Just in the last decade, total distributed solar energy production has multiplied many times over.

CONTINUE

More and more people are depending on solar power to meet their electricity **40** needs, and many of them are not waiting for their local electrical utility to install more renewable energy systems. Instead, they are participating in community solar projects or installing solar panels on their homes and lawns. This type of decentralized solar power is on the rise nationwide. **41**

Question 40

A) NO CHANGE

B) needs, but many of them are not waiting for their local electrical utility to come around

C) needs, and when their local utility doesn't step up, they look elsewhere.

D) needs.

Question 41

Which of the following provides the most effective support from Figure 1?

A) Indeed, America has shown great gains in solar energy production.

B) In fact, decentralized solar power production in 2018 was more than three times what it was just a decade earlier.

C) Decentralized solar power production has increased every year for the past decade, and it shows no signs of slowing down.

D) In fact, decentralized solar power production has increased every year for the past decade.

42 Greater reliance on renewable energy can help mitigate the damage done by fossil fuels and nuclear power. As a result, more solar power could mean a safer, healthier environment. However, **43** there are certain obstacles presented to the spread of solar power. This is particularly true with respect to the distributed electrical generation of solar energy and other renewable resources.

At this point, the writer is considering adding the following sentence:

"Increasing the amount of renewable energy produced on America's rooftops and open spaces offers several important benefits."

Should the writer make this addition here?

A) Yes, because it provides an effective introduction.

B) Yes, because it provides information that helps clarify other information presented in the paragraph.

C) No, because it would be more effective as a conclusion.

D) No, because it provides irrelevant information.

A) NO CHANGE

B) the spread of solar power faced certain obstacles.

C) solar power did face certain obstacles.

D) the spread of solar power will face certain obstacles.

Most of the technology that powers America's electrical grid is located close to power plants. Locating new renewable power sources far away from this infrastructure can be costly and difficult. However, considering the potential benefits of a cleaner, healthier environment, the investment required for the greater deployment of distributed renewable energy resources is well worth the cost. **44**

Which of the following most effectively summarizes the main point of the passage?

A) Increasing reliance on renewable energy offers important benefits to the environment and human health.

B) Renewable energy is an important part of America's overall energy mix.

C) While unsustainable, America's energy infrastructure is sure to survive well into the future.

D) By relying on renewable power, America can solve all of its energy-related problems.

CONTINUE

PRACTICE

TEST 2

Writing and Language Test

25 MINUTES, 44 QUESTIONS

DIRECTIONS

Each passage below is followed by a number of questions. For some questions, you will be asked to consider how the passage may be improved. For others, you will consider how the passage may be edited to correct errors in sentence structure, word usage, grammar, or punctuation.

Some questions will direct your attention to an underlined portion of the passage. Others will direct you to a location in a passage or ask you to consider the passage as a whole.

Read each passage carefully. After reading the passage, choose the answer to each question that most effectively improves the quality of writing of the passage or improves its conformance to standard written English. Most questions include a "NO CHANGE" option, which you should select if you think the best choice is to leave the applicable portion of the passage as-is.

Questions 1-11 are based on the following passage:

The History of Mountaineering

(1)

1 Throughout history, the legendarily dangerous sport of mountaineering has attracted adventure enthusiasts from all over the world. This recreation generally requires an adventurer to scale a high point in a mountainous region often climbing all the way to the summit. All this is often just for the pure pleasure of the journey.

Which choice best introduces the topic of this paragraph?

A) NO CHANGE

B) The sport of mountaineering has a long and exciting history.

C) Mountaineering is legendarily dangerous.

D) Because it is so treacherous, mountaineering attracts only the bravest adventure enthusiasts.

(2)

Mountaineering is a unique sport in that the challenge is provided by nature alone. **2** It involves testing one's strength, courage, and resourcefulness. As a result, mountaineering tends to attract people who are both adventurous and athletic.

(3)

3 Modern mountaineering is far different than it was in the past. Today, there two common styles of **4** mountaineering including: expedition and alpine. A single person or small group can typically accomplish an alpine-style mountaineering trip. Expedition mountaineering, on the other hand, typically involves a large amount of gear and a large team of people. Expedition mountaineering is most often reserved for attempts at summiting enormous heights.

Question 2

The writer is considering deleting the underlined sentence. Should the sentence be kept or deleted?

A) Kept, because it shows the impact of courage on resourcefulness.

B) Kept, because it provides an effective transition for including further relevant information.

C) Deleted, because it ignores the fact that many people climb mountains with paid guides.

D) Deleted, because it interrupts the paragraph's description of the development of modern mountaineering.

Question 3

To make this passage most logical, paragraph (3) should be placed:

A) where it is now

B) after paragraph (4)

C) before paragraph (2)

D) before paragraph (1)

Question 4

A) NO CHANGE

B) mountaineering, including: expedition

C) mountaineering: expedition

D) mountaineering; expedition

CONTINUE ►

(4)

Early attempts at summitting mountains were inspired by practical motives. Brave men and women scaled mountains so that **5** they could build religious monuments or make new discoveries. **6** In fact, during the eighteenth century, philosophers and scientists alike made expeditions into the European Alps in hopes of making important scientific discoveries. As a matter of fact, it was **7** not, a great adventurer – but rather a great scientist – who paved the pathway for the sport of mountaineering.

Question 5

A) NO CHANGE

B) he

C) she

D) themselves

Question 6

A) NO CHANGE

B) In fact, philosophers

C) During the eighteenth century, philosophers

D) Philosophers

Question 7

A) NO CHANGE

B) not a great adventurer, but rather a great scientist – who

C) a great scientist – who

D) a great scientist – not a great adventurer – who

Horace-Bénédict de Saussure, a French scientist, ushered in the era of mountaineering as a profession when he offered prize money for the first person to ascend Mont Blanc, France's highest mountain. In 1786, Michel-Gabriel Paccard and Jacques Balmat summited the mountain and collected the prize money. This was the first recorded act of professional mountaineering. **8**

The sport of mountaineering made its way across Europe, and in the nineteenth century a British adventurer named Sir Alfred Wills successfully summited the Wetterhorn peak in Switzerland. After returning to England in 1857, Wills founded the Alpine **9** Club, which kicked off the golden age of mountaineering and facilitated the spread of the sport throughout the world. Around this same time, mountaineering teams in North America were also making their first assents. Adventurers peaked Pico de **10** Orizaba; the tallest mountain in Mexico, in 1848; Mount Saint Elias in 1897, and Denali, the highest mountain in North America, in 1913.

Question 8

At this point, the writer is considering adding the following sentence:

"However, the first recorded alpinist was an Italian poet named Petrarch, who reached the top of Mount Ventoux in 1336."

Should the writer make this addition here?

A) Yes, because it provides an effective transition.

B) Yes, because it provides information that helps clarify prior statements.

C) No, because it would be more effective as an introduction at the beginning of the paragraph.

D) No, because it provides distracting information.

Question 9

A) NO CHANGE

B) Club, that establishment

C) Club; this establishment

D) Club. The establishment of the club

Question 10

A) NO CHANGE

B) Orizaba, the tallest mountain in Mexico, in 1848;

C) Orizaba, the tallest mountain in Mexico, in 1848,

D) Orizaba, the tallest mountain in Mexico, in 1848

CONTINUE

Thanks in part to modern equipment and techniques, today's climbers have been able to push the final frontier of mountaineering. **11** Everest - the tallest mountain in the world - was summited in 1953. Since then, the sport of mountaineering has remained both a recreation and a passionate pursue for adventure seekers around the world.

At this point, the writer is considering changing the underlined sentence to the following:

"Climbers summited Everest – the world's tallest mountain - in 1953."

Should the writer make this change here?

- A) Yes, because it provides an effective transition.

- B) Yes, because it improves clarity, tone, and voice of the sentence.

- C) No, because it would be more effective as a conclusion at the end of the paragraph.

- D) No, because the information is irrelevant, and the underlined portion should be deleted

Questions 12-22 are based on the following passage:

Literary Man of Action Mark Twain

Mark Twain is one of the most famous American authors of the nineteenth century. He is celebrated for his renowned literary works, such as *The Adventures of Tom Sawyer, Adventures of Huckleberry Finn, The Prince and the Pauper, Life on the Mississippi,* and others. Unlike the typical professional writer, **12** he lacked a formal education. **13**

Mark Twain was born as Samuel Clemens in Florida, Missouri on November 30, 1835. After Twain turned four, the Clemens family moved across the state to Hannibal, where **14** he would remain until age seventeen. The bustling city of over one thousand people inspired many of the settings in Twain's fiction, such as the town of "St. Petersburg" in *Tom Sawyer* and *Huckleberry Finn.*

Question 12

A) NO CHANGE

B) Twain

C) their

D) he himself

Question 13

Which choice provides the best conclusion for this paragraph?

A) NO CHANGE

B) Indeed, most of Twain's work was inaccurate and ill-informed.

C) Rather, Twain's most famous works were inspired by his own personal experiences.

D) However, what Twain lacked in education he made up for in creativity.

Question 14

A) NO CHANGE

B) they were housed until age

C) they lived until Twain was

D) he was until age

CONTINUE

In 1859, Twain put his writing career on hold to take a job as a steamboat pilot on the Mississippi River. Twain enjoyed the social status and high pay that accompanied his career, but everything changed when the Civil War broke out in 1861. **15**

At first, Twain had a difficult time establishing **16** <u>in the West</u>. Twain tried and failed at prospecting for gold and silver in Nevada and California. Penniless, Twain secured a position as a reporter for the *Virginia City Territorial Enterprise.* **17** <u>It wasn't long before</u> Twain had become a notorious storyteller throughout the American Frontier.

Question 15

At this point, the writer is considering adding the following sentence:

"That summer, Twain boarded a west-bound stagecoach looking for his next adventure."

Should the writer make this addition here?

A) Yes, because it provides information that helps explain what comes next.

B) No, because it provides a more effective introduction and should be placed at the beginning of the sentence.

C) Yes, because it provides information that helps explain a prior statement.

D) No, because it provides irrelevant information.

Question 16

A) NO CHANGE

B) himself in the West

C) a family in the West

D) himself

Question 17

A) NO CHANGE

B) Known by man, woman, and child alike,

C) Before long,

D) DELETE the underlined portion

During **18** this time, Twain developed his famous narrative **19** style, in comparison by the author's comical, friendly, flippant, and sardonic personality. Despite his love of the West, Twain's adventurous spirit got the best of him, and he sailed for the Mediterranean in 1867. While in Europe, the young writer spent five months humorously characterizing his foreign travels for American newspapers. By **20** 1869, Twain had spun the tales of his journeys into a bestselling book: *Innocents Abroad*. Twain returned to America the following year to settle down with his new wife, Oliva Langdon. The couple settled down in Buffalo, New York where Twain continued to write and publish for many years.

Question 18

A) NO CHANGE

B) his time in the West,

C) the Western times,

D) time out West,

Question 19

A) NO CHANGE

B) style. It encompasses

C) style, that encompasses

D) style, which encompasses

Question 20

A) NO CHANGE

B) 1869, Twain had spun the tales of his journeys, into a bestselling book: *Innocents*

C) 1869, Twain had spun the tales of his journeys into a bestselling book *Innocents*

D) 1869, Twain had a bestselling book: *Innocents*

Up until his death in 1910, Twain **21** continued to share his distinct writing skills with the world. His legacy continues to live on through his work, which remains a celebrated piece of the American literary cannon. **22**

A) NO CHANGE

B) would continue to share

C) had shared

D) shared and provided to others

Which of the following most effectively summarizes the main point of the passage?

A) Mark Twain's adventurous nature led him to many experiences that enriched the authenticity of his writing.

B) Mark Twain's work is an important part of America's cultural and literary history.

C) While sometimes controversial, Mark Twain's writings have engaged literary audiences for centuries.

D) By relying on wits and literary strategy, Mark Twain was able to become one of America's most legendary authors.

Questions 23-33 are based on the following passage:

The Eradication of Smallpox

Historically, communicable diseases **23** has been among one of the greatest threats to human survival. Smallpox, a disease caused by the variola virus, once decimated human populations. It was a devastating disease. Over 300 million people died of smallpox in the twentieth century alone. **24** Remarkably, however, the World Health Assembly declared the disease eradicated in 1979. Although it took centuries, the **25** suppression of smallpox is one of the greatest successes in modern public health.

Question 23

A) NO CHANGE

B) have

C) has

D) have been

Question 24

At this point, the writer is considering adding the following sentence:

"Children were particularly susceptible to the disease; before an effective treatment was developed, over 80 percent of youths infected with smallpox would eventually die from it."

Should the writer make this addition here?

A) Yes, because it provides effective support for a prior assertion.

B) Yes, because it provides information that helps clarify key terms.

C) No, because it contains a modifier error.

D) No, because it provides irrelevant information.

Question 25

A) NO CHANGE

B) reduction

C) obliteration

D) decline

CONTINUE

26 A long and global history has been established of cultures who work to prevent the spread of smallpox through traditional practices. **(1)** The practice of variolation or exposing healthy people to mild forms of smallpox, dates back to the fifteenth century. **(2)** Variolation proved to be effective at reducing the severity and likelihood of death from the disease. **(3)** However, it did not prevent the spread of the disease. **27** In this way, variolation was an important step towards developing a cure for smallpox. Containing this highly-contagious affliction required further medical innovation.

English surgeon and scientist Edward Jenner devoted his professional life to investigating the origins of smallpox infections. **28** By investigating the causes, Dr. Jenner sought insight into how to prevent it. However, it took a risky medical experiment to prove Dr. Jenner's groundbreaking theories on the prevention of smallpox.

In 1796, Dr. Jenner infected an eight-year-old boy with cowpox, a relatively harmless relative of the smallpox virus. A few months later, the researcher exposed the same boy to smallpox. The boy showed no infection. **29** He gained protection from the terrible disease without ever contracting it. In this single groundbreaking experiment, Dr. Jenner proved that smallpox, a terrifying disease, could be prevented.

Question 26

A) NO CHANGE

B) Historically, cultures around the globe have worked to prevent

C) Major global efforts have been aimed by cultures at preventing

D) Cultures around the globe have recorded

Question 27

To make this passage most logical, the underlined sentence should be placed:

A) where it is now

B) before sentence (1)

C) before sentence (2)

D) before sentence (3)

Question 28

A) NO CHANGE

B) By investigating the causes of the disease,

C) Investigating the causes of the disease,

D) DELETE the underlined portion

Question 29

A) NO CHANGE

B) Gaining

C) Rather, he had gained

D) Rather, he gains

News of Dr. Jenner's discovery soon made its way across Britain and then all around the world. Despite scientists and doctors doing their best to spread the smallpox vaccine, ending the scourge of smallpox once and for all required a monumental worldwide effort.

By the mid twentieth century, doctors were able to track every smallpox outbreak around the world. With the help of global health organizations, doctors across the planet undertook a painstaking process of **30** mass vaccination and isolating contagious individuals. **31** When an outbreak was detected, all of the individuals living in the area were vaccinated. This process was arduous, but it worked. By the 1970s, smallpox outbreaks were contained to only small areas of the world. Smallpox was finally eradicated in 1979 after doctors finally tracked down the last known case of smallpox, treating it, and preventing its spread.

Question 30

A) NO CHANGE

B) mass vaccination and isolation of

C) mass vaccinating and isolation of

D) massive vaccinating and isolating

Question 31

The writer is considering deleting the underlined sentence. Should the sentence be kept or deleted?

A) Kept, because it provides an effective transition between one concept and the next.

B) Kept, because it shows the impact of vaccination on public health.

C) Deleted, because it ignores the global coordination required to address an outbreak effective.

D) Deleted, because it provides irrelevant information.

Figure 1 shows the number of smallpox patients in the United States during the first half of the twentieth century.

Figure 1: Reported Cases of Smallpox in the United States (1900-1950)

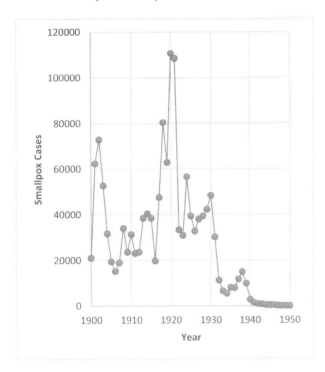

32 The annihilation of smallpox saved millions of people from a painful and potentially deadly affliction. Wiping out smallpox is a testament not only to Edward Jenner's ingenuity in developing the world's first effective vaccine but to all of the people involved in the global effort to eradicate smallpox. 33

Question 32

Which of the following provides the most effective support from Figure 1?

A) Smallpox was completely eradicated in 1979.

B) During the early 1900s, smallpox outbreaks in the United States peaked at well over 100,000 cases per year.

C) At one time, smallpox outbreaks in the United States peaked at well over 1,000,000 cases per year.

D) By 1940, smallpox had been completely eradicated in the United States.

Question 33

At this point, the writer is considering adding the following sentence:

"Without the innovations of cultures practicing variolation and the support of the worldwide medical community in spreading the vaccine, this incredible scientific feat never could have been achieved.

Should the writer make this addition here?

A) Yes, because it provides data that helps clarify other information presented in the paragraph.

B) No, because it provides a more effective introduction.

C) Yes, because it provides an effective conclusion to the paragraph.

D) No, because it provides irrelevant information.

Questions 34-44 are based on the following passage:

The Rite of Spring

Ballet is an elegant expression of performance **34** art; and, like most art forms, it has been prone to attract controversy. Consider the example of Igor Stravinsky's ballet, *The Rite of* **35** *Spring. This groundbreaking piece of art was met with shock and awe when it premiered* in Paris, France in 1913. The Russian-born Stravinsky pushed the limits of what was considered acceptable with respect to ballet movements and orchestral accompaniments. In fact, when the curtains went up, the audience in Paris was appalled **36** with what they saw and heard. However, the performance stirred deep emotions, making the premier of the ballet one of the most memorable and significant dance performances in world history.

Anticipating a controversial event, the audience was unsettled from the moment the curtain went up. The orchestra started with a strange, high-pitched solo followed by other instruments joining into a jarring crescendo of intense sound as the dancers took the stage. They danced unconventionally with halting, violent movements. The music and choreography were so novel and unusual that the crowd was incredulous at what they **37** were hearing and watching.

Question 34

A) NO CHANGE

B) art. And, like most art forms, it

C) art: Like most art forms, it

D) art; like most art forms, it

Question 35

A) NO CHANGE

B) *Spring*. This groundbreaking piece of art was considered to be shocking, particularly at its premier

C) *Spring*. Audiences looked upon this groundbreaking piece of art with amazement when it premiered

D) *Spring*, which premiered

Question 36

A) NO CHANGE

B) at

C) for

D) in

Question 37

A) NO CHANGE

B) had seen and heard

C) saw and heard

D) were about to see and hear

CONTINUE ▶

Stravinsky's ballet is a testament to the beauty and power of the season, but its themes unnerved early audiences. **38** *The Rite of Spring* centers on an ancient ceremony to honor the Earth and **39** Spring that culminates in a young girl sacrificing herself through dance, an expression intended as a gift to the god of the season. To communicate this powerful story, Stravinsky developed a musical score and choreographed accompanying dance moves **40** that was unlike any the audience in Paris had ever seen.

Question 38

At this point, the writer is considering adding the following sentence:

"Stravinsky based the ballet's choreography, in part, on Russian pagan rituals."

Should the writer make this addition here?

A) Yes, because it provides an effective introduction to new concepts.

B) Yes, because it provides information that helps clarify other information presented in the paragraph.

C) No, because it provides a more effective conclusion.

D) No, because it provides irrelevant information.

Question 39

A) NO CHANGE

B) Spring, and the ceremony

C) Spring. The ceremony

D) Spring, which

Question 40

A) NO CHANGE

B) that is

C) that had been considered

D) DELETE the underlined portion

Whether due to the strange dancing, the overwhelming music, or the shocking break from tradition, Stravinsky's first audience erupted in commotion mid-performance. They hurled vegetables and other objects onto the stage. The auditorium was so loud with **41** shouting, the dancers were unable to even hear the orchestra. At least forty audience members were ejected from the **42** theater, because of their behavior. At the end of the evening, one thing was certain: the premier **43** was a noteworthy affair.

Question 41

A) NO CHANGE

B) shouting, but the

C) shouting that the

D) shouting, or the

Question 42

A) NO CHANGE

B) theater that evening.

C) theater because of their behavior.

D) theater.

Question 43

A) NO CHANGE

B) had been

C) is

D) would be

CONTINUE

Stravinsky frustrated and confused *The Rite of Spring's* first audience, but only because the ballet was ahead of its time. Despite its provocative debut, *The Rite of Spring* remains in production over a century later. **44**

At this point, the writer is considering adding the following sentence:

"The musical scores and choreographies that drew so much controversy and ire in 1913 are now regarded as among the most significant compositions of the twentieth century."

Should the writer make this addition here?

A) Yes, because it provides an effective conclusion.

B) Yes, because it provides information that helps clarify other information presented in the paragraph.

C) No, because it would be more effective as an introduction.

D) No, because it provides redundant information.

CONTINUE

PRACTICE

TEST 3

Writing and Language Test

25 MINUTES, 44 QUESTIONS

DIRECTIONS

Each passage below is followed by a number of questions. For some questions, you will be asked to consider how the passage may be improved. For others, you will consider how the passage may be edited to correct errors in sentence structure, word usage, grammar, or punctuation.

Some questions will direct your attention to an underlined portion of the passage. Others will direct you to a location in a passage or ask you to consider the passage as a whole.

Read each passage carefully. After reading the passage, choose the answer to each question that most effectively improves the quality of writing of the passage or improves its conformance to standard written English. Most questions include a "NO CHANGE" option, which you should select if you think the best choice is to leave the applicable portion of the passage as-is.

Questions 1-11 are based on the following passage:

Avant-garde Art Challenges Convention

Can art change the world? For avant-garde artists, art may be among the only things that can foster real change. Avant-garde artists attempt to open peoples' eyes to the need for change through **1** radical, and sometimes socially unacceptable, creative efforts.

Question 1

A) NO CHANGE

B) radical, creative

C) radical and sometimes socially unacceptable creative

D) radical – but sometimes socially unacceptable – creative

CONTINUE ►

2 Avant-garde art is sometimes shocking; as a result, great contributions from avant-garde artists are often dismissed by the mainstream. However, it is by challenging the mainstream that avant-garde artists leave their mark on the world. **3**

Question 2

Which choice best introduces the topic of this paragraph?

   A) NO CHANGE

   B) Avant-garde artists are constantly breaking from convention.

   C) Avant-garde art is a type of abstract, conceptual art that many people find fascinating.

   D) Avant-garde is a term that describes art that pushes the boundaries of commonly-accepted social standards.

Question 3

At this point, the writer is considering adding the following sentence:

"By boldly and courageously sharing their art, avant-garde has made waves throughout art history."

Should the writer make this addition here?

   A) Yes, because it provides an effective transition.

   B) Yes, because it provides information that helps clarify prior statements.

   C) No, because it would be more effective as an introduction at the beginning of the paragraph.

   D) No, because it contains a grammatical error.

CONTINUE

For avant-garde artists, their chosen medium is a means **4** <u>of</u> which they can shape the minds of their viewers. Avant-garde art does not restrict creative expression to a certain style. Rather, avant-garde art is often meant to pave a path for change in the world. Sometimes, artists look to foster these changes in response to extremely violent or traumatic events. **5** <u>Consider the example of Dadaism, or Dada; artists developed this avant-garde artistic style in response to the changing and chaotic circumstances facing people in the modern world.</u>

After witnessing the atrocities of World War I, many artists began to see the world as a place where rationality, fairness, and reason were no longer relevant. Dada artists rejected the concept of **6** <u>rationality; instead, they created</u> art they believed reflected reality.

Question 4

A) NO CHANGE

B) by

C) for

D) in

Question 5

The writer is considering deleting the underlined sentence. Should the sentence be kept or deleted?

A) Kept, because it provides an effective transition between one concept in the passage and the next.

B) Kept, because it shows the impact of art on social change.

C) Deleted, because it ignores the fact that many people enjoy avant-garde art.

D) Deleted, because it interrupts the paragraph's description of avant-garde art.

Question 6

A) NO CHANGE

B) rationality. They created instead

C) rationality; instead they created

D) rationality, instead they created

Avant-garde **7** art was notably unconventional and jarring. Confusing collages, word cut-outs arranged in a random order, and "readymade" art – everyday objects transformed into deep artistic expressions – defied the expectations of even the most seasoned art appreciators. Consider one infamous example of Dadaism: Marcel Duchamp's 1917 sculpture, *Fountain.*

(1) The sculpture was nothing more than a plain, white porcelain urinal signed "R. Mutt 1917." **(2)** Though a urinal hardly qualifies as art most of the time, Duchamp's mere conception of this idea as an artistic expression was revolutionary. **8** **(3)** Duchamp changed the very concept of art, and in doing so he laid the groundwork for artists in the future to take creative risks. **(4)** *Fountain* is now considered to be one of the most influential artistic works of the twentieth century. After all, calling a urinal a sculpture and having most of the world agree could certainly pave the way for other creative visionaries to push the boundaries of acceptable artistic expression. **9**

Question 7

A) NO CHANGE

B) art of the Dada era

C) artists

D) DELETE the underlined word

Question 8

To make this passage logical, sentence (3) should be placed:

A) where it is now

B) after sentence (4)

C) before sentence (1)

D) before sentence (2)

Question 9

Which choice provides the best conclusion for this paragraph?

A) NO CHANGE

B) In fact, Duchamp sparked an entire artistic revolution.

C) Rather, Duchamp's most celebrated works diverged from avant-garde style.

D) However, what Duchamp lacked in skill he made up for in creativity.

For Duchamp and other avant-garde artists like [10] himself, beauty is not just aesthetic. Rather, beauty can grow from the profound meaning that an artistic expression represents. Avant-garde art represents a dismissal of convention and a break from the mainstream. [11]

A) NO CHANGE

B) he

C) him

D) it

Which of the following most effectively summarizes the main point of the passage?

A) Avant-garde's replant nature causes people to question deeply-held viewpoints.

B) Avant-garde artists are an odd bunch of people who are unable to fit in with the rest of society.

C) Like all great art, avant-garde art challenges people to question the status quo.

D) Avant-garde artists challenge people to reconsider the traditional viewpoints and wisdom they have always maintained.

Questions 12-22 are based on the following passage:

Chocolate: One of the World's Most Popular Foods

(1)

Today, chocolate is a beloved treat found all over the world. **12** Available almost anywhere food and beverages are sold, it comes in bars and candies, dark and milk, sweet and bitter – flavors to suit just about any palette. Anyone who has ever tried the sweet, earthy flavor of a great piece of chocolate can easily understand why chocolate is a cherished part of nearly every culinary culture. **13** Western Europeans – the Swiss in particular – love eating chocolate; in fact, the average Swiss person eats nearly 20 pounds of chocolate per year!

Question 12

A) NO CHANGE

B) It's available almost everywhere, and it

C) Available almost anywhere, it

D) It

Question 13

At this point, the writer is considering deleting the underlined sentence. Should the writer make this change here?

A) Yes, because it would edit irrelevant and extraneous information.

B) Yes, because it would improve clarity and logical flow of the paragraph.

C) No, because it would omit an effective conclusion from the end of the paragraph.

D) No, because the information is relevant and effective support.

(2)

[14] Notably however, most of the chocolate consumed in the modern world is almost unrecognizable from [15] its original form. Before modern chocolate was developed, cacao beans were usually processed and mixed into a liquid. Unlike the sweet treat chocolate is today, the original chocolate drink derived from cacao beans was thick and bitter. Served either hot or cold, the ancient chocolate drink found various uses across many cultures.

Question 14

To make this passage logical, paragraph (2) should be placed:

A) where it is now

B) before paragraph (1)

C) after paragraph (3)

D) after paragraph (4)

Question 15

A) NO CHANGE

B) chocolate's

C) it's

D) their

Question 16

At this point, the writer is considering adding the following sentence:

"In fact, there is archaeological evidence of chocolate being used for ceremonies, celebrations, and even medicinal uses in cultures around the world."

Should the writer make this addition here?

A) Yes, because it provides information that helps explain what comes next.

B) No, because it provides a more effective introduction and should be placed at the beginning of the sentence.

C) Yes, because it provides information that helps explain a prior statement.

D) No, because it provides irrelevant information.

(3)

[17] The roots of chocolate have been traced back over two thousand years to the plateaus of Central America. In this part of the [18] world, which is also called Mesoamerica, ancient peoples discovered how to domesticate the cacao tree. The Olmec, Mayan, and Aztec people all developed many unique ways to use cacao. When the Spanish conquered the Aztecs in the sixteenth century, [19] they brought chocolate to Europe.

(4)

Before being introduced to the continent by the Spanish, Europeans had never seen or tasted chocolate. However, the tasty substance quickly grew popular – especially among the rich. European colonists attempted to meet the growing demand for chocolate by establishing cacao plantations in Central and South America. [20]

Question 17

A) NO CHANGE

B) Experts have traced the roots of chocolate

C) Researchers have traced chocolate's origins

D) Chocolate originates

Question 18

A) NO CHANGE

B) world, formerly

C) world – also

D) world that is too

Question 19

A) NO CHANGE

B) the conquerors

C) the native peoples

D) it

Question 20

Which of the following provides the most effective conclusion for the paragraph?

A) NO CHANGE

B) Soon, the world's increasing appetite for chocolate demanded new innovations for meeting growing demand.

C) Indeed, chocolate is among the sweetest and richest commodities traded on world markets.

D) The wealth generated by chocolate made many people rich, but at the cost of great social injustice.

CONTINUE ▶

During the Industrial Revolution, improved cacao bean processing methods led to innovations. Chefs and scientists alike experimented with new chocolate recipes. In fact, famous names in chocolate like Nestle, Lindt, Hershey's, and Cadbury all got their start in the late nineteenth century. During this time, people got to taste the world's first chocolate and milk chocolate bars.

The chocolate found in stores today may be a far cry from the variety enjoyed by the early Mesoamericans, but it is more common than it has ever been. **21** Most of the world's cacao beans are grown in West Africa. The Ivory Coast is the leading cacao producer in the world. With improved production techniques and the introduction of cacao farming to the African continent, chocolate became less expensive and more widely available. **22** The overwhelming consumption of chocolate today illustrates the lasting power of a food that people have enjoyed for thousands of years.

Question 21

A) NO CHANGE

B) Most of the world's cacao beans are grown in the Ivory Coast.

C) Most of the world's cacao grow in the Ivory Coast, a nation in West Africa.

D) Most of the world's cacao beans are grown in West Africa; the Ivory Coast is the leading cacao producer in the world

Question 22

A) NO CHANGE

B) Chocolate lovers everywhere

C) Chocolate may not be as popular as it once was, but this

D) Food cultures across the world use many varied ingredients, which

CONTINUE

Questions 23-33 are based on the following passage:

Modern Firefighters are Everyday Heroes

Firefighters, with their bulky protective gear weighing them down and trucks blaring as **23** they are running into a burning building, represent the epitome of heroism. While everyone else is fleeing from danger, modern firefighters **24** did their best to save the people and animals affected by a fire and, if possible, save the building as well. Fortunately for everyone in modern society, most modern cities have firefighting infrastructure in place. This includes important public safety tools like fire hydrants as well as full-time, professional fire fighters. Though taken for granted today, **25** the concept of firefighting is less than two centuries old.

Question 23

A) NO CHANGE

B) they have run

C) they were running

D) they would run.

Question 24

A) NO CHANGE

B) do

C) does

D) had done

Question 25

At this point, the writer is considering rewriting the underlined portion of the sentence to the following:

"professional firefighting has evolved in several key ways since it was established centuries ago."

Should the writer make this addition here?

A) Yes, because it provides an effective conclusion to the paragraph.

B) Yes, because it provides information that helps clarify key terms.

C) No, because it contains incorrect or illogical information.

D) No, because it provides irrelevant information.

CONTINUE

Professional firefighting began in ancient Rome over 2000 years ago, **26** where an industrious man named Marcus Crassus created and funded his own fire department. Far from being altruistic, Crassus used his fire department to extort money from the owner of a burning building. **27** If the building's owner did not pay his price, then Crassus let the structure burn to the ground. This early effort at professional firefighting involved unsavory business practices**28**; regardless, Crassus' model of a mobile fire department immediately ready to respond to a public emergency laid the foundation for future firefighting.

Question 26

A) NO CHANGE

B) because

C) when

D) DELETE the underlined word

Question 27

A) NO CHANGE

B) When payment was considered insufficient,

C) After investigating the causes of the fire,

D) At a whim,

Question 28

The writer is considering deleting the underlined portion of the sentence. Should the underlined portion be kept or deleted?

A) Kept, because it provides an effective transition between one concept and the next.

B) Kept, because it shows the impact of firefighting on public safety.

C) Deleted, because it ignores the modern technologies involved in firefighting today.

D) Deleted, because it provides irrelevant information.

CONTINUE

In modern times, buildings are constructed according to strict health and safety standards. In centuries past, however, cities were highly flammable. Fires were a **29** plausible fear in pre-modern cities. **30** They were capable of destroying an entire community. European cities like London and Paris experienced multiple large fires that left thousands of residents homeless. These costly and destructive disasters were devastating, and in many ways, they inspired innovation in firefighting.

Question 29

A) NO CHANGE

B) likely

C) trustworthy

D) credible

Question 30

A) NO CHANGE

B) Unchecked, blazes could destroy

C) Without effective assistance, firefighters could not stop anything from destroying

D) In those days, they could destroy

31 While these early versions of the professional firefighters we know today put out fires effectively, they were not able to help everyone. Much of this is due to the fact that early fire companies were aligned with insurance **32** companies who would mark an insured building with their company sign. Thus, if a fire started, a company would respond quickly. However, the company would often leave the building burning if **33** they were not a customer of the insurance company.

Modern firefighting has come a long way from the ragtag teams of volunteer fire companies that protected people based on their insurance interests in centuries past. Today, fire companies no longer fight for their heroic positions or let uninsured buildings burn to the ground. Now, fire companies are almost always publicly-funded services that treat most fires with equal focus and energy. Although most of America's firefighters are still volunteers, they have raised the bar for heroism by risking their lives to save others every day.

Question 31

At this point, the writer is considering adding the following sentence:

"The precursor to today's modern firefighters, private volunteer firefighters, formed companies after the Great Fire of London in 1666."

Should the writer make this addition here?

A) Yes, because it provides data that helps clarify other information presented in the paragraph.

B) No, because it provides a more effective conclusion.

C) Yes, because it provides relevant contextual information that helps explain why firefighters are heroic.

D) No, because it provides irrelevant information.

Question 32

A) NO CHANGE

B) companies that

C) companies, which

D) companies. The insurers

Question 33

A) NO CHANGE

B) the owner of the building was not

C) the owner of the building is not

D) it was not

Questions 34-44 are based on the following passage:

Facebook Inc.

Facebook is a social media and networking website used by billions of people worldwide. Facebook's founder, Mark Zuckerberg, built the original version of the website in **34** 2004. They created the site while enrolled as students at Harvard University. Today, Facebook is among the largest and most profitable technology companies in the world.

Initially, **35** Facebook membership was limited to students at select universities. Since then, membership has ballooned into the billions. **36** Today, over two billion people use Facebook at least once per month.

Question 34

A) NO CHANGE

B) 2004 as a student enrolled at Harvard University

C) 2004; at the time he was enrolled at Harvard.

D) 2004 – even though at the time he was still enrolled as a student at Harvard.

Question 35

A) NO CHANGE

B) only students at select universities could become members of Facebook

C) Facebook's membership was composed of only students

D) Facebook limited its memberships to students

Question 36

At this point, the writer is considering adding the following sentence:

"However, since 2006, Facebook has allowed anyone over the age of 13 years old to register."

Should the writer make this addition here?

A) Yes, because it provides an effective transition.

B) Yes, because it provides an effective introduction to new concepts.

C) No, because it provides a more effective conclusion.

D) No, because it provides irrelevant information.

CONTINUE ▶

Even though signing up for an account is free, the billions of people **37** that use Facebook or its popular subsidiaries – including Instagram, WhatsApp, and Oculus VR – provide a critical source of revenue for the company behind the website. Rather than charging people to use its services, Facebook charges advertisers **38** for running targeted ads on the data-driven platform. In 2018, Facebook Inc. earned over $55 billion in revenues and held total assets valued at over $97 billion. **39**

Question 37

A) NO CHANGE

B) which

C) who

D) in

Question 38

A) NO CHANGE

B) running

C) that will run

D) to run

Question 39

At this point, the writer is considering adding the following sentence:

"Most of this revenue originated from paid advertisements that the platform places on the screens of selected users."

Should the writer make this addition here?

A) Yes, because it provides an effective conclusion.

B) Yes, because it provides information that helps introduce other information presented in the paragraph.

C) No, because it would be more effective as an introduction.

D) No, because it provides redundant information.

Figure 1, below, shows the share of Facebook's total annual revenue in the year 2018 attributable to advertising revenue, compared with all other sources.

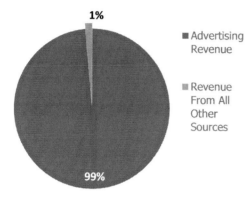

FACEBOOK ANNUAL REVENUE BY SOURCE

- Advertising Revenue
- Revenue From All Other Sources

By 2015, more than two million advertisers were paying Facebook to circulate their information. The following year, this figure increased to three million active advertisers. Advertisers value Facebook for its capacity to direct information to targeted users based on their browsing habits, interactions, and purchases on the platform. **40**

Facebook's advertising division creates a real value for both consumers and the small businesses who make up the majority of Facebook's advertisers. However, as technology often does, the social media platform's targeted marketing systems have raised novel concerns regarding **41** our relationship with technology.

Question 40

Which of the following provides the most effective support from Figure 1?

A) The degree to which advertisers value Facebook's services is reflected in the fact that nearly all the multi-billion-dollar company's revenues originate from advertising.

B) During the early 1990s, the early pioneers of the internet never would have believed that it would one day be home to sites worth billions of dollars.

C) At one time, paid advertising options were limited to print, television, radio, and word-of-mouth.

D) Some of Facebook's revenues – albeit a very small proportion – originate from sources other than paid advertising.

Question 41

A) NO CHANGE

B) your

C) society's

D) the

Because Facebook relies on user information to **42** ad value to its advertising platform, privacy advocates have raised concerns regarding the circumstances under which Facebook uses and releases member data. It has also been criticized as a platform for the facilitation of the spread of illegal or copyrighted materials, the spread of propaganda and hate speech, and the incitement of crimes. Unanticipated social challenges are consistently arising as a result of this worldwide **43** technology, and Facebook is constantly changing its policies and settings regarding user privacy and identity verification. As Facebook works to keep up with the pace of social and economic change it **44** has fostered, time will tell whether the platform will survive.

Question 42

A) NO CHANGE

B) ads

C) add

D) have added

Question 43

A) NO CHANGE

B) technology; Facebook

C) technology; and Facebook

D) technology. In response, Facebook

Question 44

A) NO CHANGE

B) will have

C) have

D) DELETE the underlined word

PRACTICE TEST 4

Writing and Language Test

25 MINUTES, 44 QUESTIONS

DIRECTIONS

Each passage below is followed by a number of questions. For some questions, you will be asked to consider how the passage may be improved. For others, you will consider how the passage may be edited to correct errors in sentence structure, word usage, grammar, or punctuation.

Some questions will direct your attention to an underlined portion of the passage. Others will direct you to a location in a passage or ask you to consider the passage as a whole.

Read each passage carefully. After reading the passage, choose the answer to each question that most effectively improves the quality of writing of the passage or improves its conformance to standard written English. Most questions include a "NO CHANGE" option, which you should select if you think the best choice is to leave the applicable portion of the passage as-is.

Questions 1-11 are based on the following passage:

The Mountain Pine Beetle Epidemic

1 The mountain pine beetle epidemic is a serious threat to forests in the Rocky Mountain region of North America. In the last two decades, millions of acres of forested land across the United States and Canada have been devastated by pine beetles. While mountain pine beetles are a natural part of the forest ecosystem, modern human fire suppression practices have amplified this natural process.

The writer is considering deleting the underlined sentence. Should the sentence be kept or deleted?

A) Kept, because it shows the impact of pine beetles on a specific region.

B) Kept, because it provides an effective introduction to the paragraph that follows.

C) Deleted, because it ignores the fact that several invasive species threaten America's forests.

D) Deleted, because omitting the sentence would make for a more effective introduction to the passage.

2 Adult beetles begin by laying their eggs under the bark of a pine tree. After the eggs hatch, the larvae feed on the inside of the bark **3** <u>over the winter, growing into adults</u>. The cycle continues the following summer as new adult beetles emerge from infected trees ready to travel to any healthy pine tree nearby.

Which choice best introduces the topic of this paragraph?

A) NO CHANGE

B) A pine beetle is only the size of a grain of rice, but don't underestimate its impact based on size.

C) As a species, the beetles have changed Rocky Mountain forests through their breeding process.

D) Pine beetles can have devastating impacts on forest ecosystems thanks to their voracious appetites.

A) NO CHANGE

B) as they grow into adults over the winter.

C) while growing into adults.

D) over the winter because they grow into adults.

CONTINUE

Each spring, adult pine beetles from the prior year's spawn **4** will have found a new living pine tree and start burrowing under its bark. **5** Whenever pine beetles infest a tree, the tree dies; even worse, one infected tree houses enough beetles to infect two trees nearby. The pine beetles will continue this process until there are no more living trees **6** nearby. Or until fire or extreme cold halt the cycle.

The mountain pine beetle epidemic presents a serious ecological threat. In the last two decades, millions of acres of forested land across the United States and Canada have been devastated by pine beetles. While mountain pine beetles are a natural part of the forest ecosystem, modern human fire suppression practices **7** has amplified this natural process.

Question 4

A) NO CHANGE

B) had found

C) are finding

D) find

Question 5

A) NO CHANGE

B) Each time

C) Every time

D) While

Question 6

A) NO CHANGE

B) nearby; or

C) nearby or

D) nearby, and

Question 7

A) NO CHANGE

B) have amplified

C) will have amplified

D) amplifies

The vast swaths of trees killed by the pine beetles are unsightly, and they pose risks for the health of forests and humans **8** themselves. Due to the density of dead, dried trees left in the beetles' wake, fire risk is one of the primary consequences of pine beetle **9** infestations – and human fire suppression tactics over the past century may have unwittingly contributed to the pine beetle's spread. Fortunately, however, **10** to prevent fires and scenic damage, there are a few interventions that can be taken.

By starting and managing controlled burns, forest management professionals can stop the pine beetle's unabated growth by cutting off their food source. In some areas, like campgrounds and parks, pesticides can prevent the beetles from entering the live tree. However, for the hardiest pine beetles, there is little humans can do to stop their momentum completely. The tiny beetle will eventually exhaust its food supply and become a much smaller, and less significant blight on the landscape. Until then, the blighted pine forests that have become prevalent in many parts of the Rocky Mountains **11** is the new normal.

Question 8

A) NO CHANGE

B) alike

C) indeed

D) DELETE the underlined word.

Question 9

A) NO CHANGE

B) infestations, and

C) infestations; indeed

D) infestations. Unfortunately,

Question 10

A) NO CHANGE

B) preventing fires and scenic damage requires interventions humans can take

C) humans can intervene to prevent fires and scenic damage

D) there are a few interventions humans can enact to prevent fires and scenic damage

Question 11

A) NO CHANGE

B) is being

C) were

D) will be

CONTINUE ▶

Questions 12-22 are based on the following passage:

The Ancient Glory of the Olympic Games

(1)

Every four years, the most elite athletes from among over two hundred participating nations gather for the world's most diverse and well-known international sports **12** competition: the Olympic Games. Inspired by ancient ceremonies, the Olympic Games embody several key tenants of honor and athleticism in traditional sports. However, this staunch commitment to the nobility of tradition is balanced against the unyielding wills of the world-class athletes who are constantly pushing the boundaries of their sports.

(2)

13 The first recorded Olympic Games took place in Olympia, Greece in 776 BCE. Starting in that year, representatives of the sovereign states of ancient Greece gathered to hold a series of athletic competitions in honor of the god Zeus **14** once every four years. Like contestants in the modern games, these ancient athletes competed in various events, including races and wrestling matches. The Ancient Greeks also held their Olympic Games once every four years, which is another similarity between the ancient Games and those celebrated today.

Question 12

A) NO CHANGE

B) competition, the

C) competition; the

D) competition. The

Question 13

At this point, the writer is considering adding the following sentence:

"The modern Olympic Games were inspired by ancient athletic competitions."

Should the writer make this addition here?

A) Yes, because it provides an effective transition from the prior paragraph.

B) Yes, because it provides information that helps clarify prior statements.

C) No, because it would be more effective as a conclusion at the end of the paragraph.

D) No, because it provides irrelevant information.

Question 14

A) NO CHANGE

B) every four years

C) in a four-year series

D) DELETE the underlined portion.

CONTINUE

(3)

Inspired by the ancient Greek competition, Baron Pierre de Coubertin founded the International Olympic Committee in 1894. Two years later, the Committee held the first modern Olympic Games in Athens in 1896. **15**

(4)

The modern games are meant to mirror many of the traditions developed by the ancient Greeks. However, updates and new additions to the festivities have helped the Olympics maintain **16** its engagement with modern audiences. For example, today's Olympic Games are divided into two sets of events, the Summer Games and the Winter Games. **17** The Winter Games were created by the International Winter Olympic Committee in 1924. The Paralympics, a popular multi-sport event designed to promote the rehabilitation of individuals with physical injuries, was created to run parallel with the Olympic Games starting in 1960.

Question 15

Which choice provides the best conclusion for this paragraph?

A) NO CHANGE

B) The Greek Olympic Games stand out as events punctuated by glory and nobility – two things that the modern games seek to emulate.

C) This launched a tradition that has been celebrated around the world for over a century.

D) Unfortunately, some participants in the Olympic Games have failed to maintain the spirit behind the original event.

Question 16

A) NO CHANGE

B) they're

C) their

D) it's

Question 17

A) NO CHANGE

B) The International Olympic Committee created this portion of the event

C) The International Winter Olympic Committee creates the Games

D) The Winter Games were created by Olympic Games officials

CONTINUE

(5)

Today, the Olympic Games create an international spectacle that **18** attract thousands of competitors and billions of spectators. **19** The 2016 Summer Games held in Rio de Janeiro, Brazil, attracted an audience of over 3.5 billion viewers who tuned in from around the world to cheer on their favorite athletes. Just as they did in ancient times, the Olympics bring together athletes from diverse cultures to compete for national glory and personal pride. **20**

Question 18

A) NO CHANGE

B) attracts

C) will attract

D) can attract

Question 19

At this point, the writer is considering changing the underlined sentence to the following:

"The Summer Games held in Rio de Janeiro attracted over 3.5 billion viewers from around the world."

Should the writer make this change here?

A) Yes, because it provides an effective transition.

B) Yes, because it improves clarity, tone, and voice of the sentence.

C) No, because it would be more effective as a conclusion at the end of the paragraph.

D) No, because it eliminates relevant information.

Question 20

To make this passage most logical, paragraph (4) should be placed:

A) where it is now

B) before paragraph (1)

C) before paragraph (2)

D) after paragraph (5)

CONTINUE ▶

21 The competitions and ceremonies that characterize the modern Olympic Games may have evolved, but at their core they remain true to the ideals of the original competition. The ancient Games maintained a strict adherence to the glory of pure athletic competition leaving all political qualms aside. No matter what one nation's position may be towards any other, they are all equal on the Olympic fields. **22**

At this point, the writer is considering adding the following sentence:

"The Summer Games held in London, England in 2012 hosted over 10,000 competitors from 204 independent nations."

Should the writer make this addition here?

- A) Yes, because it provides information that helps explain what comes next.

- B) No, because it provides a more effective conclusion and should be placed at the end of the sentence.

- C) Yes, because it provides information that helps explain a prior statement.

- D) No, because it provides information that interrupts the logical flow of the passage.

Which of the following most effectively summarizes the main point of the passage?

- A) The glory of athleticism has inspired billions of people to watch the Olympic Games every year.

- B) Despite modernization, today's Olympic Games maintain the spirit of the ancient competitions upon which they are based.

- C) While sometimes controversial, the Olympic Games have endured for centuries.

- D) By relying on skills, endurance, athleticism and strategy, anyone can become an Olympic athlete.

Questions 23-33 are based on the following passage:

Saving Wild Tigers

Over the past century, several animal populations, including the wild tiger, 23 have been put in danger due to human practices. 24 The leaders of many countries that are home to native tiger populations have taken major strides to protect these impressive beasts, but more must be done to save tigers from extinction in the wild.

Question 23

A) NO CHANGE

B) have

C) has

D) has been

Question 24

At this point, the writer is considering adding the following sentence:

"Deforestation, climate change, and poaching have all contributed to the demise of wild tiger populations."

Should the writer make this addition here?

A) Yes, because it provides effective support for a prior assertion.

B) Yes, because it provides information that helps clarify key terms.

C) No, because it contains a modifier error.

D) No, because it provides irrelevant information.

The tiger's natural habitat typically ranges from tropical, evergreen, and temperate forests, to mangrove swamps, grasslands, and savannas. **25** However, the wild tiger populations are being threatened due to extreme habitat loss. In fact, the wild tiger has lost nearly 93% of its historical range. This staggering loss in native habitat has **26** impacted global tiger populations. In the last century alone, the world has seen populations drop from 100,000 to just over 3,000 wild tigers.

Question 25

At this point, the writer is revising the underlined sentence to the following:

"Despite this expansive range, habitat loss threatens wild tiger populations."

Should the writer make this change here?

- A) Yes, because it provides more effective support for the passage.
- B) Yes, because it improves language, clarity, and tone.
- C) No, because it provides inaccurate or unsupported information.
- D) No, because it provides redundant information.

Question 26

- A) NO CHANGE
- B) obliterated
- C) annihilated
- D) devastated

(1) Wild tigers are predominately solitary 27 creatures. And the loss of their roaming space has forced them to compete for space with other tigers and predators – including humans. (2) In human-dominated areas, tigers are at greater risk of being captured or killed by poachers. 28 This migration into residential areas is especially troubling to conservationists since poachers are among the biggest threats to wild tiger populations. (3) Although some countries have initiated strong efforts aimed at preserving these remarkable creatures, tigers still fall victim to poachers.

Question 27

A) NO CHANGE

B) creatures; and the

C) creatures, and the

D) creatures – and the

Question 28

To make this passage most logical, the underlined sentence should be placed:

A) where it is now

B) before sentence (1)

C) before sentence (2)

D) after sentence (3)

CONTINUE

Figure 1, below, shows the number of wild tigers poached in India – one of the few nations home to wild tigers – between 2008 and 2018:

Figure 1: Tigers Poached in India

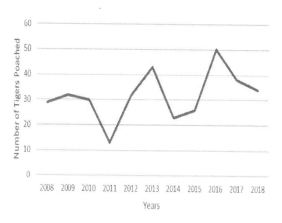

Unfortunately, poachers are not the only threat to tiger populations. Despite the factors working against them, tigers have started to climb their way back from the brink of extinction. In 2010, the governments of thirteen nations home to native wild tiger populations executed the Global Tiger Recovery Plan. **29** This plan outlines the policies nations can follow to protect native wild tigers and support the recovery of their populations. **30** The Global Tiger Recovery Plan is only one of many international initiatives world leaders have put in place in recent years to help support endangered species.

Question 29

Which of the following provides the most effective support from Figure 1?

A) In that same year, Indian authorities recorded a sharp decline in tiger poaching.

B) Rising sea levels attributable to climate change threaten to wipe out large swaths of tiger habitats.

C) India has many laws protecting wild tigers from the impacts of poaching.

D) In 2016, the world saw a sudden rise in the number of tigers poached in India.

Question 30

The writer is considering deleting the underlined sentence. Should the sentence be kept or deleted?

A) Kept, because it provides an effective transition between one concept and the next.

B) Kept, because it shows the diverse threats facing wild tigers.

C) Deleted, because it ignores the fact that poaching is preventable.

D) Deleted, because it provides redundant information.

After the Global Tiger Recovery Plan was executed, tiger populations showed a small increase for the first time in over a century. **31** Although wild tigers are on the rise, poaching, deforestation, and climate change **32** continues to impact tiger populations. Many of the preventable causes of wild tiger population decline can be addressed effectively with strong conservation laws. As a result, conservationists and lawmakers alike have a great deal of work ahead of **33** themselves to prevent the extinction of this critical wild species.

Question 31

At this point, the writer is considering adding the following sentence:

"Since conservation efforts went into effect, the overall estimated wild tiger population has increased from 3,200 to 3,890."

Should the writer make this addition here?

A) Yes, because it provides data that helps clarify other information presented in the paragraph.

B) No, because it provides a more effective conclusion.

C) Yes, because it provides effective support for a prior statement.

D) No, because it provides irrelevant information.

Question 32

A) NO CHANGE

B) continue

C) continuously

D) continued

Question 33

A) NO CHANGE

B) itself

C) them

D) it

CONTINUE

Questions 34-44 are based on the following passage:

Standing Rock and the Dakota Access Pipeline

In early 2016, protestors rallied around the environmental and social impacts of a proposed infrastructure development **34** project, which was the Dakota Access Pipeline. The controversy started when the United States Army Corps of Engineers accepted an application filed by a Texas-based oil and gas developer. The proposed pipeline **35** would run from western North Dakota to southern Illinois, crossing both the Missouri and Mississippi Rivers and part of Lake Oahe near the Standing Rock Indian Reservation.

The Standing Rock Tribe, acting as a sovereign nation, saw the pipeline as a threat to the region's clean water, their ancient burial **36** grounds, and it is likely a violation of the Fort Laramie Treaty, which guarantees the undisturbed use and occupation of reservation lands.

Question 34

A) NO CHANGE

B) project that was the

C) project: the

D) project known at the time as the

Question 35

A) NO CHANGE

B) ran

C) had run

D) should have run

Question 36

A) NO CHANGE

B) grounds. Further, the pipeline likely violated the

C) grounds – and a likely violation of

D) grounds. Furthermore, it was thought to likely be a violation of

The Standing Rock Sioux Tribe sued the U.S. Army Corps of Engineers to stop the pipeline. The Judge denied **37** their claim; later the same day, however, the U.S. government voluntarily halted the project. **38** Shortly after taking office, President Trump signed a presidential memorandum authorizing the Army Corps of Engineers to proceed with the Dakota Access Pipeline project. **39** Despite these unanticipated new challenges, protestors rallied at Standing Rock.

A) NO CHANGE

B) the tribe's

C) the tribes'

D) the tribes

At this point, the writer is considering adding the following sentence:

"This was a significant win for the Standing Rock Sioux, but unfortunately their victory was short-lived."

Should the writer make this addition here?

A) Yes, because it provides an effective transition to new information.

B) Yes, because it provides information that helps clarify prior information presented in the paragraph.

C) No, because it provides redundant information.

D) No, because it provides irrelevant information.

A) NO CHANGE

B) Because of

C) Like

D) In response to

As a reaction to the government's surprising approval of the Dakota Access Pipeline, Standing Rock Sioux elder LaDonna Brave Bull Allard rallied support. Tribal **40** members, youth groups, including the Oceti Sakowin Youth and Allies and One Mind Youth Movement, and other allies established a protest camp as a center for cultural preservation and nonviolent resistance. Before long, protests **41** will spread nationwide.

Question 40

A) NO CHANGE

B) members; youth groups, including Oceti Sakowin Youth and Allies and One Mind Youth Movement; and

C) members, youth groups – including Oceti Sakowin Youth and Allies and One Mind Youth Movement – and

D) Members – youth groups, the including Oceti Sakowin Youth and Allies and One Mind Youth Movement – and

Question 41

A) NO CHANGE

B) are spreading

C) had spread

D) is spreading

The Oceti Sakowin Youth and Allies group rallied in Washington D.C., collecting 140,000 signatures opposing the pipeline. The group got attention for their cause by planning and **42** had carried out a two-thousand-mile footrace from North Dakota to the nation's capital. **43** Over the course of the following summer, thousands of people traveled to the camp set up by the original protestors to unite with the cause. Since then, protests and marches have taken place in local communities around the country. **44** Cities have declared opposition, and some have ceased to renew contracts with corporations who support the pipeline. This event became paramount by gaining both national and international attention and facilitated the national conversation for environmental projects that cross over Native American lands.

Question 42

A) NO CHANGE

B) carrying

C) would carry

D) attempting to carry

Question 43

A) NO CHANGE

B) By the end of summer 2017,

C) By the end of the following summer,

D) During summer 2017,

Question 44

The writer is considering deleting the underlined sentence. Should the sentence be kept or deleted?

A) Kept, because it provides an effective transition between one concept and the next.

B) Kept, because it points to future conflicts between cities and corporations.

C) Deleted, because it interrupts the flow of the paragraph.

D) Deleted, because it provides information that is not related to the pipeline.

PRACTICE TEST 5

Writing and Language Test

25 MINUTES, 44 QUESTIONS

DIRECTIONS

Each passage below is followed by a number of questions. For some questions, you will be asked to consider how the passage may be improved. For others, you will consider how the passage may be edited to correct errors in sentence structure, word usage, grammar, or punctuation.

Some questions will direct your attention to an underlined portion of the passage. Others will direct you to a location in a passage or ask you to consider the passage as a whole.

Read each passage carefully. After reading the passage, choose the answer to each question that most effectively improves the quality of writing of the passage or improves its conformance to standard written English. Most questions include a "NO CHANGE" option, which you should select if you think the best choice is to leave the applicable portion of the passage as-is.

Questions 1-11 are based on the following passage:

Improving the World's Food Systems

(1)

The planet's population is already very large, and it continues to grow. In order to feed this growing population, the world will need to increase agricultural production. However, our current agricultural systems are not designed to carry the weight of such a massive global population. **1**

Which choice provides the most effective conclusion for this paragraph?

A) NO CHANGE

B) In order to meet the growing worldwide food demand, the world must rethink common agricultural practices.

C) This means that sustainable food growth practices are more important now than ever before.

D) Thus, we must turn back to the sustainable agricultural practices developed by our ancestors.

(2)

As counterintuitive as it may seem, many of our agricultural practices **2** are bad for the environment. For example, agriculture is responsible for a substantial proportion of the total greenhouse gas emissions. **3** According to the EPA, agricultural activities were responsible for nine percent of the greenhouse gases emitted from the United States in 2016. Further, the increasing need for agricultural land increases the risk of deforestation, and many of the fertilizers and pesticides used in industrialized agriculture pollute the environment. In fact, agricultural runoff has been linked to 'dead zones,' which are places where no sea life exists in oceans and lakes due to a lack of sufficient dissolved oxygen in the water. One such dead zone in the US occurs in the Gulf of Mexico, where fertilizer run-off enters via the Mississippi River. As the world population continues to grow, food demand will **4** increase and require an expansion of agricultural activities that harm human health and the environment.

Question 2

A) NO CHANGE

B) harm

C) have harmed

D) will have harmed

Question 3

The writer is considering deleting the underlined sentence. Should the sentence be kept or deleted?

A) Kept, because it provides effective support for a prior statement.

B) Kept, because it shows the impact of agricultural activity on climate change.

C) Deleted, because it ignores the fact that there are many activities that contribute to climate change.

D) Deleted, because it interrupts the paragraph's description of improving agricultural sustainability.

Question 4

A) NO CHANGE

B) increase, requiring an expansion of agricultural activities that harm human health and the environment.

C) increase and expansion of agricultural activities that harm human health and the environment will be observed.

D) increase.

(3)

5 Agriculture depends on climate and weather conditions perhaps more than any other industry. Climate affects the location, timing, and productivity of crop, **6** livestock and fishery systems at local, national, and global levels. Increased temperatures, water stress, disease, weather extremes, and similar environmental issues pose significant challenges **7** for farmers and ranchers. The U.S. produces nearly $330 billion per year in agricultural commodities, and any increasing threat raised by climate change, pollution, pests, or pathogens can cost agricultural producers substantial sums of money.

Question 5

To make this passage most logical, paragraph (3) should be placed:

A) before paragraph (1)

B) before paragraph (2)

C) after paragraph (4)

D) where it is now

Question 6

A) NO CHANGE

B) livestock; and fishery systems at local, national, and global scales.

C) livestock – and fishery systems at local, national, and global scales.

D) livestock, and fishery systems at local, national, and global levels.

Question 7

A) NO CHANGE

B) at

C) to

D) in

(4)

There is little question that the world will need more agricultural land in the coming [8] years but how much will be enough? By 2050, the global demand for grain production is projected to increase nearly fifty percent. If the agricultural industry does not find a way to grow more food on less land, it is unlikely [9] they will be able to keep up with global food demand.

A) NO CHANGE

B) years – but what is enough?

C) years – but how much will be enough?

D) years – but how much will be enough.

A) NO CHANGE

B) it will be able to

C) they will have been able

D) they will not

(5)

The world's unsustainable agricultural systems do not just threaten global food supply; they threaten water as well. Many common agricultural practices are wasteful, which results in the overuse of water for irrigation. Staple crops such as wheat, rice, sugar, cotton, and maize need a great deal of water for irrigation. Increasingly severe weather events and droughts triggered by global climate change causes crops to guzzle up groundwater even **10** faster, especially in already dry places, which are becoming drier due to global warming effects. **11**

A) NO CHANGE

B) faster; especially in already dry places, which are

C) faster – especially in already dry places, which are

D) faster. This is a particular threat in dry places, which are

Which of the following most effectively summarizes the main point of the passage?

A) In order to feed a growing world population, the way we grow our food will have to improve.

B) World agricultural systems are critical components of global economic infrastructures.

C) The ecosystem is interconnected, and unsustainable agricultural practices affect all the different components of it.

D) If we do not improve transportation and distribution of agricultural commodities, mass starvation will be a problem very soon.

Questions 12-22 are based on the following passage:

Crowdfunding

[12] Many of the challenges new business owners face are beyond their control as they have nothing to do with their products, services, or ideas. For example, one of the most common barriers to starting a new business is [13] access to capital. Crowdfunding, a new type of enterprise financing, provides a way for entrepreneurs to raise money without having to rely on banks or traditional sources of venture capital.

At this point, the writer is considering adding the following sentence:

"Entrepreneurs are a creative and dynamic group of people, but they cannot be expected to be able to solve every problem facing new business owners."

Should the writer make this addition here?

A) Yes, because it provides an effective introduction.

B) Yes, because it provides information that helps clarify prior statements.

C) No, because it would be more effective as a conclusion at the end of the paragraph.

D) No, because it provides irrelevant information.

A) NO CHANGE

B) a lack of access to capital.

C) lacking access to capital.

D) failing to obtain access to capital.

Unauthorized copying or reuse of any part of this page is illegal.

CONTINUE

251

14 Many new business owners fund their new enterprises using loans. However, due to complex and lengthy application and credit review processes, business loans can be difficult to obtain. Instead of taking on debt, some entrepreneurs choose to raise money by selling shares of their company to co-owners or venture capitalists. **15** While this can be a quick and effective way to raise money for early operations, it also places entrepreneurs at risk of losing control of the companies they founded.

Question 14

Which choice provides the best introduction for this paragraph?

A) NO CHANGE

B) Indeed, access to capital is one of the most significant barriers being faced by new businesses.

C) Access to capital is particularly difficult for some people due to historical discrimination.

D) Entrepreneurs can fund new enterprises using a number of different methods.

Question 15

At this point, the writer is considering adding the following sentence:

"Venture capitalists are investors who fund new and expanding businesses in exchange for a stake in the venture."

Should the writer make this change here?

A) Yes, because it defines a key term.

B) Yes, because it improves clarity, tone, and voice of the sentence.

C) No, because it would be more effective as a conclusion at the end of the paragraph.

D) No, because the information is irrelevant.

CONTINUE

Fortunately for burgeoning new enterprises, there are ways to fund a new or growing venture without taking on the burden of debt or the pressure of pitching to venture capitalists. Crowdfunding – a new type of grassroots funding – allows entrepreneurs to source capital from the entire **16** world rather than a select group of investors. In fact, crowdfunding has made anyone with a laptop and an internet connection a potential venture capitalist.

(1) Crowdfunding is a financing model **17** where someone raises small amounts of money from a large number of people. **(2)** Websites and social media platforms designed to facilitate crowdfunding have already helped millions of people use crowdfunding to launch their new businesses. **(3)** Popular crowdfunding campaigns have raised money for new inventions and discoveries **18** as varied as the perfect potato salad to the Oculus series of virtual reality products. **19** Because there is a greater diversity of investors on crowdfunding platforms, crowdfunding can be an effective way to raise money for a unique new business idea that mainstream investors may not appreciate.

Question 16

A) NO CHANGE
B) world, rather
C) world - rather
D) world. Rather

Question 17

A) NO CHANGE
B) that an entrepreneur can use to raise
C) people use to raise
D) in which entrepreneurs can raise

Question 18

A) NO CHANGE
B) as diverse as
C) ranging from
D) including

Question 19

To make this passage most logical, the underlined sentence should be placed:

A) where it is now
B) before sentence (1)
C) before sentence (2)
D) before sentence (3)

CONTINUE

Thanks to modern crowdfunding platforms, nearly anyone with a laptop and an internet connection can invest in start-up businesses or new products. **20** This has been a positive development for investors and entrepreneurs **21** alike; as it helps new businesses get funded and allows small investors to put their money towards products and services they really want.

Popular online crowdfunding platforms connect millions of people across the world to new products and business ideas. These websites help entrepreneurs surmount the barriers to business ownership that prevent many great ideas from coming to **22** market. Likewise, they allow consumers to help fund the development of the unique products and services that they really want.

Question 20

A) NO CHANGE

B) The crowdfunding phenomenon

C) They

D) It

Question 21

A) NO CHANGE

B) alike;

C) alike as

D) alike,

Question 22

A) NO CHANGE

B) market; likewise allowing

C) market. Furthermore, they allow

D) market and allow

Questions 23-33 are based on the following passage:

The Domestication of Dogs

Dogs are a species of domesticated animals that **23** had evolved from the wild wolf. For over 12,000 years, domesticated dog breeds have lived by people's sides as faithful companions. In fact, dogs have found important niches in numerous branches of society. **24** They can be particularly effective team members in activities like search and rescue, hunting, and ranching. Certain dog breeds are even **25** enlisted in the military and police forces. Countless canines are helping their human companions with important tasks every day, but most dogs in the United States live the leisure life of a household pet.

A) NO CHANGE

B) have evolved

C) has evolved

D) evolved

At this point, the writer is considering adding the following sentence:

"For example, certain dog breeds are trained as service animals for people with a disability or who either need emotional or physical support."

Should the writer make this addition here?

A) Yes, because it provides information that helps clarify key terms.

B) Yes, because it provides effective support for a prior assertion.

C) No, because it contains a modifier error.

D) No, because it provides irrelevant information.

A) NO CHANGE

B) participants

C) enrollees

D) members

Thanks to their pleasant and loyal nature, dogs have become one of the most popular household pets in North America. Figure 1, below, shows the number of different types of pets in North American households.

Figure 1: Household Pets in North America

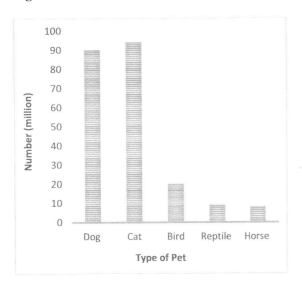

People across the United States and Canada love dogs. **26** In fact, the only other household pet to rival the popularity of the animal that **27** became known as "man's best friend" is the housecat, which brings a whole new meaning to the comic rivalry between cats and dogs! However, their popularity is not the only thing that makes dogs **28** unique; dogs are also the first species of animal and only large carnivore humans ever domesticated.

Question 26

Which of the following provides the most effective support from Figure 1?

A) The number of dogs owned in North America is steadily growing.

B) Nearly 60 million North American households currently own a dog.

C) Nearly 90 million dogs live in homes across North America.

D) By 2010, there were nearly 90 million dogs living as household pets in North America.

Question 27

A) NO CHANGE

B) has become

C) had become

D) will become

Question 28

A) NO CHANGE

B) unique; in fact, dogs are

C) unique. They are

D) unique. They were

Dogs have become an integral component to millions of American families, and it is easy to forget that the domesticated dog that plays in backyards and lounges on couches today is a descendent of the grey wolf. **29** To be more specific, the genetic divergence between dog and wolf took place between 20,000 and 40,000 years ago. **30** However, dogs were not actually domesticated by humans until 15,000 years ago when nomadic peoples began domesticating grey wolves **31** to help them hunt. Over time, the ancient grey wolf's lineage split into the more than four hundred different dog breeds people know and love today.

Question 29

A) NO CHANGE

B) In fact, the

C) Although, the

D) The

Question 30

At this point, the writer is considering adding the following sentence:

"This was during or before the last glacial maximum."

Should the writer make this addition here?

A) Yes, because it provides data that helps clarify other information presented in the paragraph.

B) No, because it provides a more effective introduction.

C) Yes, because it provides an effective conclusion to the paragraph.

D) No, because it provides irrelevant information.

Question 31

A) NO CHANGE

B) for the purposes of hunting.

C) to assist hunters.

D) for help.

CONTINUE

Over time, **32** after their domestication, dogs began to play an increasingly important role in human civilizations across the world. In hunter-gatherer societies, they aided in hunting prey and protecting against predators. **33** Today, dogs remain a key part of human society.

A) NO CHANGE

B) once domesticated, dogs

C) domesticated dogs

D) domesticated dogs have

At this point, the writer is considering adding the following sentence:

"And nearly eight thousand years ago after the domestication of livestock people began breeding and using sheep dogs to help heard and guard livestock."

Should the writer make this addition here?

A) Yes, because it provides data that helps clarify other information presented in the paragraph.

B) No, because it interrupts the flow of the paragraph.

C) Yes, because it provides an effective conclusion to the paragraph.

D) No, because it provides irrelevant information.

Questions 34-44 are based on the following passage:

Lucille Ball: Comedy Legend and Media Pioneer

Lucille Ball is among the most celebrated comedic actresses **34** who ever graced the small screen. Many of Ball's television personas reflected her signature slapstick comedic style. **35** Indeed, Ball's acting abilities were not all that made her stand out. In addition to **36** eliciting side-splitting laughter from audiences across the globe, Ball possessed the skill and tenacity required to break gender barriers in the business of television.

Question 34

A) NO CHANGE

B) whomever

C) whoever

D) ever to

Question 35

A) NO CHANGE

B) However,

C) Thus,

D) DELETE the underlined portion.

Question 36

A) NO CHANGE

B) eliciting

C) getting

D) receiving

CONTINUE

Lucille Ball was born in Jamestown, New York in 1911. She lost her father to **37** typhoid, a dangerous infectious disease, when she was just a small girl. **38** Their family relocated many times when Lucy was young. However, **39** she knew from an early age that she was destined for the stage. When she was only fifteen years old, the tenacious and persistent young actress convinced her mother to enroll her in drama school in New York City. After a few years, Ball moved from New York to Los Angeles, **40** finding roles in several major productions. While working as an actress in Los Angeles, Ball met Desi Arnaz, a Cuban bandleader and actor. By 1940, Ball and Arnaz were married.

Question 37

A) NO CHANGE

B) a dangerous infection

C) typhoid, an infectious disease,

D) typhoid,

Question 38

A) NO CHANGE

B) Her

C) Ball's

D) Lucy's

Question 39

A) NO CHANGE

B) from an early age she knew that the stage was her destiny.

C) from an early age she knew that she was destined for the stage.

D) she knew that she was destined for the stage.

Question 40

A) NO CHANGE

B) which is where she worked

C) where she found roles

D) when finding roles

It is difficult to imagine anyone watching more than a few minutes of any of Ball's many television comedies without bursting into laughter. Ball's television persona, the wacky redhead Lucy Ricardo, was always cooking up schemes that ended in hilarious disasters. Whether trying to keep up with the automated assembly line at a candy factory or crushing grapes by **41** hand, or rather, by foot, at a vineyard in Italy, Lucy's unique brand of physical comedy could always get a laugh. **42**

A) NO CHANGE

B) hand, by foot rather

C) shouting that the

D) hand – or rather, by foot – at

At this point, the writer is considering adding the following sentence:

"However, offscreen, Lucille Ball was a serious businessperson and a shrewd television producer."

Should the writer make this addition here?

A) Yes, because it provides an effective conclusion.

B) Yes, because it provides information that helps clarify other information presented in the paragraph.

C) No, because it would be more effective as an introduction.

D) No, because it provides redundant information.

Rather than sell the rights to their show outright, Ball and Arnaz maintained full ownership of the *I Love Lucy* program. Maintaining control of the production required intense work, and networks almost **43** wouldn't allow it. However, maintaining control over their show allowed the stars the freedom to make a show that rang true with audiences at the time and remains popular to this day.

44 Lucille Ball was both talented and shrewd. In 1962, she purchased Arnaz's share of their production company and became the first female owner and CEO of a major television production company. Ball went on to produce several popular television shows, and her presence on America's television screens has had a permanent impact on audiences and the media business alike.

Question 43

A) NO CHANGE

B) would not

C) refused to

D) attempted to

Question 44

At this point, the writer is considering adding the following sentence:

"In addition to being one of the most iconic sitcoms in American television history, Ball's most popular production, *I Love Lucy*, broke new ground in several important ways."

Should the writer make this addition here?

A) Yes, because it provides an effective introduction.

B) Yes, because it provides information that helps clarify other information presented in the paragraph.

C) No, because it provides redundant information.

D) No, because it provides irrelevant information.

CONTINUE

PRACTICE TEST 6

Writing and Language Test

25 MINUTES, 44 QUESTIONS

DIRECTIONS

Each passage below is followed by a number of questions. For some questions, you will be asked to consider how the passage may be improved. For others, you will consider how the passage may be edited to correct errors in sentence structure, word usage, grammar, or punctuation.

Some questions will direct your attention to an underlined portion of the passage. Others will direct you to a location in a passage or ask you to consider the passage as a whole.

Read each passage carefully. After reading the passage, choose the answer to each question that most effectively improves the quality of writing of the passage or improves its conformance to standard written English. Most questions include a "NO CHANGE" option, which you should select if you think the best choice is to leave the applicable portion of the passage as-is.

Questions 1-11 are based on the following passage:

The Cuban Missile Crisis

(1)

Threat of nuclear war has terrorized world leaders and the global public for decades. In 1945, only two nuclear bombs **1** existed. Twenty years later, the United States had built nearly four thousand bombs, and the Soviet Union possessed over five hundred. The two victors and one-time allies during WWII were now bitter enemies fully immersed in the Cold War. The Cold War heated up with the Cuban Missile Crisis of 1962, which until that time was the closest the world **2** ever came to nuclear war.

Question 1

A) NO CHANGE

B) existed; twenty

C) existed and twenty

D) existed; but twenty

Question 2

A) NO CHANGE

B) ever had came

C) ever had come

D) would ever come

CONTINUE ▶

(2)

3 The Cuban Missile Crisis has roots in global politics. In 1961, President John F. Kennedy sent American forces on a secret invasion of Cuba. The invasion was initiated as an attempt to overthrow the Cuban leader Fidel Castro's communist, anti-U.S. regime. The plan failed miserably and elicited global outrage. In response, Nikita Khrushchev, the Chairman of the Soviet Union, offered to place nuclear missiles in Cuba. A communist nation and a U.S.S.R. ally, Cuba accepted the offer and began building missile launch sites. When U.S. surveillance planes spotted the missile sites, the Cuban Missile Crisis officially began. **4** President Kennedy was faced with a daunting challenge.

Question 3

Which choice best introduces the topic of this paragraph?

A) NO CHANGE

B) Nuclear bombs are among the most destructive creations of mankind.

C) The Cuban Missile Crisis developed in response to a failed political coup.

D) The Cuban Missile Crisis was sparked by a failed political coup.

Question 4

The writer is considering deleting the underlined sentence. Should the sentence be kept or deleted?

A) Kept, because it shows the impact of political dealings on national security.

B) Kept, because it provides an effective conclusion.

C) Deleted, because it ignores the fact that diplomacy and national security are inherently related.

D) Deleted, because the prior sentence makes a more effective conclusion.

---

(3)

5 Instead of conflict, President Kennedy found an alternative option; despite meeting with military advisors who urged immediate action by force, President Kennedy decided to blockade all shipping operations around Cuba. The blockade would prevent weapons from entering the **6** island. The blockade avoided direct military conflict while also preventing dangerous nuclear weapon materials from proliferating. President Kennedy's nonviolent approach proved effective, and the Soviet Union eventually agreed to not supply Cuba with nuclear weapons.

Question 5

A) NO CHANGE

B) America's leaders found an alternative option;

C) Instead of conflict, President Kennedy met

D) Despite meeting

Question 6

A) NO CHANGE

B) island, avoiding direct military conflict while also

C) island, which, avoiding military conflict in a direct manner, also engaged in

D) island; and avoiding direct military conflict while also

(4)

(1) **7** If Kennedy **8** <u>did</u> nothing, the Soviet Union would have nuclear missiles merely 90 miles away from the U.S. within close range of U.S. cities. **(2)** President Kennedy had run the risk of appearing weak in the eyes of Khrushchev and **9** <u>his</u> fellow world leaders. **10** **(3)** However, if he had responded with military force by bombing the sites and invading Cuba, he risked escalating tensions and triggering a nuclear war. **(4)** Indeed, the leaders of both the U.S. and the Soviet Union were prepared for whatever conflict was necessary including the possibility of total nuclear annihilation.

Question 7

To make this passage most logical, paragraph (4) should be placed:

A) where it is now

B) after paragraph (2)

C) after paragraph (1)

D) before paragraph (1)

Question 8

A) NO CHANGE

B) had done

C) does

D) would do

Question 9

A) NO CHANGE

B) Khrushchev's

C) the

D) their

Question 10

To make this paragraph most logical, sentence (3) should be placed:

A) where it is now

B) before sentence (1)

C) before sentence (2)

D) after sentence (4)

CONTINUE

The Cuban Missile Crisis serves as a reminder of the potential consequences of intervening in the domestic politics of foreign nations. However, the peaceful outcome that resulted also goes to show the potential effectiveness of **11** diplomacy, an effective strategy of foreign relations. Thankfully, the world leaders Kennedy and Khrushchev chose to diffuse the situation instead of escalating it, perhaps avoiding the worst war in world history.

Question 11

A) NO CHANGE

B) diplomacy; an

C) diplomacy that is an

D) diplomacy, which is an

CONTINUE

Questions 12-22 are based on the following passage:

The Iditarod Trail Sled Dog Race

The Iditarod Trail is a 1,049-mile path that runs through the back woods of Alaska. The trail travels through snow, ice, frozen tundra, mountains, and **12** <u>forests – and every year, teams</u> of the world's most elite sled dogs race its entire length. **13** <u>To complete the race, a team of sled dogs and their driver, called a musher, must handle some of the most inhospitable conditions in the world.</u> The race begins in the relative metropolis of Anchorage and ends in the tiny settlement of Nome. Along the way, the dogs and mushers brave the environment with a mixture of courage, endurance, and support.

Question 12

A) NO CHANGE

B) forests – and, every year, teams

C) forests, every year, teams

D) forests; and every year, teams

Question 13

At this point, the writer is considering changing the underlined sentence to the following:

"Completing the race successfully requires effective coordination between a team of sled dogs and their driver, called a musher."

Should the writer make this change here?

A) Yes, because it defines key terms used in the passage.

B) Yes, because it improves clarity by omitting extraneous words.

C) No, because it would be more effective as a conclusion at the end of the paragraph.

D) No, because the revision introduces irrelevant information.

14 The first dog sled race was held in 1973, and the use of the Iditarod Trail dates back hundreds of years. Aboriginal Native Alaskans used parts of the Iditarod Trail for as long as they occupied Alaska. However, **15** the Trail's popularity was considered to be greatest during and following the pinnacle of the Klondike Gold Rush. During this time, dog sleds were the primary means of winter travel in the northernmost U.S. state.

Today, contestants participate in the Iditarod Race for enjoyment and competition. However, the annual event takes some of its inspiration from the heroic efforts of sled dogs in Alaska's history. In 1925, dog sled relays raced hundreds of miles to a remote Alaskan city in order to provide vital medicine to treat a diphtheria outbreak. The statue of the famous lead dog, Balto, in New York City's Central Park, commemorates this journey. Like the journey the sled dog teams took in 1925, the spirit of adventure **16** is present.

Question 14

Which choice provides the best introduction for this paragraph?

A) NO CHANGE

B) The first dog sled race on the Iditarod was held in 1973, but by then native peoples had already been using the Trail for hundreds of years.

C) By the time the first dog sled race was held in 1973, native peoples had already been using the Iditarod Trail for hundreds of years.

D) Racing the Iditarod is one of the most grueling endurance challenges a person can face.

Question 15

A) NO CHANGE

B) Trail's popularity was thought by many to be at its peak

C) Trail experienced the popularity

D) Trail's popularity peaked

Question 16

A) NO CHANGE

B) remains a vital and essential component of this epic dog sled journey.

C) remains critical in this epic event.

D) remains in this epic event that was inspired by the relay races run almost a century before.

CONTINUE

To complete the course, dogs and mushers must be prepared to transverse dangerous icy conditions and temperatures that can drop to 100 degrees below freezing. Mushers and their faithful dogs must press on, racing for over a thousand miles with little sleep. **17** Despite challenging conditions such as this, the winning time for the race has dropped from 20 days in 1973 to less than 10 days today. The winning team receives prize money and valuable **18** sponsorships, but the glory of prevailing under such challenging circumstances is often the only prize top competitors seek.

Question 17

At this point, the writer is considering adding the following sentence:

"Additionally, teams must carry a heavy load: survival gear, an axe, snowshoes, dog food, and dog boots."

Should the writer make this addition here?

A) Yes, because it provides an effective transition.

B) No, because it contains a punctuation error.

C) Yes, because it provides effective support for the main topic of the paragraph.

D) No, because it provides irrelevant information.

Question 18

A) NO CHANGE

B) sponsorships but the glory of prevailing under such challenging circumstances

C) sponsorships; the glory of prevailing under such challenging circumstances

D) sponsorships – but, the glory of prevailing under such challenging circumstances

The mushers may take the prizes and awards, but many Iditarod fans believe the dogs are the true winners of the race. Indeed, the Iditarod Race relies on the dedication and courage of the sled dogs. Most of the sled dogs are Siberian **19** huskies and they generally weigh between thirty and sixty pounds. The dogs are elite athletes with astounding physical **20** endurance, and racers take care to ensure they stay in good health. The dogs are thoroughly examined by a veterinarian before the race to make sure they are fit to run. If a dog becomes injured or exhausted during the race, **21** they are carried in the sled basket. Veterinarians are available throughout the race course to treat sick dogs ensuring no animals are harmed during the competition.

Question 19

A) NO CHANGE

B) huskies and generally they

C) huskies; generally, they

D) huskies, generally they

Question 20

A) NO CHANGE

B) endurance, and mushers take care to ensure their teams stay in good health.

C) endurance; and racers take care to ensure they stay in good health.

D) endurance and mushers take care to ensure their teams stay in good health.

Question 21

A) NO CHANGE

B) it was

C) they would be

D) it is

CONTINUE

The Iditarod Trail Sled Dog Race is one of the most unique competitions in the world. It was inspired by a remarkable journey that dog sled teams took to deliver medicine across Alaska's backcountry, and it remains a true adventure fit only for the fiercest competitors. Mushers and their teams face real danger and appalling conditions over the course of the grueling race. 22

Question 22

At this point, the writer is considering adding the following sentence:

"Above all, the Iditarod Race is an example of how powerful the human and dog spirit can be when presented with some of the most challenging circumstances imaginable."

Should the writer make this addition here?

A) Yes, because it provides an effective conclusion.

B) Yes, because it provides information that helps clarify other information presented in the paragraph.

C) No, because it would be more effective as an introduction.

D) No, because it provides redundant information.

Questions 23-33 are based on the following passage:

Míriam Colón

Míriam Colón was an award-winning actress and founder of the Puerto Rican Traveling Theater in New York City. **23** Throughout her career, Colón helped create opportunities for Hispanic actors and actresses.

Early in her career, Colón **24** was a Broadway performer. Though the stage was her first love, she soon began appearing in movies and on popular television shows. Today, Colón is still widely known for her role as Mama Montana in the 1983 *Scarface* film. However, among Latino audiences one of her best-known **25** films was her role in in the 2013 drama *Bless Me, Ultima*, based on Rudolfo Anaya's Chicano literary classic. Colón played a New Mexican healer in the film, and for many she remains the most memorable part of this contemporary classic.

Question 23

At this point, the writer is considering adding the following sentence:

"A pioneer for Latino and Latina actors everywhere, Colón broke barriers across the entertainment industry."

Should the writer make this addition here?

A) Yes, because it provides effective support for a prior assertion.

B) Yes, because it provides an effective transition.

C) No, because it contains a modifier error.

D) No, because it provides irrelevant information.

Question 24

A) NO CHANGE

B) is

C) had been

D) has been

Question 25

A) NO CHANGE

B) contributions

C) parts

D) acting

Colón was born in Ponce, Puerto Rico on August 20, 1936. She grew up in San Juan where she began acting while still enrolled in high school. **26** She was limitlessly passionate and audited acting classes at the University of Puerto Rico. At only fifteen years old, she debuted as an actress in *Los Peloteros,* a film about baseball produced in Puerto Rico. **27** To the surprise of many, formal acting institutions immediately recognized her talent. At age seventeen, Colón became New York's Actors Studio's first Puerto Rican member in 1953.

28 Launching her professional acting career as a teenager, Colón worked consistently in film and television. Over the years, she appeared on many popular shows including *Gunsmoke, Bonanza,* and *Law & Order.* She even had a recent role in the television series *Better Call Saul.*

A) NO CHANGE

B) Her passion for acting was pursued with enthusiasm, and her next step was auditing

C) A limitlessly passionate actor Colón began auditing

D) Even as a high school student Colón was limitlessly passionate and audited

A) NO CHANGE

B) Although many were surprised, formal

C) To many's surprise, formal

D) To the surprise of many formal

A) NO CHANGE

B) From the time she launched

C) Despite launching

D) While launching

CONTINUE

Colón had a very successful acting career, but the establishment of the Puerto Rican Traveling Theater group is her most significant legacy. The theater group became possible following the success of the play *La Carreta*, a collaboration between Puerto Rican dramatist and writer René Marqués, director Roberto Rodríguez, and Colón as lead actor. The attention she received as start of the play allowed Colón to form one of the first permanent Hispanic theatrical companies, which worked to make bilingual theater more accessible. **29** The acting troupe originally made its way around New York City in a self-contained bus and a flat-bed truck with drop-down side wings that extended into a stage. **30** Colón established the company's home in 1976 in an empty firehouse where it is still located today. Today, the company continues to tour and produce bilingual theater for neighborhoods across New York City.

Question 29

The writer is considering deleting the underlined sentence. Should the sentence be kept or deleted?

A) Kept, because it provides an effective transition between one concept and the next.

B) Kept, because it shows the method by which the troupe traveled.

C) Deleted, because it would function better as an introduction to the paragraph.

D) Deleted, because it provides irrelevant information.

Question 30

A) NO CHANGE

B) Colón established the company's home in an empty firehouse

C) In 1976, Colón established the company's home in an empty firehouse,

D) In an empty firehouse Colón established the company's home in 1976

Colón created the Puerto Rican Traveling Theater as a stage to highlight the tradition of Latino and Puerto Rican playwrights, actors, and directors. Some of Colón's other achievements include receiving a 1993 Obie Award for lifetime achievement in off-Broadway theater. She also received the 2015 National Medal of the Arts from President Barack Obama. **31**

At this point, the writer is considering adding the following sentence:

"However, the Puerto Rican Traveling Theater remains Colón's most impactful legacy.

Should the writer make this addition here?

A) Yes, because it provides data that helps clarify other information presented in the paragraph.

B) No, because it provides a more effective introduction.

C) Yes, because it provides an effective transition.

D) No, because it provides irrelevant information.

CONTINUE

The theater is credited for **32** the development of hundreds of Latino artists legitimizing cultural connections through the Spanish-speaking world and encouraging multicultural community engagement. Colón died on March 3, 2017 at the age of eighty, but her impact on the entertainment industry remains significant, even after her passing. **33**

Question 32

A) NO CHANGE

B) helping to develop the careers of

C) to develop the careers of

D) developing the careers of

Question 33

Which of the following most effectively summarizes the main point of the passage?

A) Despite her passing, Colón's legacy remains.

B) Colón's work is an important part of America's cultural history.

C) Colón's acting career speaks volumes for her accomplishments.

D) In addition to her own accomplishments, Colón opened doors for Latinos across the entertainment industry.

CONTINUE

Questions 34-44 are based on the following passage:

Vaccines and Public Health

Vaccines **34** work by introducing a weakened or deactivated form of pathogen to a patient's immune system. The immune system responds **35** by antibodies that fight the pathogen allowing it to quickly recognize and respond when a stronger version of the pathogen is reintroduced.

Widespread vaccinations have greatly reduced the spread of disease in countries all over the world. For example, **36** vaccinations have resulted in bringing down the number of people infected by smallpox in the United States each year from 16,000 to zero; likewise, polio vaccines reduced cases of the devastating disease from 29,000 to none at all. **37** Vaccines are easily accessed in the United States; for this reason, mortality rates from infectious diseases have dropped dramatically.

Question 34

A) NO CHANGE

B) work when they introduce

C) work with

D) introduce

Question 35

A) NO CHANGE

B) with

C) for

D) in

Question 36

A) NO CHANGE

B) vaccinations have resulted in a reduction

C) vaccinations have reduced

D) vaccinations have lowered the level of

Question 37

A) NO CHANGE

B) Vaccines are generally easy to access in the United States and thus

C) Vaccines are easily accessed, so

D) Because vaccines are easily accessible in the United States,

CONTINUE

The dawn of modern vaccination began in 1796 after Edward Jenner produced the first vaccine to inoculate patients against smallpox. **38** **39** After the smallpox vaccine was produced it was systematically distributed to the public resulting in complete eradication of the disease from the world in 1979. The next milestone for vaccinology occurred when Louis Pasteur developed the first inactive anthrax vaccine as well as a live attenuated cholera vaccine. These groundbreaking inventions and Pasteur's other innovative work ushered in the dawn of bacteriology.

Question 38

At this point, the writer is considering adding the following sentence:

"Although, some evidence suggests that ancient Chinese healers practiced some form of smallpox inoculation as early as 1000 CE."

Should the writer make this addition here?

A) Yes, because it provides an effective introduction to new concepts.

B) Yes, because it provides information that helps clarify other information presented in the paragraph.

C) No, because it interrupts the paragraph's description of the development of modern vaccines.

D) No, because it provides irrelevant information.

Question 39

A) NO CHANGE

B) Public health officials systematically distributed the smallpox vaccine

C) Once public health officials had systematically distributed the vaccine,

D) Once the vaccine was systematically distributed,

CONTINUE

After Pasteur's experiments, scientists started work on a slew of new antitoxins and vaccines. They developed vaccines for many **40** diseases, such as: tetanus, diphtheria, plague, typhoid, and tuberculosis. During the middle of the 20th century, scientists even started making rapid discoveries that led to the production of vaccines for formerly devastating childhood diseases such as measles, mumps, polio, and rubella.

Figure 1, below, shows an estimated annual morbidity for several infectious diseases before and after vaccines were developed to **41** prevent them.

Figure 1: Estimated Annual Morbidity

Disease	Before Vaccine	After Vaccine
Diphtheria	21,000	0
Influenza	20,000	243
Hepatitis A	117,000	11,050
Hepatitis B	66,000	11,300
Measles	530,000	61
Mumps	162,000	982
Pertussis	200,000	13,500
Pneumococcal	16,000	4,160
Polio	16,300	0
Rubella	48,000	4
Smallpox	29,000	0
Tetanus	580	14
Varicella	4,000,000	500,000

Vaccines have been very effective at stopping certain diseases from infecting patients. **42**

Question 40

A) NO CHANGE

B) many diseases, including: tetanus

C) many diseases; tetanus

D) many diseases, such as tetanus

Question 41

A) NO CHANGE

B) treat

C) reduce

D) cure

Question 42

Which of the following provides the most effective support from Figure 1?

A) For example, smallpox was completely eradicated in 1979.

B) For example, diseases like diphtheria, polio, and smallpox have been completely eliminated.

C) Measles and mumps were once devastating childhood diseases.

D) Although for some diseases, such as tetanus, there were very few reported cases to begin with.

CONTINUE

43 The practice of vaccinating redefined the landscape of infectious disease treatment. In some cases, vaccination led to the eradication of diseases that once terrorized civilizations across the globe. Unfortunately, however, certain regions of the world still struggle to manage with the public health issues created by preventable diseases. **44** As the history of modern vaccination has demonstrated, preventable diseases can be effectively addressed through diligent research and effective coordination.

Question 43

A) NO CHANGE

B) Introducing vaccination into medicine

C) Vaccination introduction for diseases

D) Vaccination

Question 44

At this point, the writer is considering adding the following sentence:

"In these places, public health officials must do more to ensure that vaccinations are effectively distributed to people in need."

Should the writer make this addition here?

A) Yes, because it provides an effective introduction to new concepts.

B) Yes, because it provides an effective transition that improves clarity and flow.

C) No, because it interrupts the paragraph's description of the challenges facing countries with public health challenges.

D) No, because it provides irrelevant information.

CONTINUE

PRACTICE
TEST 7

Writing and Language Test

25 MINUTES, 44 QUESTIONS

DIRECTIONS

Each passage below is followed by a number of questions. For some questions, you will be asked to consider how the passage may be improved. For others, you will consider how the passage may be edited to correct errors in sentence structure, word usage, grammar, or punctuation.

Some questions will direct your attention to an underlined portion of the passage. Others will direct you to a location in a passage or ask you to consider the passage as a whole.

Read each passage carefully. After reading the passage, choose the answer to each question that most effectively improves the quality of writing of the passage or improves its conformance to standard written English. Most questions include a "NO CHANGE" option, which you should select if you think the best choice is to leave the applicable portion of the passage as-is.

Questions 1-11 are based on the following passage:

The Art and Science of Beekeeping

(1)

Beekeeping, also known as apiculture, is the practice of caring for, managing, and supporting a bee colony. Beekeepers, or apiarists, keep bees to pollinate their crops and flowers or to collect honey and other natural byproducts the hives produce. **1**

Which choice provides the best conclusion for this paragraph?

A) NO CHANGE

B) From beeswax and honey to pollen and royal jelly, bees produce a number of things people use every day.

C) Bees do many important things for both people and the environment.

D) From providing valuable substances like honey, beeswax, and royal jelly to pollinating crops, bees perform several important activities for both humans and the environment.

(2)

A beehive consists of a queen bee, her drones, and the hive workers. The hive is populated by the offspring of a single queen bee. Drone bees are male bees with the sole purpose of spreading genetics within the colony by mating with the queen bee. **2** <u>Worker bees are female bees who perform most of the day-to-day activities that keep the hive going: foraging, feeding the younger bees, producing and storing honey, making wax, cleaning, and guarding the hive against intruders.</u>

(3)

3 The honeybee is seeing a decrease in population every year. Unfortunately, the cause of their declining population is largely unknown, but some believe strong contributing factors are the climate and colony collapse disorder. The collapse of bee populations worldwide would create an environmental disaster of life-threatening **4** <u>proportions. Bees</u> are a critical part of the ecosystem.

Question 2

The writer is considering deleting the underlined sentence. Should the sentence be kept or deleted?

A) Kept, because it provides information that helps explain a prior statement.

B) Kept, because it provides an effective transition between one concept in the passage and the next.

C) Deleted, because it ignores the fact that there are many important pollinators besides bees.

D) Deleted, because it interrupts the paragraph's description of beehives.

Question 3

To make this passage most logical, paragraph (3) should be placed:

A) where it is now

B) after paragraph (4)

C) after paragraph (5)

D) before paragraph (2)

Question 4

A) NO CHANGE

B) proportions because bees

C) proportions, because bees

D) proportions; bees

CONTINUE ▶

(4)

During the warmer months, the queen bee lays **5** the eggs. Worker bees stay active by buzzing around to collect pollen from plants and flowers for the hive. **6** In foraging, worker bees cover themselves in pollen, store it on their legs, and bring the golden granules back to the hive. Any pollen **7** left on their backs, and not stored on their legs, is transferred from flower to flower. The bees then turn the collected pollen into honey and store it in the hives. During the winter months, the colony will typically eat through forty to sixty pounds of stored honey.

Question 5

A) NO CHANGE

B) her eggs

C) eggs

D) some eggs

Question 6

A) NO CHANGE

B) While foraging,

C) Although

D) Foraging,

Question 7

A) NO CHANGE

B) left on their backs is

C) left on their backs – not stored on their legs – is

D) not stored on their legs is left on their backs and

CONTINUE

(5)

Domesticated colonies are made up of thousands of bees, and it is a beekeeper's duty to keep the entire colony healthy and productive. **8** A beekeeper regularly assesses the health of the hive, checks for mite infestations, and treats the hive if it has any problems. Beekeepers may also feed bees, clean and construct their hives, raise and replace queen bees, and replace combs. Of the 20,000 known bee species worldwide, the species most common among beekeepers is the *Apis* **9** *mellifera, commonly* known as the European honeybee. In addition to producing copious amounts of sweet honey, these bees are relatively docile and only sting as a last resort, since once they sting, they die.

Question 8

At this point, the writer is considering adding the following sentence:

"They typically live in manmade hives, which can be located almost anywhere including private gardens and rooftops."

Should the writer make this addition here?

A) Yes, because it provides an effective transition.

B) Yes, because it provides information that helps clarify prior statements.

C) No, because it would be more effective as an introduction at the beginning of the paragraph.

D) No, because it interrupts the paragraph's description of beekeeping activities.

Question 9

A) NO CHANGE

B) *mellifera,* which are commonly

C) *mellifera.* This bee is commonly

D) *mellifera*; commonly

CONTINUE

(6)

Without bees, many ecosystems would collapse. Humans and most animals rely directly or indirectly on pollination from honeybees. Bees ensure human food security by pollinating crops and creating honey. In fact, thirty percent of the world's most common food crops and ninety percent of flowers rely entirely on the honeybee's pollination services to grow. **10** Bees are directly influenced by the local environment around them, which plays a large role in their behavior and success. **11**

At this point, the writer is considering changing the underlined sentence to the following:

"Because bees are influenced by the environment around them, human activities can have a major impact on their behavior and success."

Should the writer make this change here?

A) Yes, because it provides an effective conclusion.

B) Yes, because it improves clarity, tone, or voice of the sentence.

C) No, because it would be more effective as an introduction to the paragraph.

D) No, because it the information is irrelevant.

Which choice provides the best conclusion for this paragraph?

A) NO CHANGE

B) In order to prevent the potential collapse of critical food and ecological systems, honeybee protection is critical.

C) Preserving honey bees is critical as they provide important benefits for beekeepers and natural ecosystems alike.

D) Without honeybees, life as we know it would change forever in ways we would prefer not to see.

CONTINUE

Questions 12-22 are based on the following passage:

Running a Marathon

A marathon is a footrace spanning twenty-six miles and three hundred eighty-five yards. Each year, hundreds of these races are held around the world with hundreds of thousands of runners competing to win. Over time, the marathon has grown in popularity and marathon runners have drastically improved their skills. **12** While many marathon runners are fierce competitors, the event is generally seen as a fun and rewarding activity. Notably, however, the recreational sprit of the modern marathon is a far cry from the experience of the first person to have ever run the race. **13** But for the first marathoner, Pheidippides, his marathon was not for fun; it ultimately cost **14** him his life.

Question 12

At this point, the writer is considering adding the following sentence:

"In fact, the marathon has become the premier long-distance race and is the longest running race at the Olympic Games."

Should the writer make this addition here?

A) Yes, because it provides information that helps explain what comes next.

B) No, because it provides a more effective introduction and should be placed at the beginning of the sentence.

C) Yes, because it provides effective support.

D) No, because it provides irrelevant information.

Question 13

A) NO CHANGE

B) The first marathoner, Pheidippides, did not race for fun;

C) The first marathoner, Pheidippides, did not enjoy his race;

D) For the first marathoner, Pheidippides, his race was not for fun;

Question 14

A) NO CHANGE

B) himself

C) the runner's

D) DELETE the underlined word.

15 The marathon has its origins in the journey Greek soldier Pheidippides took to deliver news from Marathon, Greece to Athens, Greece. Pheidippides was a news courier in the ancient Greek armies. In 490 BCE, he was ordered to run from Athens to Sparta to request **16** the Spartans help against the invading Persians. As legend has it, Pheidippides ran over 150 miles each way to Sparta and back, then the next day he ran another 25 miles to another Greek city, Marathon, and back to Athens to deliver news of the Athenian victory. Immediately after relaying the news, Pheidippides collapsed and **17** died after the race had been run, more than 325 miles in a span of just a few days. This story may be more legend than truth, but the fact remains that Pheidippides' heroic efforts inspired the modern marathon.

Question 15

Which choice provides the best introduction to this paragraph?

A) NO CHANGE

B) Marathons today can trace their origins back to Pheidippides, an ancient Greek soldier.

C) Today, marathon prizes are awarded in honor of Pheidippides, an ancient Greek soldier and news courier.

D) DELETE the underlined sentence.

Question 16

A) NO CHANGE

B) the Spartan's

C) the Spartans'

D) their

Question 17

A) NO CHANGE

B) died; he had run

C) died; he ran

D) died. After running

Harkening back to the ancient legend, **18** organizers added the marathon to the first Olympic Games in 1896. This **19** first modern Olympic marathon took place on the same route Pheidippides took from Marathon to Athens. **20** **(1)** A Greek citizen named Spyros Louis beat sixteen other competitors to win the gold medal in the first Olympic marathon event, completing the race in just under three hours. **(2)** The first Olympic marathon prompted an enthusiasm for running and an increase in competition. **(3)** However, it was not without its scandals as **21** well. In fact, the bronze medal winner in the first Olympic marathon was disqualified after officials learned he took a carriage for part of the race. **(4)** Regardless, glory won the day.

Question 18

A) NO CHANGE

B) organizers of the first modern Olympic Games added the marathon race to the events

C) when they planned the first modern Olympic Games, the marathon race was added

D) the first modern Olympic marathon race was held

Question 19

A) NO CHANGE

B) modern Olympic marathon

C) marathon

D) race

Question 20

To make this passage most logical, sentence (1) sentence should be placed:

A) where it is now

B) before sentence (3)

C) before sentence (4)

D) after sentence (4)

Question 21

A) NO CHANGE

B) well. The

C) well; in fact, the

D) well, in fact, the

22 On the same course that Louis ran to win the first Olympic marathon, Stefano Baldini placed first in the event in 2004 with a time of just under 2 hours and 11 minutes. Baldini's time was 48 minutes better than Louis' and he raced against 100 of the most elite long-distance runners in the world. In 2018, Eliud Kipchoge broke the marathon world record with a time of 2 hours, 1 minute, and 39 seconds – a staggering pace of a four minutes and forty seconds per mile. The competition and popularity of marathon running is so great that even an above average amateur runner could break Louis' gold medal time from the 1896 Olympics. What remains remarkable is that the marathon's origins can be traced back to Pheidippides' heroic running journey in ancient Greece.

Question 22

A) NO CHANGE

B) On the same course which Louis had ran to win

C) On the same course, which Louis ran to win,

D) On the same course which Louis ran to win

Questions 23-33 are based on the following passage:

Eruptions of the Semeru Volcano

Standing at 3,676 meters above the coastal plains, the Semeru volcano, also referred to as "Mahameru" or "The Great Mountain," is the highest volcano in Java, Indonesia. The Semeru Volcano is also one of the most active volcanos in the "Ring of Fire," a geological hot spot for volcanic eruptions and earthquakes. **23** The Semeru volcano typically erupts several times each hour releasing gases that rise several hundreds of meters above the volcanic crater.

The center for activity in the Semeru volcano is at the Jonggring Seloko **24** crater, which appears on the southeast side of the volcano. Around the Jonggring-Seloko vent, regular ash plumes collect and occasionally collapse in avalanches of soot. Pyroclastic and lava flows can travel down the southeast side of the ravine. **25** And similar to its neighboring volcano, Merapi, the Semeru volcano has claimed numerous lives.

Question 23

At this point, the writer is considering adding the following sentence:

"The Ring of Fire consists of volcanic island arcs and ocean trenches that encircle the Pacific Basin."

Should the writer make this addition here?

A) Yes, because it provides effective support for a prior assertion.

B) Yes, because it provides information that helps clarify key terms.

C) No, because it interrupts the paragraph's description of the Semeru volcano.

D) No, because it provides irrelevant information.

Question 24

A) NO CHANGE

B) crater that appears on

C) crater on

D) crater,

Question 25

A) NO CHANGE

B) Along with a neighboring volcano, Merapi, the

C) Not unlike its neighboring volcano, Merapi, the

D) DELETE THE UNDERLINED SENTENCE

In the past, even moderate to moderately-large eruptions of the Semeru volcano **26** have devastating impacts. For example, **27** two eruptions that took place in 1909 and 1981 were characterized as moderate to moderately-large. These eruptions produced pyroclastic and lava flows, which resulted in secondary mudflows that killed nearly six hundred people. **28** More recently, throughout the 19th and 20th centuries, most of the volcano's eruptions have been small to moderate.

Question 26

A) NO CHANGE

B) has

C) have had

D) will have had

Question 27

A) NO CHANGE

B) two eruptions, taking place in 1909 and 1981 respectively, were measured by scientists as moderate to moderately-large.

C) two eruptions, occurring in 1909 and 1981, reached moderate to moderately-large levels.

D) two eruptions, taking place in 1909 and 1981, were characterized as moderate to moderately-large.

Question 28

A) NO CHANGE

B) Throughout

C) While throughout

D) Fortunately, throughout

In recent years, the Semeru volcano has had occasional lava flows trickle down its sides and into the surrounding ravines. [29] However, some people are growing increasingly concerned that the volcano is ready for a larger eruption. The volcano's eruptions are incredibly frequent and hard to predict, but eruptions have been lasting longer and longer in recent years. In fact, the volcano [30] has been in almost constant eruption since 1967.

Question 29

The writer is considering deleting the underlined sentence. Should the sentence be kept or deleted?

A) Kept, because it provides an effective transition between one concept and the next.

B) Kept, because it shows the impact of planning on emergency prevention.

C) Deleted, because it ignores the fact that volcano eruptions release toxic gases.

D) Deleted, because it provides irrelevant information.

Question 30

A) NO CHANGE

B) has been constantly in eruption

C) has been erupting almost constantly

D) has erupted almost constantly

Figure 1, below, shows the number of eruptions recorded at the Semeru volcano between 1829 and the present day.

Figure 1: Eruptions of the Semeru Volcano

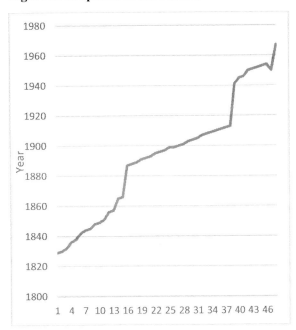

The Semaru volcano's activity raises red flags. **31** Only time will tell if the Semeru volcano will settle down after over half a century of constant activity. However, **32** until then, visitors to the scenic area are taking their lives into their own hands.

Which of the following provides the most effective support from Figure 1?

A) The number of eruptions of the Semaru volcano has consistently increased over the past century.

B) The Semaru volcano erupted over forty times in the year 1960.

C) The Semaru volcano is erupting with increasing frequency.

D) The number of eruptions of the Semaru volcano has become concerning.

A) NO CHANGE

B) then,

C) until that,

D) DELETE the underlined portion of the sentence.

The Semeru volcano has been the site of numerous deaths. **33** Regardless, the beauty of the landscape surrounding the volcano makes the area a popular hiking destination for travelers and adventurers. However, hiking in this area is incredibly risky because the volcano has been in near continuous eruption since 1967.

At this point, the writer is considering adding the following sentence:

"In the last 30 years, more than 500 people have fallen victim to the Great Mountain's eruptions.

Should the writer make this addition here?

    A) Yes, because it provides data that helps support a prior assertion.

    B) No, because it provides a more effective introduction.

    C) Yes, because it provides data that helps clarify information that follows.

    D) No, because it provides irrelevant information.

Questions 34-44 are based on the following passage:

The Sistine Chapel

Under the direction of Pope Sixtus IV, the Sistine Chapel was built in 1479 near the Belvedere Courtyard in the Vatican City. The papal chapel was built to serve as a place for the cardinals of the Catholic Church to congregate for the election of a new pope. The Sistine Chapel is still used for this purpose, **34** among others.

(1) **35** When the Sistine Chapel first opened its doors - between the years of 1508 and 1512 - its ceiling was blue and speckled with golden stars. **36** (2) In 1512, Pope Julius II asked Michelangelo to paint the ceiling of the Sistine Chapel so that it would no longer pale in comparison to the chapel's decorated walls. (3) The chapel walls were adorned with large tapestries by Raphael and masterpieces painted by renowned artists such as Pietro Perugino, Domenico Ghirlandaio, and Sandro Botticelli. (4) These masterpieces made the cathedral's ceiling seem plain by comparison, and church officials felt as if something had to be done.

Question 34

At this point, the writer is considering revising the underlined to the following:

"but the cathedral's lavishly decorated ceilings are what has earned it fame over the centuries."

Should the writer make this change here?

A) Yes, because it provides an effective transition.

B) Yes, because it provides information that helps clarify other information presented in the paragraph.

C) No, because it would be more effective as an introduction.

D) No, because it provides redundant information.

Question 35

A) NO CHANGE

B) Between the years of 1508 and 1512, the Sistine Chapel's original

C) The Sistine Chapel's original

D) Between the years of 1508 and 1512, the

Question 36

To make this passage most logical, sentence (2) sentence should be placed:

A) where it is now

B) before sentence (1)

C) before sentence (4)

D) after sentence (4)

CONTINUE

37 During the time, Michelangelo had already become famous for his work as a sculptor. His depictions of the Pieta and the statue of David earned the artist recognition across Europe. **38** As a result, many critics expected the artist to fail at his monumental task. However, the supposedly inexperienced painter left all of Rome in awe with his final creation. In fact, Michelangelo created what is now considered to be a cornerstone piece **39** in High Renaissance art.

Question 37

A) NO CHANGE

B) By the time the church sought his assistance,

C) Meanwhile,

D) DELETE the underlined portion.

Question 38

At this point, the writer is considering adding the following sentence:

"While Michelangelo was esteemed as a sculptor, he was not particularly well-recognized for his work as a painter.

Should the writer make this addition here?

A) Yes, because it provides an effective transition.

B) Yes, because it provides relevant support.

C) No, because it provides redundant information.

D) No, because it provides irrelevant information.

Question 39

A) NO CHANGE

B) to

C) of

D) for

CONTINUE

Michelangelo's masterpiece centered around nine scenes from the Book of **40** Genesis. The story beginning with scenes of the creation of the world, followed by the creation of Adam and Eve and the expulsion from the Garden of Eden; the rendition concludes with the story of Noah and the flood. Michelangelo's frescoes **41** of the creation of Adam and the banishment of Adam and Eve from the Garden of Eden **42** represent the most important scenes on the ceiling of the Sistine Chapel.

Question 40

A) NO CHANGE

B) Genesis, the story beginning

C) Genesis. The story begins

D) Genesis; the story begins

Question 41

A) NO CHANGE

B) depicting

C) making

D) demonstrating

Question 42

A) NO CHANGE

B) has been representing

C) represented

D) was widely considered to represent

One particular fresco decorating the ceiling of the Sistine Chapel, the *Creation of Adam,* is among the most famous depictions of High Renaissance art in the world. [43] Its popularity rivals the iconic standing of Leonardo da Vinci's *Mona Lisa*, and Michelangelo's depiction of the hands of God reaching out to Adam continue to be reproduced in modern film, art, and media to this day. [44]

Question 43

A) NO CHANGE

B) As popular as Leonardo da Vinci's *Mona Lisa,*

C) Its popularity rivals the iconic standing of the *Mona Lisa,* and

D) DELETE the underlined portion.

Question 44

Which of the following most effectively summarizes the main point of the passage?

A) Michelangelo's Sistine Chapel represents the pinnacle of High Renaissance art.

B) Although everyone expected him to fail at painting the Sistine Chapel, Michelangelo produced one of the world's most popular works of art.

C) Because it is so beautiful, the Sistine Chapel attracts millions of visitors every year.

D) Michelangelo's masterpiece, the Sistine Chapel, is an intricate piece of High Renaissance art that remains popular around the world today.

CONTINUE

ANSWER KEYS

&

EXPLANATIONS

ALL 7 PRACTICE TESTS

Writing Test 1 : Answer Key

1. C	28. B
2. B	29. A
3. A	30. D
4. D	31. C
5. C	32. A
6. C	33. A
7. B	
8. B	34. B
9. B	35. C
10. B	36. B
11. C	37. B
	38. C
12. A	39. D
13. A	40. A
14. B	41. D
15. C	42. A
16. A	43. D
17. C	44. A
18. D	
19. D	
20. A	
21. B	
22. A	
23. B	
24. B	
25. C	
26. D	
27. D	

WRITING & LANGUAGE TEST 1
Answers & Explanations

Passage 1

Question 1

C is the best answer.
The key to a good **topic sentence** lies in its being an effective **lead in** to the major **theme** that is being addressed in that paragraph. In this selection, sentence 2 talks about why people find nonfiction boring. Sentence 3 discusses what some authors do to make nonfiction interesting. Therefore, the **most suitable topic sentence would be one that puts forward a summary** of those ideas: how writers make nonfiction engaging. In addition, the title of the passage has the **KEYWORD** "engaging." So, you can also choose an answer with this keyword **(KEYWORD CONNECTION TECHNIQUE).**

A is incorrect because **it implies that the current topic sentence is effective**, which – as stated above – it is not. The current topic sentence **does not effectively lead into the major themes** being dealt with in that paragraph. The main idea of the paragraph is not about the definition of "nonfiction writing." Instead, it's about how writers make nonfiction engaging by "breathing life in to facts."

B is incorrect because it captures **one part of the argument** presented in the paragraph (readers finding nonfiction boring), but it does not address another part to the argument (how some writers make nonfiction engaging).

D is incorrect because it is **irrelevant** to the content that follows in the rest of the paragraph. The paragraph is not about author's **"careers."** The word career is not even mentioned in the paragraph.

Question 2

B is the best answer. This sentence speaks about the time that McPhee has dedicated to his career. Using that **starting point,** the reader is told about the various stories that he has written in that time. Because of the way in which the sentence has been used, it **provides an effective transition** between one concept in the paragraph and the next. It should be kept!

A is incorrect because the lines that follow this one **do not speak about** the investment of time in a career. Instead, they speak about the various stories and topics that McPhee has address in six decades.

C is incorrect because this statement and the lines following it **have nothing to do with comparing** McPhee to other writers. It is simply a statement to evidence the **duration** that this writer has spent working on his craft.

D is incorrect because this paragraph **does not describe nonfiction writing.** It is a description of McPhee and the various stories that he has written. Therefore, this answer **does not accurately reflect** the contents of the paragraph in question.

Question 3
A is the best answer.
No change is needed in this sentence because it accurately uses the **colon (:). A COLON is used to introduce a list, an explanation of the previously stated idea, or a quotation.** Here a colon is used to explain or clarify the common theme that McPhee's stories share. Immediately after the colon, it is said that, "each is a subject about which McPhee himself became fascinated." This phrase explains the previously stated idea regarding the "commonality" in all of McPhee's stories.

> B is incorrect because of a **missing colon** between the words, "commonality" and "each." As the colon rule suggests, **before a new clause is introduced as a clarification to a preceding clause, the two need to be linked with a colon.**
>
> C is incorrect because a comma is used **when listing items** or **when adding an additional phrase in the middle of an already existing sentence.** Since the sentence here does not fit either category, a comma is **an unsuitable punctuation.**
>
> D is incorrect because the second clause seeks to clarify the preceding one. **Semicolons act as a pause, similar to a period, when connecting different parts of the same sentence.** Unlike a colon, **a semicolon does not have to be used to clarify the information that comes before it.** So, while a semi-colon **could technically** be used in this sentence, a colon is **more suitable.** Furthermore. a **semi-colon is only used between clauses that EACH have their own subject, verb and object.** Since this condition is not met here, the semi-colon is a less suitable option.

Question 4
D is the best answer. This choice, first and foremost, **varies vocabulary.** Since the previous sentences ends with the term "fascinated," the next one begins with a **synonym** (a word that means the same thing), i.e., "captivated." In addition to the **vocabulary choice,** this sentence is **active** and tells us what the writer's captivation allowed him to **build into his style.** So, while the current sentence gives credit to the fascination, this choice **gives credit to the writer.**

> A is incorrect because it **implies** that the current sentence is **sufficient.** But as we see above, **there are ways to make the text more engaging.**
>
> B is incorrect. This choice would create **an abrupt transition** between the lines rather than allowing the subject of one sentence to **fluidly** become the object of the next.
>
> C is incorrect because it **repeats the word** "fascinated" and, as described above, it is generally advised to **avoid word repetition** so close together. Furthermore, like the original sentence, this choice makes the writer **passive** and his fascination **active** when clearly it is the writer who is active in the development of their style.

Question 5

C is the best answer. Since this sentence marks the beginning of a new paragraph, using **the third person pronoun** ("he") lacks a **point of reference**. In each new paragraph, **the reader needs to be reminded who the subject is before a pronoun can be used to refer to them.**

A is incorrect because the pronoun "he" **is used at the start of a new paragraph.** This can **cause confusion for readers.** Who does the "he" **refer** to?

B is incorrect for two reasons: because it uses the pronoun to begin a new paragraph and because the "himself" **is unnecessary here. "Himself" is a reflexive pronoun. REFLEXIVE PRONOUNS only need to be used when the subject and the object of a sentence are the same.** In this sentence, McPhee is the subject, while the Pulitzer Prize is the object. Therefore, a reflexive pronoun like "himself" is not needed.

D is incorrect because of the **reflexive pronoun rule mentioned above. The subject and the object of the sentence need to be the same for the reflexive pronoun to be used.** For example, "He writes the stories himself because he does not trust his interns to do it right." Here "he" is both the subject and the object making it necessary to use a reflexive pronoun like "himself."

Question 6

C is the best answer. As you'll recall, a comma is used **when adding an additional phrase in the middle of an already existing sentence.** Here the existing sentence is "He has been nominated for the Pulitzer Prize four times." The additional phrase is "the highest honor in literature." This additional phrase is considered a **"non-essential"** element because it's an extra detail.

For example: Donald Trump, the president of USA, likes to play golf. Here, the comma phrase "the president of USA" is an extra detail that must be set off with **DOUBLE COMMAS.** So, remember to use **double commas when adding an additional phrase in the middle of an existing sentence.**

A is incorrect. **DASHES are used to set off material for emphasis, to indicate sentence introductions or conclusions or to mark bonus phrases that are not integral to the meaning of a sentence.** So, while using dashes **both before and after** "the highest honor in literature" might work grammatically in this context – to set off material for emphasis or to indicate a bonus phrase -- using it only **before** the phrase makes this punctuation unsuitable.

B is technically accurate. However, with the current sentence, given that there is only one additional phrase to be added to an existing sentence, commas are the more simple and elegant choice. As a general rule, **dashes are used when a sentence is already overrun with (has many) additional phrases that are already separated by commas.**

D is incorrect because the additional phrase is introduced with a comma but is left "hanging" at the end. Thus, the additional phrase runs into the second part of the existing sentence taking away from the meaning of the words.

Question 7

B is the best answer. By **connecting the clauses** that serve as the other's subject and object (see explanation below) and by using **", which" to include a non-essential element to the content**, this is the most suitable answer. **A NON-ESSENTIAL ELEMENT** (bonus phrase) is one that is not **absolutely necessary** for the sentence to make sense. Here, while it helps to know that the author took twenty years to write this book, **it is not essential to the content of the sentence.**

A is incorrect. The second part of this sentence is currently made up of multiple clauses that have **not been separated from each other through punctuations or conjunctions.** Therefore, it makes the sentence extremely difficult to understand. We can see that two of these clauses "a set of books" and "about the geology of North America" serve as **subject and object** with the third clause "written over the course of twenty years" being **additional information.** Therefore, the sentence needs to be rewritten to connect the subject and object directly adding the extra information at the end. Furthermore, **it is incorrect to use a COMMA before "that,"** when "that" is being used to add an additional element to the sentence.

C is incorrect because while it does connect the subject and the object (the books with their topic), the additional information about the time it took to write the book is not demarcated with the necessary punctuation. This **lack of punctuation** makes the sentence harder to read/understand.

D is less correct. Although this choice does function **grammatically** (the comma before "that" has been removed), this choice uses the **passive voice** by saying "that was written by him" rather than "he wrote." **As a general rule, the ACTIVE voice is preferred to make the text more engaging for the reader.**

Question 8

B is the best answer. Paragraph 1 talks about non-fiction in general and introduces us to McPhee. Paragraph 2 describes the topics McPhee writes about and ends by talking about qualities in his writing. The current Paragraph 3 talks about his successes as a writer and references specific books written by him. Given this, since Paragraph 4 says more about his writing style and his use of particular strategies, **it belongs above Paragraph 3.** This would create **an effective transition** from that paragraph's ending lines about what sets McPhee's writing apart to this paragraph's more detailed consideration of those aspects.

All the other answer choices **disrupt the flow** between the paragraphs. Given that this passage has a pattern of moving **from the more general to the more specific** moving, this paragraph anywhere other than above Paragraph 3 would not be an effective choice.

When attempting to think about **paragraph flow between and within paragraphs,** it is generally advisable to **start from the general and move to the specific.** In this particular example, for instance, you could consider the following as a structure for flow:
Paragraph 1: general content about nonfiction and ending with specific mention of McPhee
Paragraph 2: general content about McPhee's approach to topics and ending with specific mention of stylistic qualities
Paragraph 3 (should be): general explanations of those stylistic qualities and end with specific examples of their use in specific works

Question 9

B is the best answer. The **KEYWORDS** "rather than" **imply a comparison between** a focus on characters **and** something else. Given the qualities of nonfiction (of being based on facts) and given the other options presented, this is the most suitable answer.

A is incorrect because the **reflexive pronoun seems misused. REFLEXIVE PRONOUNS only need to be used when the subject and the object of a sentence are the same.** Here, the subject is "the characters of the story," not "he." Therefore, not changing the current wording is not an option.

C is incorrect because in the **context** of the previous sentence of how he brings in a "human element" into his nonfiction it is **meaningless** to say that he focuses on his characters rather than the "author."

D is incorrect. Although technically it would work to say "anything else," the term is **extremely vague.** As a general rule, **it is better to avoid terms like "anything else," "etc," and "and so on."** Clearly mention **what you need to say even if that means listing multiple things.**

Question 10

B is the best answer. Since the sentence that comes before it presents **a complex idea** regarding McPhee's **focus on people through facts, it is good practice to give an example that SHOWS the readers what is meant by this.**

A is incorrect. The additional sentence is **not required as a transition because the current sentences transition well even without it.** The reason this additional sentence is needed is to better clarify an idea and not as a transition.

C is incorrect. The last line of a paragraph is generally considered **a transition sentence** that takes the reader from the idea presented in one to the idea contained in the next. Ending a paragraph with an example **is often not a good idea** since it is too specific to make **an effective transition to the next paragraph. Transition sentences like topic sentences are better when they are more general allowing the reader to prepare for the ideas that follow.**

D is incorrect because the information contained in this statement is **not irrelevant.** The example effectively **matches with the content that is described earlier.** By describing how McPhee gathered information by working with "wacky scientists," we gain insight into his process, a process that is notable for valuing people more than facts. Therefore, by providing such information, the additional sentence is **relevant.**

Question 11

C is the best answer. The sentence before this one already mentions that McPhee is a "respected professor" which already implies that he is passing on his love for writing to the next generation. The underlined sentence, therefore, is **redundant** because it simply **repeats existing information** in a different way.

A is incorrect. To say that the underlined statement shows the impact of mentorship on a successful career **is an ASSUMPTION** since what is spoken of here is only Mchphee and his work as an educator. We are not told anything about mentorship as a larger concept.

B is incorrect. This sentence is **not needed to transition** from "for over forty years" to "among his former students." In fact, the underlined sentence **interrupts the flow** of the paragraph.

D is incorrect. Once again, this statement makes **ASSUMPTIONS about the larger implications of the text, i.e., that the underlined sentence SHOULD say something** about the role of mentorship (in general) in making people successful writers. There is no need for the sentence to address these large ideas since they are **outside the scope** of what is being discussed in the passage.

Passage 2

Question 12

A is the best answer. As mentioned earlier, the **DASH** is used **to indicate sentence introductions or conclusions** and **to mark text for emphasis.** Here, the dash is used to emphasize the four preceding nouns, which introduce the sentence. Furthermore, **colons** are used to introduce the clarifying part of a sentence (which here is "the mountain lion"). **A COLON is used to introduce a list, an explanation of the previously stated idea, or a quotation.** By using the appropriate punctuation marks to introduce relevant sections of the sentence, no change is required here. **Note: avoid using "such as," "like," and "including" when using a colon.**

B is incorrect because what comes **after a colon must clarify the preceding section.** The phrase "each of these terms [...]" does not serve to **clarify** as much as to emphasize and connect the preceding terms. Therefore, the colon is not an appropriate choice here.

C is incorrect because **dashes, when used on both sides of a phrase, are most often used as an equivalent of parenthesis** (additional information). Here, the information put forward in "each of these terms [...]" is **not** parenthetical but integral to understanding the information in the sentence.

D is incorrect because without a punctuation mark after the word "cat," **the sentence loses meaning,** and we are unable to tell what "the mountain lion" is being said in reference to.

Question 13

A is the best answer. Sentence number 13 functions to strengthen the argument presented about mountain lions in the previous sentence. Thus, **"in fact"** is an **extremely suitable choice** to communicate that the ideas are connected, and this sentence is going to help make the previous one's argument stronger.

B is incorrect. "For example" is used precisely **to provide an example of an idea that came before it.** In this case, that would mean including a specific instance that showcases a mountain lion as a fearsome predator. However, since line 13 is used to state a general idea about these creatures, "for example" would be an unsuitable choice.

C is incorrect because the word "although" **implies** that the following information somehow **discredits** (makes less true) the information that came before it. This is clearly not the case in the text.

D is incorrect. "Moreover" suggests the introduction of an **additional element of information** that strengthens what comes before it **but also offers something new.** Since line 13 does not offer new information – it offers a different account/perspective of the same information – this is not a suitable choice.

Question 14

B is the best answer. In order to know whether or not this paragraph needs an additional concluding sentence, **look at the paragraph that comes after it** and **see if the addition is necessary to make the transition to the next paragraph more effective.** In this case, since the next paragraph speaks about human pursuit of animals and the current end of the paragraph speaks about mountain lions being hunted to execution with no resolution about whether that happened or not, it would be well-advised to include a concluding sentence as the one here. This sentence addresses both the one that comes before it and the one that comes after.

A is incorrect. As explained above, because of the **shift in focus** (onto hunters and hunting) in the next paragraph and the **current concluding line that leaves the issue of extinction unresolved,** a change is needed.

C is technically correct. However, the structure of this sentence with the term "fortunately" included in the middle of it is **less elegant** than Option B. Furthermore, it is **more powerful to end with a positive statement like** "proven resilient to the threats against it," **rather than a more ambiguous one that ends with terms like** "almost certain."

D is incorrect because this sentence does **not function as an effective transition** between the two paragraphs and the ideas that they contain.

Question 15

C is the best answer. Since the preceding sentence sets out a very **specific idea** about US states putting bounties on cats, there is the need for an additional **transition sentence** that will take the reader from this paragraph to the next one. Furthermore, since the following paragraph begins with a sentence about where mountain lions have had to run to, **ending the previous paragraph with a similar idea gives that paragraph both an effective conclusion and transition.**

A is incorrect because this line **is not an effective introduction** especially since the following paragraph has a **topic sentence** that resonates (shows similarities) with this one.

B is incorrect because there is **no explanation that is offered in the additional sentence.** All that is described is the effect of the policy on the mountain lion. There is no explanation regarding the hunters' intent to pursue the creatures. To choose this option would mean making an **ASSUMPTION** about the content in that statement.

D is incorrect because the information in this sentence is **clearly linked to the content of the existing paragraph.** By saying that the policy forced mountain lions into different areas, the reader is informed about the tangible effects of the bounty that was imposed on these creatures in different US states at the time. Therefore, this information is **NOT irrelevant because it allows us to understand the bigger picture of the situation.**

Question 16

A is the best answer. Since the sentence speaks about the past and refers to "hunting and habitat encroachment" as a **singular entity**, "had driven" is indeed the grammatically correct choice.

B is incorrect. "Drove" is the **simple past tense of the verb "to drive,"** while "had driven" is the **past perfect" tense of the verb "to drive."** While technically both tenses are appropriate in this case, the **past perfect tense** ("had driven") is more **active and places the emphasis on the doer of the action** (humans). On the contrary, the past tense is less active and places the emphasis on the action (the hunting). Since humans are behind the act of hunting, it is more suitable to place emphasis on the doer and thus use the past perfect tense.

C is incorrect. This is the **present perfect tense** and refers to a more recent occurrence. Since we are discussing the early twentieth century, the **past perfect tense is a lot more appropriate.**

D is incorrect. This is the **present continuous tense** and refers to something that is happening **now.** Once again, since we are talking about a particular period in US history, this is not the appropriate tense to use.

Question 17

C is the best answer. Beginning with "By the 1950s" is effective since it allows the reader to connect the ideas presented in the previous sentence ("by the mid twentieth century") and establish a mental timeline of events. Furthermore, saying that the population "had sunk" carries more weight and is a **more active** phrasing by saying "had sunk," it is implied that some form of measurement and evaluation were carried out (and thus, don't need to be mentioned).

A is incorrect because the current sentence structure is confusing to read and uses **redundant terminology** ("measured and discovered").

B is technically correct since it encompasses the same information as the correct answer. However, as mentioned above, using "By the 1950s" to begin the sentence and using a word like "sunk" communicate a more **active and dynamic** process. In this option, the use of the term "were considered" instantly makes its articulation **more passive.**

D is incorrect because **the information in this sentence is relevant and necessary to the argument** that is being put forward. Given that it was a "historical low," the underlined sentence helps the reader **establish an understanding of the timeline** in relation to mountain lions' survival in the United States.

Question 18

D is the best answer. "Adaptability" is a more concise (precise) way of saying "ability to adapt." As a general rule, **when it is possible to say the same thing with fewer words, do that!**

A is incorrect because as mentioned above, it uses more words than are needed to make the same point.

B is incorrect because "adept ability" does not mean anything. The word "adept" means to "be able" which means the same thing as "ability." Therefore, this is a **redundant** use of words.

C is incorrect because the term "adoption" has an entirely different meaning than "adaptability."

Question 19

D is the best answer. Currently, line 19 is extremely short and interrupts the **flow** between the sentences around it. By changing this sentence into a dependent clause, we are able to include ideas from this sentence and the one that follows it all while keeping a **flow** of ideas between them. A **dependent clause provides a sentence with additional information but cannot stand alone as a sentence.**

A is incorrect because as mentioned above, line 19 is short and abrupt by adding new information that does now allow a **flow of ideas between the lines around it.**

B is incorrect because transforming the sentence this way would make it extremely long with multiple commas and multiple independent clauses. This would make the sentence harder to read and understand. **Stylistically, brevity is preferred especially when listing facts about something (as compared to an interpretation or an analysis).**

C is incorrect because replacing the entire underlined section simply with "Mountain lions" would erase the additional information about their grace and power and both of which are helpful in helping to create an **image** of a mountain lion in the reader's mind.

Question 20

A is the best answer because a COLON (:) is used to introduce a list, an explanation of the previously stated idea, or a quotation. Since "prey" is followed by a list of animals that serve as mountain lions' prey, no change is needed.

> B is incorrect because in order to use a **SEMICOLON,** the phrases on either side of that punctuation mark need to be **complete sentences, i.e., each phrase needs to have its own subject, verb, and object.** This condition is clearly not met in line 20.
>
> C is incorrect because the **DASH** is used **to indicate sentence introductions or conclusions** and **to mark text for emphasis.** Technically, the dash could work here (to emphasize the nature of the mountain lions' prey). However, since the structure of the sentence so clearly fits the conditions for a colon, that is more suitable.
>
> D is incorrect because the extra dash before "and moose" adds an unnecessary emphasis on moose, an emphasis that seems **irrelevant** because the moose also preys like all the animals listed before it.

Question 21

B is the best answer. There needs to be **VERB TENSE CONSISTENCY in a sentence.** Since the verb in the first part of this sentence uses the **past tense** ("eliminated"), the second verb also needs to be so in order to have consistency (hence, "started").

> A is incorrect because there is a change that needs to happen to have **verb tense consistency** throughout the sentence.
>
> C is incorrect because **the use of a gerund is generally seen as being passive (rather than active).** Therefore, although "started protecting" is technically accurate, it is less **active** than saying "started to protect."
>
> D is incorrect because once again it would cause **verb tense inconsistency** between the past tense ("eliminated") and the future tense ("will protect").

Question 22

A is the best answer. The **dependent clause at the beginning of the sentence** allows the addition of **context to the following independent clause.** The latter states that a balance between human and animal protection must be struck. The dependent clause heightens the importance of that balance by stressing the increasing numbers of those populations.

B is incorrect because **erasing the dependent clause** would take away the **context** that it gives to the following independent clause.

C is not suitable because it **randomly** deletes one part of the information (about growing human populations) and this deletion changes the **implication of the sentence. The idea of "striking a balance"** makes less sense because this choice **represents** only one population (the lions) as growing.

D is incorrect because in order to use a **SEMICOLON,** the phrases on either side of that punctuation mark need to be **complete sentences, i.e., each phrase needs to have its own subject, verb, and object.** This condition is clearly not met in this choice since "Both mountain lion and human populations continue to expand" has a subject and a verb but no object.

Passage 3

Question 23

B is the best answer. The **KEYWORD CONNECTION** to look for here is "passage" with "passable." The word "possible" **remains ambiguous in this context** leading the reader to wonder what exactly is possible. "Passable" though immediately connects to the idea of "passage" and helps situate the reader in the context of the passage.

> A is incorrect because of the reasons mentioned above, i.e., "possible" being ambiguous, is unclear what the possibility is referring to.
>
> The words "plausible" and "probable" in options C and D both refer to the **likelihood of something occurring**. Like the term "possible," these two terms evidence a lack of clarity that is addressed with the use of "passable."

Question 24

B is the best answer. The information provided in this additional sentence helps us better understand the Northwest Passage. Although it is not the most effective transition between the sentences that comes before it, it does **add context** to the following sentence, i.e., that the Norwest Passage is "thawing." Without this added clarification about the icy nature to the Passage, the term "thawing" would be **hard to understand.**

> A is incorrect because the new sentence does not add on to anything that was said **before it since what comes before it just frames the context of the Northwest Passage.** The additional sentence only **helps to frame what comes after,** i.e., descriptions of how the terrain is changing because of global climate change.
>
> C is incorrect. If this sentence were to be used to conclude the paragraph, the structure of the ideas would be **incoherent** (not understandable). Doing this would mean ending the paragraph speaking about the terrain while the earlier sentences have already described how that terrain is changing.
>
> D is incorrect because the information provided is indeed **relevant** toward understanding more about the Northwest Passage and its conditions. It allows us to better understand the "icy and treacherous" terrain of the Passage, which in turn allows the reader to **become more informed about the context that is being described.**

Question 25

C is the best answer. This rephrasing of the sentences links the ideas within them **without the need** for any extra punctuation marks or clauses.

A is incorrect because we currently have two independent clauses that are clearly linked to each other. As in, the Passage is thawing due to the impacts of global climate change.

B is incorrect because in order to use a **SEMICOLON,** the phrases on either side of that punctuation mark need to be **complete sentences, i.e., each phrase needs to have its own subject, verb, and object.** This condition is clearly not met in this choice since "Now the Northwest Passage is thawing" does not have a subject.

D is technically correct since the usage of the **comma** to add an idea is grammatically acceptable. However, generally **when it is possible to avoid the use of punctuation marks through a rephrasing of the text, do so! Punctuation marks, in general, make a reader slowdown in their processing of the information.**

Question 26

D is the best answer. The **KEYWORD** "rescue mission" in this context **is immediately understandable as an effort to rescue someone/something that has gone missing.** By restating that the mission "was looking for [...]," we are provided with redundant (useless, repeated) information.

A is incorrect because **it is an ASSUMPTION** and has nothing to do with what has been mentioned in the text. There is no evidence here to **imply** anything to do with the impact of "fate" on "discoveries." Therefore, this answer choice is **irrelevant.**

B is incorrect because in its **redundancy** this phrase **negatively affects** the transition that might occur between the ideas around it. It interrupts the flow rather than allowing an **effective movement** in the flow of ideas.

C is incorrect because the success or failure of the mission based on the paragraph thus far would be a matter of **ASSUMPTION.** We do not know and are not told about the fate of the rescue mission. The mission is used to **contextualize** the nature of the Passage; the outcome of the mission is not the focus of the statement.

Question 27

D is the best answer. The line marked 27 fits best at the very end of the paragraph. It allows the paragraph to go from an early, disastrous attempt to expeditions that went missing to missions that caused damage to hurdles caused by weather to an account of the first successful voyage. In order to understand the importance of this first success, it is important for the reader to first see all the different kinds of challenges that they had to deal with. Furthermore, since the following paragraph speaks about how more voyages were made possible, ending with information about the first successful attempt **creates an effective transition to the next paragraph.**

The remaining three answer choices are **unsuitable for the same reasons.** They would **break the flow of argumentation in the paragraph. They would not allow for an effective transition into the net paragraph. They are less effective in helping the reader understand the significance of the first successful voyage.**

Question 28

B is the best answer since we are referring to the crew members of the ship, the singular entity that is the subject of the sentence.

A is incorrect because "their" implies a **plural** subject, which is not the case. "Their" would be used only if the sentence were to be speaking about multiple ships rather than one.

C is incorrect because the contraction "it's" represents "it is" and in the context of this sentence, and "it is" would render the phrase **meaningless.**

D is incorrect because the pronoun "his" **would be used to refer to a human subject.** Not an object like a ship.

Question 29

A is the best answer. The added information would help the reader **transition** from the first like that talks about technological advancements and the next line which **implies** the declining need for such technology given the melting of the ice. Currently, these two lines are placed side by and causes a **break in logic** where the reader jumps from thinking about the need for technology to the reason for its declining necessity. By adding a sentence about the use of the icebreaker, the reader will be able to follow the **flow of the ideas** with more ease: the need for technology → the technology that was developed and used → the declining need for that technology.

B is incorrect because using the additional statement as an introduction, **before framing the use of technology,** would cause a break in transition for the reader (especially in relation to the previous paragraph).

C is incorrect because this additional sentence **does not summarize the passage since a summary would mean a consolidation of existing ideas.** Instead, this statement provides new information.

D is incorrect because it is **incorrect** to say that this information is **irrelevant as it clearly provides the reader with new information regarding the other facts being presented. The presentation of new information that fits within the context of a text – if presented well – is always relevant in allowing the reader to gain more insights (knowledge) from the work.**

Question 30

D is the best answer. The underlined section is **redundant.** If the passage becomes "more maneuverable over time," it is **implied that an icebreaker will be needed less and less.** There is no need to **restate this information. Whenever possible, avoid repeating the same idea even if you are using different words!**

A is incorrect because it suggests **keeping the redundancy and repeating the same idea in different ways. This is not considered good practice in writing since it makes the work cluttered (messy) and harder to understand.**

B is incorrect for two reasons. First, it does not eliminate the **redundancy.** Second, "less and less" icebreakers is incorrect; the correct term would be "fewer." **As a general rule, "fewer" is used in the context of things that can be counted (fewer icebreakers); "less" is used in reference to things that cannot be counted (less ice).**

C is incorrect for the same reasons as B. There is also a **superfluous** (useless) "and thus" that has been added in this option that only serves to complicate the sentence structure further.

Question 31

C is the best answer. Since it is said that scientists "speculate" – **implying that they are not completely sure** – the possibility being described in the paragraph's concluding sentence needs to show that uncertainty. Therefore, it is important to retain "could" rather than use "will." In addition, the current version of the sentence is **passive** because of using a gerund (becom**ing**). Whenever possible, **do NOT use the gerund (verb form ending in 'ing') since it automatically renders the subject more passive.** Since this answer choice uses "become," it is more active and thus, a better choice. Finally, there is an **unnecessary insertion of the collective pronoun** "we," which is not needed because "we" has not been used anywhere else in the paragraph. It's use at this stage is **unnecessary.**

A is incorrect because as stated above the **passive voice** of the sentence is less effective in communicating the idea. Whenever possible, **the active voice is preferred.** Unless, of course, an expert writer makes the intentional choice to write passively as a very specific technical choice.

B is incorrect both for the use of the word "is," which **implies an ASSUMPTION** given the scientists' uncertainty about what will happen. It is also unsuitable because of the **passive voice** that is taken on through the use of the **gerund** (becoming).

D is incorrect because of the **collective "we"** that is used here – **an unnecessary addition** given the absence of a narrative viewpoint anywhere else in the paragraph.

Question 32

A is the best answer. The sentence works well as it is now. The use of "that" is made necessary by the presence of "will," **sentence connectors that imply cause and effect.**

Given the cause and effect **context** of the sentence, none of the other answers are suitable choices. Using "in," "with," or "when" would **completely change the meaning of the sentence.** In this case, **replace the underlined word with the given choices.** Read the resulting sentence. Does it still make sense?

Question 33

A is the best answer. DASHES are used to set off material for emphasis, to indicate sentence introductions or conclusions or to mark bonus phrases that are not integral to the meaning of a sentence. In this case, the phrase between the dashes serves to be emphasized (since it was the first time in history that this had happened) but it is also a **bonus phrase** that is not integral to the meaning of the sentence. Even without knowing it was the first time that this happened, we would be able to understand the rest of the sentence.

B is incorrect because **if the COMMA was to be used,** it should be used on both sides of the phrase "for the first time in history." **Using a comma on one side and a dash on the other** is **not recommended.**

C is incorrect. **A COLON is used to introduce a list, an explanation of the previously stated idea, or a quotation.** Since none of these conditions are met by the phrase "for the first time in history," this answer can be excluded.

D is incorrect because having only one comma, and that too at the beginning of a bonus phrase, leads to a **lack of clarity in the rest of the sentence.**

Passage 4

Question 34

B is the best answer. In the current sentence, "it's hard to even imagine what life would be like without electricity" lacks clarity. The reader needs to reread the sentence to understand the point that it is making. By using the revised phrase, the line would gain more clarity and direction; it would have a clear voice. **Most times, it helps to be brief and to find a more ACTIVE way of saying something.** The potential of being brief is exactly what this example proves.

A is **DEBATABLE** because the sentence, as it is, provides an **effective introduction.** It is just not as clear as it could be because of the way in which the sentence has been structured.

C is incorrect. There is nothing **irrelevant** when speaking about plugs and batteries to mention what electricity does in today's world. In fact, this is simply a way of rephrasing the idea that has already been presented in the text.

D is incorrect because the clarity in the proposed revision makes a transition that is as/more effective its functioning as a transition **to the next line.**

Question 35

C is the best answer. The infrastructure that provides electricity is referred to as a **singular entity,** which necessitates the use of "is." Furthermore, since we have been discussing ideas in the **present tense** ("people rely on [...]"), it is clear that the author is referring to an ongoing problem that is happening now.

A is incorrect because "are" would be used only if the infrastructures that provide electricity were **referred to as plural entities.**

B is incorrect because it speaks in the future tense and is **inconsistent with the focus on the present** that has been displayed in the rest of the paragraph.

D is incorrect because once again there would be a **verb tense inconsistency** with what has already been established earlier in the passage as a focus on the present.

Question 36

B is the best answer. The added information would help us understand just how much electricity in the United States is generated from nonrenewable sources. This information **adds to the context** put forward by the previous sentence and helps us better understand the **implications of that information.**

A is incorrect because the **transition** between the sentences, as it is now, is already effective. Adding this information is not needed for structural reasons but for the content it provides. It gives the reader a very real idea about the use of nonrenewable energy sources in the United States.

C is incorrect because this statement **is not relevant as a conclusion to this paragraph** since the paragraph eventually moves to talking about efforts to use renewable energy. By placing this sentence at the end of the paragraph, the flow would be completely disrupted, and this would make it harder for the reader to contextualize the information.

D is incorrect because this information is **NOT irrelevant.** The statistics that are provided in this statement help the reader to better understand the sheer (extreme) extent to which nonrenewable sources of energy are being used in the United States.

Question 37

B is the best answer. When "that" is used in a sentence, what follows is usually **an essential element of the sentence.** In this case, the information that follows "that" **IS** an essential element of the sentence. However, the error here is the placement of the comma before "that"; **commas are only used before the word "which" when used to add non-essential elements to sentences.** However, since there is no answer option that allows us to keep "that" while removing the comma, "which" preceded by the comma is the best option.

A is incorrect because of the **comma that precedes** "that."

C is incorrect because of the nature of the clauses. **An independent clause expresses a complete thought; a dependent clause expresses an incomplete thought.** In this sentence, the second part of the sentence is a **dependent clause** and the first **is an independent clause.** In this case, the conjunction "and" is technically correct in allowing us to connect the independent with the dependent clause. However, since the process of combustion is **directly responsible for the release of dangerous chemicals** – rather than being a separate idea, in addition to the release of dangerous chemicals – "which" is more suitable.

D is incorrect. If "this" were to be used, we would have to place a period after the word "combustion" and start a new sentence with the word "This." Such an addition would make this sentence into two sentences (**two independent clauses**).

Question 38

C is the best answer. Since the sentence is speaking of multiple sources of electricity, the **plural nature** of the subject means we need to use "do not." "Does not" would be used to refer to a **singular** source of electricity.

A is incorrect because the agreement between the subject and the verb **is inaccurate** ("does not" refers to a singular subject and not plural subjects).

B is incorrect because "doesn't" is a **contraction** of does not and exhibits the same issues as the answer above.

D is correct since "don't" is a contraction for do not. However, **contractions are seen as being informal in tone and it is recommended that, whenever possible, you refrain (stop yourself) from using contractions like don't (for "do not"), can't ("cannot")**, or won't (for "will not").

Question 39

D is the best answer. The **KEYWORDs** to pay attention to here is "most effective."

Choices B & C are easy to eliminate because they would both require making **ASSUMPTIONS** that cannot be explained by the Figure provided. For instance, Choice B describes particular kinds of solar panels and the locations of their installation. Neither of which is **referred to in any way** in the Figure. Similarly, Choice C asks the reader to **infer** information about energy sources, and this too is not mentioned anywhere in the Figure.

Choice A can be validated by the Figure as can Choice D. What makes Choice D the better answer is that it provides **more impactful information** that tells us about the shift in solar energy production over a longer period of time. This information is more useful for the reader since it **allows a broader understanding** about the topic rather than just knowing what happened in 2008, which is the information that is provided in Choice A.

Question 40

A is the best answer. This is best identified by looking at the sentence that **comes after this one,** which talks about people taking charge of their own renewable energy systems. Given this context, the underlined segment **serves to emphasize** the inefficiencies in the current system and to highlight the agency of citizens. The **central theme** of the paragraph can be defined as the ways in which people are looking to decentralize solar power.

B is incorrect because the word "but" would be misleading **given the tone of the paragraph.** "But" would imply that the people are at fault for not waiting for their local utilities. However, given the remaining material in the paragraph, we know that this is not the **tone** that is taken by the author.

C is incorrect because the phrase "when their local utility doesn't show up" shifts the **focus** of the line from "the people," to the "utility." The people are made more **passive** in this particular use of language and since the **tone of the passage** is positive (toward the people's efforts) it is more effective to eliminate this choice.

D is incorrect because it **deletes important information** that tells us how people are not waiting for someone else to take care of their problems. Deleting this would **detract from** (lessen) the impact of the central theme of the paragraph.

Question 41

D is the best answer. The graph immediately shows us that solar production has increased every year for the past decade. **Pay attention to the KEYWORDS** "distributed" and "decentralized." The Figure uses the word "distributed" and from what is described in this paragraph – about how people are taking matters into their own hands – we understand that "distributed" is used to mean "decentralized."

A is incorrect. While this answer is **DEBATABLE because there have been great gains shown in solar energy production,** this is an extremely general statement that is less preferable to choice D, which gives a specific time frame in which the gains have occurred.

B is incorrect because it asks us to make an **ASSUMPTION** about the statistics – information that cannot be discerned from the nature of the Figure. To say that something was "**more than three times**" something else, we would need more precise numerical information. We cannot guess or assume based on what we see in the current Figure.

C is incorrect because it is an ASSUMPTION **to say** that "there are no signs of it slowing down," just from the Figure that has been presented here. There is no data in the Figure to help us **know for certain** how the trend that is currently depicted might change in the future.

Question 42

A is the best answer. Since the first two sentences of the paragraph focus on the **benefits of renewable energy,** adding this sentence would help make a **more effective introduction.**

B is incorrect because the information provided here **does not necessarily** help clarify anything else in the paragraph. It simply serves to make a more effective **topic sentence** that captures what the following sentences describe.

C is incorrect because the paragraph moves on to speaking about **obstacles in the way** of renewable energy, and this added sentence **would not fit with the current content. Adding this sentence as a conclusion, therefore, would disrupt the flow of the text and make it harder for the reader to** contextualize the information.

D is incorrect because the information in this sentence is **NOT irrelevant. By talking about where these alternative energy sources are being built – "rooftops and open spaces" – this statement gives the reader new knowledge to help better understand the themes being dealt with in the passage.**

Question 43

D is the best answer. Since we are talking about the impacts of solar power on the future, the **future tense** is the most appropriate to use here ("will face"). Furthermore, this sentence structure is **active** in its use of solar power as the subject.

A is incorrect because the current sentence structure is **passive,** and the verb tense is in the **present** ("are", instead of "will"). This is not in agreement with the **verb tense usage** that is established in the first line ("can help," i.e., **future tense).**

B is incorrect because it uses the **past tense** ("faced). This is not in agreement with the **verb tense usage** that is established in the first line ("can help." i.e., **future tense).**

C is incorrect because the **tense usage is once again inconsistent.** "Did face" **could be used to imply past or present tense.** In either case, the term does not fit with the established future tense.

326

Question 44

A is the best answer. Using the **KEYWORD CONNECTION TECHNIQUE** for the term "benefits," we are immediately able to identify this as the most suitable answer.

B is incorrect because it is an **ASSUMPTION** that is not evidenced anywhere in the passage. The passage focuses on the challenges and costs of renewable energy and the worthy investment that it is despite the costs. Nothing is mentioned about the "energy mix."

C is incorrect because it is a statement that is not evidenced by anything in the passage. In fact, saying that America's current infrastructure will "survive well into the future" is making an ASSUMPTION that **contradicts the ideas being put forth about the dangers of using non-renewable sources of energy.**

D is incorrect because it makes an **ASSUMPTION.** Nowhere in paragraph is it mentioned that "all" of America's energy-related problems will be solved by shifting now to renewable energy.

Writing Test 2: Answer Key

1. A	28. B
2. B	29. C
3. A	30. B
4. C	31. A
5. A	32. B
6. C	33. C
7. D	
8. D	34. D
9. D	35. D
10. B	36. B
11. B	37. C
	38. B
12. B	39. C
13. C	40. D
14. C	41. C
15. A	42. C
16. B	43. B
17. C	44. A
18. B	
19. D	
20. A	
21. A	
22. A	
23. D	
24. A	
25. C	
26. B	
27. D	

WRITING & LANGUAGE TEST 2

Answers & Explanations

1. **A is the best answer.**

To find the **TOPIC SENTENCE**, always read the rest of the paragraph and find the "Relevant Keywords." This paragraph contains words such as **"Adventurer" and "Pure Pleasure of the Journey."** We can use the **"Keyword Connection"** technique and chose an answer choice that contains words most similar to "Pure Pleasure" and "Adventurer." Choice A contain words such as "Adventure" and "Enthusiasts." The word "Enthusiasts" describe people as being highly interested in the mountaineering activity. The topic of the passage is the sport of mountaineering and how it has developed into a popular activity.

B is incorrect because of the **words "Exciting History."** This paragraph does not discuss specific details from the past that make the history "exciting." It's mainly about the sport of mountaineering and how it has developed into a popular and adventurous activity.

C is incorrect because of the **word "Dangerous."** Although it mentions it is a dangerous sport, the topic of the paragraph is not about how dangerous the sport of mountaineering is. Instead, it's about how the sport of mountaineering that became a popular activity for adventure enthusiasts. The paragraph does not focus on the "dangerous" part of the sport.

D is incorrect because of the **word "Treacherous,"** which is extreme. Treacherous means deception or betrayal. Although mountaineering is a dangerous sport, the sport is not betraying or deceiving anyone. The word **"Treacherous"** is not relevant to the paragraph or passage.

---

2. **B is the best answer.**

When it comes to **"Adding or Deleting Line"** questions, think of **"Relevancy."** Chose keywords that are relevant to the paragraph's focus. Words such as "Strength, Courage, and Resourcefulness" are relevant **Keywords** because they describe the adventurous and athletic type of people the sport of mountaineering attracts. The words **"Adventurous" and "Athletic"** are in the last sentence of this paragraph. Thus, choice B sets up an effective transition for further relevant details. Specifically, the proposed addition provides an effective transition between the unique nature of mountaineering and the type of people it tends to attract.

A is incorrect because "shows impact of courage on resourcefulness" is not relevant. When someone is resourceful, he or she can come up with quick solutions. **No sentence in this paragraph describes the "IMPACT"** of courage on resourcefulness.

C is incorrect because of the word "Paid Guides." The **Keyword "Paid Guides" is irrelevant** because the paragraph does not mention anything about paid guides.

D is incorrect because this paragraph does not discuss **"Development of Modern Mountaineering."** Instead, it discusses the unique nature of mountaineering and the type of people it tends to attract. It attracts people who are courageous and resourceful.

3. **A is the best answer.**

For **"Paragraph Placement" questions**, think of **"RELEVANCY"** and place the paragraph where it is relevant and makes sense. The passage begins with an introduction to the topic of the popularity of modern mountaineering (Paragraph 1), continues with a description of the activity (Paragraph 2), follows with an explanation of the development of modern mountaineering (Paragraph 3), and then closes with some of the great achievements made possible through the sport (Paragraph 4).

B is incorrect because Paragraph (4) introduces the history of the mountaineering by starting the sentence with "Early attempts at." So, every paragraph after this should be about the history of the mountaineering. Paragraph (3) starts the sentence with "Modern mountaineering." Therefore, it cannot be placed after paragraph (4) since everything after paragraph (4) should be about the past and not modern mountaineering.

C is incorrect because we cannot place paragraph (3) before paragraph (2) since the passage should begin with the topic of the popularity of modern mountaineering (Paragraph 1), then continue with a description of the activity (Paragraph 2) and not discuss how modern mountaineering is different than it was in the past (Paragraph 3).

D is incorrect because Paragraph (3) is an introductory paragraph. We cannot place paragraph (3) before paragraph (1) since this paragraph (3) is not a logical introduction of the topic of the popularity of modern mountaineering. Paragraph (1) correctly introduces the topic of the passage, which is about the sport of mountaineering and how it has developed into a popular activity.

4. **C is the best answer.**

The colon properly introduces a list or provides an explanation of a previously stated idea.
Expedition and alpine are in the list of two common styles of mountaineering. Before a
colon, you must use a full sentence. A full sentence is **Subject + Verb + Object (SVO)**. Follow
this setup (SVO: List or Explanation). **Avoid using phrases (such as, like, including, etc.)**

A & B are in incorrect because a colon already introduces a list. You don't have to write
"including" to show what those two styles of mountaineering are. **Avoid using phrases (such as,
like, including, etc.) when using a colon.**

D is wrong because semicolons are not used to list. They are used to separate two closely related
full sentences. A full sentence is **Subject + Verb + Object (SVO)**. Follow this set up when **using
semicolon → SVO ; SVO**. Two full sentences can also be separated by periods (SVO . SVO) After a
semicolon, it should be a full sentence. Here in Choice D "Expedition and Alpine" is not a full
idea."

when using a colon.

5. **A is the best answer.**

The **Keywords "Brave men and women"** indicate more than 2 people. So, chose a plural
pronoun, "they."

B and C are incorrect because "he" and "she" are singular pronouns, but "Brave men" is plural.

D is incorrect because although "themselves" is plural, it uses the reflexive version of the
pronouns incorrectly. **A reflexive pronoun is used in contexts where the subject of a sentence is
also its object.** For example, they were dancing around the fire to keep themselves warm. Here,
the subject "they" also became the object. Think like this. The subject does the action, and the
object receives the action. In this case, the subject is doing the action (dancing) and receiving the
action as well (keeping themselves warm, not anyone else). Hence, "themselves" is a reflexive
pronoun.

6. **C is the best answer.**

Think Relevancy! The first sentence starts in this paragraph as "Early attempts." This paragraph is about mountaineering history. So, keywords such as "Eighteenth century" is relevant because it indicates past.

B & D are incorrect because it does not contain the **word "Eighteenth century"** to indicate that it's discussing past early attempts at summitting mountains.

A is incorrect because it uses too many commas, which makes it excessively wordy. Also, remember that the transitional phrase **"In fact" is used when you are giving more detailed information about the previous sentence. You also use it to draw attention or emphasis to the previous sentence.** The previous sentence states "Brave men and women scaled mountains so that they could build religious monuments or make new discoveries." However, the sentence after this does not provide more detailed information regarding specific discoveries. It simply states, "in hopes of making important scientific discoveries," which is not giving more detailed information.

"In Fact," Example → My friend John was pretty upset at me while I was away from town. In fact, he blocked me on Facebook. Here, you emphasize and give more information by using the transitional phrase "In Fact." You are emphasizing how upset John was and what specific thing he did as a result.

7. **D is the best answer.**

When there is **punctuation** being used as a sentence separator, there must be two of the same forms to indicate the beginning of the added portion and the end of it. Thus, if there is a dash in the middle of a sentence, there must be a second dash.

A and B are incorrect because they both involve two different sentence separators, one being a comma and the other being a dash. If a comma is used, the second punctuation must be a comma as well. The same goes for the dash. Hence, neither A nor B can be correct because of the different separators.

C is incorrect because it uses an **unnecessary dash**. Dashes are supposed to be used to separate a thought or insert a new idea, similar to a comma. In this answer choice, it would've been correct if the dash was absent but putting the punctuation makes the reader pause, which is incorrect.

8. **D is the best answer.**

Think relevancy! The passage prior to this section talks about Michel-Gabriel Paccard and Jacques Balmat winning the title of the first person to ascent Mont Blanc. The point of this sentence was to discuss how mountaineering was a growing sport. Adding an extra sentence at the end to discredit the prior message would just distract from the point of the passage.

A and B are incorrect because if the sentence were added, it would just provide a confusing **distraction** for the reader. It is not an effective transition nor would it clarify any previous points.

C is incorrect because this sentence does not apply to the paragraph. Additionally, beginning a paragraph with the word "**however**" would pose a distraction and confuse the reader. "However" is a comparison word, so it must be used when referring to the difference between one thing and another.

9. **D is the best answer.**

Instead of writing a long sentence, it's often best to end a sentence with a period, and then begin a new one. This allows the reader to identify when to pause in their reading. Using too many commas can be confusing, which is why D is the best answer.

A and B are incorrect because when there are two commas in the middle of a sentence, this acts as a sentence separator where additional information is to be added. One way you can identify whether this is correct or not is by deleting the part of the sentence between the commas and seeing whether this still makes sense, therefore why both A and B cannot be correct.

C is incorrect because a semicolon is used improperly. **Semicolons** should be used to combine two sentences that are directly related with two independent clauses. In this case, the sentences, while related, are not referring to the same exact subject at hand.

10. **B is the best answer.**

To identify the proper grammar, you must first read the parts of the sentence before and after the underlined portion. This sentence contains a list of places such as **"Pico de Orizaba"** and **"Mount Saint Elias."** This question is specifically asking to identify whether to use a comma or a semicolon in two different locations. We can understand that a comma should be used to separate appositives from the rest of a sentence. Thus, choice B is the best answer because the phrase in question, "the tallest mountain in Mexico." It is a phrase that happens in the middle of a sentence. This can be checked by noting if the phrase between the commas can be omitted and still make sense. For example, "Adventurers peaked Pico de Orizaba in 1848..." is still accurate. Lastly, at the end of the underlined section, a semicolon should properly be used to separate smaller sections of text where commas are already present.

A is incorrect because a semicolon is being used to separate a phrase in the middle of a sentence. Semicolons act as a pause similar to a period, so instead of a semicolon, a comma must be used when adding an additional phrase in the middle of an already existing sentence. This adds depth in a proper way rather than making the reader pause.

C is incorrect because this section ends with a comma. When listing things after a comma has been previously used in a sentence, a semicolon must be used. Instead of confusing the reader with many pauses, using a semicolon can allow for a proper pause.

D is incorrect because it does not contain a comma punctuation following the year 1848. This indicates that that section of the sentence would continue, when in actuality, it begins mentioning a new place in the list.

11. **B is the correct answer.**

Think about readability. The easier something is for a reader to understand, the better the flow of the passage will be. By switching up the phrasing of the sentence to put the verb and subject first, it allows readers to understand the point of the sentence more. Because of this, B must be the correct answer choice.

A is incorrect because this is less of a transitional phrase and more directed at providing depth to the prior sentence. It clarifies the point that climbers have continued to push boundaries. Transitions are typically used when you're switching from one topic to another, yet this paragraph stays consistent in topic. Therefore, A is incorrect.

C is incorrect because if you were to end on this sentence, it would leave readers hanging. If you bring up a topic and idea, it must be followed with some form of analysis. This would also end a paragraph abruptly ultimately making c the wrong choice.

D is incorrect because the information is not irrelevant and should not be deleted. If this sentence were excluded, the following sentence would have been unsupported.

12. **B is the correct answer.**

Focus on the **subject agreeability**. The first sentence in the passage talked about Twain, and the second sentence referred to him as "he." For readability, it's best to switch back and forth every other sentence from the name of the proper noun, in this case who is Twain, to their general pronoun. This makes for an easier read and therefore why B is correct.

A is incorrect because the prior sentence has a list of different names of books. Saying **"he"** could confuse the reader and allow them to believe that the writer is referring to someone other than Twain.

C is incorrect because that pronoun does not agree with the proper noun. Twain is singular, and therefore this must be reflected in the pronoun. **"Their"** is a plural pronoun, and this does not fit into the context of the passage.

D is incorrect because it is too wordy and redundant. The best way to identify this is to see if one of the words could be removed and it would still have the same meaning. The word **"himself"** can be removed and is therefore the incorrect answer choice.

13. **C is the correct answer.**

This paragraph seems to end abruptly, so you must look for a concluding sentence that transitions effectively from the previous sentence to the next paragraph. **Transitions** are important because they provide a seamless connection for the reader to follow while going from paragraph to paragraph. Because the next section talks about how some of Twain's pieces of writing are inspired by his own life as a child, you can identify that C is the correct answer.

A is incorrect because if there were to be no change, the paragraph would end abruptly and lack a **transitional sentence**. It would jump irregularly from one thought about Twain lacking education and go straight into his past life. Because A would provide no transition for the reader, it cannot be the appropriate choice.

B is incorrect because it provides unnecessary and irrelevant information to the passage. The paragraph focuses on Twain's most renowned accomplishments. Including this sentence would just discredit him and provide information that does not relate to the following paragraph.

D is incorrect because the following paragraph refers to **Twain's past experiences** rather than his creative abilities. In order to determine this, it's important to read both the prior and following paragraph. You can identify that the first paragraph discusses his ability to write great pieces of literature, and the end paragraph mentions how his past experiences are highlighted in his writing. Thus, you can deem D to be incorrect.

14. C is the correct answer.

When writing, using pronouns that agree with the subject of the sentence is important. This sentence begins talking about "**Twain**," but then switches to "**Clemens family**," which is plural. Because the plural noun was the last to be used, this should be represented in the sentence following. Thus, C is correct because it refers to the plural form, "they," yet specifically indicates that Twain himself changed age.

A is incorrect because the pronouns do not match up to the subject of the sentence. Commas were used prior allowing the idea of the Clemens family to be introduced. This indicates the plural form of the pronoun must be used, "**they**," instead of "**he**."

B is incorrect because the pronouns are incorrectly matched. In B, it says "**they were housed until age**." It is important to understand that the Clemens family is a plural noun and cannot be grouped together in a single age.

D is incorrect because the pronouns are not used correctly. The Clemens family was last mentioned; therefore, a plural pronoun must be used. Additionally, saying "**where he was**" is a vague statement and doesn't accurately depict what Twain was doing throughout this time.

15. A is the correct answer.

Focus on transitions. If a paragraph seems to end abruptly and the following sentence does not directly relate to the previous sentence, it is likely that there is a sentence that could be added. When you have questions like these, you must always read both the paragraph that the question is located in as well as the following paragraph. This will give you the appropriate context of the passage section. Once you have this oversight, the ability to choose the correct answer is apparent. Since the last sentence discusses how things changed for Twain when he moved, a transition must be included to seamlessly move into the topic of the West in the following sentence. Because of this, we can determine that choice A is the correct choice.

B is incorrect because it states that the additional sentence should not be added. Because the last sentence ends in a vague statement about how everything changed after the Civil War, we know that there must be a transition included here. Additionally, this answer choice states how the sentence would be better suited for an introductory sentence. This is not true as this would provide for a choppy read. Hence, we can rule out choice B as an appropriate answer choice.

C is incorrect because if this sentence was added, it would not provide additional support of previous information, but it would add a new idea into the passage. This would play the role of a transitional sentence to **support the following paragraph**.

D is incorrect because it claims the sentence looking to be added is irrelevant, yet it provides vital information about Twain. This sentence includes how Twain moved towards the West. Without this valuable piece of information, the following sentence would lead readers into confusion as it discusses him having a difficult time establishing himself there. Including this sentence is a necessary piece of information. Therefore, this choice is incorrect.

16. **B is the correct answer.**

Pronouns are an important part in identifying how this is the correct answer. Because Twain is mentioned, we know that the writer is referring to a singular pronoun. Because of this, we can understand that the correct answer must use the word "**himself.**" Without this, it provides an incomplete sentence and can allow the reader confusion. Saying that Twain had a difficult time establishing himself in the West provides readers with the reason in why this was true and gives them a full depiction of the scenario. Therefore, we can identify B as the correct answer.

A is incorrect because it fails to **provide a pronoun** in the sentence. Without this vital piece of writing, it allows confusion and room for readers to lose focus. It does not provide a noun either making it possible to wonder what exactly Twain had a difficult time establishing while in the West. Because of this, the sentence cannot remain the same.

C is incorrect because it provides irrelevant information for the passage. Nowhere does the writer mention Twain's family in this passage and it cannot be mentioned properly. If Twain's family were to be mentioned here, it would provide an unnecessary piece of text that would just cause confusion. Hence, choice C is incorrect.

D is incorrect because while it includes the proper pronoun, it does not include the location. By mentioning that Twain had a difficult time establishing himself, it does not discuss why this was. The location must be included to provide a complete understanding of the context of the scenario, which is why D cannot be correct.

17. C is the correct answer.

Word choice must be highly thought of regarding this question. Because the end of this passage discusses the short period of time that it took for Twain to become a notorious storyteller with the Virginia City Territorial Enterprise, the underlined phrase must depict this period of time. There are better and more concise ways to say similar things, and "**before long**" is an example of that. Instead of saying that it took a short period of time, these two words convey the same meaning. Hence, C is correct.

A is incorrect because the phrase is overly long and redundant. These questions ask for the best answer choice, and there is a shorter, more efficient way to say a similar phrase. What was said in four words could've been said in two. Therefore, A is not the best choice.

B is incorrect because again, similar to answer choice A, this answer is redundant. It uses a lot of words to describe that it was well-known how notorious Twain was as a writer. Additionally, instead of discussing the speed in which he became this well-known, it provides the outcome of his actions. For an appropriate read, avoiding this long, drawn out and pointless choice makes the piece better.

D is incorrect because an alteration of the underlined portion is needed in order to make full sense. Without this piece of valuable information, the sentence could be easily confused. This is because it provides no reason, time, or know-how regarding why Twain became the notorious storyteller that everyone came to know.

18. B is the correct answer.

This is another question that fully focuses on **word choice**. In order to choose the correct answer, one must be able to identify if all of the necessary information is provided in the sentence. This means that a time frame should be included as well. Yet here, it is not. The current sentence mentions "**this time,**" yet it does not specify what that time frame is. This can provide confusion for the reader. Because of this, mentioning that the time Twain spent in the West is what led him to develop his style is an important factor of the sentence.

A is incorrect because the specific time frame is not mentioned, and the current choice is very vague. By not mentioning this, it allows the reader to be confused about the specific time frame in which the author is referring to. Specifics must be used in advanced writing in order to confirm the reader can follow the story being told.

C is incorrect because it refers to the time Twain spent in the West as a specific time period. Therefore, the word "**Western**" is capitalized. Western is not a time frame, and this choice cannot be appropriate.

D is incorrect because it provides a formal type of writing compared to the prior voice which was much more authoritative. There is no subject pronoun mentioned, so this can be deemed as a vague statement that refers to anybody. In order for a sentence to make sense, it must include the proper pronoun, so readers can follow who is being talked about. Hence, D cannot be the correct answer choice.

19. D is the correct answer.

Separating sentences properly allows people to write and read smoothly. This involves the use of punctuation. Understanding the right time to use a period, compared to a comma, is an important concept because it will determine whether readers take a long or short pause. D is the correct answer because it uses a comma to properly separate two sections of an argument. Additionally, it utilizes the word "**which**" to show it will continue to explain the prior statement.

A is incorrect because the word "**comparison**" is not the proper word to use. "**Comparison**" means to relate two or more things to another, which is not happening in this sentence. They are listing features of Twain's writing style. Hence, A is incorrect.

B is incorrect because the words "**It encompasses**" signifies that he is currently partaking in that writing. Considering Twain passed away, he should only be referred to in the past tense. This use of the present tense makes choice B incorrect.

C is incorrect because the word "**that**" comes after the comma. This implies the sentence is referring to a specific object, which it is not. When referring to ideas and features, "**which**" is proper.

20. **A is the correct answer.**

The best pieces of writing are explanatory, yet they utilize the proper grammar. This is exemplified in choice A. A comma is properly placed after the year 1869 because as a rule, commas must be placed after a year is mentioned in the beginning of a sentence. This choice is also correct because it uses a colon to introduce the title of Twain's book. Additionally, the author accurately uses descriptive language by describing that Twain "**spun the tales of his journeys**" into his book. Thus, no change should be made and making choice A the correct one.

B is incorrect because there is a comma placed where there should be no punctuation. Adding the comma after "**journeys**" creates an incorrect pause in the reading and does not follow accurate rules of grammar. Commas should only be used to separate a thought or when there is additional information being added not directly related to the rest of the sentence.

C is incorrect because it is missing a colon before introducing the name of Twain's book, "**Innocents Abroad.**" As a rule, when anything is being introduced, especially regarding the name of a book, a colon must be used. A colon introduces a clarifying part of a sentence, which is why C is incorrect.

D is incorrect because it does not include one of the important aspects of this sentence. The purpose of the sentence is to describe how Twain's writing represented his travel abroad. Without including the phrase "**spun the tales of his journeys,**" readers may be confused at the rapid jump in ideas. Because of this, D is incorrect.

21. **A is the correct answer.**

In writing, verbs and tenses must agree. A is the correct answer because it accurately uses the past tense to describe how Twain spread his writing skills. This question was specifically looking for the correct use of words and tense as it mentioned life prior to a time of death. When this happens, it is a rule to use the past tense. Hence, "**continued**" is the proper form to use. Additionally, the word "**continue**" means to carry on. In context, this is used accurately because Twain's words were spread by him until the time of his death. Therefore, choice A is the correct answer because of the word choice and tense used.

B is incorrect because the tenses are incorrect. When the word "**would**" is used, it typically refers to the present tense. Since Twain has passed away and this section refers to his work before his death, we know that we must use past participles.

C is incorrect because the word "**had**" is not the proper way to indicate past experiences. When "**had**" is used, it means something was previously completed, which when used in combination with another past tense word, in this case "**shared**," the tenses become inaccurate and ultimately cancel out. Thus, choice C is inaccurate because of the word "**had.**"

D is incorrect because it reads in a repetitive manner. The word "**shared**" means to divide or spread with another, and the definition of "**provide**" is to give to others. Both are similar, so we call this redundant. There is no reason to use both of the options. Therefore, choice D is not correct.

22. **A is the correct answer.**

When you come across a **summary question**, there are some key points that you can follow in order to reach the correct answer. First, you have to ensure you've read all of the passage. If you're still stuck, go back and reread the first and last sentences of each paragraph. This may help you gain an even deeper understanding. Because this entire passage relates to Twain's writing and how his past and experiences were highlighted throughout his writing, A must be the correct answer.

B is incorrect because while this fact is true and can be derived based on Twain's impact, the entire passage holistically discusses how Twain got to be the prolific writer that he is. If this were to be the correct answer, the majority of the passage would be about how **Twain fit into American history**, yet this is not the case. Therefore, we can confirm that B is incorrect.

C is incorrect because there were no spots in the text that referred to Mark Twain's writing as controversial. The passage discusses greatly about Twain's past rather than how his text impacted other people. Additionally, only positive things were said about Twain's pieces in this passage. Therefore, C is not the appropriate choice.

D is incorrect because this is not true, nor is it what the passage was about. Early in the passage, the author discussed how Twain received no formal education and therefore used his past experiences to influence his writing. If he had no formal education, he unlikely focused on strategies and more so on storytelling. Additionally, the passage discusses Twain's past and what he wrote, not how he wrote it.

23. D is the correct answer.

Think word choice! When dealing with singular or plural nouns, you have to use the appropriate pronouns and auxiliary verbs that agree with this tense. This sentence begins by discussing communicable diseases, which is a plural noun. This means that the following word must be plural. Therefore, choice D is correct. **"Have"** is a plural auxiliary verb and must be inserted in order to make sense, grammatically.

A and C are incorrect because the wrong tense was used. **"Has"** is typically used around the pronouns "he," "she," "it" and "who," while "have" is usually seen surrounding "I," "you," "we," and "they." This is because the word "has" is seen as singular, while **"have"** is seen as plural. Because a plural noun is being addressed, the word "has" cannot be used. Hence, A and C are wrong.

B is incorrect because in this sense, **"have"** is a **possessive noun**. This throws off the whole sentence and confuses readers into thinking that the communicable diseases are in possession of the greatest threats to human survival. Not only does this not make sense,

24. **A is the correct answer.**

When you have a question about a sentence addition, think about evidentiary support. **Every claim must be backed up by analysis.** The prior sentence discusses how 300 million people died from smallpox, and then the next sentence jumps to them declaring the disease irradiated. Because there is little transition or explanation of this, there must be a transition between. Including additional information about the deaths of children and mentioning that this was before an effective treatment was developed smoothly transitions into the next sentence, which discusses a treatment found. Including this sentence would provide more information, and that is why A is correct.

> B is incorrect because it does not provide a **clarification of key terms**. Key terms refer to words that may not be previously defined, yet this is not what happened here. There were no definitions or clarifications included. Hence, B is wrong.
>
> C is incorrect because the sentence should be included to provide adequate information about prior statements made. Additionally, a modifier error refers to the incorrect placement of a word or phrase that would bring confusion to a reader. This is inaccurate, as mentioned before, because it would provide support for previous statements.
>
> D is incorrect because the information provided discusses smallpox further but specifies how it affected small children. This is not irrelevant information and provides support for both prior and following sentences in this paragraph. Therefore, D is incorrect on the grounds that the sentence looking to be added contains relevant information.

25. C is the correct answer.

For this question, you must be familiar with multiple words and their definitions. These questions look for the best choice of word, and therefore they may all make sense in some context, but they are not the appropriate choices. The word "**obliteration**" means to totally destroy something. Because a treatment for smallpox was created that led to the complete eradication of the disease, this must be the appropriate word. Therefore, we can conclude that C is the correct answer choice.

> A is incorrect because suppression is the wrong word. "**Suppression**" means to prevent the development of something. While this may seem accurate, it does not fully explain the severity of how the disease was stopped. Smallpox was not only reduced and stopped, but all cases were eliminated.
>
> B is incorrect because "**reduction**" is not the appropriate word to use and does not show how large of a scale this disease was. To "reduce" means to minimize. In this case, it would mean that there would still be some cases of smallpox in the world, yet this is not true. The disease as a whole was eradicated. Hence, the word "reduction" is incorrect.
>
> D is incorrect because like the other answer choices this indicates that the disease of smallpox was slowly changing rather than how it no longer existed anymore. "**Decline**" means to steadily decrease. In this case, smallpox had already declined and was no longer in existence anymore.

26. **B is the correct answer.**

Phrasing is important when choosing the best answer choice for this question. One way to help you identify the proper choice is by reading all of the answer choices in place of the current sentence and identifying which makes the most sense. Choice B **uses correct grammar and is a smooth read.** This allows readers to have no confusion when transitioning from the prior paragraph to this one. Because of this, B is correct.

A is incorrect because if there were no changes, the read would cause confusion for readers. Writers try to make their passages as smooth to read as possible, but choice A reads choppy. It is **redundant** by mentioning a "long" and "global history" together as these could be used interchangeably. It also does not provide much depth to the rest of the passage. Therefore, A is incorrect.

C is incorrect because **there is a modifier error** within the sentence. It does not read smoothly because cultures itself are not a physical nor conceptual object capable of aiming global efforts. Additionally, the wording "aimed by cultures at preventing" is a choppy sentence likely to provide confusion for readers.

D is incorrect because "culture" is not a noun capable of completing an action. The cultures themselves would not record the spread of smallpox, and this provides confusion for the reader. Because of this, choice D must be incorrect.

27. **D is the correct answer.**

When you have a question relating to sentence placement, it's important to focus on all of the surrounding sentences and the relevancy of the underlined portion. To do this, it may be helpful to read the underlined portion in all of the answer choices. After doing this, you'll have a greater understanding of what each sentence relates to. Since sentence one discusses variolation, the following sentences must do so as well. The second sentence talks about why variolation was used, yet the third sentence talks about how it didn't help prevent the spread of smallpox. This is an **improper transition** as the next underlined portion goes back to talk about how variolation was an important step in finding a cure. This backtracks, so we know that we can place this sentence after sentence two and before sentence three. Hence, D is correct.

A is incorrect because if it were left where it is now, the sentence backtracks. **This causes confusion** for the reader because the point of variolation's effectiveness would've passed and then been brought back. In order for a smooth read, it should not be kept where it currently is. Hence, A is wrong.

B is incorrect because if it was placed before sentence one, readers would be confused about what variolation was. Variolation is described in depth between both sentences one and two, so placing this sentence stating how it was an important step would make readers unsure about what was being discussed.

C is incorrect because sentence two discusses the benefit of variolation. Putting this sentence between the definition and the benefit would cause a lapse in the reader's understanding by mentioning that it was an important step without mentioning exactly how this was true. Therefore, C is incorrect.

28. **B is the correct answer.**

When you have a question about the **specific phrasing of a part of a sentence**, it's important to read the prior and following sentences. This allows you to get a deeper understanding about what the underlined portion is referring to. With this information, we can understand that the paragraph is talking about the causes of smallpox. Reading through the answer choices, you can deem B as correct because it mentions investigating the cause of the disease, which is true.

A is incorrect because if there was no change, this sentence would be vague and allow for confusion or interpretation on the reader's part. It mentions "**the causes**" without discussing what Jenner is looking for the cause of. Because of this vagueness, answer A cannot be correct.

C is incorrect because it is too repetitive along with the previous sentence which discusses how he devoted his life to determine the origin of smallpox. If this sentence was written this way, it assumes that because he was investigating the disease, he sought to prevent it while it was the opposite.

D is incorrect because if the portion were to be deleted, the "**it**" in the sentence would confuse readers about what exactly the writer was referring to. Vague statements are not good to include in writing, so "it" must be addressed more specifically.

29. C is the correct answer.

In order to find the right answer for this question, you must read the surrounding paragraph to fully understand the purpose of the section. Here, the writer is discussing how Dr. Jenner researched a boy with cowpox. **It is in the past tense**, so this underlined phrase must be as well. Because C is in the past tense, this must be the correct answer choice.

A is incorrect because it is an informal way of writing. By saying "he gained," it could be either past or present tense. To clarify this, another auxiliary verb must be used in conjunction with it. Therefore, A is the wrong answer choice.

B is incorrect because the word "gaining" is often seen as a present tense verb. This occurrence happened in the past; therefore, the verb must be in the past tense. This research is not currently happening, which is why choice B is not correct.

D is incorrect because "he gains" is in the present tense. This, similar to choice B, is incorrect because it refers to the situation as it is currently happening.

30. B is the correct answer.

When you have an underlined portion that's **looking for the best phrasing**, you must pay attention to the proper tenses. If you are in the past tense, you must also use past tense verbs to correlate and allow the reader to fully follow what's being said. Also, reading the previous and following sentences help a lot. We can understand that this section is talking about detecting all individuals affected by smallpox and curing them. Since there are two words listed, "vaccination" and "isolating," we know that both must be related in their tenses. Since they are past tense situations, the words "vaccination" and "isolation" should be used, which is why choice B is correct.

A is incorrect because if this choice was left the way it was, it would read in a confusing way. If you are using a **present participle**, which is what the "-ing" ending is, it must be in the present tense. Since this situation is discussing the past tense, we know we can eliminate this answer choice.

C and D are incorrect because in addition to using the present participle tense, they are two different ending forms of the word. Switching from "-ing" to a different tense will confuse readers and therefore if being used, it must be kept the same in both words. Therefore, choices C and D are both incorrect.

31. **A is the correct answer.**

Sentence deletion or insertion questions require you to have a general understanding of the paragraph that the question is located in. This is because if you are unaware of what's being discussed, you are likely to delete or add a portion of the sentence that would be a qualifier for the passage. This paragraph talks about isolating the smallpox disease in order to cure it. Since the underlined portion talks about vaccinating people who were detected to have smallpox, it acts as an effective transition between this and the "arduous process" that it mentions in the following sentence. Because of this transition, choice A must be correct.

B is incorrect because while the underlined portion is important to be kept in, it does not provide evidence about how public health was affected with the vaccine. This sentence discusses the fact of the matter in how once people were detected, they were vaccinated. Because there is no discussion about why public health was affected, choice B must be incorrect.

C and D are incorrect because the sentence would be beneficial to remain in the passage. Both these two choices are inaccurate as there is no irrelevant information provided nor is the point of the paragraph to discuss global coordination. The main focus of the paragraph was to explain how smallpox was cured. Because of this, C and D are incorrect.

32. **B is the correct answer.**

When you have to **analyze a chart or graph**, it helps to **look at all of the possible answer choices** to determine what you can infer from the graph compared to what you cannot. Choice B is correct because you can see that before 1940, which after that can be considered the mid - 1900's, there were two points that hit over 100,000 cases of smallpox. "Peaked" means the top points, so we can deem B as accurate.

A is incorrect because when analyzing the graph itself, we can see that it **only goes up to the year of 1950.** Because of that, interpretations can only be made using this graph between the years of 1900 and 1950. Choice A mentions the year 1979, which is much out of the graph's range. Because of this, A must be wrong.

C is incorrect because when you have a graph to observe, you must look at the boundaries. The smallpox cases on the left-hand y plane of the graph only go up to 120,000 cases per year. This means that the number **1,000,000 cannot be seen on the graph**, nor is there a point that reaches that high of a number. Therefore, choice C is not correct.

D is incorrect because if you go to the year 1940, you can see that there are some points that sit above the zero line of smallpox cases. This means that the disease could not have been completely eradicated at this time ultimately making choice D incorrect.

33. C is the correct answer.

When dealing with sentence additions, you must have a deep understanding of the previous sentences, as well as those following. Without this, you won't be sure what the specific area of the paragraph is referring to and you may make a mistake. Since this is looking to add a last sentence, we must identify whether or not the passage ends on a cliff hanger or not. This passage discusses completely eradicating smallpox but ends abruptly talking about Edward Jenner. To form a smooth ending sentence, adding this prospective sentence would help conclude the passage and summarize everything mentioned in it. Because of this, C is the correct answer.

A is incorrect because if you were to add more data or information, it would not be a successful end of a passage. This is because concluding sentences are supposed to provide a summary of what was discussed in the entire paragraph. This sentence, though, does not provide any more information and acts as a summary. Thus, A is incorrect.

B is incorrect because it does not make sense as an introduction. If it were an introduction, it would provide the summary for the entire passage at the beginning of the paragraph which would make no sense. Hence, B cannot be correct.

D is incorrect because it does not provide irrelevant information. This information is necessary to add at the end of the sentence because it provides an effective ending and ties in all the previous information from the rest of the passage.

34. D is the correct answer.

Punctuation is the most important part of this answer. Knowing when the right time to use a **semicolon** and how it should properly be used is important. A semicolon should be used, similar to a period, to separate two sections of a sentence. The only difference is a semicolon joins two different ideas. There is no need to use other conjoining words either when this is used, nor should the first word in the next sentence be capitalized. D is correct because the semicolon separates the two sentences and follows the proper structure.

A is incorrect because there is a conjunction after the semicolon. When using a semicolon, there should be no conjunction. Because one is being used, A is deemed incorrect.

B is incorrect because there is a period being used. If there was no conjunction or commas being used in this answer choice, the period would work just like the semicolon does. Unfortunately, since the phrasing begins with a conjunction, it is no longer correct. Hence, B is the wrong answer choice.

C is incorrect because the first word after the semicolon is capitalized. When you use a semicolon, the first word of the following sentence should not be capitalized. Because of this, answer choice C is not correct.

35. D is the correct answer

When looking to determine the shortest, most effective way to form a sentence with proper punctuation, you must first identify how to do this. Often times, using shorter phrases and commas are the way to go. Choice D is correct because it shows **"The Rite of Spring"** came out in the spring without the use of a lot of extra words to expand on this idea. The better you can explain something in a shorter fashion, the easier the reader will understand and follow.

A is incorrect because if there were no changes, the phrase would be long, wordy and confuse the reader from the main point of the passage. It is not important that it mentions how the art caused shock and awe as this is mentioned again in the following sentences. Because of the way the sentence is long and irrelevant, choice A is wrong.

B and C are incorrect because they end the first sentence short and continue to write **long, drawn-out sentences** attempting to explain unimportant, minute details. The shorter and clearer the sentence, the better for a reader. Because these can be confusing when reading and shy away from the point, B and C are not appropriate.

36. B is the correct answer.

Choosing the right word is vital in helping readers understand the passage or paragraph properly. You must fully read the sentence before identifying the correct word to use. In this case, choice B is right because people are typically appalled "at" something. This means that this emotion is directed at the event, which is therefore why B is correct.

A is incorrect because people do not feel emotions **"with"** something; they feel it towards something. This reaction must use the word "at" because it directs what the person or thing is affected by. Hence, A is not the right choice.

C is incorrect because the word **"for"** is often used in terms of possession or gifting. Again, the people at this event would not feel "for" what they were seeing; they would react towards it.

D is incorrect because the word **"in"** refers to a location. The location did not affect the emotion felt, and therefore choice D must be incorrect.

37. **C is the correct answer.**

This question involves **choosing the correct phrase** for an underlined portion. To find the best choice, you must read the sentences before and after the underlined portion. This paragraph is discussing how the audience was not used to this form of unique performance, and thus it caused specific reactions. Because this event occurred in the past, **the past tense must be used**. Choice C uses simple past tense appropriately; therefore, it is the correct answer.

A is incorrect because when the word "**were**" is used, it is in the second person. This passage was written in the third person, so it cannot be accurately used in regard to this sentence.

B is incorrect because the word "had" is a **past participle** that does not need to be used in this context. Past participles are used in conjunction with specific pronouns as well as their verbs. This form does not properly work in this context; therefore, B is incorrect.

D is incorrect because "were about to" indicates the **past tense but in an improper, drawn out way**. Again, the simpler you can say something, the better the reader will be able to understand. By including more words, the writing will not seem more complex; it will only make it more difficult for a reader to fully understand. Because of this, D cannot be the right choice.

38. **B is the correct answer.**

This is a **sentence addition or deletion question**. To properly handle a question like this, you must fully read the entire paragraph that the question is located in. After completed, it may help to **read the surrounding sentences with all of the answer choice options one time**. The one that makes the most sense is most likely the appropriate answer. In this case, the sentence should be added because it provides more details for the following sentences. All claims must be supported with an explanation, so by including this sentence, it would help clarify points for the reader. Because of this, choice B is correct.

A is incorrect because while the sentence should be added for clarity, the reason is incorrect. This sentence does not introduce a new concept into the paragraph. Rather, it clarifies already existent points throughout the passage. Since this answer choice indicates the sentence introduces new information, which is inaccurate, choice A must be incorrect.

C and D are both incorrect because this sentence should be added in order to introduce clarity into the paragraph. **These choices state that they are not to be included**, which is already a red flag. Choice C says that this sentence is an effective conclusion, which is not true. Conclusions are supposed to provide clarity at the end of a passage about the entire section as a whole, which this does not do. Choice D claims the information is irrelevant, which is not accurate either, as it provides support for previous claims made. Because these choices indicated the sentence should not be added, choices C and D are incorrect.

39. C is the correct answer.

Whenever a **period can be properly used**, it should be. This allows the reader to take a pause and a breather between two sentences with separate clauses. This is often more effective than commas especially when there are commas used in the previous or following section of the sentence. Having too much punctuation in a sentence can cause confusion for a reader, so using a period is appropriate in this case.

A is incorrect because if there was no change, the sentence would be **too long to follow**. Run-on sentences are long, drawn out sentences that lead to confusion in the reader. This happens when there is too much information included in a single sentence. If this was kept the way it was now, the idea of "**The Rite of Spring**" would be introduced as well as what this ballet was about. This is too much information in a single sentence; therefore, A is incorrect.

B and D are incorrect because they separate the sentence with a comma to add in more information. This, in other cases, would work. Unfortunately, there are various commas included in the following portion of the sentence. Too many commas can easily confuse a reader. When to pause should be clearly identified, yet when there is too much punctuation, this cannot be done. Because of this, both B and D are incorrect.

40. D is the correct answer.

Writing a less wordy sentence will allow readers to follow the passage smoother. **Including too many words that don't directly relate to** the purpose of the piece will just give people more to pay attention to. They are unnecessary and ultimately don't need to be included. Because this sentence focuses on how Stravinsky developed his music and choreography, we understand the point is to identify that the experience was unique for the audience. Including "that was" is unnecessary, and therefore D is the correct answer choice.

A is incorrect because if there was no change, the sentence would contain two words that **don't need to be included**. Often times, writers may believe that just because there are more words in a sentence, it could sound more intellectual. Most of the time, though, this is inaccurate. By including these words, it provides the reader with confusion and therefore should not be included.

B and C are incorrect because they are unnecessary phrases. Typically, the word "that" is used to identify or refer to a specific thing. In this case, it is not necessary to include because the next word, "unlike" fits perfectly after the word "moves." Because of this, choices B and C are not correct due to how it would make the sentence longer than it needs to be.

41. C is the correct answer.

This question refers to **punctuation**. Using the right punctuation is one of the most important parts of writing because **it helps readers pause and take breaks when necessary**. Inserting a comma in the appropriate spot, or not including one at all, sets the tone of the sentence. In this context, the author is referring to what the dancers were unable to hear. A comma is not necessary and the word that must be inserted to make this a complete sentence. Otherwise, the comma would separate two sections of a sentence that would otherwise be two different sentences. Because of this, choice C is correct.

A is incorrect because if no change was to be made, the comma would be separating two sections of a sentence that would **read as two individual sentences**. Commas should be used to insert a new idea, but a transitional word must be used after the comma. Here, it is not and therefore choice A is wrong.

B is incorrect because while there is a transitional word used, the wrong one was used. The word "**but**" is used to contrast what was previously stated. This is not happening in this sentence because the writer is justifying how the dances were affected by the way the audience acted.

D is incorrect because the word "**or**" is a comparison word. This means if this word was to be used, the writer would have to compare how loud the auditorium was to why the dancers couldn't hear the orchestra. This doesn't make sense as these are related rather than different. Because of this, choice D cannot be correct.

42. C is the correct answer.

The best choice for this question is C because it **uses proper punctuation** while explaining the reason that some of the audience were ejected from the orchestra. Without the reason being included, readers would be confused as to why they were forced to leave that night. Just by including "because of their behavior" at the end of the sentence, it clarifies the situation fully. Because of this, C must be the correct answer choice.

A is incorrect because there is an **incorrect placement of a comma** in this choice. When there is a comma, used as a sentence separator, you must make sure that the second part of the sentence can make sense alone. In this case that would mean "because of their behavior" could be seen as a separate sentence, yet this is not the case. With this, A cannot be correct.

B is incorrect because while it is grammatically accurate, it does not provide a reason as to why the audience was escorted out. This leaves the reader hanging and confused and unable to fully understand the purpose of this sentence.

D is incorrect because again, while the grammar makes sense, **it shortens the sentence too much** and does not provide any support for the previous line in the passage. In order for a passage to make full sense, it should have evidence to support previous claims. Because it doesn't have this information, D is incorrect.

43. **B is the correct answer.**

This question focuses on using the correct tenses. There are two main tenses you can expect to find in these passages. They are past and present tense. Present tense refers to things occurring currently while past tense refers to things that happened already. This passage is in the past tense because it is describing events that happened with Stravinsky's ballet. Because of this, the correct answer choice must be in the past tense. In this case, "had been" is the appropriate use of the past tense for this sentence; therefore, B is correct.

A is incorrect because the word "**was**" typically refers to a situation that was done in the past but no longer applies. This does not work in this situation because the premier is still a noteworthy affair that occurred, which is important to recognize. Because of this, answer A is not correct.

C is incorrect because the word "**is**" is used in the present tense. Since the rest of this passage was written in the past tense, this answer choice cannot be used.

D is incorrect because "**would be**" is often thought as a synonym for "trying to be." In this sentence, the performance was already considered noteworthy and therefore did not "try to be" anything. Because this wording is incorrect, choice D is incorrect.

44. **A is the correct answer.**

This question is asking **whether or not a specific sentence should be added**. To determine whether or not it should be, you must read the paragraph that the sentence is looking to be added in as well as understand what the entire passage was about. This is especially true since this is the **last sentence in the passage,** so the concluding sentence must **summarize** the entire passage well. With this in mind, you can assume the sentence should be added, as it provides an effective way to conclude and summarize the entire previous passage. Thus, answer choice A is correct.

B is incorrect because while it does say the sentence should be included, **it doesn't provide the correct reasoning** for it. The sentence looking to be included does not clarify any other information presented previously. It only provides a concluding, overall statement to leave the reader satisfied after reading. Because of this, B is not the best answer.

C and D are incorrect because they both state that the sentence should not be included in the passage. It is a great concluding sentence and therefore it would not be appropriate as an introduction, nor does it provide information that was previously mentioned throughout the passage. Since it mentioned not including the sentence, both C and D cannot be correct.

Writing Test 3: Answer Key

1. A	28. A
2. D	29. D
3. D	30. B
4. B	31. A
5. A	32. C
6. A	33. B
7. B	
8. B	34. B
9. A	35. D
10. C	36. A
11. D	37. C
	38. D
12. D	39. A
13. B	40. A
14. D	41. C
15. A	42. C
16. C	43. D
17. C	44. A
18. A	
19. B	
20. B	
21. C	
22. A	
23. A	
24. B	
25. A	
26. C	
27. A	

WRITING & LANGUAGE TEST 3
Answers & Explanations

Passage 1

Question 1

A is the best answer. There are two concepts to understand here: **COORDINATE ADJECTIVES** and the use of **COMMAS** when using such adjectives. **Coordinate adjectives** are words that are used to describe the same noun. Here, the coordinate adjectives are "radical," "sometimes socially unacceptable" and "creative"; all of which qualify the same noun, "efforts." When using **coordinate adjectives,** commas are **used to separate all the adjectives** ("radical," "sometimes socially unacceptable") **EXCEPT the FINAL ADJECTIVE** ("creative") **and the noun itself.** Since the current sentence structure follows all these rules, **no change is necessary.**

B is incorrect because **there is an unnecessary deletion of a useful descriptive phrase.** Knowing that avant-garde art can sometimes be socially unacceptable helps **contextualize** these practices for the reader. Therefore, because of this **deletion,** this choice is less suitable.

C is incorrect because it **does not follow the comma rule explained above.** Since there are multiple coordinate adjectives in this sentence, it is important to use commas to help the reader **navigate** the text. The **absence of any punctuation in this answer choice** means that it can immediately be eliminated.

D is incorrect because when **DASHES** are used to demarcate **part of a sentence,** they **emphasize that text** while also making that **text parenthetical,** i.e., it's as if that information were in parentheses, and although emphasized, not necessary to understand the statement. In this case, we see that "sometimes socially unacceptable" adds new information **that is NOT parenthetical** (it is necessary in the statement since it adds a new dimension to what is being said). Furthermore, pay attention to the use of the word "but" (rather than "and"). The use of this conjunction **alters the meaning of the sentence.** Therefore, this choice is less suitable than A.

Question 2

D is the best answer. The key to a good **topic sentence** lies in its being an effective **lead in** to the major **theme** that is being addressed in that paragraph. In this selection, sentence 2 talks about why some people dismiss avant-garde art; sentence 3 discusses why "challenging the mainstream" helps this art leave "a mark" on the world. Therefore, the **most suitable topic sentence would be one that puts forward a summary** of

A is incorrect because using the existing topic sentence does not function as an **effective transition** into the themes of the paragraph. By immediately terming avant-garde art as "shocking," the reader is not given the chance to **contextualize** that information.

B is incorrect. Although this topic sentence does allow for a transition to the following lines, **the choice of vocabulary is not careful enough.** A phrase like "constantly breaking from convention" allows the reader to make many **ASSUMPTIONS.** What conventions are we talking about? What does "constantly breaking mean"? In answer D, the phrasing is more careful "art that pushes the boundaries" (rather than "constantly breaking") and "commonly-accepted social standards" rather than "conventions." **Be extremely clear in your vocabulary choice, so that the reader understands the words as YOU mean to use them.**

C is incorrect because it **misrepresents the content that follows.** By telling the reader that avant-garde art is "conceptual" and "abstract," the text does not lead into the content that follows (about this kind of art being "shocking"). Once again, the choice of vocabulary is **unspecific** and does not give the reader a clear idea about the content.

those two ideas: why this art is dismissed and why the cause for this dismissal makes the art relevant. Choice D accomplishes both these objectives.

Question 3

D is the best answer. In reading the line carefully, we see that there is a missing word "By boldly and courageously sharing their art, avant-garde **[missing word]** has made waves throughout art history." Without a qualified after "avant-garde," the sentence is rendered meaningless. If the sentence had said "By boldly and courageously sharing their art, avant-garde **artists have** made waves throughout art history," then it would be **DEBATABLE.**

A is incorrect. The paragraph following this one speaks about the "medium" that is used by avant-garde artists. So, for this to be an **effective transition statement**, it would need to include a segue (a connection) to the medium that is used by these artists. Something like "By boldly and courageously sharing their art through **innovative media,** avant-garde **artists have** made waves throughout art history." As it stands, the sentence is **irrelevant** as a transition.

B is incorrect. By saying that this art has "made waves," the sentence is essentially **repeating** what was said in the previous sentence about leaving a "mark" on the world. So, we might even say that this sentence is **redundant** because it repeats previously articulated ideas.

C is incorrect because this sentence, by talking about the "courage" and "making waves," **would disrupt the flow of the paragraph** if used as the topic sentence. Given that the second sentence, in that case, would be about the "shocking" nature of this art, speaking of its power right before, doesn't make logical sense.

Question 4

B is the best answer. In this case, rather than a particular grammar rule, "means by which" is a particular **turn of phrase** (way of using language) that is quite common in written English. Therefore, whenever "means _____ which" is used to describe **cause and effect** (where something ("medium") is used by someone ("artist") in order to achieve something ("change viewer's minds)) **"by"** is always the **preposition that needs to be used.** Therefore, for this question, all other answers are **immediately incorrect.**

Question 5

A is the best answer. When asked questions like this one, it is helpful to MAP THE CONCEPTS in each line, to understand the potential fit of an additional sentence. Currently:

- Sometimes, artists look to foster these changes in response to extremely violent or traumatic events. [**CONCEPT:** response of art to social context]
- Consider the example of Dadaism, or Dada; artists developed this avant-garde artistic style in response to the changing and chaotic circumstances facing people in the modern world. [**CONCEPT:** Example of Dadaism, to add to the previous sentence]
- After witnessing the atrocities of World War I, many artists began to see the world as a place where rationality, fairness, and reason were no longer relevant. [**CONCEPT:** explains context of "modern world" in previous sentence]
- Dada artists rejected the concept of […] [**CONCEPT:** Connecting all the ideas mentioned above → this sentence wouldn't make sense if Dadaism was not introduced earlier]

Through **CONCEPT MAPPING**, we can see that this sentence should be kept because it provides an **effective transition.**

B is incorrect because the underlined sentence only speaks about how Dadaism responded to the world and mentions nothing about "social change." Therefore, choosing this answer would mean making an **ASSUMPTION** about Dadaism that is not evidenced in the text.

C is incorrect because of its **IRRELEVANCY.** Given that the main idea here is to speak about the response to art to social circumstances, people's enjoyment of the form has **nothing to do with** the previous or following content in the paragraph.

D is incorrect. This sentence adds to what is being said in the previous line about artists' response to their times. In order for it to be an **interruption,** the underlined sentence would give an example that has nothing to do with this idea. However, since Dadaism is used to connect to the previous sentences' concept, it **adds to the reader's understanding** and thus, **is not an interruption.**

Question 6

A is the best answer. Since the clauses on either side of the **SEMICOLON** each have their own **subject, verb, and object, the use of the semicolon is accurate.** Furthermore, since the second clause provides a **contrast** to the preceding one, the use of a connector like "instead" helps **frame that contrast for the reader** and is an effective transition word. Finally, when a clause begins with a **CONJUNCTIVE ADVERB** (like "instead," "besides," "furthermore"), **it should ALWAYS be followed by a COMMA.**

B is incorrect because it causes a **break in the flow** of the two clauses. Since the two clauses are closely related, a sentence structure that allows them to be read as **fluidly** as possible is helpful to the reader.

C is incorrect. While the use of the semicolon is accurate, this answer choice is **missing the comma** that needs to be there when a **conjunctive adverb** ("instead") **begins a sentence.** The absence of this comma makes the sentence grammatically incorrect.

D is incorrect because you cannot have two **independent clauses** connected by a comma. **COMMAS are mostly used to add emphasis within a line, to separate items in a line, and to separate dependent clauses that enhance (add to) the primary independent clause.** Since this example has two independent clauses, they must be connected with a semicolon.

Question 7

B is the best answer. In order to choose the best answer to this question, look at the lines that come **before and after it.** You'll immediately see that the line before has the **KEYWORD** "Dada." The line that concludes this paragraph also **references** Dadaism. This tells us that the **topic sentence for this paragraph needs to clarify that the following text is about** Dada artists, in specific, and not all avant-garde art, in general. This is the only answer choice that includes the **KEYWORD** in it.

A is incorrect. Without a **reference to Dadaism** in the first line, the reader is led to believe that the paragraph is about all avant-garde art. Therefore, when the reader reaches the last line where Dadaism is mentioned again, the **flow of argumentation** is confusing.

C is incorrect. Replacing the word "art" with "artists" does not solve the issue of **generalization.** Since this paragraph specifically refers to Dada artists, the **topic sentence** needs to **reference the genre** and thus, **contextualize** what is to follow.

D is incorrect because deleting the underlined word would render the sentence **meaningless.** Saying "Avant-garde was notably unconventional [...]" does not work since the term "avant-garde" is a **descriptor** that is used to describe something/someone.

Question 8

B is the best answer. Sentences (1), (2), and (4) describe specific aspects/qualities of *Fountain.* Therefore, the current location of sentence (3) causes a break in the flow of the paragraph since it takes the reader from a consideration of the specific sculpture to a consideration of Duchamp's general contributions. This is why it would be better for sentence (3) to be placed **after** sentence (4) to take the paragraph from the specific to the general in a more effective way.

A is incorrect **because a change is needed** in order to make more effective transitions between the sentences in the paragraph. Once again, **CONCEPT MAPPING** can be immensely helpful here. By tracking the concepts as being "specific" or "general," we immediately see that the "general" interrupts the "specific" and needs to be shifted.

C is incorrect. The line that transitions to sentence (1) introduces the reader to the specific piece, *The Fountain.* Adding a general line about Duchamp in between this sentence and the subsequent description of the urinal would, once again, only **serve to disrupt the flow of ideas** in the paragraph.

D is incorrect. Currently, sentence (2) **effectively transitions out of** sentence (1) by giving the reader new information about *The Fountain.* From being told that the sculpture was of a urinal, this sentence **contextualizes the absurdity of this choice in the second sentence.** Once again, adding sentence (4) here would only hinder (limit) the flow of the paragraph.

Question 9

A is the best answer. By **CONCEPT MAPPING** the sentences in the paragraph with the replacement of sentence (3) after sentence (4), we see the following: First sentence → the urinal; Second sentence → explanation of the urinal; new third sentence → **contextualization of** *The Fountain* in terms of the art world; fourth sentence → further context about Duchamp; last sentence → how the work has/might inspire other artists. With this map we see that the last line, as it is, is an effective conclusion. Therefore, no change is necessary.

B is incorrect because it is **unnecessary.** By saying that Duchamp "sparked an entire artistic revolution" we are essentially told, as it says in the current concluding sentence, that "pave[d] the way for" future generations of avant-garde artists. Adding this sentence would therefore be **unnecessary** and cause **redundancy.**

C is incorrect because the use of the words "rather" and "diverged" makes the sentence **irrelevant** in **context** of the paragraph's content. Since the paragraph tells us how Duchamp made a mark in the art world with his avant-garde work to now suggest that his work did **NOT** fit that movement would be a **contradiction.**

D is incorrect because it invites the reader to make an **ASSUMPTION.** By saying "what Duchamp lacks in skill," it is **implied that previous sentences have somehow contextualized** the author's lack of ability. However, everything that has come before only tells us the opposite and rendering this sentence **irrelevant.**

Question 10

C is the best answer. REFLEXIVE PRONOUNS (like "himself) **only need to be used when the subject and the object of a sentence are the same.** In this passage, Duchamp (and other artists

A is incorrect because the **reflexive pronoun has been used inaccurately.** As per the explanation above, consider this sentence. "He writes the stories himself because he does not trust his interns to do it right." Here, "he" is both the subject and the object making it necessary to use a reflexive pronoun like "himself." Since this **condition of subject-object agreement** is not met, the sentence does need to be changed.

B is incorrect. "He" is a pronoun and a **PRONOUN is a word that takes the place of a noun.** It **replaces** a noun whereas here, "him" **refers to a noun** ("Duchamp). "He" would only be used in place of the name "Duchamp" and since such a **replacement** would make the sentence **meaningless,** we know that this is not the right answer.

D is incorrect. "It" is used to refer to an **OBJECT, not a person.** Since we are clearly referring to people here ("artists like him") the use of "it" is incorrect.

like him) are the subject; "beauty" is the object. Therefore, this is **not the right place to use a reflexive pronoun.**

Question 11

D is the best answer. The main point to notice in this paragraph is the focus on the **KEYWORD** "beauty" and how avant-garde artists challenge themselves and their audiences to **reconside**r what "beauty" can mean. These sentences **imply that this approach to art** challenges traditionally held ideas (of "beauty") and asks people to reconsider what they might mean.

A is incorrect. Although the **tone** communicates the essential premise of the paragraph to get people to reconsider traditional ideas, this sentence is a bit of an **overstatement** in that it uses the words "question" and "deeply-held beliefs." We are **not given enough information** in this passage to evidence that avant-garde causes a questioning of beliefs but only a reconsideration of ideas. Choosing this answer would involve making an **ASSUMPTION.**

B is incorrect. The **tone** toward avant-garde artists in this line is **derogatory** (looks down on), through the use of words like "odd" and phrases like "unable to fit in"). This **contradicts** the other material in the paragraphs which speak **positively** about the way these artists push boundaries.

C is incorrect. Although the **tone** communicates the essential premise of the paragraph to get people to reconsider traditional ideas, this sentence is a bit of an **overstatement** in that it uses the terms like "challenges" and "questions the status quo." We are not given enough information in this passage to evidence that avant-garde causes a questioning of the status quo but only a reconsideration of ideas. Choosing this answer would involve making an **ASSUMPTION.**

Passage 2

Question 12

D is the best answer. Since the first sentence of the paragraph says that chocolate can be found "all over the world," the phrase "Available almost anywhere [...]" **is unnecessary** and **repetitive.** Therefore, it is **unnecessary information** that does not serve any visible purpose even that of transition. Directly beginning the following the sentence with "It comes in [...]" is far more **active** and engaging for the reader.

A is incorrect. Given the **redundancy** exhibited in the underlined phrase and the **passive** quality to the text, a change must be made.

B is incorrect. This too would cause a **repetition of information;** even more, it would be a **verbatim (word for word) repetition** of the words that are used to conclude the previous statement. **Beginning a sentence with the same words that ended the previous one is not considered good practice.**

C is incorrect. This option also, like the ones above, **demonstrates a repetition of information** that only serves as being **disruptive to the flow** of the paragraph and the ideas that it represents.

Question 13

B is the best answer. To consider the importance of this sentence, look at the lines that surround it. Considering those lines, we find that the lines before and after the underlined section speak about chocolate in general; this makes the inclusion of specific information about Western Europeans and Swiss an interruption. Therefore, in order to maintain the clarity of the paragraph, it would be better to delete this line.

A is incorrect. Although the information in the underlined section does not fit the **flow** of the paragraph, the content is still related to the **main theme of the passage,** i.e., chocolate. The title of the passage and the **KEYWORD** "chocolate" in the underlined section make this connection immediately visible. Therefore, since this sentence adds new information about the theme that is the **focus of the passage,** it is **RELEVANT** but misplaced.

C is incorrect. Given the **content** of this paragraph (a general introduction to chocolate) and the content of the next one (about the source of chocolate), the underlined sentence would **not** be an effective concluding sentence. Not only is it **not connected** to the line that comes before it, it also does **not** transition the reader to the next paragraph (which a good concluding, transition sentence would do).

D is incorrect because while the information is **relevant to the general theme** of the paragraph, it **does not provide effective support** to any of the information that comes before or after it. By highlighting the chocolate preferences of a particular part of the world, this sentence only **interrupts** the general information that we are being given about chocolate.

Question 14

D is the best answer. Let's do the **CONCEPT MAPPING.** Current paragraph (1) → general introduction to chocolate; current paragraph (2) → general introduction to the cacao bean; current paragraph (3) → geographical roots of chocolate and move to Europe; current paragraph (4) → chocolate in Europe; current paragraph; current paragraph (5) → cacao bean processing; current paragraph (6) → cacao bean production. Immediately, we notice that paragraph (2) belongs before paragraph (5), i.e., after the current paragraph (4).

A is incorrect. As we see in the concept mapping above, leaving the paragraph where it is now is **disruptive** to the flow of the larger passage. By asking the reader to jump from one topic to another, the current structure is hard to follow and thus, needs to be changed.

B is incorrect. Adding (2) before (1) **would not support the flow** of the passage which currently talks about chocolate and its global popularity in the first part of the passage before moving into a more technical conversation about cacao beans in the second part of the passage. It therefore makes sense that (2) – being an introduction to cacao beans – would be included later on.

C is incorrect because paragraph 3 **effectively transitions** into paragraph 4 by speaking about how the Spanish took chocolate from their colonies in Mesoamerica to Europe. Adding a paragraph about the cacao bean in between these paragraphs would **disrupt the current flow of argumentation.**

Question 15

A is the best answer. No change is needed since it is clear that "its" in this context refers to the subject of the sentence ("chocolate"), which is an inanimate object and thus, does not need a personal pronoun.

B is incorrect. Replacing the word "its" with "chocolate" makes this sentence become "[…] most of the chocolate consumed in the modern world is almost unrecognizable from **chocolate's** original form." The repetition of the word "chocolate" is **unnecessary** since we have just been told what the subject is. While its technically not incorrect, it is definitely an unsuitable choice.

C is incorrect. "It's" is a contraction for "it is." Replacing the word "its" with "it is" makes the sentence become "[…] most of the chocolate consumed in the modern world is almost unrecognizable from **it is** original form." Immediately, we can see that this is both grammatically incorrect and that it makes the sentence **meaningless.**

D is incorrect. Replacing the word "its" with "their" makes the sentence becomes "[…] most of the chocolate consumed in the modern world is almost unrecognizable from **their** original form." "Their" is a **third-person, personal pronoun,** i.e., the word is used to refer to a human being. Using "their" to refer to an object, like chocolate, is grammatically incorrect.

Question 16

C is the best answer. Given that the current last sentence ends with "across many cultures," adding information about its different uses in these cultures ("ceremonies," "medicinal uses," "celebrations") helps **explain** what is meant by the term "various uses."

A is incorrect. What comes next is a paragraph about the roots of chocolate in Mesoamerica and the eventual move to Europe. Therefore, this sentence about different uses of chocolate is not helpful to what comes next. That said, it does function as an **effective transition sentence** to lead us into a consideration about the use of chocolate in Mesoamerica.

B is incorrect. It would not be appropriate to place this new sentence at the beginning of the previous one since the previous sentence is necessary to **establish context.** It is because the previous sentence tells us about the "various uses" of chocolate in different cultures and that we are able to **contextualize the different uses that are listed in the newly added sentence.**

D is incorrect. The sentence talks about the uses of chocolate in different cultures and in different contexts. Because of this and because of the focus of this passage and this paragraph, the information contained here is **extremely relevant** to the content that is being put forward to the reader.

Question 17

C is the best answer. The use of the phrase "have been tracked" is in the **passive voice.** As explained earlier, **it is always preferred to use the active voice.** In this case, by making the subject of the sentence the people who did the tracking rather than the object that was tracked we are immediately able to make the sentence more **direct.** There are only two choices that allow this in the list of answers. See below for why C is a better choice than B.

A is incorrect because leaving the sentence unchanged would maintain the **passive** tone to the text while also being unclear about who it was that tracked the roots of the chocolate! For both these reasons, it is necessary to change the structure of this sentence.

B is incorrect. Although this choice **foregrounds** (focuses on) the people who did the tracking, this is a less suitable choice than C because of the phrase "the roots of chocolate." Compared to "chocolate's origins," "the roots of chocolate" is more **passive** and thus, less preferable.

D is incorrect. Replacing the underlined section with "Chocolate originates" makes the sentence both grammatically incorrect and meaningless ("Chocolate originates back over two thousand years to the plateaus of Central America"). Therefore, this answer can be eliminated.

Question 18

A is the best answer. There is no need to make any changes in this statement since it is true that Central America is, even now, also called Mesoamerica.

B is incorrect. Saying that this region was "formerly" called Mesoamerica would be **factually incorrect** since the term **implies that the name is no longer in use.**

C is incorrect. While using "also" is grammatically correct, using "which" to introduce this additional, dependent clause to the sentence leaves **less room for misinterpretation** by the reader. Since the sentence begins by saying "In this part of the world" (without re-stating that it is Central America), the "which" helps make the connection to the region that was mentioned earlier. Without the "which," the reader would be right to wonder which part of the world is being **referenced** here. Additionally, the use of punctuation in this option is incorrect. If the phrase beginning with "also" is preceded by a **DASH,** it should also be followed by one.

D is incorrect. Let's replace it and try: "In this part of the world **that is too called** Mesoamerica, ancient peoples discovered how to domesticate the cacao tree." Immediately, we notice that the sentence is harder to follow because of the lack of punctuation after "world"). In addition, the word "too" is used **incorrectly here and makes the sentence meaningless.**

Question 19

B is the best answer. The beginning of this sentence is the first time that the "Spanish" **have been referenced in this paragraph.** For anyone **unfamiliar** with Latin American/European/colonial history, this reference would seem random and disconnected **unless** the information is contextualized in some way. So, although "they" is grammatically correct, replacing "they" with "with conquerors" would **help any reader access the text** – whether or not they are familiar with the particular historical context.

A is less suitable. Although not grammatically incorrect as mentioned above, "they" does not allow the reader to **contextualize** why the Spanish are being mentioned here. Since the previous sentence spoke about the "Olmec, Maya and Aztec" peoples, it is necessary to **clarify** why the Spanish is being mentioned.

C is incorrect. This statement is factually incorrect. The Olmec, Maya, and Aztec are the native peoples to Mesoamerica and not the Spanish. Therefore, this would be **an inaccurate term** with which to contextualize the Spanish for the reader.

D is incorrect because "it" is used to refer to an **inanimate object.** Here, the subject being referred to is the "Spanish" (people) and therefore, "it" would be both grammatically incorrect and unhelpful to the reader.

Question 20

B is the best answer. Look at the **context**, which is the sentence that would come before the suggested addition and the sentence that would come after. We see that the current last sentence in the paragraph speaks about the growing popularity of chocolate in Europe while the following paragraph speaks about improved processing methods during the Industrial Revolution. Since Choice B addresses both of these topics (popularity and new innovations), it makes a great addition as the last line of the existing paragraph.

A is incorrect. If this sentence were not added, **there would be no effective transition between the paragraphs**. We would jump from a paragraph that talks about growing popularity in Europe to one that talks about cacao bean processing during the Industrial Revolution. Therefore, we see the need for a sentence to help us make the transition.

C is incorrect. By using superlatives like "sweetest" and "richest" and based on the sentence that would come before it, this answer choice seems to be an **overstatement** (exaggeration) **for which no other evidence has been provided.** Furthermore, this sentence does not provide **an effective transition** to the next paragraph.

D is incorrect. Once again, there seems to be **overstatements here** that are not based on any of the preceding information. Nothing has been mentioned thus far about people becoming rich and/or anything to do with "social injustice." Adding this sentence here, therefore, would be both **disruptive** and **irrelevant.**

Question 21

C is the best answer. The important information here is that the Ivory Coast is the largest cacao producer in the world. And being the "largest" **implies** that "most of the world's cacao beans" are grown here. Therefore, the current repetition of information can be cut out in which case the only other information to be **contextualized** would be the relationship between West Africa and the Ivory Coast.

A is incorrect because leaving the statements unchanged would mean **repeating the same information** in different ways. As mentioned above, since being the "largest producer" means the grower of the most beans, the two sentences are better off combined into one.

B is incorrect. Since the statement following that about Ivory Coast mentions the African continent, ending the previous sentence with "West Africa" allows a more **effective transition**. In addition, in order to make this **text accessible** to readers who might not know anything about the geography of the African continent situating the Ivory Coast is important.

D is less suitable. While the use of the **SEMICOLON** works in this case since both the sentences are independent clauses and have their own subject, verb, and object, we are still stuck with the repetition of information in the sentence structure.

Question 22

A is the best answer. The best way to choose an answer for a question like this is to replace the underlined section with all the given options and then decide which one might work best. Essentially, in this case, a **process of elimination** reveals that no change is needed here.

B is incorrect. In this choice, the sentence becomes "**Chocolate lovers everywhere** illustrates the lasting power of a food that people have enjoyed for thousands of years." Not only is there a **singular/plural disagreement** (between "lovers" and "illustrates") but this sentence is **meaningless!**

C is incorrect. In this choice, the sentence becomes:"**Chocolate may not be as popular as it once was, but this** illustrates the lasting power of a food that people have enjoyed for thousands of years." Apart from being a long sentence that is hard to follow, the new addition **contradicts** prior information that has been provided in the paragraph.

D is incorrect. In this choice, the sentence becomes "**Food cultures across the world use many varied ingredients,** which illustrates the lasting power of a food that people have enjoyed for thousands of years." As is immediately apparent, speaking about the general ingredients of food does not fit at all with the ongoing discussion about chocolate. This choice is completely irrelevant.

Passage 3

Question 23

A is the best answer. The underlined section is **relevant** and **appropriate** in referring to the subject of the sentence ("firefighters") and in explaining the action they are undertaking ("running"). No change is required in this sentence.

B is incorrect. "They have run" **implies** this is in the past tense and would cause a **verb tense inconsistency** with the previous part of the sentence, which uses the **present continuous tense** ("weighing them down"). Therefore, this is not a suitable answer.

C is incorrect because "were running" is the **PAST CONTINUOUS TENSE** which creates a **VERB TENSE INCONSISTENCY** with "weighing them down" (which is in the **present continuous tense**). Therefore, this is not a suitable answer.

D is incorrect because "they would run" **implies a future conditional,** i.e., they would run IF something else happened. Therefore, given the **context of the statement** and the **need for verb tense consistency,** this is not a suitable answer.

Question 24

B is the best answer. The **KEYWORDS** to pay attention here are "modern" and "save." The former tells us that the author is speaking about current times; the latter tells us that we are speaking in the **present tense.** Therefore, the **present tense of the verb "to do"** (which is "do") is the most appropriate answer.

A is incorrect because the current statement has a verb tense **inconsistency.** "Did" is in the **past tense,** while "save" **is in the present tense.** Therefore, there does need to be a change.

C is incorrect. "Does" would imply a **singular subject** (one firefighter). Since the subject here is **plural** (multiple firefighters), "does" would be grammatically incorrect.

D is incorrect once again because it is in the **past perfect tense** and causes a **verb tense inconsistency** with the present tense, "save." Furthermore, it **contradicts the term** "modern" – this term very specifically refers to an ongoing occurrence.

Question 25

A is the best answer. Look at the **context** around the underlined section. The previous sentence talks about public safety tools, and the following sentence (in the next paragraph) speaks about the evolution of firefighting over time. By rewriting the sentence with the choice here, we are able to more **effectively** take readers from the ideas in this paragraph to the ideas in the next.

B is incorrect because the choice here **does not help clarify any of the terms that have been used earlier in the text.** In fact, it introduces a new idea that helps **frame future paragraphs.** Therefore, this is not a suitable answer.

C is incorrect. The proposed rewrite tells us about the evolution of firefighting, which is **extremely relevant** to the topics that are being discussed. Furthermore, there is nothing in the sentence structure or vocabulary to suggest **an absence of logic** given what is being said before and after.

D is incorrect. By introducing us to the evolution of firefighting, the content in this statement is **absolutely relevant to the themes** being discussed in the passage. There is nothing **irrelevant** about it!

Question 26

C is the best answer. The clause that follows the **COMMA** helps add information to what came before it. Since the **contextual information** that is closest to the comma (before it) refers to a time period ("2000 years ago), "when" is a more effective connector than "where."

A is incorrect because "where" refers to information that is not directly preceding the comma and thus, leaves more room for **misinterpretation.** If the order of the sentence were reversed, and it said, "Professional firefighting began over 2000 years ago in Rome," then "where" would be the more appropriate connector.

B is incorrect. Using the word "because" would **imply** that firefighting was invented solely due to Marcus Crauss (as a person). This would be an **exaggeration** and potentially an **ASSUMPTION** because all we know is that it occurred "when" the first fire department was established, i.e., because of his action and not his personhood.

D is incorrect. If the underlined word were to be deleted, the sentence would lose meaning. It would result in **two independent clauses** – each with their own subject, verb, and object – that are not connected to each other. This would make the **context** of the events being described harder to understand.

Question 27

A is the best answer. The current sentence allows the reader to understand Crauss' way of working. If someone did not pay him the money that he demanded he would not help them with their fire emergency. This helps provide evidence for the phrase in the previous sentence, "Far from being altruistic."

B is incorrect. "When payment was considered insufficient" is more **passive** and places the **focus** on the payment (rather than the building owner). The **active voice** is always preferred when dealing with these passages.

C is incorrect. This choice **contradicts the context** of what is being said that Crauss was "far from being altruistic." Investigating the causes of the fire is **irrelevant** based on the information that is provided to us in this passage.

D is incorrect because once again "At a whim" does not help address the critique of Crauss' lack of altruism (i.e., his corruption). Instead, it presents this man as doing things without reason when he had very clear reasons for not helping someone with their fire (not getting his money).

Question 28

A is the best answer. If the underlined portion would be deleted, we would be left with a **commentary** about "unsavory business practices." However, we know that this paragraph seeks to **inform the reader** about the evolution of modern firefighting. Therefore, the underlined section is necessary to bring the reader back to the **main concepts** that are being dealt with in the passage.

B is incorrect. The underlined section tells us about the ways in which Crauss' work helped pave the way for modern firefighting as we know it (despite his corrupt business practices). The sentence **does not** mention the **general impact** of firefighting on public safety. This is an unsuitable response.

C is incorrect. This statement is **irrelevant** because the underlined section very clearly tells us how Crauss' work "laid the foundation for future firefighting." Therefore, it is not about the modern technologies that are used in firefighting.

D is incorrect because the information provided here is very clearly **relevant** in terms to the content of the passage and the paragraph. It allows us to learn about the role that Crauss played in the evolution of firefighting as we know it today.

Question 29

D is the best answer. To be "credible" means to be "believable" or to be "real." Since the previous sentence speaks about how highly flammable cities were at that time, using the word "credible" **is relevant** since it tells us that the worries were genuine and needed attention. The reason it is a better word choice than "plausible" will be explained below.

A is less suitable because "plausible" carries less **weight** than "credible." To be "plausible" means that the likelihood of something is reasonable rather than believable. It would be like saying that fires "may" happen rather than fires "could" happen. The former **implies** more uncertainty than the latter, which in this case is less suitable since fires were a real danger.

B is incorrect. To say that fires were a "likely" fear **implies** that it "probably" was a fear (rather than stating that it definitely was a fear). Once again, this choice **does not communicate the seriousness** of the threat that fires represented at the time.

C is incorrect. "Trustworthy" is an adjective that is used to describe a person's character rather than the likelihood of a fear. In this context, therefore, this word would be completely **irrelevant.**

Question 30

B is the best answer. Fires were capable of destroying entire communities **IF** they were not "checked" (i.e., controlled). The sentence as it presents fire as being singularly capable of destroying communities, but it does not give us enough **context** in which to frame our understanding of that statement.

A is incorrect because as stated above the current sentence structure speaks about fire's capability of destroying communities **without enough of a disclaimer** (that they could destroy only if they weren't controlled). While the current option is not technically incorrect, it is less suitable than the correct answer.

C is incorrect. The subject of the suggested answer here is "firefighters." However, the sentences preceding this have all talked about fires as the subject. To shift the subject so suddenly causes a **disruption** to the flow of the paragraph and therefore, is less suitable.

D, like A, is not incorrect in terms of its structure or content. However, this answer too does not provide enough **contextual support** for the idea that is being presented. That is why it is a less suitable answer.

Question 31

A is the best answer. The current first sentence of the paragraph begins with a reference to "these early versions of the professional firefighters" without providing **context** about what these early versions are. Furthermore, the previous paragraph ends with talking about how destructive past fires helped modern innovations in firefighting. Therefore, "these early versions of the professional firefighters" does not work to refer to the transition sentence either. Thus, the new addition would help **provide information that clarifies** what follows.

B is incorrect because adding this information to the last line would **disrupt** the conclusion by speaking about the event that catalyzed the formation of companies which is **after** the companies have been discussed. Therefore, this is an unsuitable answer.

C is incorrect. This sentence puts forward **information** that helps us understand the evolution of modern firefighting. Nowhere does it mention or refer to the heroism of firefighters (that was in the introductory paragraph). This argument, therefore, would be **irrelevant** in the given context of the text.

D is incorrect. Since this statement tells us historical information about the evolution of firefighter companies and given that the **central focus** of this passage is the same, the information is absolutely **relevant** to the passage/paragraph.

Question 32

C is the best answer. The clause "would mark an insured building with their company sign" is a **NON-ESSENTIAL ELEMENT** to the sentence. So, while it is useful to know that the companies marked buildings with signs, it is not necessary to know that in order to understand the rest of the paragraph. Since ,"which" is often used to introduce such non-essential elements, this is the most suitable choice.

A is incorrect because "who" is used to refer to a person. In this case, the subject is firefighter companies and as these companies are organizations, so **they are not humanized**. Therefore, "who" needs to be changed in order to make the sentence grammatically correct.

B is incorrect. Although the use of "that" is grammatically correct, "that" versus "which" might be decided based on whether what follows is considered **ESSENTIAL** or **NON-ESSENTIAL**. In this case, since information about signage can be considered **NON-ESSENTIAL** to the remainder of the paragraph, "which" is preferred.

D is incorrect. Breaking this sentence into two independent clauses is **unnecessary** especially since the information about the companies placing their signs is considered **NON-ESSENTIAL. To decide if something is ESSENTIAL or NON-ESSENTIAL,** read the whole paragraph. If this information were **NOT** in the paragraph, would it limit your understanding of its content in any way? If the answer is yes, then that information is **ESSENTIAL.** If the answer is no, it is **NON-ESSENTIAL.**

Question 33

B is the best answer. Buildings cannot be customers of insurance companies; the people who represent those buildings are the ones who are. Therefore, the owners need to be referenced in any edit of the sentence. Also, of importance is the **tense usage.** Since we are speaking about the past, it is important that any verb in the edit uses the **past tense.**

A is incorrect. Since "they" is preceded by "the company would leave the burning building," it is unclear if the term is referring to the company or the building. It cannot be the company (since that refers to the firefighters) so it must refer to the building – but as mentioned above, buildings cannot be customers (their owners are).

C is incorrect. Although this choice references the owner, it uses the verb "is." This causes **verb tense inconsistency** since the passage is very obviously referring to the past.

D is incorrect. While "it" clearly refers to the building and is thus clearer than "they" about the point of reference, we still run into the issue of who can be a customer to an insurance company. Since buildings are inanimate objects, they cannot be considered "customers."

Passage 4

Question 34

B is the best answer. This choice uses a **simple structure** to provide the information that Mark Zuckerbeg was a student at Harvard University when he founded Facebook. Without adding extra clauses and/or **cluttering** (crowding the text) with punctuation, this sentence effectively communicates the desired information. **Keep your writing as simple as possible.**

A is incorrect. First, it uses the term "they" and the **plural** "students" to refer to a single individual, Mark Zuckerberg. In addition to these grammatical errors, the current structure is complicated to follow since it breaks up two sentences that could easily be combined to make the content **flow more easily.**

C is incorrect. To use a **SEMICOLON,** you need two complete sentences and each of which has a subject, verb, and object. In this choice, the part of the sentence that follows the semicolon is **not a complete sentence.** Therefore, it is grammatically incorrect.

D is incorrect. The use of the term "even though" **implies that what follows will somehow justify/clarify what came before it.** In this case, the fact that Zuckerberg was a student is not needed to clarify anything that came earlier. It is simply an additional piece of information.

Question 35

D is the best answer. This choice is the most **active.** It states that "Facebook limited its membership to students" without adding phrases/clauses that would make the voice more **passive.** In these passages, the **active voice** is always preferred. And when two choices seem active, choose the one that is **more** active.

A, while grammatically correct, is **more passive** than the choice above. By saying that "membership was limited" rather than "Facebook limited," the subject is given less active participation in the content.

B is incorrect. The current sentence construction is **passive** because of the phrase "was limited to." Since there is a more active way to phrase the same idea as above, this choice is less suitable. **PASSIVE VOICE** is when a sentence is framed to say that a **subject receives an action.** This can be noted by the **position of the subject** in the sentence (beginning, middle, end). By placing the subject at the end of the sentence, this choice is less suitable.

C is incorrect because by saying that "membership was composed of," the **action** of limiting membership is completely ignored. Once again, this makes the sentence **passive.**

Question 36

A is the best answer. The first sentence tells us about initial restriction of membership and currently the next sentence tells us about billions of members. Adding this sentence will allow the reader to understand **HOW** that huge increase in numbers happened; it allows the reader to better understand the **context** of the information provided.

B is incorrect. There is no new concept that is being introduced following the inclusion of this sentence. The sentence that follows this one only describes the **effect** that was **caused** by this change. There is no new concept that is clarified.

C is incorrect. If this sentence were to conclude the paragraph, the preceding sentences would tell us about the increase in numbers and only give us a reason for that increase **after** that idea has been mentioned. Structurally, this is **weak** since it is important to give readers all the contextual information needed to **frame** an idea **before** it is described.

D is incorrect. This statement gives us information about **how** Facebook's users grew to the billions so quickly. Given that the increase in users is the main theme of this paragraph, the information here is **completely relevant**. Therefore, this answer can be eliminated.

Question 37

C is the best answer. Since the subject that the underlined word refers to are the people, "who" is the more grammatically correct choice.

Although grammatically correct, Choice A is less suitable since "that" is more advisable to use when what is being referred to is a non-human entity: an object, an idea, or subjects that are not human beings.

B is incorrect. "Which" is usually preceded by a **COMMA** and is used to include a **NON-ESSENTIAL** element to the sentence. In this case, the part of the sentence being referred to is an **ESSENTIAL** part of the sentence and using the word "which" would render the statement both grammatically incorrect and meaningless.

D is incorrect. Consider the sentence with this choice. "The billions of people **in** use Facebook or its popular subsidiaries [...]." Immediately, we see that the **preposition** "in" makes the sentence **meaningless.** This answer can be immediately ignored.

Question 38

D is the best answer. This is the most **active choice.** By using the verb in its infinitive form (an infinitive is an unconjugated verb that is preceded by "to" like to run, to climb, or to study). It is the most **active** form of using a verb.

A is incorrect because it is **passive.** The **gerund** form of a verb (adding "ing" at the end of the verb like running, climbing, or studying) changes the **tone** of a sentence and in this case, "for running" is more passive than "to run."

B is incorrect. Like the choice above, the use of "running" as a gerund (with or without a "for" before it) is a more **passive way** of framing the ideas in that sentence.

C is incorrect. "That will run" is written in the future tense and from the previous sentences, we know that the paragraph is discussing strategies that Facebook is using now. For example, it is said that "Facebook charges" and not "Facebook will charge." Using "that will run" will therefore cause a **verb tense inconsistency** in the sentence.

Question 39

A is the best answer. The sentence preceding this proposed addition speaks about how Facebook charges advertisers. The paragraph following this looks at the revenue received from advertisements. Therefore, adding this sentence would help bring this paragraph to a **better conclusion** while also providing an **effective transition** to the content that follows.

B is incorrect. This proposed addition will not "introduce" other information in the paragraph since the point at which it is included is at the very end. The information that is needed to **contextualize** this addition has already been introduced and explained.

C is incorrect. If used as the introductory sentence, this proposed addition would **disrupt the flow** of the paragraph. The paragraph currently makes a general introduction to revenue at the beginning before moving into a specific discussion about revenue sources. This tells us that the additional sentence belongs at the end of the paragraph.

D is incorrect. The information that is included in the proposed addition has not been stated anywhere else. In fact, by telling us more about how much of Facebook's revenue came from advertising, it helps **contextualize** the numbers given before. Information is redundant when it is repeating existing ideas or is saying something that is completely irrelevant. Since neither of those conditions is met here, this answer can be eliminated.

Question 40

A is the best answer. The Figure tells us that 99% of the company's revenue comes from advertisers. This implies that advertisers find immense value in using the platform and are willing to invest considerable resources in doing so.

B is incorrect because the Figure does not provide any information about what the pioneers thought about the future of the company in the 1990s. All the Figure shows is the share of revenue from advertisers versus other sources. Therefore, choosing this answer would involve making an **ASSUMPTION.**

C is incorrect because the Figure does not provide any information about other advertising options and their costs. All the Figure shows is the share of Facebook's revenue from advertisers versus other sources. Therefore, choosing this answer would involve making an **ASSUMPTION.**

D is less suitable. Although this information is evidenced by the image, pay attention to the **KEYWORDS** "most effective support" in the question. Choice A has more effective support because the **focus** of text marked 40 is on the advertisers and not on the other sources.

Question 41

C is the best answer. The author writes this passage as a **commentator** by talking about Facebook from the outside. The **tone** of the passage does not give away any personal relationship between the narrative voice and the content. Since "society" is the most large-scale term here, it best reflects the existing tone.

A is incorrect. The inclusion of the word "our" introduces a **collective voice.** However, since other terms that imply such collectivity like "we" and "us" have not been used anywhere in the passage or paragraph, it is **abrupt** to suddenly include such a term and thus change the **narrative voice.**

B is incorrect. Similar to choice A, "your" would be an abrupt, direct inclusion of the reader when no such effort has been made earlier in the passage/paragraph. It would be **inconsistent** in relation to the **tone** of the text. In order for "your" to be correct here, there should have multiple direct addresses to the reader in other parts of the text.

D is incorrect. Saying "systems have raised novel concerns regarding **the** relationship with technology" is extremely ambiguous since it is unclear whose relationship (to technology) is being referred to.

Question 42
C is the best answer. Here, the word "add" is used to **imply** an increase of value, i.e., Facebook uses member information to raise value for their advertisers. In this context, **add** (like the mathematical concept) is the most appropriate answer.

A is incorrect because "ad" refers to advertisement and in this sentence, if "ad" were replaced with "advertisement," you would immediately find that the sentence loses meaning.

B is incorrect because "ads" refers to advertisements and in this sentence, if "ad" were replaced with "ads," the sentence would still have no meaning.

D is incorrect. Using this answer, the sentence would read "Facebook relies on user information to **have added** value to its advertising platform." The verb tense inconsistency causes an immediate lack of meaning in the sentence. "Relies" is in the present tense whereas "have added" is in the present perfect tense (i.e., a past event that has present consequences). Because of this inconsistency, this choice can be eliminated.

Question 43
D is the best answer. By separating a really long single sentence into two different sentences and by using a phrase like "In response" to connect the ideas, this is a clear way of representing the ideas that are being spoken about.

A is incorrect. The sentence, as it is, is really long and thus, hard for the reader to follow. Although the two independent clauses are separated by a punctuation (comma) and conjunction (and), the sentence is hard to read. You will notice that this one sentence takes four lines. This is not an elegant sentence structure.

B is incorrect. The use of the **SEMICOLON** is accurate since both clauses can stand as complete sentences. Once again, it is an issue of **style. When possible, long sentences should be avoided, and their ideas should be split across multiple, shorter sentences.**

C is incorrect. Apart from an issue of **style** still being present, a conjunction like "and" is **NOT USED** after a semicolon.

Question 44

A is the best answer. The word "has" emphasizes the role that Facebook has played in the changes that are being spoken of. These are changes that are still happening in the present moment. No change is required here since this is in keeping with the content and focus on the rest of the paragraph.

B is incorrect because of a **verb tense** inconsistency that will be caused by the use of "will have." Since the preceding verbs is used in the present tense "works" and the verb in the future tense ("will survive") is qualified by saying that "time will tell," the underlined verb has to be in the present tense as well.

C is incorrect. "Have" would be used only if the subject of the sentence was used in the **plural.** Since the sentence is referring to Facebook as a **singular** entity, this would be grammatically incorrect.

D is incorrect. Deleting "has would" once again cause **verb tense inconsistency** since "fostered" would be in the **past tense** while the preceding components have been written in the **present tense.**

Writing Test 4: Answer Key

1. D
2. C
3. B
4. D
5. A
6. C
7. B
8. B
9. D
10. C
11. D

12. A
13. A
14. D
15. C
16. C
17. B
18. B
19. D
20. A
21. D
22. B

23. A
24. A
25. B
26. D
27. C

28. C
29. D
30. D
31. C
32. B
33. C

34. C
35. A
36. B
37. B
38. A
39. D
40. B
41. C
42. B
43. D
44. C

WRITING & LANGUAGE TEST 4
Answers & Explanations

Passage 1

Question 1

D is the best answer. INTRODUCTIONS work best when they start with a GENERAL TOPIC SENTENCE that eases the reader into the content that follows. Deleting the current first sentence would allow for this to happen since what is currently the second sentence is a great example of a general topic sentence that **frames the following content for its reader.**

A is incorrect. Although this sentence does provide information about a specific region, **it does not fit into its current position** because what follows are general statements about the pine beetle challenge. By placing **specific information BEFORE the general information, the flow of argumentation is weak.**

B is incorrect. When considering the flow of argumentation in a paragraph, it is often better to start with the MORE GENERAL STATEMENTS that will then help frame any SPECIFIC STATEMENTS that follow. Since the current statement does the **opposite,** it is **NOT an effective introduction to the content that follows.**

C is incorrect. Given the theme of this passage as indicated by its title "The Mountain Pine Beetle Epidemic," there is no need for the introductory statement to talk about all the species that are affecting America's forests. This answer choice is incorrect **because it asks for contextual information that might, in fact, not be useful for the reader at this time.**

Question 2

C is the best answer. Since the focus of this paragraph is the breeding process of the pine beetle, this sentence would give the reader a **general introduction** to the topic before providing **details about the breeding process.**

A is incorrect. Currently, the paragraph immediately addresses the main topic and begins speaking about the breeding process of adult beetles. **Since the previous paragraph implies nothing about what is to follow in its concluding sentence, it is imperative that the first sentence of this paragraph transitions the reader into the topic.**

B is incorrect. This answer choice focuses on the size of the pine beetle (which is likened to be the size of a "grain of rice") and does not **frame the topic of the paragraph** for the reader. As we know, a **GOOD TOPIC SENTENCE will allow the reader to immediately ascertain (identify) what is to follow.**

D is incorrect. Once again, by focusing on the beetles' "voracious appetites" rather than their breeding process, this answer does not **frame the topic of the paragraph** for the reader. Therefore, this is not a suitable choice.

Question 3

B is the best answer. By removing additional clauses, this sentence is the best choice because it is the most **direct – telling the reader all the important information without using any complications in the structure. Whenever possible, choose the simplest sentence construction!**

A is incorrect. The current construction of the sentence is **unclear.** By placing "growing into adults" as a dependent clause at the end of the sentence, the reader cannot tell if it is the chewing of the bark that helps the larva grow into an adult or if they are chewing on the bark *while* they are growing or both. Because of this lack of clarity, the sentence cannot be left as it is and needs to be changed.

C is incorrect because "while growing" is **passive. PASSIVE VOICE is when a sentence is framed to say that a subject receives an action** whereas in **ACTIVE VOICE** a sentence describes the subject as **performing** the action. "As they grow" places emphasis on the subject's action, and "while growing" places the subject in a more passive position. **Active voice is always preferred in these passages.**

D is incorrect. Pay attention to the **KEYWORD** "because." The use of this word changes the meaning of the sentence and **implies** a cause-effect relationship **that would require the reader to make an ASSUMPTION about what is being said in the text.**

Question 4

D is the best answer. In a question about VERB TENSE CONSISTENCY, look at how all the preceding and following verbs in the sentence have been conjugated. In this sentence, the verbs other than the one underlined are all conjugated in the **PRESENT CONTINUOUS TENSE** ("start burrowing." This is an immediate clue that the underlined section should be either in the PRESENT or the PRESENT CONTINUOUS TENSE and when you try both "are finding" and "find," you realize that it is only the latter which helps the sentence maintain its meaning.

A is incorrect. Currently, the underlined segment is written in **FUTURE PERFECT TENSE** ("will" indicates the future and "have" indicates the perfect tense). Using this choice, therefore, causes a **verb tense inconsistency,** which is grammatically incorrect.

B is incorrect. Once again, this choice causes a **verb tense inconsistency** and is in the **PAST PERFECT TENSE.** Therefore, this answer can be discarded immediately.

C is incorrect. Let's try it out with this sentence. "Adult pine beetles from the prior year's spawn 4 **are finding** a new living pine tree." Immediately, just from the **sound of the sentence,** you'll see that the use of the PRESENT CONTINUOUS tense makes the sentence harder to follow.

Question 5

A is the best answer. Since the sentence describes what happens each time that pine beetles infest a tree, the use of the term "Whenever" is completely **relevant** and does not need to be changed.

While choices B and C are not technically incorrect, they are less suitable answers for a simple reason. "Each time" and "every time" use one more term than is needed to communicate the same idea than "whenever does." Therefore, since **concise** (brief and direct) **terms are always preferred in such writing,** these answers are more **DEBATABLE** and can thus be eliminated.

D is incorrect. The use of the world "While" would change the meaning of the sentence. This term would **imply** that the beetles destroy the trees they infest **during the time that they are in the trees.** Now, this is **NOT entirely incorrect.** However, "during" does not covey the **extent** of what is captured by "whenever." That is, phenomena happens **every single time** that the beetles infest a tree.

Question 6

C is the best answer. While **COMMAS are useful in separating three or more words/phrases/clauses in a sentence,** the use of a comma is also dependent on the nature of the clause. In this case, we have a **DEPENDENT CLAUSE** "until fire or extreme cold halt the cycle" that follows an **INDEPENDENT CLAUSE.** "The pine beetles will continue this process until there are no more living trees nearby." In such a case, the **COMMA RULES** say that you should only use a comma **BETWEEN a main clause and a SUBORDINATE (dependent) clause** in the case of extreme contrast. Since there is no **EXTREME CONTRAST** here, a comma should not be used.

A is incorrect. Currently, the second part of the sentence (about cold and fire) **is a DEPENDENT CLAUSE** that does not function on its own. **DEPENDENT CLAUSES,** by their very nature, seek to clarify something in the preceding clause and not function as stand-alone information. Therefore, to have the two clauses as separate sentences is not a suitable answer.

B is incorrect. SEMICOLONS are used when there are independent clauses **on both sides of the punctuation. Each of which has their own subject, verb, and object.** Since this condition is not met in the example, this answer is incorrect.

D is incorrect. "And" implies that **both** conditions need to be fulfilled for the trees to be destroyed, i.e., "till there are no more living trees" **AND** "a fire or extreme cold halt the cycle." However, the **context** tells us that the trees would be destroyed if **ANY ONE** of those things happened (be it no living trees nearby, **OR** extreme cold **OR** fire).

Question 7

B is the best answer. Pay attention to whether the subject being referred to by the underlined section is in the SINGULAR or the PLURAL. Here, "amplified" refers to "fire suppression practices" (in the **plural**). Therefore, the verb should be conjugated as "have," i.e. "have amplified," **in order to be grammatically correct.**

A is incorrect because the use of the conjugation "has" would only be accurate if it was referring to a **singular subject** (one fire suppression practice). Since the sentence is very clearly referring to multiple practices, a change needs to be made.

C is incorrect because of the **VERB TENSE INCONSISTENCY** that would be caused by the use of this answer. Earlier in the sentence, we see the use of the **PRESENT TENSE** ("mountain pine beetles **are** a natural part of [...]") and therefore, using the **FUTURE PERFECT TENSE** ("will have amplified") **would cause an incorrect inconsistency.**

D is incorrect once again because of the **plural** subject and the **singular conjugation of the verb.** For "amplifies" to be used as **PRESENT TENSE rather than PRESENT PERFECT,** the subject it refers to needs to be singular. Since it is a plural subject, the correct answer would be "amplify."

Question 8

B is the best answer. The sentence suggests that there is a threat that is posed by the beetles to **BOTH** forests and humans in similar ways. The term "alike" which is one is like the other, i.e., similar, would allow us to draw this exact conclusion and therefore, is the most suitable choice.

A is incorrect because **the reflexive pronoun** ("themselves) **has been used inaccurately. REFLEXIVE PRONOUNS only need to be used when the subject and the object of a sentence are the same.** Here, "the beetles" are the subject and humans and trees are the objects making it **incorrect** to use a reflexive pronoun.

C is incorrect. Replacing the underlined word with this choice would result in a statement that reads as follows: "they pose risks for the health of forests and humans **indeed**." As we can tell from reading this statement, placing a **connector** like "indeed" at the end of a sentence takes away from its meaning. **CONNECTORS** like "indeed" are to be used **at the beginning of a sentence and followed by a comma.**

D is incorrect. If the underlined word were to be deleted, the sentence would read "they pose risks for the health of forests and humans." While there is nothing incorrect about this choice, a term like "alike" allows to establish a line of connection between two contrasting subjects ("forests" and "humans"). Because of the higher nuance (complexity) that the word allows **without making the sentence structure more complicated,** B is more suitable than D.

Question 9

D is the best answer. The current sentence has **TWO independent clauses** ("fire risk is one of the primary consequences of pine beetle infestations" and "human fire suppression tactics over the past century may have unwittingly contributed to the pine beetle's spread") and **ONE DEPENDENT CLAUSE** (Due to the density of dead, dried trees left in the beetles' wake"). This makes for one extremely long sentence that is hard for the reader to follow. Breaking this up into two sentences, therefore, is the most suitable choice.

A is incorrect. SHORT SENTENCES that are concise (short, direct) work best. **Sentences with multiple clauses** result in really long pieces of text that are, as a general rule, harder for readers to follow.

B is incorrect. Replacing a comma with a dash would not solve the problem stated above. The sentence would still be difficult to read and possibly even more difficult than it is now since the dependent and independent clauses would all be separated from each other with commas.

C is incorrect. While the **SEMICOLON** would work in so far as it separates two independent clauses (**each with their own subject, verb, and object),** the sentence remains extremely hard to follow. Furthermore, the use of the connector "indeed" also seems misplaced and does not add to the meaning of the sentence.

Question 10

C is the best answer. This is the most **active** form of sentence construction where the **subject** ("humans") are the doers of the action (intervening to prevent fire and scenic damage). As you'll recall, **active is always preferred to passive voice** because it makes the text less **dynamic** and engaging. **When a text is passive, it describes the subject as receiving an action and thus, reducing the subject's agency.**

A is incorrect. The sentence is extremely passive since it tells the reader that "interventions" can be made but does not say **who or what will have to make those interventions.** By completely taking away a subject from this sentence or rather making the interventions the subject rather than the people making them, this sentence is **extremely passive and therefore, not recommended.**

B is incorrect. Once again, this sentence is more **passive. Passive sentences also tend to place their subject toward the middle or end of the sentence** (instead of the beginning); **this is a quick way of identifying when a sentence is passive and eliminating it as a choice.** In this example, we see that "humans" are relegated (put at) the very end of the sentence.

D is incorrect. Once again, this sentence is **passive.** Placing more emphasis on the action rather than the subject, a choice that is less preferred for the reasons explained above.

Question 11

D is the best answer. The **KEYWORD here is** "Until then," a term which implies that something "will" continue to happen till something else changes. By seeing this and then looking at the different answer choices, "will be" immediately presents as the best answer.

A is incorrect. If the term "Until then" **had not been used,** the **PRESENT TENSE conjugation of** the verb "to be" (i.e., "is") would be acceptable. However, in addition to the use of "until now," there is also a disagreement between the verb and the **plural** quality of the subject. Since multiple "blighted forests" are the subject (not a single blighted forest) the **PRESENT TENSE conjugation should be "ARE," not "is."**

B is incorrect. If we use the **PRESENT CONTINUOUS TENSE** ("is being"), the sentence would read: "Until then, the blighted pine forests that have become prevalent in many parts of the Rocky Mountains **is being** the new normal." Reading this sentence reveals how this choice **impedes** (limits) **the meaning of the sentence.**

C is incorrect. Since "until then" refers to the future, the **PAST TENSE** ("were") **is IRRELEVANT** and makes the text lose its meaning. Therefore, this answer choice can be eliminated.

Passage 2

Question 12

A is the best answer. A COLON is used to introduce a list, an explanation of the previously stated idea, or a quotation. Since "The Olympic Games" seeks to clarify the ideas that have been explained before it, it is the best choice for punctuation, and **no change is needed.**

B is less suitable. While the comma is not technically incorrect, the length of the sentence and the use of the comma to separate earlier clauses in that sentence make this the less **clear choice.** With a colon, it is made **obvious** that "the Olympic Games" **clarifies** the information that came before it. **With a comma, this clarification is less clear since the reader could well think that what follows is an additional dependent clause.**

C is incorrect. For a **SEMICOLON to be used,** the clauses on either side of it have to be **COMPLETE SENTENCES** each with their own **subject, verb, and object.** Since that condition is not met in this sentence, the semicolon is not an appropriate choice.

D is incorrect because the phrase "the Olympic Games" is clearly a **dependent clause** that seeks to add to the preceding **independent clause.** Making the three words their own sentence would make it both **incomplete** and **inaccurate.**

Question 13

A is the best answer. The last sentence of the first paragraph describes the athletes who take part in the Olympics. The current first line of the next paragraph gives specific information about the first Olympic games. Including a sentence like the one that is suggested would thus be **extremely helpful**

B is incorrect. The information that is presented in this statement is **new** and does not relate to any of the previous sentences that have been put forward. Although previous sentences do mention the **KEYWORD** "ancient," which might be an indicator that this sentence is connected to, reading both more carefully will help you realize that the new sentence **does not clarify** anything that was said before. It just **builds on an existing idea.**

C is incorrect. Since the remainder of the paragraph speaks specifically about the Greeks' role in developing the Olympic Games, adding a general statement about ancient competitions that existed before the Greeks would **disrupt the flow of the paragraph** and therefore, not be a good concluding statement.

D is incorrect. Since the information provided in this statement is **directly related to the central topic of the passage and paragraph** (i.e., the Olympics), it is completely **RELEVANT.** Therefore, this answer choice can be eliminated.

Question 14

D is the best answer. Since this information ("once every four years") is presented in the last line of this paragraph, it **does not need to be mentioned here. Avoid repeating information whenever possible!**

All other answer choices to this question can be ignored since they would all cause **redundancy,** i.e., information that is **not useful** because it has been presented somewhere else.

Question 15

C is the best answer. The last line of this paragraph currently speaks about the "first modern Olympic game." The first line of the next paragraph tells us that modern games "mirror" many aspects of what was developed by the ancient Greeks. This sentence, therefore, **creates an effective transition between the two paragraphs.**

A is incorrect because there currently is no transition that takes place between the ideas presented in each of the paragraphs. Therefore, it causes a **jump in logic** for the reader, a quality that is less desirable in passages of this nature.

B is less suitable because **it repeats the similar information to what is presented in the topic sentence of the next paragraph. As we know, REPETITION OF INFORMATION** is to be avoided whenever possible. Furthermore, this sentence talks about **two specific aspects** while the next paragraph talks about **other aspects.** Therefore, because it mentions a number that is then **negated** by the following paragraph, this answer is not suitable.

D is incorrect. The information in these lines is **IRRELEVANT** both to the content that comes before it and to the content that comes after. Since "the spirit" of Olympic athletes was mentioned earlier in the passage but not in these paragraphs, this is **not the right position** for this statement.

Question 16

C is the best answer. The Olympics – emphasized by the "s" that ends the term – **refer to multiple events** that are part of the same competitive event. Since the subject of this sentence are the Olympics, "their" indicates the **plural nature** of the subject.

> **A is incorrect.** "It" is inaccurate because the word refers to a **singular subject** rather than multiple. "It" would be accurate only if "the Olympics" were to be replaced with a term like "the event," i.e., "the Olympics maintain**S ITS** engagement with modern audiences."
>
> **B is incorrect** because "they're" is a **contraction** for "they are." Replacing "it" with "they are" would render the sentence **meaningless.**
>
> **D is incorrect** because "it's" is a **contraction** for "it is." Replacing "it" with "it is" would render the sentence **meaningless.**

Question 17

B is the best answer. By saying that the "International Olympic Committee created this portion of the event," the **subject** (the Committee) **is made active** and the action of creating the game is attributed to them. **ACTIVE VOICE IS ALWAYS PREFERRED TO PASSIVE VOICE.**

> **A is incorrect** because **it is PASSIVE** in its construction. By saying that "[…] was created by the International Winter Olympic Committee" the action of creation is said to occur **to/on the subject.** Since active voice makes texts more engaging for their readers, this sentence needs to be changed.
>
> **C is incorrect because it is written in the PRESENT TENSE** ("creates") and thus causes a **VERB TENSE INCONSISTENCY.** We are clearly being told about a past occurrence that took place in 1924. Therefore, the present tense is inaccurate.
>
> **D is incorrect** for the same reason that Choice A is incorrect. **A common indicator of the use of PASSIVE VOICE is when a conjugated verb is followed by the term "by"** (i.e., "created by"). When such a construction is used, the passive voice is immediately indicated.

Question 18

B is the best answer. The **subject being referred to in this sentence** is "the international spectacle," i.e., an item that is **SINGULAR.** Therefore, the verb that addresses it needs to be in the **PLURAL form,** i.e., "attracts."

> **A is incorrect.** "Attract" would be correct only if, instead of saying "the international spectacle," the sentence said, "the international spectacles" (i.e., the plural of spectacle).
>
> **C is incorrect because it uses the FUTURE TENSE** conjugation, thus causing a **VERB TENSE INCOSISTENCY** in the sentence. From the previous part of the sentence, we know that the author is talking about the Olympic Games today (the use of the word "Today" and the conjugated verb "create"). Therefore, to use the future tense conjugation would be inaccurate.
>
> **D is incorrect** because the use of the word "can" **implies a conditional statement,** i.e., that the Olympics "can" make something happen **if** something else happens. Since this does not fit the context of what is said in the rest of the paragraph, which describes why the events are attractive and not what can make them attractive, this answer is unsuitable.

Question 19

D is the best answer. If the new version of the sentence were adopted, there would be two **vital pieces of information that would be lost:** information about when the event took place (2016) and **the intention** behind the viewers' participation ("to cheer on their favorite athletes").

> **A is incorrect** because the new addition would not make a **more effective** transition than what already exists. Because it is not **more effective** and also deletes useful information, this is not a suitable answer.
>
> **B is incorrect.** We could say that clarity, tone, and voice are improved **only if** the new sentence communicates all the same information as the current sentence but does so in a more **efficient and elegant manner.** Since this is not the case, we cannot say that the new sentence **adds** clarity, tone, or voice.
>
> **C is incorrect.** The current last line tells us about a quality of the Olympics that has stayed constant over time, i.e., its ability to bring people together. Preceding this sentence with an example, therefore, helps to **better frame** the information that is provided. Therefore, the new sentence **would not be a more effective conclusion.**

Question 20

A is the best answer. CONCEPT MAPPING is an effective way to look at the **flow of ideas** in a passage: consider each paragraph and identify its main concept. Currently, paragraph 1 gives us a general introduction to the games, paragraph 2 talks about its roots in Greece, paragraph 3 describes how the modern Olympic games came into being, paragraph 4 talks about how modern games use elements from their original form, paragraph 5 gives us a current example to evidence the link between past and current games (in terms of bringing viewers together) and paragraph 6 clearly serves to bring the passage to a close. Given this mapping, we see that there is no need to move paragraph 4 as it fits well **within the flow of the passage.**

> **B is incorrect.** We know now that the passage seeks to give us a description of how the Olympic games have evolved over time. Furthermore, the introduction **gives the reader an idea of what to expect in the rest of the passage.** Placing paragraph 4 before paragraph 1 would disrupt the flow of the passage since the reader would be invited to see the links between contemporary and ancient Olympics **without any context** about the past.
>
> **C is incorrect.** As we see in the concept mapping above, the second passage talks about the roots of the Olympics in Greece. Therefore, placing paragraph 4, which speaks about similarities between contemporary and past Olympics before the second paragraph, would **disrupt the flow of argumentation** in the passage.
>
> **D is incorrect.** The fifth paragraph gives a specific example of the Brazilian Olympics to make a case for how the **spirit of the games** have stayed the same over time. Following this paragraph with a general paragraph about how modern games mirror elements from past games would, therefore, be **disruptive** to the flow of argumentation **in the passage.**

Question 21

D is the best answer. This paragraph seeks to conclude the passage and to say how the Olympics, no matter how they've evolved, share a "core" with games of the past and how they bring nations together in the present. Including a specific example of the London Olympics to begin this paragraph would **disrupt the current flow of the passage.**

> **A is incorrect.** All the information that is needed to evidence the information that comes next about the spirit of the games remaining the same over time has already been given to the reader in the preceding paragraphs. Therefore, adding this sentence here would be **irrelevant** given the paragraph's intent to conclude the passage.
>
> **B is incorrect.** Placing this statement anywhere in the paragraph would **be disruptive to its logic** since all the other sentences here are **broad statements** that seek to **tie together** the themes that have been explored earlier in the passage.
>
> **C is incorrect** because this specific example of the London Olympics **does not help clarify** an earlier statement. The previous paragraph mentions how the games bring athletes from different countries together so, if it were to be included anywhere, this statement would belong in the previous paragraph. Since the first line of a paragraph is its **TOPIC SENTENCE** that introduces **that** paragraph, the sentence would be **nothing but disruptive in the current, suggested location.**

Question 22

B is the best answer. The **KEYWORD CONNECTION** here is the term "ancient." Since the passage has used this term multiple times, we know that it is **significant** in capturing the main idea behind the text. Furthermore, the author has repeatedly mentioned this idea in different paragraphs of the text (paragraphs 3, 4 and 5). Therefore, this is the most suitable summary of the passage.

A is incorrect. The information in this sentence about the number of viewers is the content of paragraph 5 (where the example about Brazil is mentioned). Because of its **limited presence** we can tell that the **topic, while relevant,** is not the "main point. The question asks us about the "main point."

C is incorrect. There is no mention of any "controversy" surrounding the Olympics anywhere in the passage. To choose this answer would mean making an **ASSUMPTION** about the content that is not evidenced in the text.

D is incorrect. The sentences that do speak about the athletes in this passage **speak of their skills highly** and mention the commitment that it takes to become an Olympic athlete (see the last line of paragraph 1: "world-class athletes who are constantly pushing the boundaries of their sports"). This **implies** that not everyone can be an Olympic athlete since one needs to be "world-class" to do so.

Passage 3
Question 23
A is the best answer. The subject of this sentence is "several animal populations." Because it is in the **PLURAL,** the current conjugation of "have been" is accurate and does not need to be changed.

B is incorrect. Using this choice would have the sentence read: "Over the past century, several animal populations including the wild tiger **HAVE** put in danger due to human practices." This renders the sentence **meaningless.**

C is incorrect. Like choice B, this term would also make the sentence meaningless. "Over the past century, several animal populations including the wild tiger **HAS** put in danger due to human practices."

D is incorrect because "has" does not agree with the **plural subject** and would be correct only if the subject of the sentence was in the **singular.** For example, the sentence was only about the wild tiger population rather than several animal populations.

Question 24
A is the best answer. This new sentence would help define the "human practices" that are referred to in sentence 1 and would, therefore, provide support for this prior assertion. It also creates an **effective transition** to the next line by letting us know what kinds of activities governments are trying to protect against.

B is incorrect. Although the information in the proposed addition would support a prior assertion, it does not necessarily help "clarify" particular term(s). The term "human practices" does need to be expanded on, but since what we get with this sentence are examples rather than explanations, it is not a clarification.

C is incorrect. There is no modifier error in this statement. **A MODIFIER is an optional element that changes the meaning of another element in that sentence.** Given this, we can tell that there is no modifier in this statement and therefore, no modifier error.

D is incorrect because the information that is provided here about the negative impacts of deforestation, climate change, and poaching is **EXTREMELY RELEVANT** to the content in the paragraph (human practices that are affecting the survival of animal populations).

Question 25

B is the best answer. The revised line would address the "expansive" nature of the habitats that tigers can live in by serving to make the point about their habitat loss even powerful (if they could live in so many places and 93% of them have been lost, the reader gets a sense of the **scale** of what is being spoken of). In this way, the new sentence would improve the language, clarity and tone of the paragraph.

A is incorrect because it is not "more" effective than the current sentence in terms of the support that is provided for the information that follows. In fact, it is very much the **same information** just stated in a way that is more powerful for the reasons mentioned above.

C is incorrect. The information that is provided in this sentence is evidenced by facts that are provided later on in the paragraph. Therefore, it is not **unsupported.** Furthermore, since we are not told about the **sources of information** in this paragraph, the reader is in no position to make a decision about its **accuracy.** To do so would involve making an **ASSUMPTION.**

D is incorrect because the information provided in this revised line is **new information** that has not yet been mentioned to the reader. Therefore, it certainly is **RELEVANT** to the readers' understanding of the **main topic being dealt with.**

Question 26

D is the best answer. To devastate means "to destroy" or "to ruin" something. The loss of native habitat has, as the **context suggests,** led to the destruction of tiger populations globally.

A is incorrect because the word "impacted" does not **communicate the seriousness of the situation.** To impact simply means "to have an effect on" and impacts can be both positive/negative/neutral. In this case, we are clearly given to understand that there has been a **serious negative effect** caused by the loss of habitat.

B and C are incorrect. "Obliterate" and "annihilate" are synonyms and are used to mean the **complete destruction of something.** In this context, using those words would **imply that tiger populations have been completely wiped out** and to say this would be an **EXAGERRATION/ASSUMPTION** (since there are still tiger populations existing in the world).

Question 27

C is the best answer. Given the related ideas in the two sentences, adding a comma between them would be the simplest way of addressing the current **break in flow.**

A is incorrect because it is not advised to **begin a new sentence with a CONJUNCTION** ("and"). Since the ideas in the two sentences are clearly related, providing the reader different information and **deleting the CONJUNCTION** would be the only way to separate the sentences effectively.

B is incorrect. SEMICOLONS are never followed by a conjunction (like "and"). Although the sentences otherwise fit the conditions for using a semicolon **in that they are both complete sentences with their own subject, verb, and object**, the use of the word "and" makes this an inaccurate answer.

D is incorrect. The current use of a **DASH** before "including humans" would make the addition of a dash after "creatures" **problematic.** In fact, doing so would take away the **meaning of the sentence.** When dashes are used on either side of a clause, they are used to **emphasize the information within them.** So, in this case, the dashes would emphasize "and the loss of their roaming space has forced them to compete for space with other tigers and predators" but make the following phrase "including humans" **a problematic addition.**

Question 28

C is the best answer. By placing the underlined sentence before sentence 2, **the flow of logic in the paragraph would be improved.** Currently, sentence 1 talks about how tigers' nature has led them to look for new spaces, sentence 2 talks about risks to tigers in human dominated areas, sentence 3 talks about the migration of tigers to human dominated areas, and sentence 4 talks about countries' efforts to stop poachers. **Immediately, we see that moving the underlined sentence before sentence 2** would allow a more **effective transition** to speaking specifically about risks to tigers in human-dominated areas.

A is incorrect. Currently, there is a challenge to **the flow of logic** in the paragraph because the sentence that talks about tigers' migration to human-dominated areas comes **after** the sentence about specific risks to tigers in human-dominated areas. Therefore, its position needs to be changed.

B is incorrect. The first sentence describes **why** tigers are searching for new places to live (because they are "solitary creatures" who need space to roam). Therefore, adding the underlined sentence **before** sentence 1 **would be preemptive** in talking about the migration before we know that tigers are migrating in the first place.

D is incorrect. Once again, this would **disrupt the flow of logic in the paragraph.** The last lines that explain what governments are doing to stop poaching and talking about the risks that poachers present to **migrating tigers** needs to come BEFORE the sentence that talks about what actions are being taken to stop them.

Question 29

D is the best answer. We see an obvious peak in the graph at the year 2016 immediately allowing us to see evidence for this answer in the provided figure.

A is incorrect. This choice begins with the phrase "In that same year." However, we are not given information to understand which year is being referred to. Therefore, this answer choice can be immediately eliminated.

B is incorrect. Nothing about "rising sea levels" is indicated in the graph and therefore, this answer choice is **IRRELEVANT** in answering the given question.

C is incorrect. The graph only tells us about the number of tigers poached in India over a given span of time. We are not given enough information here to associate those changes in numbers with particular laws that were/were not passed. Choosing this answer would involve making an **ASSUMPTION** for which we do have sufficient evidence.

Question 30

D is the best answer. The information that is given here is **repetitive** and this **repetition** of what has already been said a few lines earlier **is what makes the content REDUNDANT.**

A is incorrect. The sentence does not connect two concepts in the paragraph. Rather, it restates a concept ("The Global Tiger Recovery Plan") that has already been explained earlier.

B is incorrect because it is **IRRELEVANT.** This sentence speaks about a particular initiative that has been taken to protect tiger populations and does not **refer to** the "diverse threats" that tigers face.

C is incorrect because it is **IRRELEVANT.** The underlined sentence speaks about a particular initiative that has been taken to protect tiger populations and not the general ideas of how/if poaching is preventable.

Question 31

C is the best answer. By giving data, this statement provides **strong evidence** for the phrase "tiger populations showed a small increase" that is shown in the previous sentence. Adding it, therefore, would help the reader **better understand** what is meant by "small increase."

A is incorrect. The word to pay attention to here is "clarify." To clarify something means that something that was unclear before can now be better understood. While it is true that this sentence would help the reader **better understand** how the numbers have increased, it is less suitable than saying that the sentence "supports" a prior statement. Evidence is often given to **support,** not to clarify. Therefore, although technically correct, this answer is less suitable than Choice C.

B is incorrect. This sentence specifically seeks to support information given about the Global Tiger Recovery Plan and after introducing the increase in numbers, it goes on to talk about **continued struggles** to tiger conservation. Introducing this sentence at the end of the paragraph would, therefore, **disrupt the flow of logic** in the text.

D is incorrect. The information provided in this paragraph is **EXTREMELY IRRELEVANT** since it provides quantitative data to show how the Global Tiger Recovery Plan has helped increase the number of tigers in the world.

Question 32

B is the best answer. There are multiple (**PLURAL**) subjects in this sentence which include "poaching, deforestation, and climate change." Therefore, the **accurate verb conjugation would be** "continue." Any other choice would be grammatically incorrect.

A is incorrect because "continues" **conflicts with the PLURAL** subjects. "Continues" could be used only if, for example, the subject was only "poaching" or "deforestation" or "climate change." Not all of the above.

C is incorrect because "continuously" would make it **grammatically incorrect.** The sentence would then read "poaching, deforestation, and climate change **continuously** to impact tiger populations." "To impact" following this work makes the sentence meaningless.

D is incorrect. The reader is told that the information is about the present time because of the use of "are" ("are on the rise"). To use the **PAST TENSE** by saying "continued," therefore, would cause a **VERB TENSE INCONSISTENCY** and **imply** that these practices/conditions no longer continue to affect tiger populations (which as we are told in the passage, they do).

Question 33

C is the best answer. REFLEXIVE PRONOUNS are used when the subject and the object of a sentence are the same. Here, the subjects are "conservationists and lawmakers" and the object is the wild tiger populations. Therefore, "them" is the more accurate choice.

A is incorrect because the **reflexive pronoun has been used inaccurately.** As per the explanation above, consider this sentence. "He writes the stories himself because he does not trust his interns to do it right." Here, "he" is both the subject and the object making it necessary to use a reflexive pronoun like "himself." Since this **condition of subject-object agreement** is not met, the sentence does need to be changed.

B is incorrect. Apart from being another reflexive pronoun, "itself" is **inaccurate** because "it" is used to refer to inanimate objects and here, the author is clearly referring to human beings ("conservationists and lawmakers").

D is incorrect. As mentioned above, **"it" is used only to refer to inanimate objects**. Here, the author is clearly referring to human beings ("conservationists and lawmakers"). Therefore, this answer is incorrect.

Passage 4

Question 34

C is the best answer. A COLON is used to introduce a list, an explanation of the previously stated idea, or a quotation. Since "the Dakota Access Pipeline" seeks to clarify the ideas that have been explained before it, the colon is the best choice for punctuation here.

A is incorrect. The use of "which" indicates that the information that follows is a **NON-ESSENTIAL ELEMENT** (not necessary for the reader to know). However, since this is the first time the **major event being referenced in the passage** is mentioned, it is an **ESSENTIAL ELEMENT.** Therefore, this answer is incorrect.

B is incorrect. This choice would make the sentence read: "In early 2016, protestors rallied around the environmental and social impacts of a proposed infrastructure development **project that was the** Dakota Access Pipeline." As you can see, this sentence structure is **unclear** and makes it difficult for the reader to **effectively understand** the content being presented.

D is incorrect. With this answer, the sentence would read: "[…] of a proposed infrastructure development **project known at the time as** Dakota Access Pipeline." Apart from making the sentence harder to read, this change would **imply** that the name of the project changed at some point. We know from reading the rest of the passage that this is not the case.

Question 35

A is the best answer. The **KEYWORD** here is "proposed." Because the sentence calls it the "proposed pipeline," it is most accurate to use a term like "would" to describe where the pipeline was proposed to be constructed.

B & C are incorrect for the same reason. Because the term "proposed" is used, it would be inaccurate to say "ran" or "had run." A proposal by its nature is **written BEFORE a project is completed.** Using the **PAST TENSE would contradict this implied future.**

D is incorrect. SHOULD is generally used in reference to first person pronouns (I, we) and in all other cases, WOULD is the more appropriate term. Since there is no first-person pronoun in this sentence, a group of third person proposers of the plan is **implied.** "Should" would be the less correct choice. Note that the sentence would still carry the same meaning if "should" was used; it would not be as grammatically correct, though.

Question 36

B is the best answer. This answer choice effectively separates the **two different ideas** being presented in this statement; the second idea adding a different dimension to the first. By splitting the ideas into **two independent clauses** and by adding the **connector** "further," the **argument** is easier to understand. The argument is that the threats presented to indigenous communities in that area, which is a threat that is furthered (added to) by being in potential violation of the Fort Laramie treaty.

A is incorrect. The sentence, as it is, is extremely hard to follow. It presents lots of information in one **run-on sentence** and therefore, makes it difficult for the reader to see the different dimensions to the case being presented.

C is incorrect. Adding a DASH before "and" does not help make the ideas presented any **clearer.** Furthermore, **DASHES** are used to demarcate **part of a sentence.** Here, it is being used to demarcate an entire sentence that has multiple clauses. Therefore, it is not a suitable choice.

D is incorrect. Although this choice also separates the sentences and uses a connector like "furthermore," the sentence construction is **passive.** By saying "thought to be likely," there is an unnecessary, **added layer of uncertainly** (thought to be) that is added to what is already included through the use of the word "likely."

Question 37

B is the best answer. Since there are multiple entities who are being referred to in the first two lines (the tribe, the engineers, and the judge), it would help the reader to clarify who "their" refers to. The **context** allows to understand that it was the tribe's claim that was being rejected.

A is less suitable because, although grammatically correct, the use of the word "their" is **ambiguous** and does not immediately **clarify** for the reader who is being referred to.

C is incorrect. The use of the **apostrophe** (') **AFTER** "tribes" implies that there were multiple tribes who were involved in the case. But, as the first sentence suggests, it was the Standing Rock Sioux Tribe, specifically, that was suing the engineers.

D is incorrect because there is no apostrophe in this choice and this **punctuation is needed to make the word possessive.** In this case, "the claim" is the object being possessed by the tribe and hence, it is the tribe's claim. Tribes (without the apostrophe) is simply the **plural form** of tribe.

Question 38

A is the best answer. The sentence before this proposed addition talks about how the Standing Rock Sioux Tribe had a victory; the sentence after this proposed addition talks about how this victory did not last long. Therefore, this proposed addition would help the reader **effectively transition** from one concept to the next.

B is incorrect because this proposed addition does not help clarify anything that comes before it. In fact, it only **lays the groundwork** for information that comes after (i.e., about how the President overturned the earlier decision to halt the project).

C is incorrect. The information provided here about the victory being "short-lived" has **not been mentioned before.** It is the first time that the reader is being provided with this knowledge and, therefore, it is not **redundant** (useless, because of being repeated).

D is incorrect because the content of the proposed new sentence is completely **RELEVANT** to the rest of the information that is being provided in this paragraph. It is completely in keeping with the theme of the passage, which is to inform the reader about what happened with the case brought by the Standing Rock Sioux Tribe.

Question 39

D is the best answer. Since the earlier sentence speaks about a new challenge that emerged, the **connector** "in response to" helps the reader understand the **cause-effect nature** of the events, which is the memorandum (the cause) led to protests (the effect).

A is less suitable. Although grammatically correct, the usage of the word "despite" **has a different tone** than "in response to." "Despite" in this context says how even though there were unexpected struggles, the protestors rallied, which is different in meaning than saying that protestors rallied **to address/respond to** the unexpected struggles. "Despite," therefore, is more **DEBATABLE** than "in response to."

B, like A, is not incorrect. It is just less suitable. **As a general rule, beginning a sentence with the word "because" is not considered good practice.** "Because" is more useful in the middle of sentences to clarify details and is considered **passive** when used at the beginning of a sentence.

C is incorrect because it completely alters the meaning of the statement. By saying "Like these unanticipated new challenges, protestors rallied at Standing Rock," there is a **comparison** being established between the memorandum and the protests, which would require a huge **ASSUMPTION** being made by the reader since no information to that effect has been given in the passage.

Question 40

B is the best answer. When **DASHES** are used on either side of a phrase, they give it emphasis while also highlighting that this information is additional to the main content of the sentence. Given that the phrase here names the youth groups in question (content that is **additional**), the DASHES have been used accurately.

> **A is incorrect** because the use of multiple commas within the underlined phrase to separate items in a list ("Tribal members," "youth groups," and "other allies") and also the names of groups that are only associated with one item on the list (i.e., the youth groups) makes the sentence extremely unclear and hard to follow.
>
> **B is incorrect** because the semicolon has been used inaccurately. **SEMICOLONS are used to separate two complete sentences,** each with its own **SUBJECT, VERB, AND OBJECT.** Since that condition is not met here, this answer choice is unviable.
>
> **D is incorrect** because it creates **unnecessary** separations (by using a DASH before "youth groups") between the items being mentioned as part of a list. This causes a **disruption in the flow of logic** in the paragraph. Furthermore, there is an **inaccuracy** in the phrase "youth groups, the including," so the sentence **does not make sense.**

Question 41

C is the best answer. Since "spread" is the first conjugated verb to be used in this sentence, look at the conjugated verb in the previous sentence ("established"). **Since that verb was used in the PAST TENSE,** the reader is told that the events being described have already happened. Therefore, given that "had spread" is the only choice that we are given in the **PAST TENSE,** it is the obvious answer.

> **All other choices are incorrect because each of them would cause a different kind of VERB TENSE INCONSISTENCY** with the rest of the passage. The current selection uses the **FUTURE TENSE,** and choices B and D use the **PRESENT CONTINUOUS TENSE.** All of these cause verb-tense inconsistencies in the passage.

Question 42

B is the best answer. When **two conjugated verbs follow each other in quick succession, they should be conjugated the same way – VERB TENSE CONSISTENCY.** Since the first verb "to plan" is conjugated in the **PRESENT CONTINUOUS TENSE** ("planning"), the following verb ("to carry") needs to be conjugated in the same way. Hence, "carrying" is the right answer.

A & C are incorrect because they use versions of the **PAST and FUTURE TENSE** and would lead to an inconsistency.

D is incorrect because it alters the meaning of the sentence. "Attempting to carry out" works grammatically since the primary verb ("to attempt") matches the conjugation of the previous verb ("planning"). However, "attempting" **implies** that the action was **not carried out.** We know from other information provided in this passage though about the success of the group's work that the actions were definitely carried out.

Question 43

D is the best answer. It is **direct** and immediately reminds the reader of the timeframe that is being referred to. Since the date of the protests have not been mentioned so far in this passage, reminding the reader is important so as to help them **contextualize** the information. This choice is also the most direct since it uses the least amount of text to communicate the same idea, and that is that all of this took place during the summer of 2017.

A and C are less suitable because they are more **ambiguous for the reader.** By saying "the following summer," the reader is asked to remember information (about dates) that was last presented in the introduction. Even in the introduction, the year is mentioned as "2016." Therefore, since the text is not talking about the following year, it is important to remind the reader of the date.

B is less suitable than D because it is more PASSIVE. "During summer 2017" communicates the information in a more concise way than "By the end of summer 2017." When presented with two options that are **DEBATABLE, always choose the more ACTIVE choice. A majority of the time, the more ACTIVE choice** also has **FEWER words,** i.e., it is more concise.

Question 44

C is the best answer. Up until this sentence, the paragraph has focused on people who joined the protests across the country. The subjects of "cities" and "corporations" have not been mentioned anywhere. Therefore, especially with no **connector** like "Furthermore" to help the reader **contextualize why this information is being shared,** the underlined sentence only serves to **disrupt the flow of the paragraph.**

A is incorrect because the sentence **does not connect the concepts** of the sentences before and after it. The sentence before it talks about how individuals across the country joined the protest. The sentence after it talks about the attention that the protests garnered as a result of people's participation. Information about the cities' opposition, in fact, **brings a new concept into the mix** rather than clarifying existing ones.

B is incorrect. Choosing this answer would involve the reader making an **ASSUMPTION** about where the content is headed since nothing has been mentioned so far to suggest "future conflicts between cities and corporations."

D is incorrect because the information in the sentence is **definitely RELEVANT and connected to the pipeline.** It is simply **not introduced or contextualized enough** to fit in the current paragraph.

Writing Test 5: Answer Key

1. B		28. D	
2. B		29. D	
3. A		30. D	
4. A		31. C	
5. B		32. C	
6. D		33. B	
7. C			
8. C		34. D	
9. B		35. B	
10. D		36. A	
11. C		37. A	
		38. B	
12. A		39. B	
13. B		40. C	
14. D		41. D	
15. A		42. A	
16. A		43. C	
17. B		44. A	
18. C			
19. D			
20. B			
21. B			
22. C			
23. B			
24. B			
25. A			
26. C			
27. B			

WRITING & LANGUAGE TEST 5
Answers & Explanations

Passage 1

Question 1

B is the best answer. There are two qualities that make a good concluding sentence for a paragraph. **First, the sentence summarizes the last line of the paragraph it concludes, and second, the sentence transitions the reader to the topic of the next paragraph.** In this case, the last line of the paragraph describes "our current agricultural systems are not designed to carry the weight" and the first line of the next paragraph states "many of our agricultural practices are bad for the environment." Therefore, an effective concluding statement would mention the limitations of the current systems and lead into a discussion about what those practices are. In this case, we also see that that the **KEYWORD** "practices" is used in the first line of the next paragraph confirming that this is the most suitable answer.

A is incorrect because the last line of the current paragraph talks about "agricultural SYSTEMS" whereas the first line of the next paragraph uses the term "agricultural PRACTICES." Since systems and practices mean different things, we know that we need a sentence that will introduce that term to the reader before the next paragraph takes it forward.

C is incorrect. **Although this choice uses the KEYWORD "practices,"** we see that it discusses "food growth practices" rather than "agricultural practices." The latter is the term that is used in the first line of the next paragraph. Therefore, we know this is a less suitable answer.

D is incorrect. By referring to "ancestors" rather than current practices, this sentence does not **effectively transition** the reader into the topic of the next paragraph. Therefore, this choice is unsuitable.

Question 2

B is the best answer. Whenever possible, use a word that can communicate the same idea in FEWER words. Here, "are bad for" can easily be substituted by the word "harm." This would make the sentence more **DIRECT** and thus, more **ACTIVE.**

A is incorrect because as mentioned above it uses more words to make the same point. It also is **more PASSIVE** than the word "harm," i.e., the actions that are being spoken of seem "bad" but not "harmful." Therefore, these words do not communicate the **tone** as well as the word "harm" and could be changed.

C is incorrect. By using the **PAST PERFECT TENSE,** this choice creates a **VERB TENSE INCONSISTENCY.** From the last line of the previous paragraph and from the use of the word "current," it is **implied** that the author is talking about an ongoing problem. Therefore, any version of the **PAST TENSE** is unsuitable.

D is incorrect because it uses the **FUTURE PERFECT TENSE** and like the one above, this choice creates a **VERB TENSE INCONSISTENCY.** From the last line of the previous paragraph and from the use of the word "current," it is **implied** that the author is talking about an ongoing problem. Therefore, any version of the **FUTURE TENSE** is unsuitable.

Question 3

A is the best answer. Since the previous statement says that "agriculture is responsible for a substantial proportion of total greenhouse gas emissions," the underlined sentence provides effective support by providing data. This helps the reader **better contextualize** what a term like "substantial proportion" might mean.

B is incorrect. The proposed addition gives us information about the emission of greenhouse gases (in specific) and not "climate change," in general. Therefore, this answer choice is less suitable in answering the question.

C is incorrect. Although this sentence does not talk about various causes of climate change that information is **not necessary at this point in the paragraph.** Since the author is very clearly talking about agriculture and greenhouse gas emission, there is no need for the sentence to talk about all possible activities causing climate change. This would **disrupt the flow of logic in the paragraph.**

D is incorrect because the **theme of this paragraph** is not a description of how to improve "agricultural sustainability." Rather, we are told from the **topic sentence** that this paragraph deals with informing the reader about current agricultural practices' negative effects on the environment.

Question 4

A is the best answer. It is the most **ACTIVE** of all the options presented and communicates the information **with clarity.** We know that this choice is active because the actions in this sentence ("increase" and "require") are directly applied to the subject ("growing food demand").

B is incorrect because it unnecessarily **adds an additional clause** to the sentence and thus, making it **more complicated** for the reader to understand. **Whenever possible use the most simple and direct sentence structure. Often, this will mean fewer words, active voice, and the absence of a dependent clause.**

C is incorrect. In this choice, there are two issues. First, there is **a missing article** ("an") before the word "expansion," i.e., the sentence should read "increase and **AN** expansion of agricultural activities that harm human health and the environment will be observed." In addition, we observe that the sentence has become **PASSIVE** by being identified by the placement of "be observed" at the end of the sentence. Therefore, this is not the best choice.

D is incorrect because it will **delete relevant information** that tells us about **the effect caused** by the increasing food demands. This information is important in providing an **effective conclusion to the paragraph.**

Question 5

B is the best answer. For questions about the order of paragraphs and sentences, **CONCEPT MAPPING** is the best way to approach finding the right answer. In this passage, the main concept in paragraph 1 is an introduction to climate change and the challenges of current agricultural systems, paragraph 2 describes how current agricultural practices affect the environment, paragraph 3 discusses the importance of climate to agriculture, paragraph 4 emphasizes how difficult it will be to find the necessary agricultural land, and paragraph 5 talks about implications beyond food to water. Given this, we see that a description of how climate affects agriculture would be most useful **before paragraph 2** since (like the first paragraph) this paragraph is a more **general introduction to the main theme.** By better understanding the **seriousness of the problem,** the reader will be better able to understand the **importance to finding more sustainable agricultural practices.**

A is incorrect because the **main theme** of the passage is **climate change** and not the climate in general. This paragraph speaks more generally about the relationship between agriculture and the climate and, as we know, a **STRONG INTRODUCTION** tells the reader about the main theme of a text (not a related theme). Therefore, this is a less suitable choice.

C is incorrect. Paragraph 4 talks about how serious the need for agricultural land is. This is a specific problem that is being highlighted in the context of the general issue of climate change. Therefore, following this paragraph with **general information** about the importance of climate to agriculture would **disrupt the flow of logic** in the passage.

D is incorrect because as mentioned above leaving the paragraph where it is now **affects the flow of logic.** Generally speaking, **a strong essay starts with more general ideas and moves onto more specific ones.** In order to allow this to happen, the paragraph needs to be moved from where it is now.

Question 6

D is the best answer. When a sentence includes lists of THREE OR MORE ITEMS, COMMAS are used to help the reader navigate through them. This sentence is complex because there are multiple lists of three or more items. List 1: location, timing, and productivity, List 2: crop, livestock, and fishery systems, and List 3: local, national, and global levels. Therefore, commas need to be in place in all of these lists to enable the reader to navigate through them. D is the only answer choice that uses commas in all the necessary places.

A is incorrect because there is a **MISSING COMMA** after the word "livestock" which makes it more difficult to understand the different lists that are being discussed here.

B is incorrect. To use a **SEMICOLON,** the clauses on either side of the punctuation should each have their own **SUBJECT, VERB, and OBJECT.** Since that condition is not met here, this is not a suitable choice.

C is incorrect. When **DASHES** are used to demarcate **part of a sentence,** they **emphasize that text** while also making that **text parenthetical,** i.e., it's as if that information was in parenthesis, and although emphasized not necessary to understand the statement. In this case, we see that all the information included in the sentence is **RELEVANT** and **ESSENTIAL** and therefore, a dash would not be an appropriate punctuation mark.

Question 7

C is the best answer. "For" is usually used when speaking about nouns ("farmers and ranchers"). "To" is used when speaking about verbs.

> All the other answer choices, therefore, would either be inaccurate ("to") or render the sentence meaningless ("at" or "in").

Question 8

C is the best answer. There is an important shift in TONE in this line. In the previous paragraphs, the author laid out the seriousness of the problem. In this one though, specifically with the underlined part of the sentence, the tone becomes **more severe** and **implies** that **it might be too late to address this problem.** Therefore, the phrase "but how much will be enough" needs special emphasis **in relation to what precedes it.** And in such cases, the dash is the perfect punctuation choice!

> A is incorrect because the current version of the line does **not include any punctuation mark that would help the reader notice the strong emphasis of what follows** and the way in which the **tone** has become more serious. Therefore, it does need to be changed.
>
> B is incorrect because of the use of the term "what" and "is." Since we are talking about the amount of agricultural land, i.e., a **quantity,** "how much" is more appropriate than "what." Furthermore, the previous part of the sentence talks about what the world **"will need,"** i.e., **the FUTURE.** Using "is," **the PRESENT,** causes a **VERB TENSE INCONSISTENCY.**
>
> D is incorrect because although "how much will be enough" is a **RHETORICAL QUESTION,** i.e., a question that does not need an answer. It **is a question** and the use of the question mark establishes the **importance of that question for the reader.** Using a **PERIOD** at the end of the question, therefore, is less suitable.

Question 9

B is the best answer. In this question, the subject is the agricultural industry, which is a **non-human entity (being)** that is referred to earlier in the same sentence as "it." Therefore, "it" would the accurate and consistent way to continue to refer to this subject.

A is incorrect because "they" can be used only when referring to multiple individuals or things. If the sentence were to be about agriculture industries (**in the PLURAL**), then **"they" would be a suitable answer.** As it is, the underlined section does need to be changed.

Answers C and D cannot be considered for the same reason (for using "they").

In addition, answer C, by stating that "they will have been able" (i.e., the sentence becomes "it is unlikely **they will have been able to** keep up with global food demand" **is incorrect for the conjugation,** "will have been able." The word "been" refers to the **PAST TENSE** while "will" refers to the **FUTURE TENSE.** Therefore, there is a **VERB TENSE INCONSISTENCY within the same phrase.**

Question 10

D is the best answer. A sentence with **MULTIPLE CLAUSES is MORE DIFFICULT for a reader to follow.** Therefore, if a sentence can be split into two independent clauses while maintaining the necessary connection between its different parts, it is always the better choice in terms of **clarity** and **tone.**

A is incorrect because the **LENGTH** of the sentence and the inclusion of multiple clauses makes it difficult to understand. We can see that there are **two LINKED subjects** being dealt with here: how climate change is causing crops to guzzle water even faster and how the risk is **exacerbated** (made worse) in dry areas. Therefore, because there are two subjects that could be linked with a **CONNECTOR** as two **INDEPENDENT CLAUSES,** which would make the sentence **MORE ACTIVE,** a change is needed.

B is incorrect. **A SEMICOLON** is used to separate two independent clauses, each **with its own subject, verb and object.** In this case, the presence of the **CONNECTOR** "especially" is an immediate signal that a **SEMICOLON** is not a suitable choice. "Especially" signifies a dependent clause, which goes against conditions for the use of a semicolon.

C is incorrect because **a DASH is used to emphasize the content that precedes it** (or, in some cases, what comes after it). **When DASHES are used on either side of a phrase, the information within is considered PARANTHETICAL** (in parenthesis, i.e., it is **RELEVANT but not NECESSARY**). Since none of these options would fit the **TONE** and **OBJECTIVE** of the statement here, **it is not the** suitable option here.

Question 11

C is the best answer. The best way to arrive at this answer is through a **process of elimination.**

A is incorrect. Although the previous paragraph mentions a "growing demand," which **implies** population growth. This one mention is **insufficient** to make this answer an **effective summary** for the entire passage.

B is incorrect. The passage focuses on the various components of the agricultural ecosystem and how they are impacted by the changes in the weather. Speaking to the importance of "agricultural systems" in relation to "economic infrastructures," therefore, is not the main theme of the passage. This answer choice is **DEBATABLE.**

D is incorrect. The question asks us to talk about the most **effective** way to **summarize the content of the passage.** "Mass starvation" is not a term that the author spends time on and to use this statement to encapsulate (summarize) the topic of the passage would require making **extensive ASSUMPTIONS** from what has been presented in the text.

Passage 2

Question 12

A is the best answer. The **FIRST LINE OF AN INTRODUCTION** eases the reader into the content that is being dealt with in the passage. Typically, a **GOOD INTRODUCTION** starts with a **GENERAL STATEMENT** and gradually, with each sentence, **becomes more specific.** Currently, the introduction immediately begins by talking about the challenges faced by new business owners. Adding this sentence before it, would help **ease the reader more effectively** into the main topics at hand.

B is incorrect because if added at the beginning of the paragraph as indicated, there are no prior statements for this one to clarify.

C is incorrect. The last line takes us to the **specific topic of the passage,** crowdfunding. We know that this is the main topic because the title, "Crowdfunding," tells us this. Therefore, adding this line at the end of the paragraph **would not be an effective conclusion** since it would **disrupt the flow of logic** in the paragraph.

D is incorrect. This sentence helps **contextualize** entrepreneurs as a group and links **directly** to an idea that is then expanded in the passage (that they cannot address all the problems faced by new business owners). As such, this information **is extremely relevant** to the content of this paragraph.

Question 13

B is the best answer. This is the **most active** option and immediately tells the reader what one of the most common barriers to new business owners, "a lack of access to capital."

A is incorrect because the current statement is **ambiguous** (unclear). The sentence states "one of the most common barriers to starting a new business is access to capital." While the following information tells the reader that it is the **lack** of access that is the barrier, this statement is **not direct** in communicating the information. Therefore, it needs to be changed.

C is incorrect. Using a **GERUND** (a verb ending with "ing" like "lacking") **is an immediate indicator** that the sentence is more **PASSIVE. ACTIVE** sentence structures are always preferred since they more **directly link the action to the subject**.

D is incorrect. By **using more words than necessary to communicate the same idea** as "lack," this option does not have the clarity of choice B. Furthermore, the use of the gerund here also makes this a more **passive choice. Sentences are considered ACTIVE when the subject performs an action. They are considered PASSIVE when the subject receives an action.**

Question 14

D is the best answer. From talking about crowdfunding in the last line of the introduction, the current **topic sentence** talks about "loans." Therefore, adding the proposed addition **before the current first sentence** would be helpful in **easing the reader into the change in topic.**

A is incorrect because a **GOOD TOPIC SENTENCE** (the first sentence) of a paragraph allows the reader to **EFFECTIVELY UNDERSTAND the flow of logic,** i.e., how the ideas from the previous paragraph continue to this one and what the main idea of this paragraph is. Since the sentence now immediately talks about loans, it is not an **effective transition** and therefore, could be changed.

B is incorrect because it is **redundant** and repeats the same information about the lack of "access to capital" that was mentioned in the earlier paragraph to introduce crowdfunding. Adding this sentence would therefore be **repetitive** in this particular context.

C is incorrect. While not untrue, the term "historical discrimination" is not mentioned anywhere in this paragraph. Rather, the paragraph talks about difficulties with loans in a more general context. Adding this statement here would, therefore, **disrupt the flow of logic in the paragraph.**

Question 15

A is the best answer. Since the end of the previous sentence is the first time that the term "venture capitalists" is used, adding this would be extremely helpful in **improving access,** i.e., ensuring that readers know what is being discussed. Whenever possible, **define the terms that you are using** especially if they are technical terms that are only relevant to a certain field.

B is incorrect because knowing what "venture capitalists" are does not help address the voice or tone of the paragraph (or sentence). While it does add clarity, this clarity is in relation to what is put forward in the previous sentence. Hence, A is the more suitable answer.

C is incorrect. The last line describes the risk of venture capitalism as a source of funding for new business owners. Adding a description about venture capitalism **after** its risks are described will **disrupt** the flow of logic in the paragraph. Therefore, this is **not an effective concluding statement** for the paragraph.

D is incorrect because the information provided is **extremely relevant to the text in the paragraph.** By telling the reader what "venture capitalists" do, the reader is better able to understand how/why business owners use these avenues to fund their work.

Question 16

A is the best answer. To best understand the answer, break down the different components to the sentence. **When DASHES are used before and after a clause, that information is parenthetical.** Therefore, for purposes of analysis, lets remove the clause "a new type of grassroots funding." What we are left with is an **independent clause** that states "Crowdfunding allows entrepreneurs to source capital from the entire world rather than a select group of investors." The **KEYWORD** to notice here is the **CONNECTOR** "rather" which sets up a **CONTRAST** between different parts of the sentence. Therefore, it needs to be preceded by a comma, so that the reader understands the **comparison** that is being made.

B is incorrect because without a punctuation before the word "rather," the reader is not encouraged to **take a pause** and through this **pause** to **notice the contrast that is being presented.** When contrasting ideas are present in the same sentence, the **appropriate punctuation is needed to make the ideas easier to access for the reader.**

C is incorrect. Adding a **DASH** before "rather" would only serve to **confuse the reader.** Furthermore, **dashes when used on one side of a sentence emphasize what comes before (OR, sometimes, what comes after it).** In this case, we want emphasis on **both sides of the dash** and therefore, it is not the right choice.

D is incorrect. "Rather than a select group of investors" is a **DEPENDENT CLAUSE.** For a sentence to be able to stand on its own, i.e., be an **independent clause/complete sentence,** it needs its own **subject, verb, and object.** Since the clause above does not meet those requirements, this answer choice is not grammatically correct.

Question 17

B is the best answer. By using "that" to refer to the concept of "fundraising," and by using the **specific** term "entrepreneur" to replace the **ambiguous** term "someone," this answer most effectively captures the message being conveyed by this sentence.

A is incorrect because "where" is a **RELATIVE PRONOUN** that refers to a location. Here, the subject of the sentence is "Crowdfunding," which is a concept and not a location. Therefore, the current structure of the clause is unviable.

C is incorrect. There is **NO relative pronoun that is used,** which makes the sentence hard to follow. Furthermore, the use of the word "people" increases the **AMBIGUITY** of the statement and creates a **REPETITION** of vocabulary with the use of "people" later in the same sentence.

D is incorrect because "in which" and "where" refers to a location (because of the use of "in" that precedes the relative pronoun "which"). Though this is not grammatically inaccurate per se, this choice is less suitable than choice B.

Question 18

C is the best answer. For a question like this one, the best way to arrive at the right answer **is to replace the underlined phrase with each choice** and then look for two things: **grammatical accuracy and ACTIVE voice.** The option that best fits **both of these conditions** is the best answer. In this case, as will be shown below, "ranging from" is the best option. The resulting statement is both grammatically correct and **more ACTIVE** than the current construction ("new inventions and discoveries **ranging from** the perfect potato salad to the Oculus series of virtual reality products")

A is incorrect. Pay attention to the **KEYWORD** "to" before "the Oculus series of virtual reality products." Saying that something ("inventions and discoveries") is as varied as X **TO** Y is not **grammatically accurate.** In this case, it would have been more accurate to use the word **AND** (i.e. "new inventions and discoveries **as varied as** the perfect potato salad **AND** the Oculus series of virtual reality products").

B is incorrect for the same reasons as choice A. In this context, if using "as diverse as," it would be accurate to use "and" and not "to." "To" in this context implies a range of items whereas "and" states a specific point of reference in terms of diversity/variety.

D is incorrect. Once again, if using the term "including," **TO** would be grammatically incorrect. The more accurate version would use the word **AND** and it would utilize commas before and after the word "including" (i.e. "new inventions and discoveries, **including,** the perfect potato salad **AND** the Oculus series of virtual reality products"). Since neither condition is met, this answer choice is not suitable.

Question 19

D is the best answer. A **CONCEPT MAP** of each of the sentences reveals:

- Sentence 1: describes crowdfunding
- Sentence 2: platforms that facilitate crowdfunding
- Sentence 3: the variety of causes in crowdfunding campaigns with specific examples
- Sentence 4: the diversity of crowdfunding campaigns and the effect of that diversity

Based on the flow of logic in the paragraph, we see that sentence 4 would be better placed **before** sentence 3 since that would allow the reader to be introduced to the idea of "diversity" before engaging with specific examples.

A is incorrect because a general statement about diversity and its impact is placed **after** a sentence about specific kinds of diversity. Since **a solid PARAGRAPH STRUCTURE goes from more general information to more specific details,** a change would need to be made.

B is incorrect. Based on the concept mapping above, moving sentence 4 before sentence 1 means talking about the diversity of crowdfunding **before** telling the reader what crowdfunding is. Therefore, this would definitely **disrupt** the flow of ideas in this paragraph.

C is incorrect also because it would **disrupt the flow of logic** by describing how diverse causes attract nonmainstream investors **before** speaking about the platforms that facilitate crowdfunding in the first place.

Question 20

B is the best answer. By restating that the sentence is referring to "the crowdfunding phenomenon," this choice helps **improve clarity for the reader.**

Choices A, C, and D are incorrect for the same reason.

There are multiple items referred to in the sentence which are "crowdfunding platforms," "laptop and an internet connection," "start-up businesses" and "new products." Terms like "This," "they," or "it" are unclear because these terms do not remind the reader **of the subject that is being referred to. When multiple topics/items are being referred to in one sentence,** it is good practice to **restate your point of reference in the following sentence.**

Question 21

B is the best answer. By removing the word "as," this answer choice transforms the clauses on both sides of the **SEMICOLON** into clauses that each have their own **subject, verb,** and **object.** This makes the sentence structure ideal for the use of this punctuation mark.

A is incorrect because the use of the **CONNECTOR** "as" makes the following sentence a **dependent clause** rather than a **stand-alone sentence.** Therefore, in this case, the presence of the semicolon makes the sentence **grammatically incorrect.**

C is incorrect. Without any punctuation to separate the clauses, this becomes a **run-on sentence that is extremely difficult to understand. Whenever possible, avoid run-on sentences. A RUN-ON SENTENCE is a grammatically incorrect sentence in which multiple independent clauses are placed together without an appropriate CONNECTOR and/or PUNCTUATION MARK.**

D is incorrect. COMMAS are used to connect **dependent clauses** to **independent clauses.** In this statement, we see that there are clearly two independent clauses. One is about the positive nature of this development for "investors and entrepreneurs," and the second is about new businesses and small investors. While the ideas are connected, they are also **different from each other,** i.e., one of the ideas is not **dependent** on the other.

Question 22

C is the best answer. This answer choice **enhances the CLARITY** of the sentence by splitting two extremely long independent clauses into two separate sentences. In addition, it effectively uses the **CONNECTOR** "Furthermore" to indicate how the sentence that follows adds to the ideas being expressed in the clause that comes before it.

A is incorrect because the use of the word "Likewise" is **inaccurate.** "Likewise" essentially means "in the same way" and is generally used to introduce a related idea about the same subject. However, here, the following sentence speaks about "consumers" while the previous sentence speaks about "entrepreneurs." Therefore, "likewise" does not capture the additional information that is being presented.

B is incorrect. Although the use of the **SEMICOLON** is not grammatically inaccurate, the use of this punctuation mark makes the sentence incredibly long and hard to understand. Remember that **effective sentences prioritize CLARITY.**

D is incorrect because the use of the conjunction "and" does not help in making the sentence any clearer. The use of this conjunction simply creates a really lengthy statement that continues to be difficult for the reader to understand.

Passage 3

Question 23

B is the best answer. "Dogs are" is in the present tense and in the plural, so there needs to **be a present tense and plural conjugation** to have **VERB TENSE CONSISTENCY** and **SUBJECT VERB AGREEMENT.** "Have evolved" is the only answer choice that fits both of these criteria.

> A is incorrect because "had" (in the **PAST PERFECT TENSE**) causes an **INCONSISTENCY** with the use of the "are" earlier in the sentence.
>
> C is incorrect because although "has" is in the present tense, there is a disagreement with "are," which refers to the "dogs" in the plural.
>
> D is incorrect because the use of the **SIMPLE PAST TENSE** causes an **INCONSISTENCY** with the use of the "are" earlier in the sentence.

Question 24

B is the best answer. The information in this proposed sentence adds **new information** about ways in which dogs are useful to humans. Also, the use of the **connector** "for example" is a much more **effective transition** since it tells the reader that the following content will help evidence a preceding point ("found important niches in numerous branches of society").

> A is incorrect. "To clarify" means to make **something more understandable/clearer.** While the use of this new sentence will help **add new information** to the paragraph, it is not needed for the sake of **clarity** since there are already examples included in the test which help the reader understand the content.
>
> C is incorrect. There is no modifier error in this statement. A **MODIFIER is an optional element in a statement that changes/modifies the meaning of some other element in the sentence.** There is no modifier in the newly proposed addition since all the information in it is necessary (not optional).
>
> D is incorrect because the statement provides information that specifically has to do with how dogs have found a niche in human society. By putting forward an example that helps add to existing information, this sentence would be completely **relevant.**

Question 25

A is the best answer. "Enlist" is a term that is specifically used to refer to how new participants join the army or the police forces. To say that dogs "are enlisted" also **underlines** the fact that dogs do not enlist themselves. They **are enlisted** by humans to serve in those particular roles.

> All the other choices give dogs **an active agency that in this case they do not possess.** To say that dogs are "participants," "members," or "enrollees" would **imply** that the dog is making the choice to take part in these activities. To say so would be a huge **ASSUMPTION,** of course, **since we do not understand enough about canine behavior to say anything about the ability to choose** in such situations.

Question 26

C is the best answer. This is the only statement that is immediately evidenced by looking at the data shown in the graph.

> A is incorrect because the graph shows us information surrounding different pet "types" and their presence in US households. We are not given any information about a shift in numbers of any of these pet populations over time.
>
> B is incorrect. Since the graph shows us that nearly 90 million homes have a dog as a pet, this answer choice **misrepresents** the information that is represented in the graph.
>
> D is incorrect because there is no specific information about the year that is given in the graph. Saying that it represents data from 2010 would therefore be an **ASSUMPTION** that cannot be made based on the information given.

Question 27

B is the best answer. By looking at other verbs in the sentence, we see "is the housecat." The use of "is" immediately tells us that we are speaking in the **PRESENT TENSE.** Therefore, the correct conjugation for speaking of "man's best friend" will also be a version of the present tense so as to contain **VERB TENSE CONSISTENCY.** Therefore, given all the other choices, this is the only likely one.

All other answers cause **VERB TENSE INCONSISTENCY.** "Became" is in the **PAST TENSE,** "had become" **is in the PAST PERFECT,** and "will become" **is in the FUTURE TENSE.** Therefore, in this case, making sure that there is consistency in the verb tense usage throughout the sentence immediately reveals the right answer.

Question 28

D is the best answer. By splitting the sentence into two, the **clarity, tone and voice** are improved; the sentences become more active. Furthermore, this is a better answer than C because of the use of the word "were." Since the previous part of the sentence introduces information about the past (i.e., "first species [...] to ever be domesticated," "were" is a more grammatically correct choice than "are."

A and B are incorrect for the same reason.

SEMICOLONs are used to separate two INDEPENDENT clauses, each with their own subject, verb, and object. While these conditions are met, pay attention to the **length of the clauses.** Using the semicolon results in an **extremely long sentence** and such sentences **are much harder for readers to understand.** Furthermore, since the first sentence refers to a **present** occurrence and the second refers to something that took place in the **past, separating the sentences is a much more suitable choice.**

C is incorrect because although it creates two sentences and thus, enables more clarity, it uses the **PRESENT tense** "are" to speak about dogs being the first species to be domesticated. Since this clearly refers to an event in the **past,** this tense choice would not be accurate.

Question 29

D is the best answer. Connectors like "to be more specific," "in fact," and "although," closely depend on the **context of the statement.** Here, we have a line that tells us that dogs descended from the grey wolf, and the next line tells us when the genetic divergence took place. The following line tells us when domestication began happening. Looking at the **concepts** in each of these sentences, we see that there is no need **to use a connector** between the statement about dogs' lineage and when the divergence took place. The two ideas stand alone and are not dependent on each other (as the use of a connector would suggest). Therefore, **D is the only correct answer.**

A is incorrect because "to be more specific" would imply that the previous sentence presented general information about genetic divergence already. Hence, this **connector** is being used to clarify **an idea that was put forward before.** However, we see that the previous lines talk about descendance **not** genetic divergence and thus, this **connector is irrelevant.**

B while not technically incorrect is just unnecessary. "In fact,," in this case, **is superfluous** (extra) and would be the right answer choice only if D was not also presented as an option.

C is incorrect because the term "although" **implies a contrast** that is presented with the information that came earlier. Since no such contrasting information is presented. This term is **irrelevant.**

Question 30

D is the best answer. We have not been told anywhere in the passage what a "glacial maximum" has to do with the domestication of dogs. Therefore, this information immediately seems **irrelevant** since it seems to be referring to a topic that is completely outside the scope of the current passage.

A is incorrect because once again the term "glacial maximum" does not seem to link to anything else that has been said earlier in the passage. Furthermore, there is no quantitative data that is presented in this sentence. Adding it at the proposed location does not clarify anything that came before it.

B is incorrect. This paragraph discusses the links between dogs and wolves. Nothing about a glacial maximum is mentioned anywhere in the paragraph. Therefore, this would be an **irrelevant** introduction since the **topic sentence** should capture what follows in the paragraph.

C is incorrect because as above this paragraph discusses the links between dogs and wolves. Nothing is mentioned about a glacial maximum. Therefore, this would be an **irrelevant** conclusion since the **concluding sentences** should capture the main point of the preceding paragraph and take the reader to the next idea that is being discussed.

Question 31

C is the best answer. By saying "to assist hunters," the **tone** is **kept active** while also clarifying for the reader what "them" refers to. Since the preceding information references "dogs," "humans," and "nomadic peoples," it is better for **clarity** to be specific who "them" refers to.

A is incorrect because of the use of the word "them" and the **subsequent ambiguity** that is created about the **subject being referred to.**

B is incorrect. By extending the length of the phrase and by using a sentence construction that makes the action (hunting) **more passive**, this sentence is less suitable. **Remember that in passive sentences, the ACTION takes place to the subject (rather than the subject enacting the action).** When we say, "to assist," the action ("assist") is carried out by the dog. When we say, "for the purposes of hunting," the action ("hunting") happens to the dog. Therefore, the latter is much more **passive** and can be discarded as the right answer.

D is incorrect because "for help" is **ambiguous** and does not tell the reader **what kind of help** the dogs provided. Since this sentence describes the first time that dogs were domesticated, knowing **why** is extremely **relevant** to the reader.

Question 32

C is the best answer. Once again, we are looking for answer choices **that are most active** and one way of identifying the most active choice is to look simply **at the number of words that are used to make the same point.** Here, "domesticated dogs" is a **simple, effective way** of adding a clarification that since their domestication, dogs have continued to be important to human society.

A is incorrect for the same reason as B since both choices use more qualifiers than necessary to make the same point. By saying "after their domestication" and "once domesticated," these choices add the **unnecessarily qualifiers of time** (i.e., "after" and "once) which are not needed. Simply saying "domesticated" tells us that this process has already happened.

D is incorrect. Replacing the underlined section with this answer, we see that "Over time, **domesticated dogs have** began to play an increasingly important role [...]." The use of the verb "have" with "began" is grammatically incorrect. The correct use of the terms would be "have begun."

Question 33

B is the best answer. While this statement provides interesting information about sheep dogs, adding the sentence at the indicated location would **disrupt the flow of the paragraph.** The previous sentence talks about the role of dogs in hunter gatherer societies. The following sentence concludes the passage. The specific information that is included in the proposed new line, therefore, would be **out of place** in an otherwise **generalized paragraph that serves to end the passage.**

A is incorrect because the previous information speaks about how dogs served as protection from predators in hunter-gatherer societies. **Nothing has been mentioned yet** about the domestication of livestock and the role of dogs in herding cattle. Therefore, adding this sentence does not help clarify anything that came before it.

C is incorrect. **A good concluding sentence summarizes the previous content and prepares the reader for the content that is to follow.** This sentence does not fit either of these conditions and would, therefore, **not be a good conclusion.**

D is incorrect because although adding the information at the specified place would **disrupt the flow,** it still contains information **that is relevant to the central theme of the passage,** i.e., how dogs have evolved over time to serve different purposes in human society.

Passage 4

Question 34

D is the best answer. Since there is only one clear subject in this sentence, "Lucile Ball," no reference like "who," "whomever," or "whoever" needs to be used. These terms **are useful when there are multiple subjects being mention and when the usage of these pronouns is not necessary.** Therefore, since this is the only answer choice **without a pronoun,** it is immediately identifiable as the correct answer.

Question 35

B is the best answer. What is important to note here are that the two sentences seek to establish a CONTRAST, and this is indicated by the use of the word "not." The previous sentence reads "reflected her signature slapstick comedic style" and the following sentence tells us that this was NOT the only quality that made Ball stand out. Therefore, because it implies a **contrast,** "however" is the most appropriate choice for a **connector** that builds on an idea from a previous sentence but also **takes that sentence in a new direction.**

A is incorrect because a connector like "indeed" is used in order to **restate** a previously made point. In this case, since the focus of the **argumentation/logic** changes in the line that follows "indeed," it is insufficient in **capturing** the tone and concept of the text.

C is incorrect because like "indeed," **"thus"** is used to **prove/restate** an argument that comes before it. Since the sentence here **shifts the previously stated idea and builds on it,** "thus" is an inaccurate **connector.**

D is incorrect. **Since two contrasting ideas are mentioned one right after the other and in relation to each other, a CONNECTOR is essential to maintain the flow of logic in the paragraph.** Taking away the connector without replacing it, therefore, would not be a suitable choice.

Question 36

A is the best answer. "To elicit" means to evoke or to draw out a particular kind of response. Since this sentence describes the kind of laughter that Ball evoked from her audience, "eliciting" is indeed the right choice.

B is incorrect. The term "illicit" is used to refer to an action that is "wrong" either by law or by custom. An example would be "He was arrested for his use of illicit drugs." In the **context of this paragraph,** the use of this word is **completely irrelevant.**

C and D are incorrect. Although "getting" and "receiving" laughter work grammatically and also communicate the **meaning** of the sentence, they are not as **context specific as "elicit."** "Elicit" is specifically used to describe emotions that brought out because of something/someone. "Get" and "receive" are used in multiple different contexts and thus, are not as specific as the choice in A.

Question 37

A is the best answer. There are two different **descriptors** that are used to discuss "typhoid," each of which have different **connotations** (meanings). To be "dangerous" means that the disease is serious and risky. "Infectious" means that the disease is communicable from one person to another. By using two different descriptors to **describe the gravity** (seriousness) of typhoid, the sentence is accurate as it is.

B is incorrect. Not only does it change the meaning of the sentence (an "infection" is less serious than a "disease"), this choice would be grammatically incorrect as it does not use **COMMAS** before and after the dependent clause (the clause that **contextualizes** the disease as dangerous and infectious).

C is incorrect because **it alters the meaning by deleting the word** "dangerous." As mentioned above, the use of **both these adjectives** is important in communicating the seriousness of typhoid and deleting one of them, and it would affect the **tone** that the author seeks to establish.

D is incorrect because it does not allow the reader to **understand the context,** i.e., what kind of disease typhoid is. Although we could say that "dangerous and infectious disease" is **NON-ESSENTIAL** (we know she lost her father to it, so it is **additional information**) it is important to **introduce an unfamiliar reader** with the seriousness of the condition.

Question 38

B is the best answer. Since Lucy is the subject of this sentence and because her name has been mentioned later in the sentence, the pronoun "her" is the most effective pronoun to be used.

A is incorrect because "their" refers to **multiple subjects** or a **subject whose gender cannot be classified as male or female.** Since there is only one subject in this sentence (Lucy) and since she has been referred to as a girl/woman multiple times in the preceding text, "their" is incorrect.

C and D are incorrect for the same reason, i.e., the **subject's name is mentioned twice in the same sentence. When there is a clear case of subject reference like the use of their name, an additional reference to them in the same (and sometimes following sentences) only needs a pronoun.** It is clear to the reader who is being referred to and referring to them twice (be it through their first or last name) is **unnecessary.**

Question 39

B is the best answer because **it is the most active choice.** By saying that the stage was her destiny," the term "was destined" is made more active. In so doing, the **clarity and tone of the line changes by** "from an early age **she knew that the stage was her destiny."** This sentence places the focus on Ball and her knowing by making the sentence more **active.**

All the remaining answers are incorrect for the same reason, i..e, **for the use of the PASSIVE voice.** By saying that Lucy "was destined," the subject (Lucy) is described as being the recipient of destiny rather than focusing **actively** that it was Lucy's **knowing** that helped her realize her own destiny.

Furthermore, choice D deletes the **context** of an "early age." This is an important bit of information since it tells the reader about Lucy's **character** and her development as an artist.

Question 40

C is the best answer. This is the most active choice since **it directly links** to "Los Angeles," which is where Lucy found roles in several major productions.

A is incorrect. By using the term "finding roles," it is not only **passive**, but it also does not refer the reader to **the location** where she began to find more work.

B is incorrect. "Finding roles" is different than "working in productions." The former tells us about what Lucy was able to find, and the latter **implies a choice that was made AFTER** the finding. Since we are just introduced to the idea that Lucy moved to Los Angeles, "finding" fits the **context** better than "working in." In addition, "which is where she worked" is **more passive** in **tone** than simply saying "where she worked." There is an extra usage of "which is," and the addition of **WHICH** implies **that what follows is a NON-ESSENTIAL ELEMENT** to the text. However, it is **ESSENTIAL** to know that Lucy found more work in Los Angeles.

D is incorrect because "when" refers to a time and here, the point of reference is a place. Although the sentence begins with an **allusion** (reference) to time ("After a few years"), the focus is on Los Angeles and not on the years themselves.

Question 41

D is the best answer. When DASHES are used on either side of a clause, they imply PARANTHETICAL INFORMATION while EMPHASIZING that information. Here, saying "— or rather, by foot –" the author tells the reader **extra information which, while not necessary to understanding the sentence, emphasizes WHY** that particular episode was funny (it helps qualify the "physical comedy" that is referred to later).

A is incorrect. The repeated uses of COMMAS in the current sentence construction makes the sentence **hard to understand.** The reason being the author mentioning "the foot" does not come through as **clearly.**

B is incorrect. By leaving out the word "or" and by placing "rather" at the end of the phrase, this sentence both **reduces the clarity of the statement and is grammatically less suitable (connectors like "rather" most often belong at the beginning of an introduced phrase).**

C is incorrect because "shouting at the" seems **completely irrelevant** in the context of this current sentence. It would render the sentence meaningless.

Question 42

A is the best answer. This sentence would be an effective **CONCLUSION** to the paragraph because the next paragraph goes on to talk about Lucy's work as a producer. Therefore, this sentence would make an effective transition to the ideas that follow.

B is incorrect because nothing in the proposed sentence helps "clarify" concepts in the preceding paragraph. The paragraph has to do with Lucy's particular approach to comedy and does not mention anything to do with her skills as a businessperson or a producer.

C is incorrect. Given that the content of this paragraph has nothing to do with Lucy as a producer but as an actor. Using this proposed sentence as an introduction would be **IRRELEVANT.**

D is incorrect because this information has not been mentioned before and is **useful in expanding our knowledge** about the central topic of the passage (i.e., Lucy). Therefore, it cannot be classified as **REDUNDANT.**

Question 43

C is the best answer. "Refused" **is the most ACTIVE and CLEAREST** of all the different options that are provided here.

A is incorrect for two reasons. First, using a **CONTRACTION** (wouldn't, rather than would not) **is not considered good practice in a formal essay.** Furthermore, **"wouldn't allow" is a more passive TONE than "refused to allow,"** which communicates the strength of the networks' opposition.

B is incorrect. Although **this choice does not use a contraction**, it still is more passive as vocabulary than "refused."

D is incorrect because "attempted to allow" **would change the meaning of the sentence** and would mean that networks "almost allowed" Ball and Arnaz's ownership of their work to move forward unopposed. This would **contradict the tone** established in the sentence that maintains control of their show "require intense work."

Question 44

A is the best answer. The proposed sentence would be an **effective transition** that helps take the reader from a specific focus on *I Love Lucy* in the previous paragraph to other ways in which Lucille Ball created impacts in the film industry.

B is **incorrect.** An effective introductory line helps **frame** the concepts that follow. It does not "clarify" what comes after. The proposed sentence simply tells the reader that there were multiple ways in which Lucy's work broke new ground. It is the rest of the paragraph that then clarifies the ideas presented in this sentence.

C and D are incorrect because the information in this proposed sentence **is new information** and is **explicitly linked to the content of the topic.** Therefore, it is **neither redundant nor irrelevant.**

Writing Test 6: Answer Key

1. B	26. D
2. C	27. A
3. C	28. B
4. D	29. A
5. D	30. C
6. B	31. C
7. B	32. D
8. B	33. D
9. D	
10. C	
11. A	
	34. D
	35. B
	36. C
12. A	37. D
13. B	38. C
14. C	39. B
15. D	40. D
16. C	41. A
17. C	42. B
18. A	43. D
19. C	44. B
20. B	
21. D	
22. A	
23. B	
24. A	
25. C	

WRITING & LANGUAGE TEST 6
Answers & Explanations

Passage 1

Question 1

B is the best answer. The two clauses in this sentence are connected (**comparing** the number of bombs that existed in 1945, compared to twenty years later). Since the clauses on either side of the **SEMICOLON** each have their own **subject, verb, and object, the use of the semicolon is accurate.** Since the clauses are too **lengthy, combining them through the use of this punctuation mark** is a suitable choice. In fact, the first clause is rather short.

A is less suitable because **although not technically incorrect, the significantly shorter length of the first part of the sentence** ("In 1945, only two nuclear bombs existed") could disrupt the **flow** of the paragraph. **The LENGTH of sentences** has an impact on the **tone** and the feeling that is communicated to the reader. It is well-advised to have texts that are composed of sentences that have roughly the same length. **This would better to maintain the INTEGRITY** of the form.

C is incorrect because the connector "and" does not **emphasize** the comparison that is established in the sentence. "And" is used when two ideas are **similar** but here, they are clearly trying to show a difference that has occurred (in the number of bombs that exist). In addition, "and" would make the sentence **too long** and this too, like having sentences that are too short, **can be disruptive to the flow.**

D is incorrect because when a **SEMICOLON is used,** there is no **CONJUCTION** that needs to follow it (conjunctions are words like "and," "but," "or").

Question 2

C is the best answer. The KEY term to focus on here is "until that time," which references a particular moment in history (the Cuban Missile crisis). In such cases, the **PAST PERFECT**

To understand why choice A is not suitable (even though it is not grammatically incorrect), **let us look at the difference between SIMPLE PAST and PAST PERFECT TENSE** ("ever came" versus "had ever come"). Both events refer to something that happened in the past, but **PAST PERFECT is used to refer to something that happened <u>before</u> another action in the past.** In this case, the Cold War had started **before** the Cuban Missile Crisis and therefore, when speaking about what the Crisis represents in history in relation to the start of the Cold War the past perfect is more appropriate.

B is incorrect. Using "came" as the conjugated form of "to come" is **incorrect in this context. PAST PERFECT conjugations are formed by the word "had" + the PAST PARTICIPLE of the verb.** The PAST PATICIPLE of "to come" is "come," and "came is the **SIMPLE PAST.** Therefore, this choice is grammatically incorrect.

D is less suitable because, generally, **WOULD** is used to refer to something that **might** have happened but never did. When something in the past did happen like the Cuban Missile Crisis, **HAD is the better choice.**

TENSE, "ever had come," is the most suitable choice (more on this below). A **process of elimination** also tells us why this is more suitable than the other choices provided.

Question 3

C is the best answer. A GOOD TOPIC SENTENCE, a sentence that introduces a paragraph, effectively directs the reader to the main theme of that text. In this case, the **KEYWORD is** "failed," and the paragraph tells us how a failed coup (by the US in Cuba) led to this crisis. The reason why this choice is better than choice D (which also uses the word "failed") is mentioned below.

A is incorrect because the current topic sentence by saying that the Crisis has "roots in global politics" is **vague** and does not **effectively set up** the account that follows. The paragraph focuses on the US attempt to "overthrow the Cuban leader" and how the "plan failed miserably."

B is incorrect once again because it is **extremely general** and does not **introduce the reader to the contents of the following paragraph.**

D is incorrect. Although this choice also contains the **KEYWORD** "failed," it is less suitable than choice D because of the **use of vocabulary.** To say something was "sparked by" is to say that the event was started **because** of that "thing," i.e., the Cuban Missile Crisis was sparked because of a failed political coup. However, the paragraph tells us that was more complicated than that. The US coup failed, yes, but "in response" the Chairman of the former USSR offered to place missiles there. What happened, therefore, was not only because of the failed political coup but because the coup set off a series of actions and reactions.

Question 4

D is the best answer. The main theme of the paragraph is to **inform the reader** about how the Cuban Missile Crisis began. Therefore, the previous sentence by telling us how "the Cuban Missile Crisis officially began" is a far more **effective conclusion.**

A is incorrect because showing "the impact of political dealings on national security" is **irrelevant in this current context.** Furthermore, just saying that President Kennedy faced a "daunting challenge" is not evidence of such an impact.

B is incorrect because this last sentence **disrupts the flow of logic in the paragraph.** We have just been told how the Cuban Missile Crisis began. Why is there a need to speak of the challenge facing the President?

C is incorrect because the content that is included in this answer is **irrelevant to the question that is being posed.** Yes, the current last line is not about the relationship between diplomacy and national security. But given that the focus is on how the Missile Crisis began, why should this relationship be highlighted at this point in the text?

Question 5

D is the best answer because it removes all **redundancy** (i.e., an unnecessary **repetition of information).** By using the **connector** "despite," and by saying how the President's chosen option went against the advice he received, we know that an alternative option was chosen. Restating that idea, therefore, is **unnecessary.**

A is incorrect because the first part of the sentence "Instead of conflict, President Kennedy found an alternative option" **is unnecessary. It repeats information that is already stated in a later part of the same sentence.**

B is incorrect. Apart from adding an **unnecessary clause,** this phrase is incorrect because **it alters the meaning of what is being said.** As per the sentence, President Kennedy went outside what America's other leaders (i.e., the "military advisors") recommended. Saying that these leaders provided an alternative **contradicts** what is described as the President's decision to go **against** advice given to him.

C is incorrect because it renders the statement **meaningless.** Consider the following sentence. "Instead of conflict, President Kennedy met with military advisors who urged immediate action by force, President Kennedy decided to blockade all shipping operations around Cuba." As you can see, the sentence no longer carries meaning.

Question 6

B is the best answer. By using a COMMA to connect the ideas being presented, this answer choice improves **the clarity, tone, and voice** of the paragraph. Therefore, it is the most suitable answer.

A is incorrect because the ideas are **unnecessarily broken up into two sentences** with a less-than-ideal **repetition** of the subject, "the blockade."

C is incorrect. The **connector** "which" is used **inaccurately here.** First, "which" only needs to be **preceded** by a comma (not followed by one). Even if the comma used had been accurate, "which" is used to **introduce NON-ESSENTIAL elements,** i.e., elements that are interesting to know but are not necessary. Here, the information following "which" is **clearly ESSENTIAL.**

D is incorrect because **SEMICOLONS** are only used between **two independent clauses, and each of which has their own subject, verb, and object.** An immediate sign of a **misuse of a semicolon** is when a **conjunction** like "and" **is used after it** (as is the case here).

Question 7

B is the best answer. Let's map the concepts in this passage. Paragraph 1 → general introduction to nuclear weapons and the Cuban Missile Crisis, paragraph 2 → specific events leading to the beginning of the crisis, paragraph 3 → the development of the blockade, and paragraph 4 → why a response was necessary from President Kennedy. Given this map, we see that to create an **effective flow of logic,** paragraph 4 would be best placed **after paragraph 2.** This way, the reader would be told about the pressure on President Kennedy to respond before describing the nature of his response ("the blockade").

A is incorrect because where it is now, the paragraph **disrupts** the flow of logic in the passage and asks the reader to understand the "solution" before understanding the seriousness of the problem.

C is incorrect. In order to understand the pressure on President Kennedy, the reader first needs to understand how/why the Crisis began. Placing paragraph 4 after paragraph 1 would tell the reader what happened after the crisis developed, before telling us how it developed in the first place.

D is incorrect because if placed before the introductory paragraph, paragraph 4 would be **preemptive** and would describe an **effect** before telling the reader about the **cause.** This would be extremely **disruptive to the flow of logic in the passage.**

Question 8

B is the best answer. A conditional sentence contains two parts: the "if" clause, which explains the condition and the "then" clause, which explains the result. When an "if" clause is a **PAST UNREAL conditional,** something about the past that could have happened but did not, **the PAST PERFECT is used in the "if" clause.** Given this rule, "had done" is the only correct option.

A is incorrect because the specific grammar rule surrounding the use of the **PAST UNREAL CONDITIONAL** is currently being broken. Therefore, a change is required.

C is incorrect. The choice "does" would immediately cause a **VERB TENSE INCONSISTENCY.** The paragraph is explicitly talking about a past event and using the present tense would immediately pose an error.

D is incorrect. Although "would" is generally used to refer to an event that might have happened but did not, in this case, President Kennedy did not "do nothing." The **inaccurate component** is "do." Once again conjugated in the present tense, this would cause a **VERB TENSE INCOSISTENCY.**

Question 9

D is the best answer. Pay close attention to the subject here. In the beginning, when referring to Khrushchev, the only subject being referred to is President Kennedy. However, when speaking of "fellow world leaders," the points of reference are **both** Khrushchev and President Kennedy (since they both are world leaders). Therefore, "their" is the only correct answer choice here.

A is incorrect because it **implies** that President Kennedy's fellow leaders are **not** Chairman Khrushchev's world leaders and clearly, that is not the case.

B is incorrect because it **implies** that Chairman Khrushchev's fellow leaders are **not** President Kennedy's world leaders and clearly, that is not the case.

C is incorrect because the word "the" does not show any reference to whose "fellow global leaders" are being spoken of. The **KEYWORD** here is "fellow," and the reader needs to be able to understand who "fellow leaders" refers to.

Question 10

C is the best answer. The first sentence talks about what would have happened if President Kennedy did nothing. Therefore, it only fits with **the flow of logic** that the second sentence would present the alternative possibility, i.e., if President Kennedy had chosen to respond with military force.

A is incorrect because where it is now, there is a **disruption to the flow of logic in the paragraph.** Currently, the paragraph is structured as follows: sentence 1 discusses what would happen if the President did nothing, sentence 2 discusses the risk of the President seeming weak in the eyes of his colleagues, sentence 3 discusses what would happen if the President chose military force, and sentence 4 discusses how all global leaders were prepared for anything.

B is incorrect because the use of the **connector** "however" immediately tells us that this sentence responds to something else. Therefore, it cannot be placed before sentence 1 and become the introductory statement to the paragraph.

D is incorrect because sentence 4 talks about the **leaders on both sides** and not only President Kennedy. Placing this statement after sentence 4 would be **ineffective.**

Question 11

A is the best answer. The phrase "an effective strategy of foreign relations" is a **DEPENDENT CLAUSE** that is used to directly **clarify a word in the main, INDEPENDENT CLAUSE.** Therefore, the current sentence construction and punctuation choice are suitable and do not need to be changed.

B is incorrect because a **SEMICOLON** needs two independent clauses on either side and each with its own subject, verb, and object. Since the **clause following the semicolon** here is obviously a **dependent clause** that does not have **its own subject, verb, and object,** it is not a suitable answer.

C & D are not suitable because words like "that" and "which" are used to introduce **ESSENTIAL and NON-ESSENTIAL** elements to a sentence (respectively) when the elements in question are not so apparently a dependent clause that describes a term immediately preceding it. In such cases, words like "that" and "which" only serve to make the sentence harder to follow.

Passage 2

Question 12

A is the best answer. The DASH is used to indicate sentence introductions or conclusions and to mark text for emphasis. In this case, the DASH both marks the conclusion to the description of the Iditarod Trail and emphasizes its use for dog sled races (which, as we know from the title, is the main theme of the passage).

B is incorrect because the comma before "every year" is unnecessary in this case. Placing the comma before and after "every year" would give it special emphasis. In this case, the emphasis is meant to be on the dog sled race.

C is incorrect. By deleting the **conjunction** "and," this becomes a **run-on sentence. A run-on sentence includes multiple clauses that is not separated effectively with conjunctions and/or punctuation marks.**

D is incorrect because as we know, following a **SEMICOLON** with a **conjunction** is grammatically incorrect. The correct way to use the semicolon here would be: "The trail travels through snow, ice, frozen tundra, mountains, and forests; every year, teams of the world's most elite sled dogs race its entire length."

Question 13

B is the best answer. By rephrasing the sentence to be more **concise** and by taking out "extraneous" (extra) information, this is the most suitable choice. The **extra information that has been deleted** is "some of the most inhospitable conditions in this world," which is a phrase that has already been **established** by the descriptions that come earlier in the paragraph.

A is incorrect because there are **no key terms being explained in this sentence.** It is simply a way of rephrasing the information that has already been presented in a more **active** way.

C is incorrect. The current concluding sentence **is already effective** in describing how dogs and mushers come together in the dog sled races. Adding one more statement about the required coordination, one that introduces the word "musher" after it has already been used, is **not suitable.**

D is incorrect. The information contained in the revised sentence communicates **the same information as in the underlined sentence while making the construction more effective.** There is no **IRRELEVANT** information in this revision.

Question 14

C is the best answer. In order to identify the right answer, look at the sentence that follows it. In that sentence, the **focus** is on the Native Alaskans and their long-standing use of the Iditarod Trails. Therefore, the **topic sentence** should **retain the emphasis on the native communities** while also introducing the new information about the dog sled race. C is the only option that does this.

A is incorrect because the use of the **conjunction "and" does not effectively communicate the CONTRAST** that is being put forward in this statement that although the trails were used for races from 1973, the land was being used well before that. Therefore, the current sentence construction needs to be changed.

B is incorrect. The use of the **conjunction** "but" in this option better sets up the contrast. However, this **sentence construction** places **equal emphasis on both the races and the use of the land by native communities.** For the reasons above, i.e. to have an **effective transition to the next sentence,** this is less suitable than choice C. There needs to be extra emphasis on the native communities who have been inhabiting the trails for hundreds of years.

D is incorrect because **for the current paragraph, this topic sentence is irrelevant.** It does not help the reader understand the following text and thus, is not **an effective topic sentence.**

Question 15

D is the best answer. By making the same point by using **as few words as possible,** this answer choice **shows the most clarity and thus, is the most ACTIVE.**

A and B are incorrect for the same reason. **They are both PASSIVE in their construction** and include **uncertainty** when it is not needed. Phrases like "thought to be" and "considered to be" are generally **not recommended** because they **imply** that the author **might not be sure of what they are saying.**

C is incorrect because by saying that the "Trail experienced the popularity," the subject ("The Trail") is described as being a recipient of the popularity (placing the emphasis on the popularity). On the contrary, saying that the "Trail's popularity peaked, the emphasis remains on the Trail, which is the main topic of the passage.

Question 16

C is the best answer. The key lies in looking **at the context surrounding this underlined sentence.** The sentence before talks about the past. The sentence that comes after at the beginning of the next paragraph speaks about the races **today.** Therefore, the text that replaces the underlined section should connect the events of the past to the events of the present. The choice in this answer is the most **concise, active** way of doing so.

A is incorrect because the phrase "the spirit of adventure is present" does not **effectively tell the reader** what "is present" is in reference to. Given that the previous sentence was about the past, there needs to be a term/phrase included to clarify that this statement refers to how the spirit of the races continues to this day.

B is incorrect because the statement includes **repeated information.** The terms "vital" and "essential" are synonyms and there is no need to include them both. Furthermore, by ending the sentence with "epic dog sled journey," the sentence **repeats** many words from the phrase that are used in the beginning of the sentence ("the journey the sled dog teams took"). In **well-constructed sentences,** the **vocabulary choice is careful and intentional.**

D is incorrect because, like choice B, it repeats information that does not need to be restated. For example, since the year 1925 is already mentioned in the early part of the sentence, this information does not need to be repeated, "inspired by the relay races run almost a century before."

Question 17

C is the best answer. By adding this information, the reader is given a **better understanding of the conditions that make the race difficult** (which is the main topic of the passage). Not only is weather and harsh terrain a challenge, but dogs and mushers must also carry heavy loads with them. This information is extremely helpful in **contextualizing** the dog sled races for the reader.

A is incorrect because the sentence does not necessarily provide more or less of an effective transition than what already exists in the paragraph.

B is incorrect. The punctuations are used correctly. As we know, **a COLON is used to introduce a list, an explanation of the previously stated idea, or a quotation. The colon in this sentence introduces a list,** and **the use of COMMAS is correct.** They are used to separate three or more items and used after the term "Additionally," i.e., **a CONNECTOR** that is used to refer to the previous sentence's ideas.

D is incorrect. Given how closely related the **content in this sentence is** to the main topic of the paragraph, it is **not irrelevant.**

Question 18

A is the best answer. The supporting clause (introduced by "but") is effectively **preceded by a COMMA.** This allows the reader to understand that the material which follows "but" is directly related to the preceding content and seeks to clarify it. Since this **objective is reached without making the sentence hard to follow,** no change is needed.

B is incorrect because there is missing punctuation before the word "but." Since there is a **clarification** being put forward in the subsequent clause, the **shift in argumentation** needs to be preceded by a **COMMA.**

C is not suitable because there is no need to add a **SEMICOLON here in order to separate the two clauses.** Doing so and taking out the word "but" **alters the tone of the line.** The "but" **emphasizes that the real glory of the race is finishing it** and not all the other prizes that are added on. By taking away "but," the **effect of comparison is lost.**

D is incorrect. Although the DASH could be an effective choice for this sentence, the error lies in the use of the **COMMA** that comes after the word "but." The **COMMA use here is unnecessary** and because of this error, D is not a suitable answer.

Question 19

C is the best answer. There are two independent clauses in this statement and each **with their own subject, verb, and object.** The first clause is "Most of the sled dogs are Siberian huskies" and the second clause is "they generally weigh between thirty and sixty pounds." Since these are **ideas that are linked by the larger theme** (of Siberian huskies) **and yet, not building on each other,** a semicolon is an effective way of combining the two rather short statements into one, more all-encompassing sentence.

A is incorrect because the use of the **conjunction** "and" is unnecessary in this case. "And" implies a link between two ideas, i.e., where the idea after the "and" **adds to the idea that precedes it.** Since this condition is not met, choice A is not the best option.

B is incorrect. By continuing to use "and," placing "generally" in a different location, and omitting the use of punctuation, this sentence structure would be **difficult for a reader to follow.**

D is incorrect because using a COMMA **without** a conjunction or **connector** makes this sentence meaningless.

Question 20

B is the best answer. This choice uses the accurate terminology ("mushers" not "racers") and effectively uses a comma to link the ideas of the dogs' physical endurance and the mushers' care to ensure their health (and, subsequently, their endurance).

A is incorrect because the term "racers" is **inaccurate.** In the first paragraph, the author tells us that the people who "drive" the dogs are called "mushers." Therefore, in keeping with the **context that we've already been given,** "mushers" is the preferred choice of terminology.

C is incorrect. The use of "and" after the **SEMICOLON** is an immediate indicator that this choice is **inaccurate.** When semicolons are used properly, **conjunctions are not needed between the two independent clauses that they separate.**

D is incorrect because the **lack** of punctuation does not allow the reader to understand that there is a slight, interrelated **shift in argumentation that has taken place.** The sentence moves from describing the dogs' endurance to the mushers' care. Both of which refer to the importance of the dog's physical health.

Question 21

D is the best answer. The subject of the sentence is "a dog," i.e., **a dog in the SINGULAR.** Therefore, the only grammatically accurate way of referring to this dog with a pronoun is to say "it is."

A is incorrect because "they" would only be used if the subject referred to "dogs" in the **PLURAL.**

B is incorrect because the tense "was" immediately causes a **VERB TENSE INCONSISTENCY.** Since the preceding verb is in the **PRESENT TENSE** ("is injured"), this tense usage needs to be continued through the rest of the sentence.

C is incorrect because it uses "they" and "would." For "would" to be used accurately, the sentence would have to read "If a dog **was to become** injured or exhausted during the race, **it would be** carried in the sled basket." Otherwise, there is a **VERB TENSE INCONSISTENCY that emerges.**

Question 22

A is the best answer. In the paragraph as it is, the first sentence reiterates (repeats) the unique nature of this race. The second sentence talks about its roots. The third sentence talks about the difficulties that mushers and dogs face. To complete the **flow of logic in the paragraph** and to provide **an effective conclusion to the passage,** the proposed sentence would be a good addition. By using the term "above all" it draws the reader's attention to what they should take away from the passage as a whole.

B is incorrect because the information contained in this proposed sentence does not **clarify** anything that was mentioned earlier. In fact, all the information that precedes this added sentence has been **explained and framed** in the paragraphs that have come before it.

C is incorrect. Given that the current first sentence reiterates what the Iditarod Dog Sled Race is, including what the race provides before the current first sentence would **disrupt the flow of logic in the paragraph.**

D is incorrect because the power of the human and dog spirits in the face of unimaginable difficult conditions is not an idea that has been mentioned earlier in this paragraph. Therefore, because it provides content that has not been stated earlier in this paragraph, **this statement cannot be called redundant.**

Passage 3

Question 23

B is the best answer. The first line introduces us to Colón and the Puerto Rican Traveling Theatre, and the second line (currently) describes the opportunities that were created for Hispanic performers through her work. By adding the proposed line, the reader gets a chance to understand that Colón was a pioneer and that she helped break barriers for Latino/Latina performers. Therefore, this sentence especially since this is an introductory paragraph creates an effective transition for the reader.

A is incorrect because only one line is said before the proposed location of this sentence and nothing in that line is given/needs support from what is stated here.

C is incorrect. There is no modifier error here. A **MODIFIER is an optional element in a statement that changes/modifies the meaning of some other element in the sentence.** There is no modifier in the newly proposed addition since all the information in it is necessary (not optional).

D is incorrect because this sentence provides information that is directly related to why Colón is an important figure in theater. Since the content is directly linked to other ideas in the paragraph, the proposed addition is **RELEVANT** to the text.

Question 24

A is the best answer. When referring to the past in which what happened doesn't change over time like her career, "was" is the best option.

B is incorrect because "is" is in the **PRESENT TENSE** and would be inaccurate when referring to an event that has taken place in the past.

C is incorrect. When referring to the past, **"had been" is used when what happened in the past does not apply to the present.** In this case, what happened early in her career clearly does not change over time and therefore, this choice is incorrect.

D is incorrect because "has" by being in the **PRESENT TENSE** would be inaccurate when referring to an event that took place in the past.

Question 25

C is the best answer. The **KEYWORD** to consider in the existing sentence is "role," i.e., the sentence specifically refers to the character that she took on for *Bless Me, Ultima* rather than the movie itself. Therefore, "parts" is the most relevant answer choice here.

None of the other answers effectively capture this connection (between the underlined section, and a word that is a synonym for "role"). While "contributions" does come close, it is less suitable because the term is **broader in scope.** Here, we know that the contribution being referred to is a character that Colón played in one particular film. Therefore, "parts" is the most suitable option.

Question 26

D is the best answer. In this sentence, the **important information** is that Colón audited University level classes while she was still a student in high school. By including this information to **contextualize** her "limitless" passion, this answer choice best communicates all the necessary ideas in the text.

Choices A, B, and C are incorrect because they do not tell the reader that Colón audited these classes while she was still in high school. Therefore, the reader does not see an **effective transition** from the previous sentence in which her high school status is introduced. Due to their **relative lack of clarity,** therefore, none of these three choices are as suitable as the correct answer.

Question 27

A is the best answer. The "surprise of many" is **in reference to** the recognition that Colón received for her work in *Los Peloteros* from formal institutions. By accurately depicting this connection between the ideas with **clarity,** this is the most suitable answer.

B is incorrect because the use of the **connector** "although" **alters the meaning of the sentence.** It implies that "even though" many were surprised, film institutions recognized her talent. However, as we know from the sentence, many were surprised **because** film institutions recognized her talent. Therefore, "although" is not a suitable choice.

C is incorrect. When referring to a **quantitative reference** (like "many") the possessive use of "'s" does not apply. The **apostrophe followed by the letter "s" signifying possession** is generally used in reference to a **specific person/thing** and its possession of a quality/material object/emotion.

D is incorrect because a **COMMA** has not been used to demarcate the end of the **DEPENDENT/INTRODUCTORY CLAUSE** and this punctuation is necessary to help the reader understand the argument that is being presented.

Question 28

B is the best answer. The **KEYWORDS** to pay attention to in this sentence are "worked consistently." It is a phrase that tells us that something (consistent work) continued to occur for Colón from the time her career was launched (as a teenager). This answer is the only one that more accurately communicates this idea.

A is incorrect because the word "launching" is written in the **PRESENT CONTINUOUS TENSE** while "worked" is conjugated in the **SIMPLE PAST.** This leads to a **VERB TENSE INCOSISTENCY** that takes away from the **meaning of the sentence.**

Answers C and D are also incorrect for the same reason. **The PRESENT CONTINUOUS TENSE** refers to something that is ongoing in the present. **The SIMPLE PAST TENSE** refers to something that happened in the past which does **NOT** change over time. Since this passage speaks about the biography of a particular person, the **SIMPLE PAST** is the more clear and effective choice when speaking about specific times in her life.

Question 29

A is the best answer. This sentence provides information about how the group travelled until they finally found a location in NYC. Therefore, the text helps the reader better understand the concepts in the paragraph that follows.

B is incorrect because the sentence does **more** than just give information about how the group traveled. Therefore, although this answer is accurate in part, it needs to be kept not only for its content, but also for how it serves the flow of logic in the text.

C is incorrect. The paragraph transitions from focusing on Colón's work beyond the traveling theatre to going into specifics of the traveling theatre. Therefore, a sentence like this one would be **an insufficient** introduction to the paragraph.

D is incorrect because the information by relating closely to the **topic of the passage** is EXTREMELY **RELEVANT** in helping the reader better understand Colón's work.

Question 30

C is the best answer. Since there are two different time periods being **referenced** here ("1976" and "today"), the construction of the sentence should reflect the link between the past and the present. By using both of these references as **DEPENDENT CLAUSES** that begin and end the sentence, which also maintaining an **ACTIVE VOICE** in terms of Colon's establishment of the theatre in a firehouse, this is the most suitable option.

A is incorrect because although it is **ACTIVE** in its voice, the construction of the sentence does not allow the reader to clearly understand the shifts in time that are contained within its ideas. Without any punctuation to help the reader make the necessary connections, this sentence does need to be changed.

B is incorrect. By deleting the information about the year of establishment, the reader misses out on an **important piece of relevant information** regarding the development of the theatre company. The date in this context **is important in letting the reader know the timeline of events.**

D is incorrect because like option A, the sentence does not **effectively allow the reader to engage with its concepts.** The lack of punctuation is a serious hurdle in this choice.

Question 31

C is the best answer. This paragraph lists the different kinds of recognition and acclaim that Colón has received. The next paragraph returns to talking about the Traveling Theatre. Therefore, adding the proposed sentence would help the reader **make the transition between the two concepts,** i.e., the general acclaim that was received and the achievement that remains her most impactful legacy.

A is incorrect because this data is not needed to clarify anything else in the paragraph. The data that is about the honors she has received **stands on its own merit** and does not need further explanation/clarification.

B is incorrect. If this sentence were used as an introduction to this paragraph, we would remain with a problem of **transition** at the end of the paragraph where the author seeks to lead the reader from a conversation about Colón's other accomplishments to a focus on the Traveling Theatre. Therefore, this sentence would **not** be a more effective introduction than the sentence that already introduces the paragraph.

D is incorrect because the information in being closely related to the **central theme of the passage** (i.e., Colón & the Traveling Theatre) **is RELEVANT** to the text.

Question 32

D is the best answer. This answer retains the **ACTIVE voice** by ensuring that the theater is described as taking charge of the "developing" that occurs **and is clearer.** By mentioning that we are speaking about **career development** and not "development" in general, the vocabulary choice is much more specific and targeted.

A is incorrect because the term "**development**" **is ambiguous** and does not tell the reader what kind of development is spoken of. **Furthermore, this choice is more passive** and takes away the **active** nature of the subject (the theatre). **Passive sentences make subjects the recipients of action** (here, "development" is used in **reference** to the Latino talent rather than the theatre) **whereas active sentences describe the subject as carrying out that action. Whenever possible, USE THE MORE ACTIVE CHOICE.**

B is incorrect. By adding one more term ("helping") into the mix, the **ACTIVE** tone is diluted, and the theater is no longer credited with developing the talent; it is credited with **helping** develop talent. As you can see, the **tone** shifts with words of qualification (like "helping") by taking away from the power of the statement being made.

C is incorrect because of the word "for" that follows "credited" and precedes the underlined section, "to develop" would lead to a **grammatical error.** "Credited **for to develop** hundreds of Latino artists." As you will notice, the sentence loses meaning.

Question 33

D is the best answer. The passage describes Colón's various accomplishments but always reminding the reader that her most impactful work was that which also developed the careers of other Hispanic performers. Therefore, this answer choice comes closest to summarizing the passage.

A is incorrect because this statement is **an oversimplification** of the main point of the paragraph. Yes, the passage does speak to how Colón's legacy remains even after her death, but this statement does not **effectively capture** the many dimensions to her work that are described here.

B is incorrect because it is **limited** and **generalized.** Yes, Colón's work is a part of the American cultural landscape and yet, much of the focus of this passage lies in describing **why and how** her work came to be. An **effective summary cannot gloss over** (ignore) these details.

C is incorrect because once again it is limited. This choice only **references** Colón's acting career. Yet, as we've been told many times in the passage, the Puerto Rican Traveling Theater is her most significant legacy because it supported other Latino performers and artists. A summary that does not represent the **scope** of her work, therefore, is not an **effective summary.**

Passage 4

Question 34

D is the best answer because it is the most **ACTIVE** form of constructing the sentence. **ACTIVE SENTENCES speak of the subject** ("vaccines") as the doer of the action ("introduce"). Therefore, this is the most effective answer choice.

All the other answer choices here are incorrect because they all include **more passive choices** of describing what vaccines do. In **PASSIVE** sentences, the subject is given a less direct/no role in the **execution of the action. Rather, the action often happens to the subject. These sentences take away from the clarity and tone of the text and, unless used by a master author for a very specific purpose, PASSIVE sentences are always an unsuitable choice.**

Question 35

B is the best answer. The sentence clearly includes a **cause-effect relationship** because of the use of the term "**that** fight against." Therefore, the underlined word needs to be a preposition that can be used to **refer** to how that fight is carried out. Fights are carried out "with" particular tools/strategies (in this case, the "antibodies").

None of the other prepositions, when used to replace the underlined word, addresses the term "that fight against." When "for," "in," or "by" are used, these choices **negatively impact the sentence's meaning** and **make it grammatically incorrect.**

Question 36

C is the best answer. Once again, this choice is the **most ACTIVE and emphasizes the subject** ("vaccines") in the reduction of small pox infections.

All the other choices here are passive. **PASSIVE** sentences can be identified in a number of ways, the simplest of which is by looking at the number of words that the sentence takes to say the same thing. The more words there are, the more PASSIVE the sentence is.

Note that **using the PASSIVE VOICE** is different than saying that a sentence **becomes more PASSIVE.** The former refers to a particular grammatical choice that leads to a specific type of sentence construction (from subject doing the action to the subject being the recipient of the action). The latter refers to a **tone**, a way of using language in which the **ACTIVE** quality to the text is diminished, by using more words than needed and by using qualifications like ("it resulted in a reduction" rather than "it reduced").

Question 37

D is the best answer because it effectively uses an **introductory, DEPENDENT clause** followed by a comma to make the link between the easy access to vaccines and a lower infant mortality rate.

A is incorrect because of the use of the connector "for this reason" that follows the **SEMICOLON.** Since semicolons are used to separate two **independent clauses, each with their own subject, verb, and object, CONNECTORS are not needed or accurate.** Furthermore, SEMICOLONs are better used when the connection between the two clauses is **less integral to the idea that is being communicated.** Here, the easy access to vaccines is **integral** to explaining the second part of the sentence. Therefore, the SEMICOLON is not the best choice.

B is less suitable because the sentence construction is **not as concise** as it could be. As a general practice, "thus" works better when used to **begin a sentence,** i.e., when the previous sentence puts forward an idea and the following sentence beginning with thus is used to emphasize the point that has been made. Even if "and thus" is used in the middle of a sentence, it needs to be **preceded and followed by a COMMA** to emphasize its placement (the COMMA is missing in this answer choice).

C is incorrect because this sentence construction does not effectively capture the **cause-effect relationship between the two concepts being highlighted** (the easy availability of vaccines, and the lowered infant mortality rates). It is a **simplistic** sentence structure that shows less **facility** (ease) **with language.**

Question 38

C is the best answer. This paragraph very clearly states its focus on "modern vaccination" as stated in the **topic sentence** that introduces it. Therefore, adding the proposed sentence would **disrupt the flow** in logic and ask the reader to consider a different idea that is not expanded upon anywhere in this paragraph.

A is incorrect because for **an effective introduction** to occur, the new concepts being mentioned in that introduction need to be discussed in further detail later in that passage. Since this does not occur here, this answer is not the suitable choice.

B is incorrect. The information provided here is never mentioned anywhere else in the paragraph. Therefore, by its very nature, **this sentence does not help clarify any future concepts in the text.**

D is incorrect because the information here, while not **useful** in this particular paragraph, still **relates to the theme of the passage** (i.e., vaccinations). **Therefore, it is not generally irrelevant** (as this answer choice suggests). **It is simply irrelevant because it is unnecessary in this particular paragraph.**

Question 39

B is the best answer. By placing emphasis on the public health officials and **their ACTION, i.e.,** the distribution of the vaccine, this sentence has the most **clarity** of the other choices.

A is incorrect because some of the information here is **redundant** (not really useful) **and could be deleted.** For instance, it is not necessary to state that the vaccines were produced before being distributed. How could they be distributed if they hadn't been produced? The sentence also lacks a subject and does not tell us who did the distribution of the vaccines.

Options C and D are incorrect for the same reason which is the use of the word "once." By using this particular **connector** to begin the sentence, an **inconsistency** is caused with the use of the word "resulting." This will lead to a loss of grammatical accuracy. See the mismatch caused by the inclusion of the bolded answer choices and the underlined verb. "**Once public health officials had systematically distributed the vaccine** to the public, <u>resulting</u> in complete eradication of the disease from the world in 1979." The same inconsistency occurs with option D as well.

Question 40

D is the best answer. The **KEYWORDS** to notice here are "such as." The use of which makes the **COLON** an inappropriate choice. If the line were to have said, "They developed vaccines for many diseases: tetanus, diphtheria, plague, typhoid, and tuberculosis," the COLON would be used to introduce a list and as such would be appropriate. However, since the term "such as" has been used, a **COMMA is more appropriate since this connector makes what follows a DEPENDENT CLAUSE.**

> A is incorrect because of the use of the term "such as" preceding the use of the COLON. Since this connector makes what follows a **DEPENDENT CLAUSE,** the colon is no longer the right choice.
>
> B is incorrect. Once again, by using the word "including" before the use of the COLON, this answer choice is not suitable.
>
> C is incorrect because the sentence following the **SEMICOLON is not an independent clause that has its own subject, verb, and object.**

Question 41

A is the best answer. Vaccines, by their very nature, are designed to help "prevent" someone from contracting a disease, which is why as stated in the first paragraph that vaccines "are a weakened or deactivated form of pathogen" that are introduced "to a patient's immune system."

> B is incorrect because vaccines cannot be used to "treat" a disease after it has been contracted; it can only be used to prevent against it.
>
> C & D are incorrect because vaccines have the effect of reducing the **rates of occurrence** of a disease (as seen in the previously stated information about infant mortality) and of potentially eradicating it (as in small pox). However, these are results that evolve over time from attempts to **prevent** the likelihood that people will contract the disease that they are being vaccinated against. "Reduction" and "cure" are not the immediate outcomes of vaccination usage and since this sentence refers to the **direct intention of vaccines** (through the use of the phrase "before and after the vaccines were developed to […]"), prevention is the most suitable answer.

Question 42

B is the best answer. The sentence asks for evidence to support the "stopping" of certain diseases. Therefore, when looking at the Figure, we are looking for diseases that reached "O" (i.e., stopped) after vaccines were invented for them. Based on this, B is the only possible answer.

A is incorrect because there is no information provided in the Figure to help us locate information that is specific to a particular year ("1979").

C is incorrect. While this statement is not untrue based on the figure, it does not provide effective support for the "stopping" of certain diseases, which is what is asked for in this question.

D is incorrect because once again it does not provide effective support for the "stopping" of certain diseases, which is what is asked for in this question.

Question 43

D is the best answer. By simply stating the subject, "vaccinations" without any additional clarifying terms and phrases, this answer is the most **concise and ACTIVE.**

All of the other answers use "extra" text to communicate the same point. **As mentioned earlier, using more words/phrases than needed makes sentences more PASSIVE since they take away from the dynamism of its subject/action. Therefore, whenever possible, use the most SUCCINT** (concise, clear) **way of structuring a sentence.**

Question 44

B is the best answer. The sentence before the proposed addition introduces a new idea, which is how certain regions of the world struggle to make vaccines available. The sentence after the proposed addition concludes the passage by **wrapping up the passage** with general information about the vaccination. Therefore, a sentence like this one **needs to be added between the two existing statements** to improve the clarity and flow of logic in the paragraph.

A is incorrect. The "new concepts" of some countries' struggles with access to vaccines have already been introduced **before** the location where this proposed line will be included. Therefore, it does not function as an **introduction** to the ideas, but it is simply a continuation of them.

C is incorrect. The previous sentence is the one that **disrupts the flow** by introducing a new idea toward the end of the concluding paragraph of the passage. This sentence seeks to **address** the disruption caused by that sentence.

D is incorrect. Since the idea (of how "certain regions of the world still struggle to manage with the public health issues") has already been introduced in the previous sentence, this sentence's call for action from public health officials in those countries is **extremely relevant.**

Writing Test 7: Answer Key

1. D	27. B
2. A	28. D
3. C	29. A
4. B	30. C
5. B	31. C
6. B	32. A
7. D	33. A
8. D	
9. A	34. A
10. B	35. B
11. A	36. D
	37. B
	38. A
12. C	39. C
13. B	40. C
14. A	41. B
15. D	42. A
16. C	43. D
17. B	44. D
18. B	
19. A	
20. D	
21. C	
22. A	
23. C	
24. C	
25. D	
26. C	

WRITING & LANGUAGE TEST 7
Answers & Explanations

Passage 1

Question 1

D is the best answer. By listing various substances that bees produce and by stating the importance of these activities for **both** humans and the environment, this statement provides the best conclusion to the paragraph.

A is incorrect because the current last sentence tells us a few reasons why apiarists keep bees, but it does not tell us the extent of these products and the potential benefits to the world. Therefore, by giving the reader more information while also **referring** to larger ideas of bees' contributions, (to humans and the environment) the current conclusion is not as effective as it could be.

B is incorrect because this sentence restricts itself to the benefits for humans. Answer D tells us about the benefits to the environment as well. Since introductions **aim to give the reader a wholistic approach about the main topic of a passage,** the restricted information presented here is less suitable.

C is incorrect because the sentence here does not tell us what kinds of benefits bees provide to humans and the environment. **A good introduction always FRAMES the following information as extensively as possible, so that the reader has a good base from which to understand the rest of the passage.**

Question 2

A is the best answer. The **TOPIC SENTENCE of this paragraph tells us that** a hive "consists of a queen bee, her drones, and the hive workers." The sentences that come before the underlined section describe the queen bee and her drones. Therefore, a sentence explaining the worker bees is necessary so as to explain all the information that has been provided in the topic sentence.

B is incorrect because the information here is not **used for transition.** It is used to explain the composition of a beehive. As we see, the next paragraph talks about a "decrease in population" of honeybees. For the sentence here to be seen as a transition, it would have to **both** talk about worker bees and connect to the **topic of the next paragraph.**

C is incorrect. There might be pollinators besides bees but as the title of this passage clearly states, this text's focus is the "Art and Science of Beekeeping." Therefore, there is no need for this sentence to **talk about matters that fall outside the scope of this specific topic.**

D is incorrect because this sentence **does not interrupt** the flow of logic in the paragraph. Rather, it strengthens it by providing **relevant information** about the composition of beehives.

Question 3

C is the best answer. For questions about the order of paragraphs and sentences, do a **CONCEPT MAPPING,** i.e., map out the main concept of each paragraph to see where the identified selection will best fit. In this text paragraph 1 introduces bees and their many uses, paragraph 2 describes the composition of a beehive, paragraph 3 speaks about the declining population of honeybees, paragraph 4 gives more information about the queen bee and the workers, paragraph 5 speaks about the role of the beekeeper, and paragraph 6 concludes the passage by reiterating the importance of bees. From this mapping we see that paragraph 3 would best fit **after paragraph 5,** which can be evidenced by the first line of the first paragraph that states how ecosystems would collapse without bees and the last line of paragraph 3, which tells us how bees are "critical to the ecosystem." We see a **KEYWORD CONNECTION here** ("ecosystem") that provides a clue to the order of the paragraphs.

A is incorrect because in its current position, paragraph 3 **interrupts the flow of logic in the passage** by going from a description of beehive composition to speaking about declining population only to then go back to a description of the functions of specific types of bees.

B is incorrect. By introducing information about the decline of the bee population before talking about the role of the beekeeper, this choice would again cause **a disruption of flow** within the passage.

D is incorrect because this position would cause a **jump in topics** from speaking about the declining population to an explanation of the composition of a beehive only to return to the dangers of the ecosystem collapse in the concluding paragraph. **The flow of logic in a passage** needs to be extremely **fluid and clear,** so that the reader can effectively absorb all the information being presented to them.

Question 4

B is the best answer. What is currently a stand-alone sentence, "Bees are a critical part of the ecosystem," directly refers to why a decline in bee population could be life threatening. Through the use of a **connector** like "because," this connection is more **directly evidenced to the reader.**

A is incorrect because it causes an unnecessary **break in logic** by placing two related sentences side by side instead of **using a CONNECTOR** that **contextualizes** the relationship between them. Because of the absence of a connector, the reader is less likely to see the last line as a continuation of the previous idea. Instead, it would lead them to believe that the author is putting forward a new idea.

C is incorrect. The use of a **COMMA** is incorrect here. **COMMAS are always used when dependent clauses come at the beginning of a sentence.** When a dependent clause comes at the **end of a sentence,** most of the time **COMMAS are not used.**

D is incorrect because the **SEMICOLON usage** does not allow the reader to see the connection between the two ideas. It simply represents two independent clauses that might not only be related because they both speak about bees. **To show a relationship between ideas, CONNECTORS are absolutely essential.**

Question 5

B is the best answer. Since the queen bee is directly referenced as the subject in this sentence, a possessive pronoun is needed, i.e., since she (the female queen bee) is the one who lays the eggs, hers is the right possessive pronoun to use.

A is incorrect because "the" does not reference the subject of the sentence and clearly the "queen bee" is the subject that is being emphasized here.

C and D are incorrect. By not including a possessive pronoun and by using an **ambiguous** term like "some," the sentence is not given the same clarity as it is by telling us whose eggs are being laid (i.e., her eggs).

Question 6

B is the best answer. The term "foraging" obviously refers to the activity described in the previous line, which describes bees as "buzzing around to collect pollen from plants and flowers for the hive." Since this sentence describes what worker bees do <u>during</u> **the foraging process,** "while" seems to make the most logical sense.

A is incorrect because "in foraging" suggests that the following sentence might tell us about the <u>result</u> of that activity. However, what we are given information about is the entire process.

C is incorrect. The term "although" **implies that this sentence will contain contrasting ideas. Since there are no contrasts mentioned here** and only explanatory information, this is not a suitable choice.

D is incorrect because by simply using the word "foraging" the sentence is rendered **meaningless and incomplete.**

Question 7

D is the best answer. This is most the **active and direct** form of phrasing the sentence because there are no extra clauses and/or punctuation marks **and the reader gains an immediate understanding of what is being described.**

A is incorrect because the use of commas before and after "and not stored on their legs" gives this information **more emphasis.** From the sentence, we see that no part of it is more/less important than another. All of the information seeks to **add to the reader's knowledge of how bees use up pollen.**

B is incorrect. By deleting the information about bees storing pollen in their legs, the sentence becomes slightly **more difficult to comprehend.** The reader needs to understand that bees start by storing pollen in their legs (as the previous sentence also states) and **only store them on their back when they are not stored in their legs. Since there are multiple bits of information being presented here, it is helpful to repeat relevant details for the reader.**

C is incorrect because the use of **DASHES** before and after a phrase leads either to the phrase being seen as **PARENTHETICAL** (extra information) or in that phrase having special emphasis. Since neither of those intentions is desired here because all information in the sentence is **relevant and essential,** the DASHES would be less suitable. Please note that they are not grammatically incorrect but simply less suitable.

Question 8

D is the best answer. The **TOPIC SENTENCE lets us know that this paragraph will give us information about a beekeeper's duties.** The current statement expands on this idea. Adding information about a manmade beehive and its location, therefore, **interrupts the existing focus of a beekeeper's duties.**

A is incorrect because this sentence does not say anything about a beekeeper's "duty," which is the subject of the next line. In order for a statement to be an **effective transition,** it should connect concepts between two lines/paragraphs.

B is incorrect. If the term "manmade" hives had been mentioned anywhere in the first sentence, then this statement would have been helpful in clarifying the concept. However, since the term is not used in the topic sentence, the new addition does not help explain **prior concepts.**

C is incorrect because using this new sentence as an introduction would **imply** that the topic of the paragraph is "manmade hives." However, the focus here is on domesticated colonies and the duties of the beekeeper in ensuring the survival of those colonies.

Question 9

A is the best answer. Since it accurately uses punctuation and sentence structure, no change needs to be made in the underlined section. **COMMAS** have been effectively used to separate clauses while also maintaining the flow of ideas and the connection between them.

B is incorrect because "which" is generally used to introduce **a NON-ESSENTIAL ELEMENT to the sentence,** i.e., an element that is interesting to know but that is not necessary to understand. Here, given the technical name that has been mentioned before, knowing the common name is an **ESSENTIAL ELEMENT** so as to make the text accessible for the reader.

C is incorrect. By breaking the sentence in two, the **tone is altered.** The ideas presented in them **become less fluid in their structure** and cause an interruption (in terms of the form of the text) that is **unnecessary.**

D is incorrect because **SEMICOLONS can only be used when the clauses on each side of the punctuation mark have THEIR OWN subject, verb, and object.** Since that condition is not met with the phrase "commonly known as the European honeybee," this choice would be **inaccurate.**

Question 10

B is the best answer. By ending the paragraph with a "call to action" for readers, this sentence **significantly improves the tone and voice of the sentence.** Furthermore, through the use of "because," the reader is able to **make a connection between the ideas being presented in the sentence** and is able to more **effectively navigate through them.**

A is incorrect because in either case, the mention of the "influence of the local environment" seems a **sudden interruption** to the earlier flow of the paragraph. In addition, **good conclusions end with a strong, active statement that takes the reader from the passage to broader ideas about the text's implication.** By starting the final sentence of the passage with a **DEPENDENT CLAUSE,** the sentence is automatically made more passive. Therefore, this sentence is **NOT an effective conclusion.** It is, however, an improvement in tone/voice/clarity.

C is incorrect. Since this sentence brings in a new dimension, "the influence of the local environment," it is not going to be an effective introduction to the concluding paragraph. Furthermore, adding this sentence as an introduction would not help the reader **effectively transition** between this idea and the next (about the risks to the ecosystem). As such, this would not be a more effective introduction.

D is incorrect. The information included in this statement, while perhaps **unnecessary,** is not irrelevant. **The content that it contains directly relates to the central topic of the passage and to many of the aspects of this paragraph.**

Question 11

A is the best answer. The underlined sentence, as it is, functions as an effective **conclusion** to the paragraph. **Concluding sentences** take specific ideas from the preceding text and present a **more general** idea that the reader is left with. By ending the current text with this sentence, we already have an **effective conclusion** to the paragraph. Although this sentence is **not ideal** to end the passage, it is the better choice of the options that are given to us.

B & C are incorrect because they would be **REDUNDANT.** Since the introduction to the paragraph has already said that "Without bees, many ecosystems would collapse," there is no need to repeat this idea at the end of the paragraph (as B suggests). Similarly, by restating the "critical need" to save bees this choice also repeats information that has already been provided earlier in the passage.

D is incorrect because it does not **provide an effective transition** from the previous line, which specifically tells us about how local systems affect bees. There is a **jump in logic** that would be created by including this sentence after the underlined text.

Passage 2
Question 12
C is the best answer. The proposed inclusion provides support for the phrases "grown in popularity" and "improved their skills." This is achieved because the proposed sentence tells us that the marathon has both become the most "premier long-distance race" and the "longest running race at the Olympic Games."

A is incorrect because what comes next is the approach (by athletes) toward the sport, which is that they see it as both competitive and recreational. The information in the proposed sentence does not help **clarify** any of those ideas.

B is incorrect. In order to understand the popularity of the marathon, the reader needs to first be introduced to the event itself. Therefore, adding this sentence to the introduction would **disrupt the flow of logic** in the paragraph.

D is incorrect because the information in this proposed line is **completely relevant** to the content being addressed in the passage. The passage speaks about how the marathon has developed since its early days and knowing its "status" in the Olympics and as a long-distance race **helps the reader better understand the context of this event.**

Question 13
B is the best answer. The KEYWORD "fun" is repeated in this choice as in the preceding sentences and, therefore, serves to better connect the sentences.

A is incorrect because the **use of the SEMICOLON** is incorrect since the clauses on either side of the punctuation are not complete. If the first part of the sentence did not begin with the word "But," perhaps this choice would have been more suitable. Furthermore, beginning a sentence with a conjunction like "but" is also not recommended.

C is incorrect because "did not enjoy his run" is **different in meaning than** "did not race for fun." The former indicates a lack of enjoyment in an activity, while the latter speaks about the **intention** behind the runner's engagement with the activity.

D is incorrect because the sentence construction is **clumsy.** By starting the sentence with a preposition like "for" (when unnecessary), and by including an extra "his" in the phrase "his race was not for fun," this choice negatively affects the structure of the sentence.

Question 14

A is the best answer. No change is needed since the underlined word and the surrounding sentence construction support the reader in understanding the statement, i.e., that the race cost the runner his life. Since "the runner" is clearly **mentioned as the subject earlier in the sentence,** using "him" is a perfectly acceptable form of referring to "his life."

B is incorrect because **reflexive pronouns (like himself) are only used when the subject of the sentence is also the same (i.e., "he").** For example: "He writes the stories himself because he does not trust his interns to do it right." Here, "he" is both the subject and the object making it necessary to use a reflexive pronoun like "himself." Since the subject is the "first marathoner," "himself" is inaccurate.

C is less suitable. Although the use of the possessive ("'s") is **accurate,** it is less acceptable. There is no need to restate the subject ("the runner) since he has already been referred to by name and as the "first marathoner" earlier in the sentence.

D is incorrect. Deleting the underlined world would result in the sentence stating "it ultimately cost his life." This **construction is unclear** since it does not tell the reader who was "cost" his life. It is **always good form to remind the reader of who is being referred to especially when using non-specific pronouns to refer to a significant event** ("his life").

Question 15

D is the best answer. The sentence is both **confusing** and **redundant** (useless because it repeats information). Since the previous paragraph tells us that Pheidippides was the first marathoner stating that the event "has its origins" in the work of this runner is **unnecessary.** The information that he was Greek and a news courier are also both mentioned in the following line and do not need to be stated again.

A is incorrect because in addition to the redundancy explained above, the sentence is extremely **confusing for the reader.** Without using punctuations to separate information, the reader is presented with a more **challenging task.**

B is incorrect. This statement also tells us information that has been given to us before. It also contains an **error** in referring to Pheidippides as a soldier when he was actually a news courier (in the next line).

C is incorrect. This sentence, in addition to being repetitive, also refers to Pheidippides as a soldier (rather than a news courier in the armies). This is an **ASSUMPTION** since someone who delivers news/messages does not have to be a soldier. In fact, it is more likely that they are NOT a soldier and that is why they are being asked to run messages from one place to another.

Question 16

C is the best answer. The implication here is that help was being sought from Spartan citizens, i.e., multiple Spartans. The help "belongs" to the Spartans. It is **necessary to use the letter "s" at the end for the word followed by the apostrophe** (Spartans'). When using the apostrophe to show possession, if the word ends with the letter "s," the mark comes **after** the "s." For example, "citizen's" **is used to show the possession of one citizen.** "Citizens'" is used to show the same for multiple citizens.

A is incorrect because the current use of Spartans does not indicate the possessive relationship between that word and "help," i.e., the Spartans have the help that the Greeks are seeking through their news courier.

B is incorrect. If this choice were used, it would imply that the help of **one particular** Spartan is being requested. However, from the **context of the sentence,** we know that the general population (i.e., all Spartans) is being asked for help.

D is incorrect because there are multiple subjects being referred to in this statement: the courier, Athens, Sparta, and Persians. Restating whose help was being sought, therefore, is important in **ensuring clarity for the reader.**

Question 17

B is the best answer. There are **two independent clauses** in this statement: "Immediately after relaying the news, Pheidippides collapsed and died" and "he had run more than 325 miles in a span of just a few days." In this statement, where each clause has its **own subject, verb, and object,** the use of the **SEMICOLON** allows clarity while also making it apparent that both ideas are linked to each other.

A is incorrect because the use of multiple clauses separated by **COMMAS** is both **hard to understand** and makes the **tone** of the sentence more **passive** (rather than **active and engaging**).

C is incorrect. When **two past events are referred to in the same statement, the earlier occurrence should be conjugated using the PAST PERFECT TENSE** and the **relatively more RECENT event should be conjugated using the SIMPLE PRESENT TENSE.** This sentence uses the SIMPLE PRESENT ("he ran") to refer to an event that took place more in the past than the runner's death (i.e., the run itself). Therefore, in this case, the simple past is less accurate.

D is incorrect because this change would have the sentence read as follows "Immediately after relaying the news, Pheidippides collapsed and died. After running more than 325 miles in a span of just a few days." It can immediately be identified that this choice **breaks the flow** of the sentences and does not **transmit the message quite as effectively.**

Question 18

B is the best answer. This is the **MOST ACTIVE of all the choices.** It is a quality that is evidenced by the **direct attribution** of the action ("added") to the subject of the sentence ("organizers of the first modern Olympic Games").

A is incorrect because it is **unclear.** The sentence states that the organizers "added to" the Olympics but not clearly state **what** was added. This lack of clarity does not allow the reader to identify the event/events that is being referred to here.

C is incorrect. In the use of **the PASSIVE VOICE,** the action takes place **to** the subject rather than the subject carrying out an action. We see a clear example of this **passivity in this answer choice** where the main action ("the marathon race was added") is given more emphasis than the organizers who added it to begin with.

D is incorrect because it, once again, does not give the subject (the organizers) any emphasis or **agency.** In fact, this choice removes the subject from focus altogether.

Question 19

A is the best answer. The previous sentence has just introduced us to when the marathon was included in the Olympic Games. Since there are multiple events being referred to in this preceding sentence, by restating the subject of the "first modern Olympic marathon, the reader is **reminded** of the exact event that is being referred to in the content that follows. Therefore, this choice best preserves the **clarity** of the paragraph.

While choices B, C, and D are not **inaccurate,** these answers are less **clear** in their subject. Therefore, it is more likely that these choices will have the readers more confused as to the event that is being referred to (given the multiple events being referenced in the previous sentence).

Question 20

D is the best answer. Sentence (1) talks about the winner of the first Olympic marathon, sentence (2) describes responses to the first marathon event, sentence (3) puts forward a scandal, and sentence (4) talks about the glory despite the scandal. Given this **CONCEPT MAP,** it seems like the best place to add (1) is after (4). Since speaking about the "glory" right after the scandal sounds **abrupt,** adding information about the first winner would help **contextualize the text.**

A is incorrect because as mentioned above, the short phrase that ends the paragraph, "Regardless, glory won the day," **currently seems to interrupt the flow of logic in the paragraph.** It needs to be **evidenced by something in order to make its presence relevant.** Hence, a change is needed.

B and C are incorrect for the same reason. Given the description of the scandal and the current last sentence that refers to the "glory," the only **relevant location for the account about the gold medal winner is after sentence 4.** With any other choice, the reader **is left hanging** at the end of the paragraph since **there is no context about what "glory" might refer to.**

Question 21

C is the best answer. By breaking this sentence into two **independent clauses,** the **clarity is greatly improved.** We are told that there was a scandal, and then the next sentence provides evidence to support the claim.

A is incorrect because the term "in fact" is used inaccurately. "In fact," is used to **clarify a point,** i.e., "They say that A happened. But in fact, it was B that happened." This term, therefore, is often used to present a **contrasting occurrence. In this context, since what follows the use of "in fact" is evidence that exactly supports what came before it,** the connector has been misused.

B is incorrect. When a **SEMI COLON is used, connectors do not need to be used after it. By placing "in fact," after the punctuation mark, the sentence becomes inaccurate.**

D is incorrect because using COMMAS **makes the sentence unclear and hard to understand. Once again, the use of the connector "IN FACT" makes the construction problematic** since COMMAS are generally effective when adding **similar** ideas rather than **different ones** (as indicated by the connector here).

Question 22

A is the best answer. When choosing between **THAT** and **WHICH** consider whether what follows is considered **ESSENTIAL** or **NON-ESSENTIAL.** **To decide if something is ESSENTIAL or NON-ESSENTIAL,** read the whole paragraph. If this information was **NOT** in the paragraph, would it limit your understanding of its content in any way? If the answer is yes, then that information is **ESSENTIAL and THAT is used.** If the answer is no, it is **NON-ESSENTIAL and WHICH (preceded by a COMMA) is used.**

In this case, the information that follows "THAT" is clearly ESSENTIAL since it connects the reader with concepts and ideas that were previously mentioned (about Louis). Therefore, no change needs to be made.

Since all the other options here use "WHICH," we can immediately tell that A is the right answer.

Passage 3

Question 23

C is the best answer. In the current paragraph, we see that both the second and third sentences begin by speaking about "The Semeru Volcano." By adding a description of the "Ring of Fire" in between these sentences, the **flow of information about the volcano is disrupted.**

A is incorrect because it is a **description** of the "Ring of Fire" and not **supportive of it.** A description **helps the reader better understand a particular term. The** support **helps prove something that has been said before.** Since this sentence can more likely be called a **description** rather than **support,** A is not a suitable answer.

B is incorrect. While it is true that this description helps clarify the "Ring of Fire," what is **DEBATABLE** here is whether or not the "Ring of Fire" is a **key** term. **Key terms** are absolutely essential to understanding a sentence/paragraph. Here, even without a description of "Ring of Fire," the reader is able to **understand** the context of the volcano.

D is incorrect because although the information is not **necessary,** it is NOT **irrelevant.** Since the information here is still related to the central topic, it helps **inform** the reader about the context.

Question 24

C is the best answer. By making the **information accessible by using the least amount of extra words and clauses,** this choice best enhances **clarity and voice.**

A and B **unnecessarily use the terms "appear on,"** which are **repetitive** since we are given the location (the southeast side of the volcano). Adding more terms than necessary **leads to sentences sounding passive, which is never a recommended choice.** Of A and B, B is more accurate since the use of "that" implies that what follows is **ESSENTIAL,** i.e., necessary information to better understand the passage and the context.

D is incorrect. Consider the sentence that results. "The center for activity in the Semeru volcano is at the Jonggring Seloko crater, the southeast side of the volcano." The loss of the preposition ("on") and inclusion of the **COMMA** (which adds an extra clause as well) make this choice unsuitable.

Question 25

D is the best answer. The previous content in the paragraph tells us about the nature of the Semeru volcano, and the first sentence of the following paragraph tells us about the devastating impacts of its eruptions. Therefore, there is no need to add a sentence about the loss of lives here since neither does it help conclude the current paragraph (by introducing a new idea) nor does it help **transition to the next one.**

A, B, & C are incorrect because they introduce **new information** in the concluding sentence. Not only are we told about the loss of "numerous lives," we are also told about the neighboring volcano ("Merapi), which seems **irrelevant** given the other information in the paragraph.

Question 26

C is the best answer. As the only answer choice that includes a **PAST TENSE CONJUGATION** (have had is the past perfect tense), this is the only option that is **CONSISTENT** with the phrase "in the past" (at the beginning of the sentence).

All other options use **PRESENT** (have; has) or **FUTURE TENSE** (will have had) conjugations that are inaccurate in this context.

Question 27

B is the best answer. By using **COMMAS** to demarcate the mention of the years that the earthquake took place, this sentence construction **makes this information a subordinate clause that helps clarify what came before it. The use of the COMMAS also tells the reader that the information, while useful to know, is not integral to understanding the main topic of the sentence.** Furthermore **by mentioning that scientists were the ones to classify the earthquake** the sentence is made more **ACTIVE** since particular subjects are described as performing an action.

A is incorrect because the **run-on sentence** does not use any punctuation to help the reader better **process** the information. There are two bits of information being shared here. The first is the years that the earthquakes took place, and the second is how they were classified. Using punctuation will help readers better understand sentences that put forward multiple ideas.

C &D are incorrect because they are far less **precise** than the correct answer. Both answer choices do not use the word "respectively" to qualify the dates that are provided. They do not tell the reader **who** classified the earthquakes as moderate to moderately large. Therefore, these answers are not as **specific** in its choice of **vocabulary** as the correct answer.

Question 28

D is the best answer. By using the term "fortunately" to **effectively transition the reader** from the **negative tone** of the previous sentence to the more **positive tone** of this one, this answer is most suitable because of the way **it connects the ideas presented in two sentences. CONNECTORS are excellent tools to improve the flow of a text.**

The remaining three answer choices are less suitable precisely because they do not use a **CONNECTOR** like "Fortunately." Given that the previous sentence talks about the dangers of these volcanos and the loss of life that has occurred in the past, the **shift in tone** in this sentence needs to be **explicitly identified.** The shift, of course, is that the paragraph tells the reader that fewer lives have been lost to the volcanos is the 19th and 20th centuries.

Question 29

A is the best answer. This sentence transitions the reader from information about "occasional lava flows" to descriptions of the volcano's frequent eruptions.

B is incorrect because there is nothing in this sentence to suggest a **focus** on either "planning" or "emergency prevention."

C is incorrect. While it is true that this sentence does not include information about "toxic gases," to say that this is a reason for deleting the sentence would be **an overstatement.**

D is incorrect because the content in this sentence in describing people's fears surrounding the volcano's eruptions is **extremely relevant to the topic being dealt with.**

Question 30

C is the best answer. When speaking of something that is **still happening,** the most **effective verb tense to use is the PRESENT CONTINUOUS TENSE.** In this case, since the ongoing event is also being placed in reference to the past (i.e., the eruption in 1967), it is also necessary to use the **PRESENT PERFECT CONTINUOUS** ("has been going" rather than "is going"). In this way, the timeline of the event is made clear. It is an event that happened in the past that is still going on.

None of the remaining answers include both of these components.

In addition, choices A and B do not engage the verb ("erupt"). Instead, they make the verb and adverb ("eruption"). When the primary verb is disengaged this way, the sentence automatically becomes more passive.

Choice D uses the **PAST TENSE** ("erupted"), which causes a **VERB TENSE INCONSISTENCY** since the sentence is obviously referring to an ongoing phenomenon.

Question 31

C is the best answer. This information is clearly evidenced in the Figure. The volcano has been erupting with increasing frequency.

A is incorrect because of the term "consistently." We see from the Figure that the rate of increase has not been consistent. It is showing greater increase in some decades over others. To be able to say that the increases have been "consistent," the graph would be a diagonal.

B is incorrect. From the Figure, it is hard to associate an exact number of eruptions with a particular year. To do so would require the reader to make an **ASSUMPTION.**

D is incorrect because "concerning" is an **ambiguous term** that cannot be **evidenced with support from the Figure.** Therefore, this answer choice is not suitable.

Question 32

A is the best answer. The clue to the right answer lies in this phrase from the preceding sentence "will settle down after over half a century of constant activity." The **KEYWORDS in this sentence are** "will settle down," implying a time in the future. Therefore, the term "until" is necessary since it describes the wait for a future time. The term "then" is necessary since we are referring to a particular point in **time.**

B is incorrect because "then," without the addition of "until" does not capture the wait for a future moment.

C is incorrect. "Until that" would only be accurate if it was followed by "happens," i.e., "However, until that happens, [...]." This would enable the reader to understand that it is the settling down of the volcano that is being referred to. Without "happens," however, makes this choice grammatically incorrect.

D is incorrect. Without the underlined section, the sentence would lose all meaning. Saying "However, visitors are taking their lives into their own hands," without a qualification of why/how/until when they are doing this, makes the sentence **irrelevant.**

Question 33

A is the best answer. The statement, very clearly, provides data that helps the reader better understand an otherwise vague term, "numerous deaths."

B is incorrect because the statement would be a **more** effective introduction than what already exists. At best, it would be as effective as the current introductory statement (the **KEYWORD in the answer choice,** is "more").

C is incorrect because the data helps clarify information that comes **before** the statement and not something that is included **after** it.

D is incorrect because the data provided in this sentence directly relates to the themes being discussed in the passage/paragraph. Therefore, it is **EXTREMELY RELEVANT** to the text here.

Passage 4

Question 34

A is the best answer. By restating information that precedes it and by ending the statement with "among others," the reader is **effectively led** to the next paragraph.

> B is incorrect because this sentence does not help clarify **information that has been presented earlier in the paragraph.** It restates one use of the Chapel and underscores the idea that there are other uses toward which the Chapel has been put to use.
>
> C is incorrect. Without the **context to understand** what the Sistine Chapel is and what it was used for, this sentence would become **irrelevant.** Therefore, adding it as the introductory sentence would be an **ineffective choice.**
>
> D is incorrect because although this sentence **refers to information provided earlier,** it does NOT restate it. The statement would only be considered redundant if it were to directly repeat the information that came earlier.

Question 35

B is the best answer. This sentence construction keeps all the necessary components of the information that is presented while keeping it grammatically accurate and active. The necessary components to this sentence are stating the time period as being between 1508 and 1512, naming the Sistine Chapel (since it is a new paragraph) and describing the ceiling as being blue and "speckled with golden stars."

> A is incorrect because the use of DASHES before and after "between the years of 1508 and 1512" draws unnecessary emphasis to the dates. Since this **information is as important as all the other information presented in this sentence, the special emphasis is not needed.**
>
> C is incorrect because it deletes a vital bit of information about the years between which the Sistine Chapel opened its doors. This is important information for the reader to know so as to **establish a timeline of events that occurred there.**
>
> D is incorrect because this answer choice does not reference the subject of the sentence (the Sistine Chapel). This is important particularly because this is the first sentence of a new paragraph, and the subject needs to **be reiterated.**

Question 36

D is the best answer. Sentence 1 describes what the chapel looked like between 1508 and 1512, sentence 2 explains what happened in 1512, and sentences 3 & 4 continue descriptions of what the Chapel looked like and based on **context,** we are given to understand that these descriptions are also from between 1512. This is particularly important because sentence 4 speaks about how the "church officials" felt like something needed to be done by the "plain ceiling." This **implies that this occurred BEFORE** Michelangelo was invited to paint the ceiling. Therefore, the best location for sentence 2 is **after** sentence 4.

All the other answer choices **disrupt the flow of the paragraph** by talking about an event that occurs at the end of the timeline than the other sentences describe, i.e., sentence 2 takes place in 1512 while all the others are set as taking place between 1508 and 1512.

Question 37

B is the best answer. This phrase clearly establishes the **transition between the previous paragraph** and this one by telling the reader what Michelangelo had accomplished in the time leading up to the church's invitation.

A is incorrect because the term "During the time" is both grammatically incorrect and **ambiguous.** The inaccuracy is because of the use of "the" instead of "that," i.e., it would be accurate to say "during **that** time." However, even if that had been done, this sentence would be ambiguous since the time was last referred to in the previous paragraph and since this is a new paragraph, the reader should be reminded of the **timeframe being referred to.**

C is incorrect. "Meanwhile," like the previous choice, is ambiguous and does not clearly tell the reader which time period is being referred to here.

D is incorrect because deleting the underlined portion would leave the reader without any transition whatsoever while changing the subject from the Sistine Chapel to Michelangelo.

Question 38

A is the best answer. At the moment, the reader jumps from a sentence about Michelangelo's recognition to one in which the author describes how people thought he would fail. This **contrast in ideas** would only make sense if a sentence like the one proposed here is added. This would clarify the point that Michelangelo was known as a sculptor and not as a painter.

B is incorrect because it doesn't provide support for anything that has currently been said before it. Instead, **it provides useful context to frame information that comes after.**

C is incorrect because the information here has never been mentioned earlier and therefore, is not **redundant.**

D is incorrect because this information is extremely **relevant** to better understanding Michelangelo's status in that place and at that time.

Question 39

C is the best answer. Since we are speaking about a work of art (the ceiling of the Sistine Chapel) and its position as a cornerstone piece within a particular **genre of art**, the only preposition that would be **accurate** is **OF.** In referring to an art work, we would call it a "piece **of** art." It is exactly the same here except that "work" has been preceded by cornerstone and art has been qualified with "High Renaissance."

All other answer options would be grammatically incorrect since they would either alter the meaning of the sentence or render it meaningless.

Question 40

C is the best answer. Given the many ideas that are expressed here, it is more suitable to keep the sentences separate. The other aspect to pay attention to is the **VERB TENSE**. In reading the rest of the sentence, we see that the author uses the **PRESENT TENSE** ("concludes") to speak about the end of the book. In order to maintain consistency, "begins" would be the most accurate verb tense choice.

A and B are incorrect because of the conjugation of "to begin." Beginning does not reflect the **PRESENT TENSE** and in not following this condition sets up a **VERB TENSE INCONSITENCY within the sentence.**

D is incorrect because the use of **SEMICOLONS would result in an EXTREMELY LONG SENTENCE** that is hard to follow. Since SEMICOLONS have already been used to separate descriptions of the Book of Genesis, it is not advisable to make the introduction of the book also a clause that is connected with that punctuation mark.

Question 41

B is the best answer. Since the sentence later uses the word "represent" to speak about the art, the verb that describes its content needs to be something that is close to "showing," i.e., we are told what the art work shows and what it (the thing it shows) represents. Of the options that have been provided for this answer, "depicting" is the term that comes closest to capturing the relationship between what is shown and its representation.

A is incorrect because the preposition "of" is **insufficient** in describing how the story of Adam and Eve links to Michelangelo's frescoes.

C is incorrect. Using "making" in this sentence would render the statement meaningless.

D is less suitable than B because of the **connotation** of the word. "To demonstrate" is usually used to mean "to prove something." "To depict" most often means "to portray." Given that we are speaking of works of art in which topics/themes/qualities are harder to "prove," "depicting" is the word with the more suitable connotation.

Question 42

A is the best answer. No change is needed since the Sistine Chapel still exists and, therefore, using the **PRESENT TENSE** to speak of what is represented on its ceiling is completely accurate.

The other three answer choices are incorrect precisely because of their VERB TENSE (i.e., the way in which the **infinitive** "to represent" has been conjugated in choices B & C, and the way it has been qualified as an event of the past in option D).

Question 43

D is the best answer. The focus of this paragraph is the *Creation of Adam*. In this **context,** it **seems irrelevant to include comparisons of the work to Da Vinci's** *Mona Lisa.*

The first sentence in this paragraph names and identifies the *Creation of Adam*. The main premise of the second sentence is to inform the reader of its contents and to speak of this image's contemporary relevance. Given this premise, there seems to be **no need to mention** the *Mona Lisa* and because all other answer choices include this **irrelevant information,** they can be excluded.

Question 44

D is the best answer. It most effectively combines and summarizes the ideas that have been described in the passage. The sentence references Michelangelo, the Sistine Chapel, and the **continued significance** of this work of art in today's world.

A is incorrect because of **the tone** of this answer choice. While it does briefly **allude** to the major themes of the passage, it is too **abrupt** to serve as an effective concluding statement for the passage.

B is incorrect. This statement cannot be considered a **summary** of the passage. It states one idea that was mentioned once while describing public perception of Michelangelo. However, this is **insufficient evidence on which to base a claim that this is the "main point of the passage."**

C is incorrect because the focus of this sentence is on the number of visitors who go to the Sistine Chapel rather than Michelangelo who is very obviously the central focus of this passage. Including this sentence as a conclusion would be **irrelevant.**

Made in the USA
Middletown, DE
08 July 2019